Charles Bronson in *Death Wish 4: The Crackdown* (1987)

BRONSON'S LOOSE AGAIN!

On the Set with Charles Bronson

Paul Talbot

BearManor Media

Albany, Georgia

Bronson's Loose Again! On the Set with Charles Bronson
Copyright © 2016 Paul Talbot. All Rights Reserved.

No part of this book may be reproduced in any form or by any means, electronic, mechanical, digital, photocopying or recording, except for the inclusion in a review, without permission in writing from the publisher.

This book is an independent work of research and commentary and is not sponsored, authorized or endorsed by, or otherwise affiliated with, the Estate of Charles Bronson or any motion picture studio or production company affiliated with the films discussed herein. All uses of the name, image and likeness of Charles Bronson and other individuals, and all copyrights and trademarks referenced in this book, are for editorial purposes and are pursuant to the Fair Use Doctrine.

The views and opinions of individuals quoted in this book do not necessarily reflect those of the author.

The promotional photographs and publicity materials reproduced herein are in the author's private collection (unless noted otherwise). These images date from the original release of the films and were released to media outlets for publicity purposes.

Published in the USA by
BearManor Media
P.O. Box 71426
Albany, GA 31708
www.BearManorMedia.com

Softcover Edition
ISBN-10: 1593938977
ISBN-13: 978-1-59393-897-0

Library of Congress Control Number: 2015919039
BearManor Media, Albany, GA

Printed in the United States of America

Table of Contents

Acknowledgments   vii

Introduction   ix

Chapter 1: A Brief Bronson Biography   1

Chapter 2: *Hard Times* (1975)   13

Chapter 3: *From Noon Till Three* (1976)   59

Chapter 4: *Love and Bullets* (1979)   83

Chapter 5: *Cabo Blanco* (1980)   109

Chapter 6: *Borderline* (1980)   137

Chapter 7: Screenwriter David Engelbach on *Death Wish II*   155

Chapter 8: The Women of *Death Wish II*: Robin Sherwood and Silvana Gallardo   173

Chapter 9: Actor Robert F. Lyons on *Death Wish II*   185

Chapter 10: *10 to Midnight* (1983)   191

Chapter 11: *The Evil That Men Do* (1984)   217

Chapter 12: The Giggler Lives!: Actor Kirk Taylor on *Death Wish 3*   241

Chapter 13: *Act of Vengeance* (1986)   253

Chapter 14: *Murphy's Law* (1986)   265

Chapter 15: *Assassination* (1987)   301

Chapter 16: *Messenger of Death* (1988)   323

Chapter 17: *Kinjite: Forbidden Subjects* (1989)   339

Chapter 18: *Yes Virginia, There is a Santa Claus* (1991)   357

Chapter 19: *The Sea Wolf* (1993)   369

Chapter 20: *Donato and Daughter* (1993)   381

Chapter 21: Actor Robert Joy on *Death Wish V: The Face of Death*   391

Chapter 22: The *Family of Cops* Series (1995–1999)   401

Bibliography   419

Index   431

Acknowledgments

During the researching of this book, intense efforts were made to contact cast and crew members who worked on a film with Charles Bronson and extreme thanks is extended to those who agreed to be interviewed.

Special thanks to these fellow Bronson scholars for providing contact information and/or invaluable research materials: John Charles, Horace Cordier, Duke Fenady, Mark Hartley, Bobby Heckman, Mike Malloy, Bryan Moose, Chris Poggiali, Scott Ray, Robert Richardson, Edwin Samuelson, Neil Sarver, Tom Stockman, William Wilson, and Eric Zaldivar.

Thanks to Ben Ohmart and BearManor Media for publishing the book, to W. Heyward Sims for the cover design, to Sam Bruce for proof reading, and to Eric Greenwood for photo scanning and technical advice.

Thanks also for the longtime support of Marco Antonio, Stewart Baulk, Christopher Bickel, Howard S. Berger, Sam Bruce, Charles Brower, Ryan Clark, Travis Crawford, Shane Dallman, John Exshaw, Tommy Faircloth, Lee Goldberg, Greg Goodsell, Don Guarisco, Brian Harris, John Harrison, Bruce Holecheck, Troy Howarth, Chad Kaplan, Andre Joseph, Ian McDowell, Marty McKee, Zack Meekins, Lee Pfeiffer, Steve Pulchalski, Jason Stout, Dan Taylor, Nathaniel Thompson, Mark Tinta, Delmo Walters, Jr., Anthony Vitamia, and Robert Zobel.

And finally, thanks to God, my family, and all of the Bronson Brothers that bought and/or read my first Bronson book, and to all those holding this book.

Introduction

After the publication of *Bronson's Loose!: The Making of the 'Death Wish' Films*, I located and interviewed a half-dozen more alumni of the *Death Wish* sequels. This inspired an exhaustive search for more living cast and crew members who had worked with Charles Bronson on non-*Death Wish* movies. The collection of three dozen new interviews plus an abundance of ongoing, extensive research snowballed into enough material for this companion book.

Bronson's Loose Again!: On the Set with Charles Bronson covers Bronson's career after the first *Death Wish* as well as during and after the sequels. Documented herein are production stories behind some of the best Bronson films of the 1970s; his work in the 1980s (including his pictures for the notorious Cannon Films); and his return to acting after a brief hiatus in the early 1990s in television movies that featured some of the more interesting performances of his entire filmography.

For this book, I wrote only about Bronson movies for which I could secure at least one primary interview. Films that have already been extensively covered elsewhere are not discussed here. Examples: the making of *Mr. Majestyk* (1974) is discussed in Walter Mirisch's autobiography *I Thought We Were Making Movies, Not History* and in Richard Fleischer's book *Just Tell Me When To Cry*; the making of *Telefon* (1977) is detailed in Don Siegel's memoir *A Siegel Film*; and the extras on the *Death Hunt* (1981) Blu-ray (from Shout! Factory) cover everything about that film.

This book is intended to be read by those who have already seen the movies that are discussed. The story synopses in each chapter rarely run longer than one sentence—but the quotes, the anecdotes and the information contain "spoilers." Each chapter is intended to be a "stand alone" piece to be read after each film is watched (or rewatched). There is some (very) minor overlapping of information between several chapters in this book and in the previous *Bronson's Loose!* book.

When the first *Bronson's Loose!* was released, I was amazed to learn that many Bronson fans were decades younger than me and that the star's young audience continues to expand. I hope that this book will entertain the Bronson buffs who want to learn more about cult favorites like *Hard Times* (1975), the *Death Wish* sequels (1982–1994), *10 to Midnight* (1983), and *Murphy's Law* (1986). I also hope that these chapters will lead more Bronson fans to discover or reevaluate his lesser-known, underrated films like *From Noon Till Three* (1976), *Borderline* (1980), *Act of Vengeance* (1986), and *The Sea Wolf* (1993).

No other action icon ever aged as well onscreen as Bronson did. He remains one of the most exciting and unique screen personalities in film history. It doesn't get better than Bronson.

Chapter 1
A Brief Bronson Biography

Charles Bronson once said, "There's nobody who had less regard for himself than I did in my youth. There's nothing that gives a more inferior feeling than digging a hole in the ground."

The future international screen icon Charles Dennis Bunchinsky was born in Ehrenfeld, Pennsylvania, on November 3, 1921, into a family of dirt-poor coal miners. "When I was a kid, I used to take long walks in the woods while other boys were playing baseball or football. Every once in a while, I'd spot a chicken that had gotten loose from its owner's coop. I'd throw my knife at it. Then I'd chop off its head, gut the chicken, pack it in mud and cook it slowly over a fire. It really was delicious."

At sixteen, he went into the family business. The young man's time in the coal mines built up his later-to-be-famous physique, but the grueling work also left him with permanent scars on his back and periodic bouts with claustrophobia that lasted for the rest of his life. "Even now," he recalled many decades later, "when I'm in the back of a car, I can get those feelings."

In the late 1920s, older brother Joe slightly modified the spelling of his last name to "Buchinsky," and Charles (and most of the other siblings) followed suit. Charles was drafted into the Army in early 1943 and served as a tail gunner in the South Pacific. At one point he took a bullet in the shoulder, which added another scar to his already-creviced torso. "For me, being drafted was like having a fairy godfather change me into a prince. Who knows where I'd be today if I hadn't gone into the Army? I met my share of sonofabitches in the service. I remember back during World War II, when I was in gunnery school at Kingman, Arizona, the squadron had a party. This sergeant's wife wanted to dance with me. Great big fat woman. Hell, I didn't want to dance with her. *Nobody'd* want to dance with her. I told her no. Little later, the sergeant comes over to me and wants to know why I've been propositioning his wife. Apparently, she'd gone over and told him I'd been after her. I told him I hadn't propositioned her, and I wasn't interested in her that way or any other way. So he wants to fight. Fight a sergeant when I'm a private? I didn't need that and I knew it. I backed off. He follows. I back. He comes on. I back all the way down the dance floor, until I'm against the wall and I can't back any further. So I picked the bastard up and threw him. For some screwy reason, I thought if I didn't hit him, I wouldn't get in trouble. So I threw him. When he landed, he broke his arm. I got six months hard labor, carrying sides of beef into the mess hall and cans of garbage out of it."

After the war, he used the GI Bill to study acting and, billed as "Charles Buchinsky," struggled to find work. "When I got out of the Army, I got a job in [a] gambling joint in Atlantic City. Then I went out to the Pasadena Playhouse, where I tried to study speech just to improve my diction. It was rough. I was afraid that too much speech instruction would hurt me. Precise English and my kind of looks don't go together. I demonstrated toys on street corners, sold Christmas cards, and played a village blacksmith in a community theater. Another actor recommended me for a part at Fox in *You're in the Navy Now* [1951] with Gary Cooper. I got the part because I could belch on cue.

"I'd never even seen a studio before. I never went into Hollywood because you had to ride a bus to get there, and I didn't even have bus fare. But I got a lotta jobs after that. Mostly punks, construction workers, punchy fighters—all the parts nobody could play because of their educated backgrounds I could play because I was just a bum. Most actors are impersonators, but in me they got the real thing. I came along when you had to look like a part to play it. If you looked like Tyrone Power, you got romantic roles; if you had two scars on your face, you were the heavy. I thought I'd get stuck in a category playing elevator operators and doormen all my life. I never thought of myself as the romantic lead in those days."

The young actor decided to change his last name to "Bronson" after spotting that moniker on a Hollywood street sign. The name "Charles Bronson" first appeared on-screen in the Alan Ladd Western *Drum Beat* (1954), which gave Bronson a great supporting role as the villainous Native American "Captain Jack." The performance should have earned him an Oscar nod and a stardom launch. He got neither.

In 1958 he was excellent as the lead in four outstanding B-pictures: *Showdown at Boot Hill*, *Machine Gun Kelly*, *Gang War*, and *When Hell Broke Loose*—but the movies and the star received little notice. That same year, he got the title role in the half-hour TV series *Man with a Camera* (1958–1960), where he played a freelance photographer who dealt with various bad guys. "[I was] playing second banana to a flashbulb."

By the early 1960s, Bronson was a popular supporting player in hit films like *The Magnificent Seven* (1960) and *The Great Escape* (1963). In 1964 he signed with top Hollywood agent Paul Kohner—who repped the likes of Ingmar Bergman, Marlene Dietrich, John Huston and Liv Ullman. Bronson continued to work constantly, and his unique charisma was featured in major features including *The Sandpiper* (1965) with Elizabeth Taylor, *This Property Is Condemned* (1966) with Natalie Wood, and the World War II action blockbuster *The Dirty Dozen* (1967) with Lee Marvin. Much of his best work of the 1960s was on television. He had "guest star" gigs on dozens of top shows including *The Twilight Zone* (1961), *Alfred Hitchcock Presents* (1962), *Bonanza* (1964), *Rawhide* (1965), *Combat!* (1965), and *The Fugitive* (1967).

On October 5, 1968, Bronson married the British actress Jill Ireland. They had been involved since the shooting of *The Great Escape* when Ireland was married to Bronson's co-star/buddy David McCallum. Bronson and Ireland would be inseparable for the next twenty-one and a half years and would appear in sixteen films together.

Bronson was now in his mid-forties and had been acting onscreen for fifteen years. It seemed obvious that he would never become a major American star, but he was still reluctant to make overseas pictures and turned down lead roles in all three films of Sergio Leone's *Dollars* Spaghetti Western trilogy (1964–1966)—even after the first one had made Clint Eastwood a worldwide icon. Bronson finally agreed to appear in the European films *Farewell, Friend* (1968), *Once Upon a Time in the West* (1968) and *Rider on the Rain* (1970). Although ignored in the United States—where they were shelved or sparsely-released—the three movies were international blockbusters and turned Bronson into one of the biggest film superstars in the entire world. "Jill pushed me in directions I didn't want to go. She made me do *Farewell, Friend* in France with Alain Delon—which was critically and financially good. Jill convinced me to make *Rider [on the Rain]* and, ironically, it was the picture that changed my career."

With his squinty eyes, stoic expression, bulky physique, and cracked, unhandsome face, Bronson was an unlikely candidate for screen stardom, but his effortless charisma and powerful presence made it impossible for audiences to ignore him. Agent Paul Kohner worked with publicist Ernie Anderson to skillfully promote Bronson's brooding, simmering, allegedly violent persona while building up the star's filmography and wallet. By the early 1970s—with foreign hits like *Violent City* (1970), *Cold Sweat* (1970) and *Red Sun* (1971)—Bronson was one of the planet's highest-paid actors and was getting $500,000 per picture. "The best publicity breaks in the world are your successful pictures—movies that your audience liked well enough to pay three or four dollars a seat and left the theatre entertained."

Trade ad for *Red Sun* (1971), one of Bronson's biggest international hits.

The Bronson phenomenon was huge in Japan. *Red Sun* unspooled in one Tokyo theater for nine months and broke the house record set by the recent reissue of *Gone with the Wind* (1939)—which had played for a mere four months. Nearby, a massive billboard displayed a lone image: a painting of Bronson's cracked, mustached face. There was no text, just the visual promise that the latest movie with the nation's favorite star could be seen locally. In 1971 Bronson collected $100,000 for four days work shooting (in Colorado) a series of TV ads for a new cologne from the Japanese firm Mandom. These clever spots by director Nobuhiko Ohbayashi (who went on to do the 1977 cult horror film *Hausu*) perfectly captured the rugged Bronson mystique. A few weeks after the first commercial's broadcast, Mandom's product was the best-selling cologne in Japan. A rival company decided to not even bother airing its own Bronson-less ad.

"The rest of the world is more important now, as far as the movie business is concerned. More than half the gross comes from overseas. And most of the pictures being made in the U.S. these days don't interest me that much. American pictures have become narrowly nationalistic in that they show mostly only our own worst problems. Ninety-percent of the pictures being made are either subtly or indirectly anti-American. It can be just the selection of the actors in a film. They can be overly effeminate or overly something else—and its unattractive. The subject matter also leaves a lot to be desired. Take a picture like *Dusty and Sweets McGee* (1971). All it shows is the problem of drug addiction—no solution or even hope of a solution. It doesn't put junkies, who are not a majority in this country, in their proper context in society. I don't think people around the world want pictures like that from us. They want to see the kind of pictures we don't seem to make much anymore. Strong, meaningful stories where a problem or a conflict is presented, then worked through, resolved. They want to see interesting, fully developed characters. People who don't just take off all their clothes and jump into bed together at the bat of an eye."

In the early 1970s, the Bronson cult had become so insatiable in France that a half-dozen of his movies (including the old *Machine Gun Kelly*) were screening simultaneously at Paris cinemas to large crowds. No one was more surprised by Bronson's popularity than Bronson. "I don't think of myself as being ruggedly good-looking and I never have. I have never thought of myself competing with the likes of Rock Hudson."

Between takes on the sets of his movies, Bronson kept to himself while whistling, chain-smoking, bouncing a ball, or whittling. "I'm not a mixer. To tell you the truth, I'm friendless. I don't like shop talk. The idea of being invited to play tennis on somebody's swanky Bel Air tennis court is like being asked to eat garbage. There's no reason not to have friends. Just the opposite is true. There's every reason to have friends. But I don't think you ought to have friends unless you're willing to give them time. I give time to nobody. My wife is my friend. I confide in Jill if I happen to have something to confide. Worries can be running a maze through my mind, really burning in my head, and I won't even mention them to my wife."

Although Bronson was still barely known to moviegoers in his native country, his wealth enabled him to purchase a huge, Oriental rug-paved mansion in Bel Air, California and a farm in West Windsor, Vermont. The 260-acre New England estate, which was filled with antiques (including carousel horses), became the favorite retreat of the Bronson clan when the star was not shooting a picture.

At the 1972 Golden Globe Awards ceremony, Bronson was named by the Hollywood Foreign Press Association as "World Film Favorite: Male" (i.e. the world's most popular male actor) in a tie with Sean Connery of "James Bond" fame. "Hollywood has always been limited in the casting of stars. I probably would have been stuck in featured roles if I had stayed here. The money for films is borrowed on the stars' names, and traditionally the stars have been the half-baked publicity names. In Europe, there is no such problem. Most of the countries have government subsidies, so the producers don't have to borrow on their stars' names. They hire the best actors for the roles."

Newsweek: "The scripts are tommy-guns of clichés in which blood flows like red-eye, and the starlets wear bodices that pop open with the regularity of an exhibitionist's raincoat. But what the audience really digs is Bronson's tough-yet-tender act, which mixes parody and fantasy."

The critics rarely praised his performances, but Bronson was a trained, serious, and meticulous actor. He was extremely critical of his own films and performances. "My approach to acting is different than most actors. I just do it. No trickery. Just drawing on experience. Acting for me is a combination of instinct and emotional experience." Beginning in 1972, "director approval" became a non-negotiable clause in the star's contracts.

Bronson played a mob figure (his character ages four decades) in the Italian-made *The Valachi Papers* (1972). It grossed $17 million in America, but industry insiders credited the huge ticket sales to the post-*Godfather* (1972) "mafia-mania" and not to the Bronson fan base. The shot-in-the States Bronson vehicles *The Mechanic* (1972), *The Stone Killer* (1972), and *Mr. Majestyk* (1974) were all excellent, action-packed films that didn't ignite American box offices.

"The critic on one magazine wrote that I was better in *The Mechanic* than in *The Valachi Papers* because I had less to say. When a man goes out of his way to blast me that way, I figure he knows for certain that I had his wife in bed or that I've beaten a friend of his to a pulp. Why else would he write that? The critics never see my role as it is—as a man protecting his garden, killing poisonous snakes. Instead they just say it's me again committing violence. When you act, your whole body is the instrument. Those critics can't relate to this. It's a lot more difficult to act with blood on your face rather than sipping cocktails on a couch. And which one do you think the public's going to pay to see?"

Although he would (reluctantly) grant press interviews, Bronson rarely appeared on TV talk shows. "I don't like them. I was once on *The*

A Brief Bronson Biography

Dick Cavett Show [1972] to plug a picture, and he said, 'I understand you're pretty physical.' He wanted me to take off my shirt and show my scars. I thought, 'This little snot-nose is trying to trap me.' I didn't want to put myself in that position."

When *Death Wish*—starring Bronson as an enraged New York City vigilante—opened in the summer of 1974, the ticket booths exploded with $22 million in sales. The fifty-four-year-old actor finally became a box office draw in his own country and the brutal film became one of the more controversial and debated of its era. "I have made more than fifty films in my life, and some of them are really forgettable. But my favorites are *Red Sun* and *Rider in the Rain*—and if you think about it, they were two of my best, and no one got to see them. I mean no one in comparison to the millions who have seen *Death Wish* and complained about it."

Charles Bronson in *Death Wish* (1974), the star's first (and only) American box office blockbuster.

As *Death Wish* became an immediate smash, Paul Kohner encouraged Bronson to take an extended vacation at the Vermont farm while the agent ignored all scripts and offers that were being presented. Kohner insisted that no movie deal would be accepted that didn't provide Bronson with at least $1 million upfront (for a shoot lasting no more than six weeks). "I've found when a man becomes a star, after a couple of years he no longer seems to try. They get in a groove, a ditch. I remember working with people who were stars—before I was one—and watching them stalk off to their trailers because they needed a rest or a drink. It's a rut I don't want to get into and won't get into."

Robert Chartoff and Irwin Winkler, who had previously produced *The Mechanic*, met Bronson's fee and signed him for *The Ten-Second Jailbreak*—their new project at Columbia Pictures. Original director Michael Ritchie (*Downhill Racer*, 1969) quit the film over creative issues with the script (he wanted more humor) and over Bronson's insistence that Jill Ireland play the female lead. The two producers already knew not to argue with the star's casting choice—previously, Bronson had threated to walk off *The Mechanic* if his wife didn't get a role. Tom Gries (*Will Penny*, 1968) ended up directing the new Chartoff/Winkler production, which was retitled *Breakout* and ended up as an efficient action programmer with a fine, semi-comedic performance from Bronson.

The Columbia Pictures hierarchy were initially delighted to have the first post-*Death Wish* Bronson movie, but when the suits finally watched the completed *Breakout*, they thought that it was barely releasable—even after it became one of the star's biggest overseas hits when it opened in Europe in March 1975. *Breakout* became an early example of "saturation booking" after one executive suggested that the studio could salvage the American release by investing heavily in non-stop, nationwide TV ads. Columbia scheduled the film into a then-record 1,400 theaters for a simultaneous opening on May 21, 1975. To find that many available screens, the studio had to book *Breakout* into drive-ins and second-run houses in some cities—but still at first-run prices. A then-massive $4 million was spent on promotion including the ubiquitous airings of *Breakout* TV and radio spots ("the greatest escape film ever!"). Huge

A BRIEF BRONSON BIOGRAPHY

newspaper and magazine ads warned that this new Bronson movie would only be playing "special limited engagements." Fifty-grand was gambled to show a trailer during the televised Muhammad Ali vs. Ron Lyle bout on May 16.

Spanish poster for *Breakout* (1975). (Courtesy of Eric Zaldivar)

The costly, clever strategy worked, and *Breakout* became one of the "must-see" event pictures in the spring of 1975. The PG rating (despite a graphic image of a guy getting ripped apart by an airplane propeller) increased ticket sales by enabling adolescent boys to see the film at matinees. The movie collected $12.7 million in the first two weeks of release, recouped its entire production and marketing costs within a month, and ultimately grossed $16 million in America. One excited promoter said, "Stripped to the waist, Bronson's money in the bank." (A few months later, the *Jaws* marketing team at Universal Pictures recreated the *Breakout* "saturation" recipe with astonishing results.)

Over the next fourteen years, Bronson would prove to be as tireless as his movie characters. He would star in twenty-one violent action pictures and would constantly be on international theaters screens. "I don't let success go to my head. I still feel like the poor kid who grew up in the school of hard knocks. The bad thing about being famous is people notice you and point you out wherever you go. It scares the hell out of me. An actor shouldn't pick parts to please himself. He's got to think of the movie fans all around the world who want to be entertained. They pay for it all."

Chapter 2
Hard Times (1975)

Hard Times is a genuine, unforgettable masterpiece and one of the more underrated films of the 1970s. As the mysterious bare-fisted boxer "Chaney," Charles Bronson gives his best-ever lead performance and burns a hole in the screen with his charisma. First-time director Walter Hill's staging, camera compositions, gritty Depression-era atmosphere, and use of authentic New Orleans locations are impeccable.

Hill got his start in the late 1960s as a second assistant director. At the beginning of the next decade, he was a hot screenwriter with *Hickey & Boggs* (1972), *The Getaway* (1972), *The Thief Who Came to Dinner* (1973) and *The Mackintosh Man* (1973) on his resume. He said, "I met Larry [Lawrence] Gordon in the spring of 1973—he was running A.I.P.

Charles Bronson as Chaney, a mysterious bare-fisted boxer, in *Hard Times* (1975). This portrait was taken during the filming of a deleted rail yard fight scene.

[American International Pictures] then, and he told me he'd give me a shot at directing if I'd write a script for him. We had to find a subject, obviously—then he moved over to Columbia Pictures. Larry was going to have his own unit that specialized in low-budget action films. The first thing he told me was that he didn't figure he was taking a chance on me as a director: I couldn't be worse than the ones he'd been working with at A.I.P., and at least he'd have a shot at getting a good script. I was in that bullshit 'hot-writer' phase coming off *The Getaway*, so we made a deal: write for scale, direct for scale, and they couldn't make the picture without me. So it was a good bargain for everybody; they got me cheap, and I got a shot at directing. The truth is, I would've paid them for the chance." In March 1974, the thirty-two-year-old Hill left his writing job on the Paul Newman detective picture *The Drowning Pool* (1975) when he got the *Hard Times* gig.

Gordon had come across an original action script by young writers Bryan Gindoff and Bruce Henstell. The premise was based on an early-1970s newspaper article about street boxers who fought bare-fisted in underground, high-stakes bouts in the San Pedro area of Los Angeles. Gindoff had written and produced the exceptional, truth-inspired low-budget suspense picture *The Candy Snatchers* (1973), about a young woman who was kidnapped and buried alive in a fiberglass coffin. Henstell had crewed on a few low-budget pictures, including *The Candy Snatchers*.

Henstell says, (1) "Our original script fortuitously landed on the desk of producer Larry Gordon shortly after he had made a deal to produce at Columbia. He was enticed away from the world of 'low-budget' film at American International. His deal at Columbia, I was told, was that he had more or less complete control on any film he brought in at under a set figure—a million dollars, I think it was. Gordon's family were businessmen from Mississippi. He had a number of chits and favors he could call upon in from the, let us say laissez-faire, world of New Orleans to control production costs. So he was looking for a project he could shoot there, and ours happened to fit."

Hill said, "[The script] was contemporary and pretty rough stuff—very A.I.P. I thought maybe if you did it more like a Western with a kind of mythopoeic hero, it might take the edge off—give it a chance to come up-market. Larry went with that, so we made it period—set it in New Orleans. Larry had spent a lot of time there; he went to Law School at Tulane. He knew a lot about the city."

Gordon said at the time, "If it wasn't for tax shelter dollars, I don't think I'd be [shooting] in New Orleans; I don't think this film would be financed. I wanted the film here for two reasons. First, the background is very, very special. You get a great look from the extras and a great accent that you can't get anyplace else in the country. And second, I simply wanted to come back to a place I consider a second home."

Hill's own screenwriting style began to develop when he got a copy of the *Point Blank* (1967) script from that film's writer, Alex Jacobs. Hill

Jill Ireland as Lucy Simpson.

said, "I admit to a somewhat juvenile sensibility, with an emphasis on physical heroics. I tried to write in an extremely spare, almost Haiku style—both stage directions and dialogue. Some of it was a bit pretentious, but at other times I thought it worked pretty well. *Hard Times* was the first, and I think maybe the best [written in that style]. The clear narrative drive of the material and the splash-panel approach to the characters perfectly fit the design I was trying to make work."

An example of Hill's "Haiku style" in the *Hard Times* script:

Chaney drops his coat.
Silence.
The two hitters move out.
Palms up.
Cesare's man comes forward.
Chaney feints, hits him once.
Once is enough.
Out like a match.

Gindroff and Henstell's street fighting script was rewritten by Hill to take place in the 1930s. (No specific date is ever mentioned in the actual film, but Hill's screenplay gave the date as "1936," and the publicity materials and trailer later announced "1933.") At the time, the American public was in a nostalgia craze for that decade, and Hollywood produced a number of 1930s-set movies including *The Sting* (1973), *Paper Moon* (1973), *The Way We Were* (1973), *Dillinger* (1973), *Big Bad Mama* (1974), *Capone* (1975), *W.C. Fields and Me* (1976) and *Gable and Lombard* (1976)—with varying degrees of success.

Lobby card: Chaney (Bronson) visits Lucy's (Jill Ireland) apartment.

Hill said, "I wrote a draft, then rewrote it four or five times before I finally got it. But I did get it, and I knew it. I knew it was going to get an actor, and get made." His drafts were written in longhand on legal pads. *Lloyd Williams and His Brother* was a 1969 Western script by Hill that was optioned but never filmed. Elements from that screenplay ended up in *Hard Times*.

The *Hard Times* script was peppered with text that was to appear on screen. The film was to open with:

> This story is true in most details.
> The names have been changed.
> Not much else.
> It has no moral.

The screenplay was broken down into three "parts," with each part beginning with a quote:

PART ONE

> After all, characters are best explained through their behavior.
>
> Old Welsh saying

> Talk's cheap.
>
> Old American saying

PART TWO

> They speak whatever's on their mind
> they do whatever's in their pants

the boys i mean are not refined
they shake the mountains when they dance

> e.e. cummings

PART THREE

There is a code of honor among pickpockets and among whores. It is simply that the standards differ.

> Ernest Hemingway

The opening legend and the periodic literary quotes did appear in the film until they were dropped from the very final cut.

Chaney (Bronson) and manager Spencer "Speed" Weed (James Coburn) in the Louisiana bayou.

Hill said, "My favorite advice to directors about casting that I read was by the great Broadway director George Abbot, who said, 'Directors like to think there's only one actor who can play a certain part, but there's always somebody else.' I think that's true. I'd written the lead in *Hard Times* for a much younger man; I thought we'd get someone like Jan-Michael Vincent [*The Mechanic*, 1972], and I wanted Warren Oates [*Two-Lane Blacktop*, 1971] for [James] Coburn's part. But it worked out."

Speed—the flashy, self-destructive con man played in *Hard Times* by James Coburn—was described in Hill's screenplay as "A man past the first flush but who still possesses great energy." After dozens of TV episodes, Coburn (with Bronson) got a career boost with supporting roles in *The Magnificent Seven* (1960) and *The Great Escape* (1963). The lanky, 6' 2" (1.88 m) actor had a rich voice and an unforgettable presence and went on to be a major star in *In Like Flint* (1967), *The President's Analyst* (1967) and *Pat Garrett and Billy the Kid* (1973). Coburn was familiar with the *Hard Times* era—his father had lost the family garage business during the Great Depression.

Hill said, "They had offered [the lead] to a couple of actors, and they didn't want to do it. Then we sent it to Charlie [Bronson]. I said he was too old. I never really was in love with Charlie too much. A day later, which was unbelievably fast, they called back and said he read the script, liked the script, wanted to do the movie, but he had to meet me. He wanted to see if I measured up. Charlie comes out of a side room, wearing a black t-shirt, black jeans. God, he was really in shape. I started to reach out and shake hands, and he just walked by. He grabbed a small wooden chair that was there, turned it around—just one move, boom! Bam, put it down, then sat kind of backwards on the chair, leaned over the back of the chair—and he hadn't even said 'Hello.' There was a pause. He was very...Bronsonian. He shook hands and asked me why the hell I thought I could direct him. He got a million of our $2.7 million budget."

Once Bronson was cast, Hill reworked the script's dialogue to reflect

Hard Times (1975)

Bronson as Chaney.

the star's age: "Well, you look a little past it, friend"; "Hey, pops, ain't you a little old for this?"; "Hey, old man, I'm going to end it for you."

Deleted scene: Poe (Strother Martin), Chaney (Bronson) and Speed (James Coburn) arrive for a factory yard fight.

The fifty-two-year-old Bronson was easily believable as a successful street fighter because of his spectacular physical condition. Every morning, the actor would rise early, consume a cup of coffee, and begin his workout. He said, "I run. I have a sandbag hanging from a tree, and I punch it. When I'm on my farm in Vermont, I build stone walls. I chop and split wood. I help with the haying. I probably will be physical all of my days. I don't read too many novels where the hero is stronger than me. Most time, I feel I outperform them." His daily routine also included deep squats and climbing up a forty-foot rope hand-over-hand. If he was at a movie location where the weather or streets were unsuitable for running, he would jog through the rooms of his hotel suite. Bronson consumed a daily vitamin ritual supervised by his actress wife, Jill Ireland. In his prime, the 5' 8" (1 m. 72 cm.) actor kept his weight at 160 pounds (72.57 kg.). He ate small meals and only on very rare occasions would he treat himself to steak and potatoes or one-fourth of a doughnut. Once a month, he'd indulge in a small glass of the alcoholic liqueur Campari. Even before his stardom, the actor had been fanatical about his physique. In the early part of his career, before his torso became world-famous, he would ask directors to let him play some scenes shirtless.

Bronson kept his legendary physique for *Hard Times* but lost his famous hair to suit the Depression time period. He said, "Usually, my hair is long, and I wear a moustache in films. But not in this one." The shaggy hair on his head was trimmed drastically for *Hard Times*. (Receding hair was something the star never had to worry about. His thick, natural mane stayed for the rest of his life.) The mustache had been his international trademark since *Rider in the Rain* (1969). Previously, he agreed to shave it for *The Valachi Papers* (1972) to match that film's real-life character, but he would later refuse his directors' requests to lose the facial hair for *Telefon* (1977) and *Borderline* (1980).

Writer Harry Crews, who visited the set of the star's next picture *Breakheart Pass*, noted: "Bronson stands like a pit bulldog. He somehow manages that kind of balance with only two feet. It is the kind of balance only the very finest athletes, the world-beaters have....So symmetrical is he that it is impossible for him to make an ungraceful move, and it is from that symmetry that his bulldog balance comes....He is, in fact, the straight-on, tear-your-balls-off kind of guy that he so often portrays with such power on the screen."

Cast as Speed's "permanent fiancé", Gayleen, was Texas-born Maggie Blye. She says, "The very first picture I did was *Summer and Smoke* [1961]. It was a Hal Wallis production with Geraldine Page and Laurence Harvey. It was actually Geraldine who encouraged me to continue acting. She thought I was a natural and that I should continue as an actress. I did a very tiny 'one-line' in a picture with Don Murray called *One Man's Way* [1964] and then I did *Hombre* [1967]—that was my big break and I was put under a seven-year contract at Fox." After that Paul Newman Western, Blye had major roles in *Waterhole #3* opposite James

Coburn and *The Italian Job* with Michael Caine. "And then, I had all those ridiculous bombs. I did a campy movie called *Diamonds for Breakfast* [1968]. Marcello Mastroianni, poor baby, was supposed to have an English accent and speak with a Russian accent. He was so confused. We couldn't understand anything he was saying. *He* didn't know what he was saying. I play a cat burglar. This was made in 1967, the year I was dating Omar Sharif, for goodness sake. We were all over every magazine. Oh, my gosh, what a fun time. Those were the days where you didn't have to worry about security or any of that kind of stuff. Life was just so easy. It was so pleasant. Women have to learn how to handle [themselves] in Hollywood. It's not easy. I was fortunate. I was very blessed in that I had very good management and very good agents and they were quite protective.

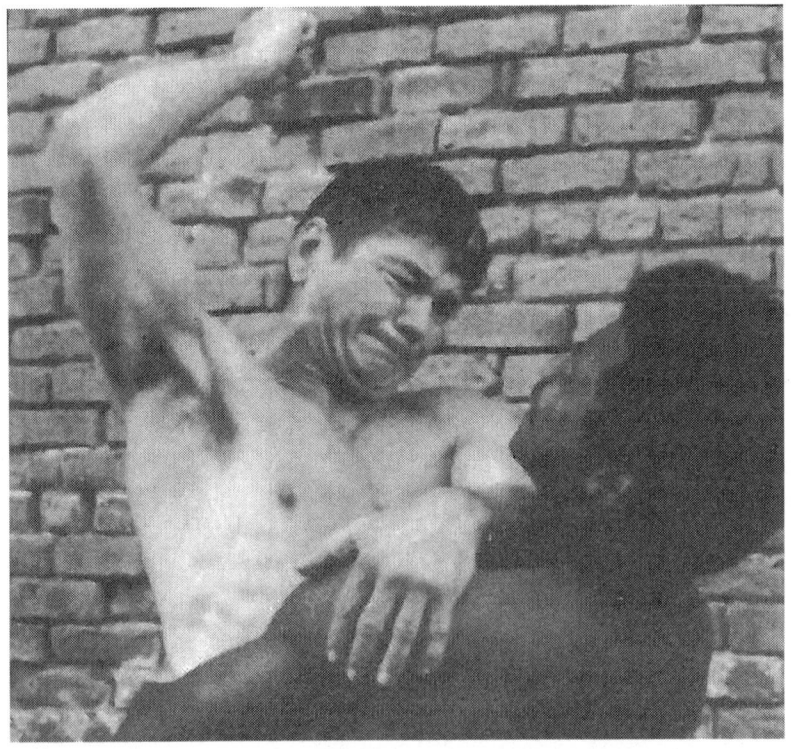

Deleted scene: Chaney (Bronson) battles Zack (Bob Minor).

"[For *Hard Times*,] I did not have an audition, I had a meeting. And it was presented to me as an offer. I remember Walter being there. Walter was great. He was always on my side. He was pulling for me to play Gayleen from the beginning. I think Walter had a little crush, maybe. He'd seen *Waterhole* and just fell in love with me in *Waterhole*. Someone told me that I was the reason why they got Coburn. I don't know what his hesitation was before they brought me into the project. He wasn't that interested and then when they told him that I was gonna be playing the love interest, he liked the idea of working together again. He knew me, so he felt comfortable with that because everyone is always more comfortable working with people that they know. And everyone always wants to have someone on their team."

Bruce Glover, a popular character actor—with credits including *Diamonds Are Forever* (1971) and *Chinatown* (1974)—was cast as the loan shark flunky "Doty." He says, "I didn't read for it. There was no audition. I just went over for an interview. I had built a rapport with a lot of people, so my reputation was getting pretty strong. I had been at it a while by then and fairly confident in what I was doing."

Glover had hard times of his own growing up in Chicago during the late 1930s and early '40s. He says, "In my working class neighborhood, I started [working] at [age] six. Worked for my dad when I was eight. He got me a job on a newsstand on the corner down from his watch repair store. I made $6 a week for six days work, every day after school and then all-day on Saturday. And I'd get that six bucks, and I really felt rich. I did every kind of job you can think of, including coal delivery. You didn't even have wheelbarrows; you just had canvas sacks. I was doing that when I was ten. We were so poor. If there was bath water, my sisters would bathe first. Then, my mother. And then, they would let me bathe. But when I was covered with coal dust, I'd get my own bath. [laughs] It made me aware that I could make money, and that it took work."

Deleted scene: Chaney (Bronson) fights at the railroad tracks.

Hard Times started shooting at the beginning of September 1974. The cast and much of the crew were booked into the Fairmont Roosevelt Hotel at 130 Roosevelt Way, an eighty-one-year-old building that covered an entire block. The hotel was named after Theodore Roosevelt. Numerous other United States Presidents would check in over the years—as would Elvis Pressley, who stayed in the entire top floor while shooting

King Creole (1957). The Fairmont Roosevelt was right next to the French Quarter, enabling the *Hard Times* company to be able to walk to almost all of the filming locations.

Blye: "They flew me into New Orleans on a Thursday. We were gonna start shooting Monday. We all had lunch. It was at one of those chain restaurants. It had that lattice stained glass atmosphere with lots of hanging macramé plants that looked left over from the 60s. [laughs] It was a fun lunch. Everybody was very 'up' and excited about starting the picture. It was charming and funny and all that good stuff. But I noticed that Charlie was just a total observer. He was like the big panther or tiger. He just watched things. Always. And you never can read him. I guess he's the perfect poker player because you cannot read the man's face at all, what he's thinking. At least I couldn't. At the end of the meal, he came up to me and took my hand and said, 'You're a really good actress. I'm glad you're in this movie. You're gonna be fine.' They had told Charlie that he could have approval. Charlie was his own cut of the cloth. This was a very, very unusual man. And I'm so glad that he got with Jill because she was a sweet, warm, very conservative lady. Very withdrawn, very reserved. But so kind and just genuinely sweet. And I liked her very much."

Gayleen (Maggie Blye) pleads with Speed (James Coburn) to leave the dice table. In the final cut, Gayleen disappears from the movie after this scene.

Jill Ireland was with Bronson in New Orleans not only as his wife, but also to play his love interest, "Lucy Simpson"—described in the script as "Eccentrically attractive, but with querulous, doubting eyes. A bit shopworn for her years." Ireland said, "You get caught in this acting thing, and you almost can't do without it. You want a job. But you can't get one. You know you can do it, but, damn it, you can't do it unless someone asks you to. It's enough to drive you to suicide when you can't work. I think I'm in so many of his pictures because no other actress would work with him. He's a stickler for punctuality, and he's always hustling me out of my dressing room to be on time. I wouldn't presume to say I was an influence on his career, but perhaps on his choice of leading lady. I think he's a fated individual, that what happened to him happened the day he was born. People can make it easier for you, ease your general burdens, but I don't think they can make it happen." Her $75,000 salary was a fraction of what Bronson was paid for the film, but she also got over $100,000 worth of jewelry that her husband bought for her from the hotel's lobby. The Bronsons' three-year-old daughter Zuleika was with them for the entire shoot. Their five other children, who were in private schools, were flown to the set every weekend. A wall on one of the Fairmont's halls was ripped out prior to the Bronsons' arrival to create a suite big enough for the family.

Blye: "I did [research] on my own in terms of the hair. I had just played Elizabeth Taylor and Henry Fonda's daughter [in *Ash Wednesday*, 1973] and my hair was long for that part. It was below my shoulders to my bra line. I wanted to cut it, because I don't like to wear wigs. Jill loved to wear wigs. In all of her films she has a wig on, she's never without it. You don't even know because they were so beautiful. She had a beautiful collection. I went ahead and cut it off and made it in that 1932 [style] with the waves on the side. A lot of people didn't know me with the dark hair. They knew me with blonde hair. That's a big contrast. As it turned out, I did another picture for A.I.P. right after that with Harris Yulin and Dale Robertson—*Melvin Purvis: G-Man* [TV, 1974]. I was playing

Deleted scene of Speed about to get busted at an illegal craps game.

Kate Kelly, Machine Gun Kelly's wife. So [the hair] was perfect for both of them."

Hill said, "Writing does not train you for the following essentials in directing: Verbally transmitting your ideas to other people. Suffering fools. Practical problem-solving of a physical nature. Leadership that falls somewhere between being the first of equals, or a ruthless tyrant—depending on your character and the role you choose to play. Most of all, a sense of how to deal with the actors, to give them confidence they're in good hands and are in an environment to do their best work."

Strother Martin played the "hophead" doctor "Poe." Martin was an astonishing character actor from pictures like *The Man Who Shot Liberty Valance* (1962), *The Wild Bunch* (1969) and *Butch Cassidy and the Sundance Kid* (1969) and was probably best-known as the sadistic prison ruler in *Cool Hand Luke* (1967). He said at the time, "When bizarre roles come along, I'm often the first actor considered for them. [Character roles] aren't conducive to delusions of grandeur. There is no fear of an ego trip as there is with leading men. It does put you in touch with and make you appreciative of the slob side of yourself because it is so frequently brought to your attention." Martin had small roles in the early Bronson pictures *Drum Beat* (1954) and *Target Zero* (1955) and would act later with the star in *Love and Bullets* (1979).

Deleted scene: Gayleen (Maggie Blye) flirts with Chaney while Speed is in jail.

Much of New Orleans had not been modernized, and few areas had changed at all since the 1930s. Among the numerous locations seen in *Hard Times* were Magazine Street (where Ireland's character lived), The Cornstalk Hotel in the French Quarter (used as the residence of Coburn's character), the Irish Channel area (used to depict the rough area of town), and the St. Vincent de Paul Cemetery on Desire Street. That graveyard location had above-ground tombs and was seen previously in the "tripping" sequence in *Easy Rider* (1969). Hill later shot parts of *Southern Comfort* (1981), *Johnny Handsome* (1989) and *Bullet to the Head* (2012) in Louisiana and used the cemetery again for the climax of *Johnny Handsome*. The backwoods fight scene was shot near Lafitte, Louisiana, where Canjun-tongued extras with interesting haggard faces were used.

Blye: "Every single thing to do with the art direction and the set decoration was spot-on perfect. It really was. It should have been nominated. Some of the original walls, restaurants and buildings that we used are now gone because of Katrina." (Hurricane Katrina destroyed much of New Orleans in 2005.)

Lobby card: Chaney (Bronson) fights Street (Nick Dimitri).

The whorehouse exterior was shot on Jackson Street. The pressbook insinuated that the interiors were shot at a real whorehouse, and an anonymous crew member insisted that "about eighty-percent of the girls employed as 'atmosphere' extras were the genuine article." One actress in the scene who was definitely *not* "the genuine article" was brunette model Laura Misch, a "Bunny" at the New Orleans Playboy Club who had recently shot a brief role in *Mandingo* (1975) and posed as the centerfold for the February 1975 issue of *Playboy*.

The movie's fine photography was by Philip Lathrop (*Point Blank*), a specialist in location shooting who shot Hill's next film, *The Driver* (1978) entirely at real Los Angeles locations. He explained the *Hard Times* shoot: "It's a wholly different type of treatment because you're working on actual sets, and you have to invent a lot of different things that you need not do in the studio, where you can remove a wall or have lights above on the scaffolds. But it gets done."

Bruce Glover: "Coburn was like 'the guy.' His dressing room was like the 'green room' for everybody. Everybody hung out in there and had a great time with Coburn. He was a great storyteller, very sociable kind of person. It's a tough business, and people like Coburn make it a lot easier. Bronson was a whole different case. I liked Bronson in spite of the fact that he was not an easily likeable guy. The first time I had any encounter with him, I was standing on the sidewalk talking to Strother. And suddenly I felt a hand on my chest and a hand on my back pushing me off the sidewalk. It was Bronson going, 'Don't block the sidewalk.' [laughs] Strother saw that I looked kind of angry and goes, 'Oh, don't be worried. He just was checking you out to see how you were built.' [laughs] And I think that was accurate—he was checking out this fairly rugged-looking guy. He had that quality of guys who are very combative types. Bronson had that quality to him. Now on the set, he was very easy to work with and very much the pro. His acting was terrific, and I think it's one of the best things he ever did. I was very fascinated by him because he reminded me of my grandfather and coal delivery people. The fact that I had delivered coal gave me a certain rapport with Bronson because he had worked in a coal mine.

"Working-class people have a different attitude and ideas. Bronson, to me, was a working-class guy made good. I was curious about him. I was very admiring of him. There's something inspirational about a guy like Bronson because you can see that he came up the tough way—the early films, where he had like two or three lines. He had a presence and eventually built himself into a sizeable star doing rather terrific work. There was a kind of shield there, a cautiousness. And who knows what kind of crap he might have gone through with the hierarchy of Hollywood when he first started out here. There's a lot of great people working in the business, but there's some really *mean* people."

Deleted scene: After their breakup, Chaney (Bronson) encounters Lucy (Jill Ireland) at a bar.

Hill said, "[Bronson] was a touchy guy. He was kind of professionally mean. He never said much; he was very quiet. He always seemed to be angry about something, never fully stated what the problem was. But I'll tell you something. It was almost like magic, some kind of catnip—he was enormously attractive to small children. Kids would look at him, and they would come right over and sit on his lap. And he loved kids; he loved children; he had about seven. He was such a mean-looking guy, but kids weren't afraid of him. I used to say it was like King Kong, like a gorilla. He had this magic effect on children. But he didn't like adults very much."

Blye: "[Bronson] was just total professional. He had been trained over there at the Pasadena Playhouse. There was no 'star' situation, nothing like that. He had respect for you, you had respect for him. And you just did the work. Charlie and Jill had a 'reader' that the company employed for them. And the reader would break down the script for them [and] help them so that they knew their lines."

During exterior shoots, the set was roped off and guarded by a dozen off-duty, uniformed cops. Bronson would occasionally allow local kids to duck under the rope and approach him. He gave one boy a signed dollar bill and autographed the denim shirt of a teenaged girl.

Deleted scene: Chaney (Bronson) considers beating up Lucy's new boyfriend.

Glover: "Bronson would just sit in a chair, picking up the sun near his dressing room. He had that whole 'tough guy' thing going constantly. I would see somebody come up to Bronson and go, 'Can I get your autograph?' And Bronson would say, 'I don't give autographs.' 'Well, can I get a picture with you?' 'I don't do pictures.' 'Can I at least shake your hand?' 'I don't shake hands.' [laughs]"

Blye: "Charlie was just like a mute, for God's sake. He wouldn't say anything, period. And if he did, it was inaudible and that was another way of letting the citizen know that he was not available. He would give you that steely-eyed look and you knew not to proceed any further. If you did, you were a fool. [laughs]"

Glover: 'I wouldn't go and intrude on [Bronson] because I had seen what he did with people who had just come out of nowhere. But if there was a bunch of people with him and he was having conversation, then I would go over and join and be there every chance I got. One time, he was sitting alone at a table, and I was sitting a good ten, fifteen yards away, and he looked at me and gestured me over, and I sat at the table with him, and he said, 'You know, I noticed that every time there's people talking with me, you come over and you join in. Why do you do that?' I said, 'Well, Charlie'—I called him "Charlie' on the set, there was no ego—'I come in only when you're already open to people talking to you. I figure I'll learn something.' And he nodded. I suppose I could have opened up the conversation and talked to him more. But I was very cautious. I'd seen the way he was. I don't think he had any problems with me. I think he kind of liked me because I was good in the film."

Larry Gordon said during production: "You know there aren't many superstars who will work with a first-time director, but Charlie is the most professional star I have ever worked with. He's always thinking of the picture."

The *Hard Times* opening scene of Bronson pouncing off of a moving boxcar was filmed at the Chalmette railroad yards. A special stuntman was brought in to perform the action or at least demonstrate to the star how to land properly. Bronson dismissed the stuntman with, "I know more about jumping out of boxcars than he does. I was a rails rider back in the Depression. I was a kid then. It was in Pennsylvania. The only way to get out of town was to hop a freight. I was caught once and thrown in jail because I said I was sixteen. If I had admitted to being only fourteen, I'd have been sent to the work farm, which was worse. It was the pit of the Depression, remember. Every man I knew was looking for work. I worked in the mines myself, getting peanuts for two shifts a day. It was so bad back then, nobody had anything worth stealing. So, at least I wasn't tempted to try that. Men and boys 'bumming' around like that were called hobos. That's what I play in *Hard Times*. A drifter. A hobo who's searching for something."

Blye: "I could tell you a story about Charlie that was pretty startling. We were down around the dock. It was backstreet. There was a rope tied around it. It was dark in that area. I went over and managed to get to my chair and sit down. If you're not working, you're fighting mosquitos. I went over there to put on more lotion. Charlie comes over and he sat down in a chair next to his makeup man [Phil Rhodes]'s chair. Well, this guy comes stumbling up and he's really out-of-it and Phil Rhodes steps in and cuts him off. All of a sudden, Charlie motions him and this guy comes over to Charlie and they talk. It seems like it's pretty intense, whatever was going down. Charlie took off a jacket and gave it to him. He tried to give him some money and he wouldn't take it. The man took a jacket from Charlie, that's the one thing he would take. And then he went on just shuffling down the road in the middle of the night. It was just the strangest encounter. They called Charlie in because he had to go to work. The makeup guy gathered up his box to go in right after him and I said, 'Who was that?' And he said, 'That was his brother. He hadn't seen him in twelve years.' Can you imagine? It was just a bizarre story because you would have never, ever, in a thousand-trillion years known that they were related. I've never told anybody that story."

The mysterious sibling was Bronson's sixty-three-year-old brother,

Roy. Exactly one year later, Bronson was shooting *St. Ives* (1976) in a seedy area of Los Angeles when the grizzled Roy came out of nowhere to hug his famous brother. Bronson said at that time, "He told me he saw all my pictures and that he tells all his friends I'm his brother. He's an alcoholic and he's been one for years. He has no address and I don't know where he lives. He started speaking to me in Lithuanian. But I don't speak the language. I guess he forgot that, although my mother used to speak it when we were kids. Since I last saw Roy he had lost one foot. He said he was working and sober and had a job as a gardener when he cut his foot with a sickle while cutting grass. He didn't look for a doctor but took care of it himself. He was paid off for the job, picked up a wad of money and went off on a bender. He ignored the injury, the foot got gangrenous and they had to operate. They tried to fit him with an artificial foot but it didn't work so they had to do further surgery, amputating his ankle. I offered to pay his medical bills, but he keeps saying no thanks. He won't take money or help. [As children,] we had no heating. We kept warm by huddling close to other bodies. I came out of the hardships a stronger man—I guess Roy suffered most, he was the oldest. It's sad. Roy knows he is probably killing himself with the booze, but you can't help anyone if they don't want to be helped."

Six years later, Bronson would see his less-fortunate brother one final time when the limping Roy showed up on the Los Angeles/skid row set of *Death Wish II* (1982) to approach the star and accept some cash. Shortly thereafter, Roy was fatally stabbed in the buttocks. His decayed corpse was found in a sleazy hotel room.

Glover: "Everyone working on [*Hard Times*] was quite terrific to work with. Mike McGuire [*Report to the Commissioner*, 1975] and I had done a season of repertory years before, in 1964, in Syracuse, New York. A terrific guy, wonderful actor. Maggie Bly, she's a terrific gal. That scene on the newsstand with Coburn was one of my favorite acting moments ever because Coburn was so good and made me look so powerful and scary. He was just the greatest guy to work with. Just fabulous. Coburn had always played hero types, the superior guy that always won out, and now he's playing this semi-nerdy guy—one of the best things he ever did. That scene on the newsstand was a 'teaching' moment. My character was trying to *teach* Coburn to live up to being a man and paying off what he agreed to pay off. It wasn't a villain that enjoyed hurting people. It was a lesson plan. Acting is very simple; you just think the thoughts of the character, be in the environment, and let it happen to you. Let things in, instead of worrying about pushing out. Walter is a terrific talent, and I really enjoyed working with him, even though I pissed him off a bit because I improvised a line for that scene where I said, 'Sell your sister, but get the money.' And he got mad at me because I added a line to his dialogue. 'Sell your sister' was my improvised line. [laughs]"

Newspaper ad.

Blye: "The thing that Walter does, which is terrific in my opinion, is that once he casts someone, then he gives them total, free reign to explore the whole character and have fun in the creative process. And if he disagrees or if he wants to change something, he's very polite. He takes you aside and you have a quiet conversation so everybody doesn't hear. That's a very good, safe place for an actor. He is unique like that. He's a very patient director. Actors would pay money to get directors like that. That's the truth of it. Strother Martin, Jimmy [Coburn] and myself all hung out together. We were like the three musketeers. That was the first time that I met [Martin] and he was like a father figure to me. He would give me advice. We went to dinner every night together, we'd go to a different restaurant, we'd watch all the ball games on Sunday. We'd be piled up in Jimmy's room, placing bets and ordering a lot of room service—all night long. [laughs] It was fun. It was that time of the year and Jimmy was such a football fan. On location in New Orleans, they knew that I was part of the cast. So they were asking me for autographs all over the place. And the paparazzi was chasing us around. They seemed to be very eager to create something between Jimmy and myself. Jimmy, I couldn't even [describe] in a word. Magnificent. Wonderful. The best. My buddy, my friend, my mentor. He taught me so many things about acting, taught me so many things about life."

The fight scenes were all very sparsely described in Hill's script. The director had a detailed list of shot compositions planned before each day's filming. Extensive blocking and choreography were done prior to shooting. Max Kleven was the film's stunt and fight coordinator and played the Cajun pool player that attacks Chaney. No doubles were used for Bronson or any other actors in the fight scenes.

Hill said, "[Bronson] was in remarkable physical condition for a guy his age. He had excellent coordination and a splendid build. His one problem was that he was a smoker, so he didn't have a lot of stamina. I mean, he probably could have kicked anybody's ass on that movie, but he couldn't fight much longer than thirty or forty seconds."

Bronson had been a chain smoker since age nine. For the film *Chato's Land* (1972), he had the costumer sew a pouch in his loincloth to hold his tobacco and pipe. After the *Hard Times* shoot, Bronson periodically chewed tobacco to try to cut down on smoking, but it would be another four years before he was able to stop completely.

Glover: "Robert Tessier, the bald-headed guy in one of the fights, was an Algonquian Indian." The bulky, 6' 1" (1.85 m) Tessier was cast as "Jim Henry," one of the tougher opponents battled by Bronson's character. Tessier had been a Silver Star paratrooper in the Korean War before breaking into movies as a grip, stunt man and bit-part actor. He was in a half-dozen low-budget biker pictures before getting in bigger films like *The Longest Yard* (1974) and *Doc Savage: The Man of Bronze* (1975). Tessier looked especially imposing when he shaved his head, as he did for *Hard Times*. Both Tessier and Strother Martin came on the movie via Meyer Mishkin, the aggressive talent agent known for his stable of rough-looking character actors. "Mighty Meyer" had represented the pre-stardom Bronson and Coburn.

Tessier said, "When I'm playing a heavy, a real bad guy, I try to project evil. I look around and I hate every 'mother' I see, especially if I'm going to have to fight with another actor pretty soon. I've had some actors come up after a scene and say, 'Jesus, I thought you were really pissed off there for a minute'...[During the scene] where James Coburn was trying to make a deal, and I'm in the background squeezing a ball, without anything to say, I was just projecting what I was thinking, 'Fuck you. I'll get your guy. I'll murder him in the first round.' That's doing my homework. I don't just show up on the set. When they're having dialogue, I'm having my own dialogue in my head...But if I'm just *there*, thinking about the chick I met last night, or 'will I get laid tonight,' there's absolutely nothing. They could just take a mannequin out of a window and put it there."

The Bronson/Tessier bout was filmed at a battered warehouse on Chartres Street in the Ninth Ward near the Mississippi River. Tessier recalled that while shooting his big *Hard Times* fight scene, he never touched Bronson, but the star accidentally punched him for real "about seven or eight [times], plus he broke my nose when he kicked me. He was getting in too close. Actors have a tendency to get in close, even though it's a make-believe thing, and you don't *need* to be close because it's the camera angles that make it look real....I didn't get pissed at all. It was a mistake. He was supposed to kick me in the stomach with his right foot, then I bend over and he kicks me in the face with his left foot. What he did was kick me in the stomach with his right foot, then kicked with his right foot again. If he'd kicked with his left, he would've missed me. I was down holding my stomach when I saw the wrong foot come up, and it was just too late. He's not stupid, and he's kind of well-coordinated—it was just something that happened." Tessier would be cast in Bronson's next picture *Breakheart Pass* (1975).

Glover: "Here's an interesting moment: Tessier had that fight scene with Bronson, and Tessier told me that Bronson [really] hit him a little bit. And when he did that, he grabbed Tessier and hugged him and rocked him and went, 'I'm sorry, I'm sorry, I'm sorry, I'm sorry'—very tenderly apologizing. When we were doing the film, Robert had already been sentenced for a drug thing. He was a motorcycle gang guy, and he was sentenced to at least three years in prison, and they were letting him finish the film before he had to go serve his time. When Tessier came out of prison, he asked me to coach him for a couple opportunities he had, acting wise. He's passed on now." Tessier died in 1990.

Blye: "My character, in the script, was supposed to be leaving town and going to Florida. And then [Coburn's Speed character] comes down there after her. In the original draft, you see us all get together in Florida. You see Chaney walking into the ring—he's got this fight and we're all back together as a team. But that was before Lester Persky came in. He was the money. He was brought in because Larry Gordon was falling apart. Financially, we weren't making it. They brought him in to save the day. I never met the man. He was the silent money partner. Because of hanging out with Coburn, I was privy to that kind of information."

Lester Persky was a flashy, New York advertising legend who had recently formed the Persky-Bright Organization with fellow stage producer Richard S. Bright. The duo had raised financing for a number of Columbia Pictures' films including *The Last Detail* (1974), *Shampoo* (1975) and *The Man who Would Be King* (1975). From 1974–1976, Persky-Bright would invest $25 million into a package of major films that netted over $100 million. The pair attracted backers by protecting the investment with tax shelters. Persky said in 1976, "We work on the old-fashioned theory that if you have your own money up, your decisions are more sound." Persky-Bright was credited on *Hard Times* with "production services."

Blye: "The only way we could even continue with the film then was to do it however [Persky] wanted it. If he was gonna put his money up, then it was gonna be done his way. And his way was making it more commercial and that meant, of course, adding fight scenes. He added two. I'm not saying that wasn't a good choice, just that it was different. And that, of course, took away the character development that was written in terms of Chaney—what Walter had written for the depth of Chaney's character. [The original script] was multi-layered. We're talking about two different movies. I heard that [Bronson] was very disappointed. What does it add to his character? Nothing. He's got two extra fights. We've already seen how great [a fighter] he is. He felt that he'd never ever have another chance to possibly be nominated for an Academy Award or a Golden Globe. He had never been nominated for anything, which is so wrong. He was such a good actor."

Nick Dimitri played "Street," Bronson's last opponent in the film. The 6' 2" (1.88 m) Navy veteran was a bodybuilder and stuntman who had played bit parts as guards, hoods, boxers, and gorillas in dozens of movies and TV episodes. Dimitri had worked with Bronson before when he played a boxer in *Kid Galahad* (1962) and did stunts for *Breakout* (1975). *Hard Times* was his biggest role and one of the rare times he received billing. His later work included a memorable bit as a bartender knocked out by Steven Seagal in *Out for Justice* (1991).

This final battle of the movie was shot at a warehouse on the river on Tchoupitoulas Street. It took seven days to film. Bronson and Dimitri were sprayed with baby oil to simulate sweat. Between takes, Bronson would sit on the floor, do pushups, or, literally bounce off the walls while Coburn, Martin and crew members would watch football on a tiny portable TV. Hundreds of Styrofoam crates filled with real oysters were on display to make the set look like a genuine fishery. Under the hot lights, the oysters became rancid and were doused with Lysol in an unsuccessful attempt to control the stench.

Glover: "That place stunk because those were real fish. It was an amazingly stinky place. I saw [Bronson] jump five feet up on a wall and bounce off the wall with kicks. Powerful work, and he had the body for it. That guy was a bull. I totally admired his stamina, his physique. I was always impressed by his ability. He was older than me, and I thought, 'Gee, look what this guy's doing.' It was inspirational to me."

Towards the end of the shoot, producer Gordon was reading a trade paper and saw a huge ad for *The Streetfighter* (1974), the brutal karate picture that New Line Cinema had just released in the States. Columbia Pictures had considered *The Streetfighter* as an alternate title for *Hard Times*—against the wishes of Gordon, Hill and Bronson. Gordon said, "I must say that I could see the commercial possibilities of 'Charles Bronson as The Streetfighter' but this ad finished that title. It's very interesting to be talking to the press every day about our picture *The Streetfighter*, and pick up the paper and find out it's [already] playing."

Glover: "It was a very interesting experience being in New Orleans at that time. You could really see that you were in the South by the way blacks related to certain situations. And that was very instructive, in a way. Strother invited me to go to a restaurant. And I went, and there was this very formal black waiter, and he was 'Steppin Fetchinit' all over the place. And I said to Strother, 'Is he kidding us? What is this? A joke?'

I remember the hotel we were staying in was rather terrific. They had a lot of good art objects on various floors. They were rather terrific things, like sculptures and stuff. And they started disappearing. I imagine that people working on the film were stealing them. [laughs] Somebody was. And the hotel had a nice little restaurant downstairs. They had a rather elegant big, full grand piano."

Hard Times wrapped in mid-December after seven weeks in New Orleans. Hill said, "I shot it in thirty-eight days. It seemed like about a year and a half. I got along pretty well with Bronson, not so well with Coburn, loved Strother Martin. I had written a rather exotic character; Strother asked me if he could just play it like Tennessee Williams. I said, great, and that took care of it. Strother could be very waspish, but he was a gentle soul. He gave me a special edition of Whitman when we finished."

Tennessee Williams himself sent word to the *Hard Times* set asking Bronson to star as an ailing mariachi singer in *The Red Devil Battery Sign*, the playwright's odd new script. Bronson, who had unsuccessfully auditioned decades earlier for a touring production of Williams' *A Streetcar Named Desire*, was flattered, but there was no way that a stage production could be fit into his schedule of movie commitments. Anthony Quinn took the role in the ill-fated play, which closed in Boston in 1975 before its planned Broadway opening.

After the *Hard Times* shoot, Bronson and Ireland went to their Vermont estate for Christmas. Bronson said, "My friends are not in the movie business. I prefer to spend time with my neighbors in Vermont, where we have a farm. My wife and I call Vermont home. Those Vermont hills are quiet and majestic. We spend all the time there together with our children that we possibly can. We have a spread of about 300 acres in a remote part of the state. It gives us plenty of privacy. There's enough room so we can be on our own and all of us together. We don't bother anybody, and nobody bothers us. The Vermont air is clean and crisp and, for me, it's a great place to paint." On the last week of February 1975,

Bronson and Ireland reported to the Idaho set of *Breakheart Pass*, their next co-starring vehicle.

Future director Roger Spottiswoode (*Tomorrow Never Dies*, 1997) was the editor of *Hard Times*. Critic/historian Roger Ebert once wrote, "One day I met the soundmen on *Hard Times* and watched them pounding a leather sofa with ping-pong paddles to create the sounds of blows landing."

Glover: "They did add an extra scene after they were finished filming—that scene where me and that terrific black actor [Frank McRae] go to Coburn, and I hold Coburn while my henchman beats the crap out of Coburn's car. We shot that a good six weeks after the film was completed. We went over to Paramount, and we filmed that little section. I still had the hairstyle."

In March of 1975, an early cut of *Hard Times*—without music or a completed sound mix—was rush shipped from Columbia Pictures for a promo screening at a theater owners' convention in Europe, where the market for Bronson pictures was insatiable, and where the star's newest release, *Breakout*, was becoming his biggest international grosser.

Columbia Pictures planned to release *Breakout* in American theaters in July of 1975 and then open *Hard Times* a mere five weeks later in August to cash-in on the star's post-*Death Wish* (1974) heat. Agent Paul Kohner pleaded with the studio and producer Gordon to add more time between the dates. Gordon said, "As long as there's a nickel left in *Breakout*, the theater owners are not going to run *Hard Times*. But we've got to get it to them. They're hot for it, and we've got to get it to them." Ultimately, *Breakout* was bumped up to open in May and *Hard Times* was held until the fall.

On Friday, July 18, Columbia held special screenings of *Hard Times* for exhibitors and theater managers in thirty American cities. The response was positive and the film was shorter than the version shown earlier at private European screenings, but Gordon and Hill decided to make some further trims. *Hard Times* was ultimately cut down to a tight ninety-three minutes (including credits). A number of vignettes were shortened and some were deleted completely.

In the final version of *Hard Times*, Blye's Gayleen character is last seen one-hour into the film at a gambling hall when Coburn's Speed loses a huge sum of money. She then inexplicably disappears for the entire third act of the movie. In the earlier cuts, that gambling sequence was followed by another craps game that gets busted by the police. Speed assaults a cop and ends up in the city jail for ten days before being released and captured by henchmen.

Blye: "I had a scene that was cut with Charlie and Strother in the bar and I started to come on to Charlie. 'What are we gonna do now that he's in the slammer?' And Strother is trying to figure out a way to keep Chaney so that he doesn't drift off down the road and they lose him as their number-one star boxer. The whole scene with Jimmy and myself, when I go to see him when he's in prison, was all cut. And the scene with Jimmy and Strother and Charlie, when they come to see him in prison. There was this whole, long sequence of going into the jail room with all of the bars and there's a conference table in the center. You're able to touch each other and he's able to nuzzle me on the side of my neck. He's trying to make up to me and so forth. And I tell him that it's the end. 'I'm gonna hit the road and I'm going down to Florida. I was there for you every step of the ride and then at the end, you wouldn't stop the gambling and this is it. I'm leaving.' And she did. [This explains why Speed is eager to go to Miami in the final scene.] Another scene that bit the dust was with Jill Ireland. Jill and I had a scene together [in] that night [scene] where we're all dancing."

The very last scene to be dropped by Hill for his final cut of the film was a factory yard battle between Bronson and black stuntman/actor Bob Minor.

SPEED
Opponents are harder and harder to come
by. You don't mind fighting Black do you?

Hard Times (1975)

CHANEY
Just as long as the money's green.

SPEED
That's exactly the way I look at it.

The sequence was dropped so late in the editing process that Minor is still listed in the end credits and a photo from the fight turned up on a lobby card and in the novelization. (The bout does not appear in any released version of *Hard Times*.) The factory vignette was one of the two fights that had been added during production at the insistence of financer Lester Persky. The other battle added by Persky, which had Bronson beating an opponent near the railroad tracks, was edited out of the film earlier in the editing process.

Hill said, "When I turned my cut over to Columbia on *Hard Times*, they had two little notes: I said no, and they said fine." Others were not happy with the final version, especially not Bronson and Ireland—who gave the second-best performance of her career in *Hard Times* (besides the later *From Noon Till Three*, 1976). The film originally had one final scene between Chaney and Lucy where the boxer made one last attempt at reconciliation. That vignette was dropped completely. Every other scenes with both Bronsons were cut in half.

After seeing *Hard Times* for the first time, Bronson confronted Gordon and Hill at the Columbia studio commissary in Burbank and said, "We could have had a good picture if you hadn't hacked it to death." Movie journalist Liz Smith wrote, "Both Charles and Jill turn somewhat sullen with disappointment just thinking about *Hard Times*. They feel it was butchered and left Bronson without a story line, simply barechested, punching violently and again a vulnerable target for his critics." Hill later said, "We had kind of a falling out over the film. He thought I'd been a little too—how do I put this? Too draconian in my editing of his wife's scenes."

Advertising herald handed out to potential ticket buyers on the street.

Blye: "[The final cut] completely eviscerated all that Walter had put in the third act to bring in summation of these characters. I could see their reasoning to put in another fight, but I couldn't see their reasoning to cut the whole gully out. Anyway, it's all yesterday's news. [laughs] Everybody's been through it. Everybody's had their stuff cut. I know that I was just so saddened by it. Not just because of my part, but because I could see how much that Charlie was counting on it. I knew his conversations that he had with Coburn. Coburn shared with me what Charlie had said in terms of believing in Walter as a director and in what he thought this film could be, how it could really be good for both of them. I thought their chemistry together was just dynamite. I loved Coburn in this. I know it's like a character that he'd played before but he never played it this well. He was just too slick for his own good. [laughs]"

Strother Martin said, "Sometimes what starts out as a large part ends up as a very small one. It can come as a great shock if you aren't prepared for it when you go into a theater to see your new film. I was hacked from seven scenes in *Hard Times*. If you see the director before the film is released, and he says your part has been drastically cut, you have time to adjust. But when you're sitting in the theater and discover you've been wiped out, it's like a cold bucket of water in the face. I think *Hard Times* would have been a better film if they'd been a little more generous to me. That's one of the sad things you go through. It was one of the best parts I ever had. I just loved that part, and damn it! James Coburn went on the floor, too. They [cut] twenty-five minutes of story out of that. What we were all doing really hard was, all of us supporting players, we were trying to get Charlie nominated because we all like him as an actor, and we all liked this story. I couldn't believe they would cut it that bad." Among the moments cut from Martin's performance was most of his barroom recitation of Edgar Allan Poe's poem "The Bells" and him singing the popular British music hall song "The Man Who Broke the Bank at Monte Carlo" while the posse drives away from the backwoods roadhouse.

Bronson planned on having total control over his own Depression-era script that he had written with Ireland. *Dollar Ninety-Eight* was an autobiographical character study set in a coal mine town of the 1930s. Bronson was to produce and direct as well as star with his wife. "There's a lot of injustice I know about," he said in 1975 while discussing the project. "I keep a personal code about dignity and making things better for other people." This script would go through multiple drafts and be read by several studios and production companies for well over a decade without being made.

Hard Times co-writers Bruce Henstell and Bryan Gindoff were among those approached to work on *Dollar Ninety-Eight*. Henstell: "My partner and I were encouraged by Bronson's agent, Paul Kohner, to develop a story set in the hard-scrapple coal fields of Bronson's birth. But before long, the coal field project died." Henstell and Gindoff went on to write a 1977 episode of *Hunter*. Gindoff later wrote and produced the teen comedy *Losin' It* (1983) and a few years later had a script in development at Paramount for a never-made comedy that was to star Eddie Murphy as a kiddie-show host.

Hard Times opened in the United States on October 8, 1975. For promotion, theaters were provided with facsimiles of a newspaper front page with a photo of Bronson fighting Tessier under the headline "Chaney KO's Skinhead." Other suggested publicity gimmicks were: setting up a craps table in theater lobbies; hiring a shoeshine man to set up in front of the theater and give free shines; convincing a local restaurant to have a "Hard Times Special" with menu items offered at 1930s prices and/or a cup of coffee for a nickel with the third refill costing another five cents—as seen in the movie; and hiring local musicians to perform Dixieland standards like "When the Saints Go Marching In" on a flatbed truck that travels through town—with the bass drum reading "Hard Times Dixieland Jazz Band" and the players wearing "Hard Times" T-shirts. A novelization, which included the scenes cut from the final film, was released in American by Dell Publishing and in Britain by Star. It was a nicely-embellished book with internal monologues by Chaney that gave his backstory.

American paperback novelization.

Vincent Canby, *The New York Times*: "a terrific directorial debut for Walter Hill. The movie recalls classic Westerns about godlike heroes who come out of nowhere, set things straight and then move on, as well as more mundane movies of the thirties about men working at their jobs.... [Bronson] is to acting what a monolith is to sculpture." Richard Eder, *The New York Times*: "*Hard Times* is a stylish, sharp movie. Its characters are taut and springy and it is frequently funny." Jeffrey Lyons, CBS-TV: "A tough-nosed, no nonsense, gutsy look at the underbelly of America as it existed back in the 30s. A fine picture." Frank Rich, *New York Post*: "Working from this plain story, screenwriter Hill has made an enviable directorial debut and given Bronson the best starring vehicle he's ever had....[T]his picture might not be nearly as effective as it is, were it not for Bronson himself. The star's granite presence is properly exploited for its resonant possibilities for the first time. The tension hidden in the actor's body and the secrets locked behind his cold, sad eyes link Chaney to our most romantic image of the woeful hard-times hobo." *Variety*: "*Hard Times* is to be admired as a sincere attempt to broaden Bronson's role spectrum....Jill Ireland is excellent in a touching performance as a down-and-out girl." Kathleen Carroll, *New York Daily News*: "The film is hardly a triumph, but it is so well suited to Bronson's low-key intensity, his stubborn silences and icy aloofness, that it becomes easily the best thing he's ever done." Jay Cocks, *Time*: "Surprise: a good Charles Bronson movie. *Hard Times* is unassuming, tough and spare, a tidy little parable about strength and honor....This time, the stolid performer manages to achieve an authentic, scruffy street dignity. *Hard Times* is the best script Bronson has enjoyed since he became box office....Hill is responsible for Bronson's finest performance to date. If this seems a modest compliment, *Hard Times* is evidence that there may be larger ones on the horizon."

Pittsburgh Press: "Bronson and Coburn are so well-cast the picture zips along largely on the strength of their chemistry. Brooding, inarticulate Bronson is the ideal contrast for fast-talking, laughing-eyed, wise-cracker Coburn. *Hard Times* is as brutal a fist-to-the-chin flick as has come along in some time.... The movie is rather good lowbrow entertainment." (The reviewer also noted that the picture was playing to sold-out houses in Pittsburgh.) *Lawrence* (KS) *Journal-World*: "*Hard Times* is reminiscent of those kung-fu flicks which were the rage a year or so ago. There is a lot of physical violence, all accompanied by standard fist-meets-flesh sound effects.... Bronson looks like a generic throwback, a Neanderthal with speech capabilities, and that's really all that's required of him." *Pittsburgh Post-Gazette*: "*Hard Times* should have an easy time at the box office. It delivers just what it promises, and action audiences who don't expect more will be satisfied...[but] it could have been...an effective, meaningful drama instead of just a slugfest.... The role is so tailored for Bronson it would verge on self-parody were it not for the dark animal presence of the deadly serious actor.... The fights that are the only substance of the film are curiously old-fashioned. While the beefy actors look convincing, they absorb dozens of blows to the face with scarcely a cut.... This is preferable to the sadism of films like *Mandingo*, however." *Lakeland* (FL) *Ledger*: "This writer gets absolutely no thrill from seeing a movie whose only purpose is to have the characters beat the mud out of each other.... To the film's credit, half the fights are over quickly and none are as vicious and demeaning as the big fight in *Mandingo*." *Evening Independent* (FL): "It ought to signal easy money for the theaters that show it. If the word gets out, that is. *Hard Times* is one of this year's sleepers.... It is about as good as it possibly can be for the kind of film it is.... His face like a slag heap swallowing lemons, Bronson says little and lets his fists do the talking.... The fight scenes, though curiously unbloody, thud with painful reality.... The story is no more complicated than a piece of *True* magazine fiction, but it is honest, unpretentious, ringing with principal."

Hard Times was the rare Bronson picture that collected accolades. Columbia prepared special newspaper ads that featured quotes from the reviews. Blye: "We got really good notices. From all the best critics. I was very surprised at that. The studio just didn't give it any juice. If they don't pump it with that publicity machinery, then forget it. If it didn't make the 'do-rey-me'—to use Jimmy's words—in the opening weekend, then they were done with it. I never had a picture that was popular when it came out. And that included *Hombre*. Everything turned out to be a cult film. *Waterhole #3* was discovered later. *The Italian Job* was discovered later. But the interesting thing about my career is that I always worked with icons. It's just amazing to me. It truly is."

Japanese poster. Outside of America, the film was called *The Street Fighter*.

Hard Times (1975)

Japanese program.

Bronson was asked by black feminist Michele Wallace how the *Hard Times* setting compared to modern America. He replied, "Jesus, how can people be having hard times? You don't have a job, you get welfare. During the old depression you see there wasn't any such thing, and you were handed a shovel even if all you did all day long was lean on it. Now all you have to do is go down and collect your check. Welfare is the wrong thing. If there are no able-bodied workers in the family, they deserve the welfare. But if somebody can be put to work and is healthy enough to work, he ought to get a job, no matter what it is."

Hard Times never shared a double-bill with *The Streetfighter*, the martial-arts picture that caused Columbia to change the title of their Bronson vehicle, but on some Milwaukee screens, *Hard Times* was paired with another Japanese karate epic: *Lightning Swords of Death* (1974).

The total gross for *Hard Times* in the States was $5 million. When the movie was released later in the United Kingdom, the title reverted to *The Streetfighter* to avoid confusion with Charles Dickens' classic *Hard Times* novel (1854). *Films & Filming*: "[The movie] can be safely recommended to anyone who enjoys watching grown men beating hell out of one another, which means it should please a pretty large public." In Australia, Japan, and most other markets, the moniker *The Streetfighter* was used. By the end of 1976, Columbia Pictures' two Bronson movies, *Breakout* and *Hard Times*, had collected over $50 million in total worldwide ticket sales.

The television premiere of *Hard Times* was on September 24, 1977, on *NBC Saturday Night at the Movies*. The network brought the film back again on Sunday, April 17, 1979, for *The Big Event*. Some violence in the fight scenes was edited for the broadcasts. *Hard Times* was first released on home video in the early 1980s. During the video rental heyday, you couldn't walk into a rental shop that didn't have *Hard Times* on the shelf.

Trade papers had announced that Bronson was going to star in another Larry Gordon/Columbia Pictures production that would begin shooting in fall 1975, but the star never worked with his *Hard Times* producer or director again.

Hill said, "I'd occasionally run into Charlie around town, and even though the picture had done well, I never quite knew where we stood. Talking to him was kind of like being in a movie. There was one party, maybe five years later, and he was staring at me from across the room—like a gunfighter in a bar in a Western. I thought, 'Is that son-of-a-bitch just going to stare at me forever? Ah, fuck it. I'll go talk to him.' I went over and shook his hand, and once I'd done that, everything was fine. We had a nice chat. A year later, at another party, he passed me and cut me dead; wouldn't even say hello. A year after that, we ran into each other again, and it was like we were old friends. So he ran hot and cold."

Hill went on to be one of the finest (and underrated) directors of the 1970s and '80s, with classics like *The Driver* (1978), *The Warriors* (1979), *The Long Riders* (1980) and *Southern Comfort* (1981). Gordon made six more features with Hill and became one of the more-powerful producers in cinema history, with a string of blockbusters including *Predator* (1987) and *Die Hard* (1988).

Neither Blye nor Glover saw Bronson after filming *Hard Times*, but they did encounter Coburn before that star died in 2002. Blye: "I went to [Coburn's] Christmas party a couple of years. We'd run into each other at different things that were happening in the business. He was still working a lot and doing voice-overs. And then he did some good pictures, got the nomination [for *Affliction*, 1997]. That was wonderful. There'd be different events and red carpet things and I'd see him. [Strother Martin and I] stayed friends until he passed away [in 1980]. We'd get together every once in a while and meet up at Musso and Frank's, the famous Hollywood restaurant up on Hollywood Boulevard."

Glover: "I would bump into Coburn afterwards. I could always tell that he didn't remember who I was or that we'd worked together. Of course, he did so many films. I would see him at the Academy all the time. He was a bit stressed out with his hands, he was having these terrible arthritic problems with his hands. They were swollen up. But he was a very gracious guy. He would always pretend that he knew who I was. *Hard Times* was a great experience. A fascinating movie. The experience is in my top five, and I've done seventy-two films and maybe 150 television shows."

Blye: "[*Hard Times* is] almost a film for all mankind. It's not a political film. Isn't the title *Hard Times*—like Charles Dickens? It's not the same story, I don't think. [laughs] But the essence is 'the haves and the haves not.'"

---

(1) All quotations in this book that were taken from interviews conducted by the author are introduced in the present tense (i.e. "Henstell says") or with a colon (:) (i.e. "Glover:") to distinguish them from excerpts from previously-published interviews, which are introduced in the past tense. This includes the quotes from those who died before this book was published.

Chapter 3
From Noon Till Three (1976)

"Probably unlike most directors who worked with Charlie—and were scared for their lives and ran—I had a very good experience, which was hard won," says Frank D. Gilroy, writer/director of the 1976 offbeat Western *From Noon Till Three*, which ranks as the most unusual of all Charles Bronson vehicles.

Gilroy started writing television plays in the 1950s and TV episodes in the 1960s. His 1964 stage play *The Subject Was Roses* won Broadway's "triple crown": the Pulitzer, the Tony and the Drama Critics Award. Gilroy wrote a number of screenplays and directed the movies *Desperate Characters* (1971), a low-budget drama with Shirley MacLaine, and *The Turning Point of Jim Malloy* (TV, 1975). As he explained in his 2007

Charles Bronson as the sneaky outlaw Graham Dorsey in *From Noon Till Three* (1976).

memoir: "Ninety-percent of my career has been failure. I've been dead broke six times, and if I don't sell something soon it'll be seven....I'm a working writer with a family to support who, to make a buck, has written for such TV series as *The Rifleman, Have Gun will Travel, Wanted: Dead or Alive* [all 1958]."

Gilroy says, "I used to read a lot about the West and, at some point, I read about the Coffeyville Raid [1892], in which a gang robbed two banks simultaneously that were across the street from each other. In the course of going in to do that raid, one guy's horse went lame, and they had to drop him off, thinking they would pick him up on the way back. And when they went and pulled the raid, it was a disaster. I often wondered about the guy they dropped off. [laughs]" Starting with this real-life premise, Gilroy created a fictional novella, which was published by Doubleday and Company in 1973 as *From Noon Till Three: The Possibly True and Certainly Tragic Story of an Outlaw and a Lady Whose Love Knew No Bounds.*

The first section of Gilroy's book is a "Letter to the Editor" written in 1881 by rich widow Amanda Starbuck describing her intense three-hour love affair with Graham Dorsey—an outlaw who held her captive while his posse robbed the local bank. The second part of the novella is a "Publisher's Note" from 1973 explaining that the Starbuck letter became an international love story sensation and inspired a classic song, while the woman's mansion became a successful tourist attraction. The final section of the book explains that in 1973 a moldy stenographic pad dated 1882 was discovered in an attic and contained the story that a dying, bullet-ridden man claiming to be Graham Dorsey dictated to a stenographer at gunpoint. The alleged Dorsey recited that the famous Starbuck letter was an outrageous fabrication of what had actually happened and that it embellished his height, manners, looks, and background. ("Just because I enjoyed that afternoon doesn't mean I go along with her account of what took place.") The story in the pad ended with the alleged Dorsey dropping dead. He had been shot in a bar for claiming to be Graham

Dorsey. The novella concludes with the publisher suggesting that the readers make their own decision as to which story is true.

From Noon Till Three didn't attract any attention from Hollywood until Gilroy met with producer M.J. (a.k.a. Mike) Frankovich, who agreed to listen to a brief pitch. Frankovich had been a bit part actor in the 1940s before becoming a producer of B-movies and serials. He became head of production at Columbia Pictures in the early 1960s and at the end of that decade went back to producing with hits like *Cactus Flower* (1969), *The Love Machine* (1971) and *$* (1971). Almost all of the films from Frankovich Productions were based on published novels or popular plays. Gilroy said, "Mike bought the book and agreed to let me direct."

For the screenplay, Gilroy followed his novella closely and kept most of his original dialogue, but he combined the separate viewpoints of the book into one chronological story. There were some changes. In the book, Dorsey convinces Amanda that he really is her supposedly dead lover by reciting "intimate details of [their] previous lovemaking." In the script, he proves his identity by exposing his "manhood" (off-screen). Other alterations included: dropping the part about Amanda giving birth to Graham's stillborn child; Dorsey's ultimate fate; having Amanda's story being told via a book instead of a newspaper letter; and girls in a convent reading the scandalous bestseller. The screenplay calls the book *Amanda and Graham* but in the final film it is called *From Noon Till Three*.

The movie version was first announced (without a studio or stars) in July 1973. Early the next year, Frankovich set up *From Noon Till Three* at United Artists, where his production *Report to the Commissioner* (1975) was also being made.

While Gilroy and Frankovich searched for their male and female leads, Bronson was looking for another movie to star in with his wife, Jill Ireland. Bronson had often insisted that his wife be cast in his films, and she had already appeared in a dozen of his vehicles. Ireland said at the time: "That's part of our plan of keeping the family together, and that's why Charlie and I work in the same pictures. It can be terribly destructive to a marriage for the husband or the wife to be gone for weeks on a location, so I go with Charlie whether I'm working or not. And he has said that if I got a picture by myself, he would accompany me. Charlie is such a strong actor that it would be easy for him to overwhelm an actress who wasn't familiar with his style. I am, and I know how to reach his level of energy. I like to watch husband-and-wife teams. I think there's a deeper gut level in their performances."

Bronson added, "I think the audience likes it. They think they might see something private; there is a sense of the voyeur....you can have your real-life love scene in your dressing room or, as on location, a boxcar. I prefer working with Jill. She is such a professional, and we know each other so well that we can get to the heart of a scene much faster. It saves the director's time. [We rehearse at home] only if it's a difficult scene. We might rehearse the lines but never the business. It's better to keep it spontaneous when you're working with the actual props."

Graham (Bronson) licks chicken grease off the fingers of widow Amanda Starbucks (Jill Ireland). The licking action was improvised during the shooting of the scene.

The star was very supportive of his wife, personally and professionally. When the unauthorized biography *Charles Bronson Superstar* was published by Dell in the fall of 1975, Bronson tried to buy and destroy every copy because of the unflattering image that the paperback presented of Ireland. (He was unsuccessful, and the book is still widely available on the collectors market.)

Bronson said, "I'm feeling very confined and limited in making picture after picture on the same subject: action and violence. I want a different type of role—changing my image would be a real challenge at this point for me. Actors who make action pictures are respected more for the money their movies make but not for the quality of their performances. I'd like to let people know I can do more than that. Play some softer love scenes. Something lighter and less tense than my usual."

The *From Noon Till Three* script described the Graham Dorsey character as "late thirties, a thoughtful brooding man whose face stops well short of being handsome." Although Bronson was a huge box office draw at the time, had already given some comedic performances, and had been in seventeen Westerns, he was not initially considered for the role. Gilroy: "He was not a first choice, because it seemed beyond anything I had ever seen him do. I wanted Jack Nicholson [*The Last Detail*, 1973]— I wanted that roguish element. But Mike Frankovich got in touch with Charlie. I had great misgivings. [laughs] I was not immediately drawn to the idea because I had never seen him do anything that had humor in it. Charlie was very protective of Jill. And he was looking for something for the both of them. So we met. I remember Mike Frankovich and I having tea with the Bronsons. They were a genuinely loving couple. And we all looked at each other and thought, 'Okay, let's take a shot at this.'"

United Artists had just produced *Breakheart Pass* (1976) with the Bronsons and were happy to sign the couple again. Bronson's *From Noon Till Three* contract paid him close to $1.5 million in upfront salary in addition to ten percent of the gross receipts over $10 million and almost half of the net profits. Ireland said, "I hope he has a long life and time to do all the things...and enjoy the money he's made." Ultimately, his staggering percentage points on *From Noon Till Three* ended up meaning nothing when the film ended up performing poorly. Ireland collected her standard $75,000 fee (with no points).

Gilroy: "On my other movies, I always had a rehearsal period. And I felt that in [Bronson's] case and Jill's, it was especially essential to have a week to ten days just going over [the script]. I put that in the contract, and his agent approved it. [laughs] Charlie only heard about that three days before we were to begin, and he came storming into my office and said, 'What's this rehearsal shit?' I said, 'Didn't your agent tell you? That's the way I work.' He had to honor the contract. We get to the first day of rehearsal. The beginning was very, very dicey. It's Charlie, Jill, the script supervisor, and me sitting around a table. We were using one of the buildings on the lot. Smoke was coming out of Charlie's ears. He hated it. The truth of it was, he had never rehearsed in his life. Never. I think he had this fantasy that a lot of actors have: 'It will destroy my spontaneity.' I would say that one of the worst days I spent in show business was that first day of rehearsal. [laughs] Mike Frankovich was one of the old 'all hands.' He wanted to be on top of everything, and he said, 'I want to come to the rehearsals.' I said, 'I'm not doing secret work. Come in whenever you want.' He came in and sniffed the air at that first rehearsal and said, 'Everything seems under control.' [laughs] We never saw him again until we shot.

"Charlie was really cantankerous, and he kept saying, 'If I stand up, I can say it better.' I said, 'Charlie, look, if you can't say it just sitting at a table, it's not going to work.' And I just kept going at it as nicely as I could. We broke for lunch that day, and he said to me, 'You direct a few more pictures, you'll give up this rehearsal shit.' I said, 'Charlie, it's my hope that after this picture, you're gonna *want* rehearsal.' So we do the afternoon, and it isn't much better. They didn't seem to know when they were getting it and when they weren't. We ended that day on a very dark note, and I called my wife and said, 'I think I'm paying for all my sins. If this doesn't change in the next couple of days, I don't know what the hell I'm gonna do.' Charlie was so angry, he went to his agent and tried to get me fired. And his agent, Paul Kohner—not that he really believed in me—didn't want to break a contract. So the next day we came back in. Suddenly, Charlie realized that the purpose of rehearsal was to allow you to explore, to make mistakes, to try something. And the day started to get better. He realized you could experiment. That's the whole idea of rehearsal, so that you don't get in front of the camera and start rehearsing. That's why some pictures shoot so long. On the fourth day or so—there was nice weather, and we were sitting outside—I wanted to go over something with Jill, so I said, 'Charlie, why don't you just take a walk.' He went away, and I worked with Jill, and when he came back, he brought us a bowl of cherries. He loved that I was treating her and him seriously as actors. I don't think many directors took him seriously. He had, unconsciously even, such an intimidating air that [directors thought,] 'Let's shoot. Let's get it over with. Let me get out of here.' From then on, the rehearsals paid off handsomely. He was never gonna be Jack Nicholson, but Charlie really reached and he trusted."

United Artists had no studio space of its own, so the film was shot on the Warner Bros. ranch and in the Warners studio beginning in June of 1975. The director of photography was Lucien Ballard, a legend in the field who had shot Three Stooges shorts in the 1930s as well as numerous features like *The House on Telegraph Hill* (1951), *The Killing* (1956) and *The Wild Bunch* (1969). He had recently lensed Bronson's *Breakout* (1975) and *Breakheart Pass* (1976). Gilroy: "He was a top cinematographer. And he had worked with Charlie before. I had a little trouble with Lucien in the beginning because he was used to being in control. And I had won Charlie during rehearsals. Once in a while, I would want something and Lucien didn't want to do it. He finally realized that Charlie was with *me* now and trusted *me*. And then Lucien and I were fine. I remember socializing with Lucien and his wife after." Ballard's nighttime interiors and exteriors for *From Noon Till Three* are especially impressive.

From Noon Till Three (1976)

Graham (Bronson) waltzes with Amanda (Jill Ireland). A framed print of this image was displayed in the homes of the Bronsons and of writer-director Frank D. Gilroy.

On the set, Bronson told the *Los Angeles Times*: "I have hostility towards the [press]. One reason is that I envy it and secondly, I think it has too much freedom. Freedom of the press is tremendous. I don't read it anyway....You're indoctrinated to believe the printed word. I could talk to my wife and give her a piece of information and she won't believe it as readily as she would if she read it....I used to be what many consider an angry person. But what is it that directs you? Time, I suppose. Psychologists say if a man reaches the age of forty and hasn't made it yet, he's going to have a problem. And if he has made the success he's been trying for, he will mellow out. I'm not a Charles Bronson fan. I don't think I turned out the way I thought I would turn out when I was a kid. It's a disappointment. I'm a disappointment to me. My image, my sound, everything else. A big disappointment." As Bronson finished a light lunch, he added, "I have to fight weight and my appetite all the time."

Between takes, Bronson chewed sunflower seeds constantly to compensate for the loss of cigarettes. A chain-smoker for thirty-five years, Bronson gave up cigarettes "cold turkey" after having breathing problems the previous year while shooting the fight scenes in *Hard Times*. The star enjoyed his *From Noon Till Three* change-of-pace role. When columnist Marilyn Beck visited the set, he told her, "[Critics] are trying to get the public to stay away from my pictures, as if the violence in them would influence anyone. They act as though I'm to blame for every beating a woman receives from her husband."

Producer Frankovich said, "Everyone is afraid of Charlie, but all you've got to do is get past his rough exterior and you find a pussycat. Let's just say that Charlie's had to learn to act the hard way—in commercial movies that haven't called for sensitivity or finesse. Believe me, Bronson's going to pleasantly surprise a lot of people with his performance in this film, which comes off rather like a sophisticated *Cat Ballou* [1965]." Gilroy: "Charlie was a very taciturn guy. He didn't say much. [laughs] He could just sit in a room with people and be perfectly calm. And because he didn't talk much, I'd see him make people nervous all around the room just by sitting there. He was a very imposing guy."

When writer Roger Ebert visited the Warner Bros. ranch one morning, Ireland said: "You'd think they'd have a little more consideration. I was called for the crack of dawn, and they're not going to need me until after lunch. Yesterday was as hot as this morning is cold. The heat sat on my heat like a bowl of porridge. One day you freeze, the next day you swelter, and every day, you watch for rattlesnakes. I've played prostitutes, wives, girlfriends [in Bronson movies]. I suppose I could go on and on forever, and people would never recognize me. The public's not women-oriented. They come to see Charlie. They could see me today and not recognize me tomorrow. I don't care, as a matter of fact, what people I don't know think of me. Maybe that's why I never really made it. Here I am, after I thought I'd quit acting for once and all, with my very best role. I'm happy with it. I want to make it work, I want to be good, but maybe it doesn't mean the whole world, right?...I've recently been offered two roles, but neither fits my lifestyle right now. One would be shot in Mexico, and Charlie doesn't want to work there anymore. And the other one doesn't really seem to be any good. One thing I've learned from Charlie is not to take a role just to indulge yourself because you're just using yourself up." (She ended up turning down both non-Bronson projects.)

Ireland told visitor Vernon Scott, "I don't think I've established my own identity with the public, but then I haven't tried very hard to push my career. Charlie has never used any muscles to get me into pictures when the producer didn't think I was right for a part. In one movie he insisted I play a role even though I was against it. Whenever I appear in a film with him it's because Charlie believes I'm the best actress for the part. He's always very complimentary of my work. Once in a while when I tell him I'm thinking about quitting, he says, 'No. You're one of the best actresses around.'"

Gilroy: "About halfway through shooting it, we break for lunch, and I'm in my trailer. There's a tap on the door, and it's Charlie. He offered me his and Jill's next two movies to direct. Now, here was a problem for me. I'm primarily a theater guy. I had to go with my gut on this. I said, 'Charlie, I'm bowled over and flattered and honored, but I have another direction intended for my life at this point.' Because I knew if I took two pictures, there goes three-four years of my life. He took it as an insult. He couldn't imagine anybody turning down two movies. I had a lot of trouble with him the rest of the day. I had to take him aside and say, 'Charlie, look me in the eye. I am really flattered.' I was being sincere. And finally, he realized how it was with me, and we proceeded."

After watching a reel of rough-cut scenes when she came to the set, movie reporter Liz Smith wrote: "I must say there are scenes so enticing that I predict Bronson's usual audience will be enlarged by millions, including little old ladies in tennis shoes who usually shy away from anything more violent than a root beer float."

Gilroy kept track of the schedule by tossing away his script pages that were shot each day. "Because I rehearse, I usually don't have to do many takes because I know what the actor is capable of. There was a scene in the picture that was complicated with movement, and we couldn't get it: [Ireland] holding a candle and coming downstairs. Finally, when we got up to about ten takes Jill came to me and said, 'Frank, you know, we're not used to doing more than one or two.' I said, 'Jill, look. I know what you guys are capable of in this scene. Now, do you want me to settle for what I think is less than the best you can do?' 'Oh, no,' she said. So we kept on shooting, and I think it was the most takes I've ever done of anything. The number stays in my head: seventeen. But we got it. We were on schedule. I think we even came in under budget. It was altogether a happy shoot. Charlie really stood on his tip-toes. For Charlie to smile, you don't know how hard that was for him. [laughs] I think he almost got applause." Gilroy got Bronson to smile, but at one point the script called for Bronson to cry, which the actor would not do. The vignette of Bronson licking chicken grease off of Ireland's fingers was added during the shoot.

Newspaper ad.

In early September 1975, Elmer Bernstein, whose long career included the scores for Bronson's *The Magnificent Seven* (1960) and *The Great Escape* (1963), signed on as the composer. A few days later, on the last day of shooting, Bernstein was on the set for a newly written scene where he and lyricist Alan Bergman played tunesmiths plugging their song "Hello and Goodbye." (Gilroy's script had its own song and lyrics: "I loved Graham and he loved me and we lived together from noon till three.") After the first take, Bronson said, "Jill *could* sing that song. She has one of the most beautiful voices you'll ever hear." In the final film, the song (co-written by Marilyn Bergman) was reprised over the end credits by Ireland. United Artists Records released Ireland's version as a single, but it was not a hit and did not become as ubiquitous as it was in the movie.

Bronson rarely went to a film's "wrap party," but he showed up at the *From Noon Till Three* event with Ireland and three of their four sons. Ireland said, "Charles and I have loved making this movie so much. Right, Charlie?" Bronson added, "Yeah, Frank Gilroy is a prince." The star originally planned to take a break for the rest of the year after finishing *From Noon Till Three*, but he decided to squeeze in the detective movie *St. Ives* (1976), which started shooting two weeks later. From May 1974 to December 1975, Bronson shot five features in a mere nineteen months. After *St. Ives* was completed in late December, Bronson finally took a long hiatus from movie making until *The White Buffalo* started shooting in April 1977.

In January 1976, Bronson and Ireland optioned the movie rights to *Will There Really Be a Morning?* (1972)—the autobiography of mentally ill 1930s film star Frances Farmer. The Bronsons planned to produce the film later that year as a starring vehicle for Ireland, who said, "Someone in my family suffered through a similar tragedy." Bronson said, "Whatever work we do will be staggered so Jill and I don't face a separation. The family comes first. That's what it's all about, what we're working for." The couple never got to produce the film before their option expired.

Meanwhile, Gilroy completed *From Noon Till Three*. He says, "I was used to getting final cut. I couldn't get it here. And I lost several things that the producer, for whatever ridiculous reason, insisted on. I'm not saying it would have made any *huge* difference. These [cut] scenes were largely towards the end. They might have been a little bit harsher than what was presented." Gilroy's original conclusion had Bronson dancing in a mental institution with "a heavily made-up HAG wearing high heels and a ratty fur piece over her hospital gown" who believes herself to be Amanda Starbuck. The final movie closes with a freeze-frame of Bronson's face superimposed with the Dorsey/Amanda waltz from earlier.

Even with the altered ending, *From Noon Till Three* turned out to be a flawless film, one of the more unusual Westerns ever made, and a definite curio. Bronson is fantastic in one of his finest performances, especially in the later scenes where his character breaks down mentally. Ireland gives her best-ever performance.

United Artists had originally planned to distribute *From Noon Till Three* nationwide during the 1976 Easter weekend, but the studio became nervous about this odd Bronson picture and cancelled the wide release. United Artists opened their other Bronson Western, *Breakheart Pass*—originally intended for Christmas 1975—in the spring of 1976 with a "saturation" booking in 254 American theaters. While *From Noon Till Three* sat on the shelf, Warner Bros. gave their easy-to-sell Bronson action-mystery *St. Ives* a wide release in the major territories from July through September of 1976.

At the end of 1976, United Artists started cautiously releasing *From Noon Till Three* on a region-by-region basis. In October, it opened in Los Angeles, Chicago, Florida, and Washington, D.C. In November, it played Maine.

The studio did their best to announce that *From Noon Till Three* was an atypical Bronson movie. A press release noted: "He's got a physique of tempered steel and the scarred, roadmap face of a matinee idol left out too long in the war. He looks like he can lick any man in the world

Alternate newspaper ad.

and put away a quart of scotch with the other hand. He is the highest-paid movie actor in the world—legendary gunfighter, tough guy, street brawler, and all-round guaranteed, pure box-office macho on seven continents. And now he's going to charm and delight a world full of fans as a lover, as a funny guy, and yes, even as the world's most unlikely coward in a great and unexpected entertainment. A classic movie ad campaign once bore the catchphrase, 'Garbo Talks!' Now one could coin another slogan: 'Bronson laughs!' *From Noon Till Three* will bring movie audiences a number of firsts, including the usually stoical, placid-faced Bronson breaking out in laughter! *Noon* is a comedy movie. That stamps it far from the genre of Bronson films to date and is a refreshing change. [I]t proves that behind that steely-eyed visage, Bronson has a keen sense of humor and a rarely-displayed knack for timing and delivery of comedy lines."

Two different one-sheet posters were designed, including one showing Bronson and Ireland lying in bed with a quartet of hanged outlaws dangling over them ("If only the gang could see me now!") and another with a cartoon depiction of the opening dream/robbery sequence ("It'll keep you on the edge of your saddle!"). Alternate ads were provided to newspapers with various taglines like: "An unusual Western starring an unusual Bronson"; "Bronson is as good with a punch line as he is with a punch"; "Romeo and Juliet were two lovebirds. Graham and Amanda were two cuckoos"; "Graham Dorsey became a legend after his death. The trouble was he was still alive"; and "Their love was so deep, so strong, so pure, it couldn't possibly be true (and it wasn't)." Several of the publicity stills had Bronson smiling or dressed in tuxedo and top hat. A movie tie-in paperback of Gilroy's book was released by Avon.

Charles Champlin, *Los Angeles Times*: "Bronson eases the narrow glint in his eyes to become a comic actor and fall guy, likable and charming....[The movie] is a curious piece of business, even farther off-trail than most off-trail Westerns....In a real sense, the movie is not Bronson's but Jill Ireland's. It is a lovely chance to evolve from the sad and straitlaced widow to the sensuous woman to the greedy living legend and she brings it off attractively and competently....[T]he punch line of the last sardonic joke is unfortunately the weakest of Gilroy's inventions, so that the carry-away feelings probably do an injustice to the movie's middle distances....*From Noon Till Three* gets good marks for freshness and ambition and high marks for the Bronsons in fresh and entertaining guises. Gilroy as director tells his story well, although a different director might have asked Gilroy the writer for a stronger finish."

UPI: "The results are surprisingly funny in this very entertaining... very offbeat and stylized western fantasy. What is most surprising is that Bronson and wife Ireland should fit so well into the straight-face but satirical proceedings." *Variety*: "an offbeat and amiable, if uneven and structurally awkward, western comedy." *Box Office*: "Bronson fans may be disappointed, but others could be pleasantly surprised. The leads are given a chance to be more animated than usual, which will also shock those who thought Bronson and Ireland were incapable of more than one emotion. Ms. Ireland is called upon to be highly dramatic and comic and proves to be very adept at both." *Independent Film Journal*: "[A] well-intentioned failure...*From Noon Till Three* amounts to little more than a personal showcase for Mr. and Mrs. Bronson, one that probably proved far more enjoyable and worthwhile for them to make than it will be for audiences to sit through." *Miami Herald*: "Mrs. Bronson conveys the right edge of inviting gullibility throughout; her hubby constantly strives to be James Coburn-cocky, something even Coburn would have a difficult time doing with this material."

Because *From Noon Till Three* didn't attract crowds or major accolades in its initial bookings, United Artists didn't open it in New York City until Friday, January 28, 1977. (It was co-billed in most theaters there with *The Return of a Man Called Horse*.)

Gilroy: "The studio didn't know really what to do with this picture. It wasn't a traditional 'Charlie Bronson movie.' There was something different about it, obviously. Not knowing what to do with it, they really botched it. Vincent Canby, the movie critic of *The New York Times*—who never really gave good reviews—had to go to a theater on 47th Street and pay his own money because they didn't preview it. And, by God, he loved the movie, and he gave us a great review."

Vincent Canby, *The New York Times*: "*From Noon Till Three* is neither a conventionally comic Western nor a conventional comedy, and it certainly isn't a conventional Bronson film. More than anything else, I suppose, it is an ebulliently cheerful satire of contemporary myth-making and celebrity, cast as a fable of the Old West. Not all of it is equally successful, and it takes its time making certain points, which, being made, are made again; yet its intelligence and its narrative shape are immensely satisfying....[Gilroy] obtained two remarkably attractive, absolutely straight performances from Mr. Bronson, who is funny without ever lunging at a laugh (as Burt Reynolds often does under similar circumstances) and from Miss Ireland, whose cool, somewhat steely beauty are perfectly suited to the widow who manages almost immediately to transform a real-life experience into mass-media material with plenty of spin-off."

Tom Allen, *Village Voice*: "The pits. Frankly, I could never fully trust anyone capable of writing such a trite, tricked-up novella and then ham-handedly directing the film version."

In fifty-nine theaters in the New York City area, *From Noon Till Three* grossed a mere $65,000 in its first week. Bronson didn't give up on the film. He paid for a two-page ad in the trades featuring a still of Ireland surrounded by quotes from the many critics that had praised her performance. She got no nominations.

"Hello and Goodbye" received a Golden Globe nomination for "Best Original Song." Ireland said, "[Five-year-old daughter] Zuleika was my little buddy and biggest fan. She loved the song and thought her mother had the most beautiful voice in the world. I would sing the lyrics to her every night before she went to sleep." On January 29, 1977, Ireland was in Los Angeles to sing the piece live at the Golden Globe awards

Canadian newspaper ad.

ceremony. She wore a black velvet gown designed by Bob Mackie and had rehearsed the previous day with Paul Williams on piano. "Evergreen" from *A Star is Born* (1977), co-written by Williams, won the award. The absent Bronson was in Helsinki shooting *Telefon* (1977).

In a piece on potential Academy Award nominees, the *Los Angeles Times* listed Gilroy's script as a possible nominee for "Best Adaptation," but the film received no Oscar nominations, not even for the song.

From Noon Till Three hit Missouri screens in January. It was in Milwaukee and parts of Canada in February. In June, it played Arizona. *Milwaukee Sentinel*: "One of the best Bronson films of the last four years....A sly comedy that will no doubt upset some Bronson fans."

Gilroy: "Charlie was inflamed that the studio had really thrown it away. He wanted me to join him in a lawsuit against the studio. I said, 'Financially, I can't afford to do that.' We stayed in touch. It was always a good feeling. We were actually friends."

The final United States gross for *From Noon Till Three* was less than $1 million. *Breakheart Pass*, Bronson's other 1976 Western for United Artists, collected a little over twice as much, but it was still a box office disappointment, as were the studio's two other offbeat (and bigger-budgeted and better-marketed) 1976 Westerns: Robert Altman's *Buffalo Bill and the Indians* with Paul Newman and Arthur Penn's *The Missouri Breaks* with Marlon Brando and Jack Nicholson. The lone Western hit of the year was Clint Eastwood's *The Outlaw Josey Wales*. Bronson would make one final Western: *The White Buffalo* (1977), which became another flop.

From Noon Till Three producer Mike Frankovich's other 1976 Western, *The Shootist* with John Wayne, also failed despite grossing double what his Bronson picture did. Frankovich said at the time, "Westerns have been having a tough time for two reasons. One is the hangover from saturation on TV, years and years of the home screen crowded with cowboys. Two is the spaghetti Western, which saturated theater markets with lots of action and laughs and a heavy load of violence. You can't go on killing people on the screen without drawing adverse reaction from the audience. Americans are too concerned about their own personal safety; they don't want to see unlimited mayhem in movies." Frankovich produced no further features in any genre.

Despite the commercial failure of *From Noon Till Three*, Bronson's status as a screen draw was not in jeopardy. *Breakheart Pass* was a huge success in foreign territories, and *St. Ives* was a modest hit in the States, where it collected $4 million. At the end of 1976, a poll taken among film fans in sixty countries named him as the most popular movie star.

In the summer of 1977, United Artists had *From Noon Till Three* on the bottom of a double-bill with the phenomenon *Rocky* (1976) for bookings in second-run houses and drive-ins. (1)

The broadcast premiere of *From Noon Till Three* was on *The CBS Wednesday Night Movie* on November 16, 1977—a little over a year after its first theater dates. (The brief vignette insinuating that Bronson displayed his genitals was omitted.) Bronson fans (and non-fans) that had missed it in theaters were finally exposed to the picture, and it began to develop a deserved cult following. The film was belatedly released on VHS by MGM in 1993.

Gilroy continued his successful theater career. He returned to filmmaking with *One in Paris* (1978), which he wrote, produced, and directed (and even handled the New York City distribution for). In 1981 Gilroy had another offbeat film at United Artist: his original noir comedy *The Edge*. When Bette Midler signed on, she nixed Gilroy as the director and had his script rewritten. The movie was ultimately directed by Don Siegel as *Jinxed!* (1982), with Gilroy billed under the pseudonym "Bert Blessing." Gilroy died in 2015. His three sons—Tony, Dan and John—are all successful screenwriters.

Looking back on *From Noon Till Three* in 2014, Gilroy says, "We were all pleased with what we did. I'm sitting here looking at a beautifully framed picture: Charlie and Jill, in costume, dancing in *From Noon Till Three*. It was their favorite movie they made together."

From Noon Till Three (1976)

One-sheet poster for the obscure compilation feature *The Wild West*. (Courtesy of Chris Poggiali)

---

(1) In 1977 Bronson "starred" in another Western. *The Wild West* was a tedious hodgepodge of cowboy-movie clips compiled by Laurence Joachim—a distributor of martial arts epics, kiddie matinees, and a pair of Bruce Lee "features" cobbled from the *Green Hornet* TV series (1966). For *The Wild West*, Joachim slapped together faded scenes from old Republic

Pictures-owned Westerns. The poster had a collage of legends including Bronson, Clint Eastwood and John Wayne who were prominently billed over-the-title. Wayne pops up frequently in the compilation, but Bronson (via three clips from *Showdown at Boot Hill,* 1958) and Eastwood each appear for less than ninety-seconds. This "movie" received no American theatrical bookings but in the late 1980s, *The Wild West* was released to American videotape stores with another misleading ad campaign that gave no indication that the film was a compilation.

Chapter 4
Love and Bullets (1979)

When Charles Bronson was at the hottest point of his stardom in the 1970s, his name could attract millions of dollars in financing to any film he was attached to. Sir Lew Grade was among the moguls who signed Bronson in the hopes of securing an international blockbuster. *Love and Bullets* was the result.

The Jewish-British Grade's long career started when he was a dancing star in British music halls during the late 1920s. In 1934 he became a talent agent, then in 1954 he formed the production company ITC (Incorporated Television) and began producing for TV. By the late 1970s, the knighted Grade was a wealthy legend with a string of small-screen successes including dozens of big-name variety specials; top

Charles Bronson as Lieutenant Charlie Congers, an American cop sent to Switzerland, in *Love and Bullets* (1979).

shows like *The Saint* (1962–1969), *The Prisoner* (1967) and *The Muppet Show* (1976–1981); and the mini-series *Jesus of Nazareth* (1977). He had also dabbled in small features like *Desperate Characters* (1971)—directed by Frank Gilroy, who made Bronson's *From Noon Till Three* (1976)—and *The Possession of Joel Delaney* (1972). Grade had big hits with *The Return of the Pink Panther* (1975) and *The Pink Panther Strikes Again* (1976).

Dapper, diminutive, stocky and bald, Grade smoked a dozen $25 cigars daily and was chauffeured around London in his huge Rolls Royce Phantom VI. He was shrewd, clever, tireless and (mostly) beloved. Grade wrote in his memoir: "By the end of the 1970s, I felt I'd gone about as far as I could in TV and had met most of the challenges the medium had thrown at me. It was time to take some different risks….By this time I was really beginning to become more and more involved in movies. In fact I was, as they say, hooked!" From 1977 to 1982, the mogul would "present" almost eighty feature films.

Bronson's agent, Paul Kohner, met with Grade at the 1976 Cannes Film Festival to discuss *Maximilian and Juarez*—an epic, $16 million television miniseries that the agent was developing with his son, producer

Pancho Kohner. The historical script dealt with the monarch Maximilian I and his battles with Mexican president Benito Juarez. Bronson was to play Juarez, and if the project had gotten made, it would have given the actor his best-ever role. The Kohners' plan was to televise the complete miniseries in America and England, then release a shortened version as a theatrical feature in other territories. This method had worked successfully for Grade's miniseries *Moses the Lawgiver* (1974) and Bronson's three-hour TV movie *Raid on Entebbe* (1976). Grade immediately informed the press at Cannes that he was producing a Charles Bronson epic. *Maximilian and Juarez* never went into production and was never seen on big or small screens, but Grade was back at Cannes the following year—and this time Bronson was with him.

Pancho Kohner recalled that when *Maximilian and Juarez* fell through, Grade presented Bronson and the Kohners with "a screenplay Lew had already bought and wanted us to do. We read it, didn't like it and, anyway, it was going to need a heavy rewrite. A good friend, the writer Wendell Mayes, once told me he had a great title for a Charles Bronson movie, *Love and Bullets, Charlie*—like the sign-off at the end of a letter. One day we all had lunch together at MGM, told him the story, and Charlie said he would be happy to do it. I rang Lew there and then. He wanted a 'Bronson film,' liked his image and thought this could be very commercial." Mayes was an Oscar-nominated screenwriter with exceptional action credits like *Von Ryan's Express* (1965), *The Stalking Moon* (1968), *The Poseidon Adventure* (1972) and Bronson's *Death Wish* (1974). All of Mayes' prior (produced) scripts had been adapted from novels. *Love and Bullets, Charlie* was his only original screenplay to be shot.

Bronson said at the time, "I like directness. I don't like being over-emotional. In the entertainment I seek for myself and in real life, I like it when a man is a man. I like to do stories about people's strengths rather than their weaknesses. Weakness is becoming an end these days. Look at that dude Gary Gilmore. They should have shot that punk as soon as he said shoot me. [Other stars are] all too busy trying to stretch something out of nothing. I can play the character better because of the roundness of my experience—because of the things I've been through. All those method guys—like that De Niro, Stallone, and what's his name, Pacino—they're all the same. They even look the same.

"When I know someone is going to pay $3.50 or more for a ticket, I try to really give them something special. When I pick my pictures, I don't read scripts in the ordinary way. I see them up there on the screen, not as words on paper. I try to see the story happening in images the way the audience will. And that's how I choose the scripts for my movies. There are lots of roles I turn down that I'd love to play. But I don't think the audience would enjoy seeing me in those parts."

Grade said, "I'm not very good at scripts, I can't read a script. I skim through a few pages, I get a feeling, a flavor. What's important is the package. What's it about? Who's doing it? Who's in it?"

Bronson and Grade signed a contract in January 1977. In mid-May at the Cannes Film Festival, Grade held a luncheon for 150 distributors at the Hotel du Cap at Cap D'Antibes. Motioning with his ash-dripping cigar, the mogul explained to the crowd that his ITC Entertainment would be spending $125 million on eighteen films to be produced in the next year. The first would be *Love and Bullets, Charlie*—the inaugural movie in a two-picture Bronson/Grade deal—to be followed by a then-unnamed action movie shot in the Caribbean starring Bronson and Sophia Loren. (Grade's 1976 Loren vehicle *The Cassandra Crossing* had been a top-grosser on the international market.) The upcoming roster also included two thrillers based on Robert Ludlum novels as well as a movie version of the best-seller *Raise the Titanic*. The Ludlum acquisitions were never shot. Like the other flashy, independent moguls Bronson worked with before (Dino De Laurentiis) and later (Menahem Golan)—Grade announced many films that didn't get made.

Charles Bronson
and
Jill Ireland
in John Huston's
Love & Bullets, Charlie
Produced by Pancho Kohner
Directed by John Huston
Written by Wendell Mayes
Production designed by Stephen B. Grimes

Pre-production trade ad listing the original director.

Grade passed out champagne, cognac, and fresh flowers to the distributors and slipped hefty tips to the waiters. Publicist Ernie Anderson, whose clients included Bronson and Ingmar Bergman, remarked that what Grade handed out as tips at the party was more than what Bergman had spent on his last two movies. (Bronson said at the time: "Everything is weakness and sickness to Bergman. Everybody has some mental problem, and all they can think about is suicide.")

Bronson's wife Jill Ireland, who was scheduled to co-star in *Love and Bullets, Charlie*, graciously worked the crowd—although she had recently broken her foot and was on crutches (adorned with diamonds). Bronson was characteristically dour and unsociable at the party although he grew to be fond of Grade. A framed portrait of the mogul would soon hang in the star's home and would stay there until Bronson's death. By the time the luncheon was over, Paul Kohner had convinced Grade to commit to a third Bronson picture: the Depression-set *Dollar Ninety-Eight*, which would co-star Ireland. Actor/composer Paul Williams was to play the Baptist preacher brother of Ireland's character and would also write songs for her to sing in the film. This proposed project (also referred to as *98* and *$1.98*) was based on an outline that the Bronsons had first written in 1974. Several screenwriters would write multiple drafts up until the late 1980s, but the film was never made.

Hollywood columnist James Bacon wrote: "Instead of a busty starlet, the star of this year's Cannes Film Festival was Lord Lew Grade and his Churchill cigar....Grade reminds me so much of Michael Todd. Everything is done first cabin all the way." Grade had been holding court at lavish Cannes press conferences since 1974 and would do so until 1980.

Love and Bullets, Charlie would be the third Bronson movie (after *St. Ives*, 1976, and *The White Buffalo*, 1977) to be produced by Pancho Kohner. The film was announced to be shot in Zurich, Zermatt, Paris, Amsterdam, Managua, London, Rio de Janeiro, Dallas, New York, Houston, Washington, D.C., and Chicago. Ultimately, Switzerland would be the lone European location. Phoenix, Arizona and Hollywood were the only American locations that were used. Some scouting and pre-production did take place in Rio de Janeiro, but nothing was filmed there.

Grade raised at least sixty percent of his films' budgets by pre-selling them to distributors spread out in various international territories—often in deals that were extremely convoluted. Among his backers was the Boston-based 600-house theater chain General Cinema. Hence, a number of Grade's movies could play only in General Cinema venues in some areas. The budget for *Love and Bullets, Charlie* was announced as $8 million, although some insiders speculated that Grade exaggerated his costs by more than double. Bronson's reported fee was $1.5 million, a percentage of the profits, and all on-location expenses for himself and his family. Grade was able to partially protect the investment in his Bronson movie from guarantees collected from American network and pay-TV channels (including Home Box Office).

Cover of the elaborate pressbook shipped to international distributors while the film was in production.

Despite the prominent "Sir Lew Grade Presents" billing and the ubiquitous pizazz he showed in public, the mogul took a "hands-off" approach to his movies. Director John Boorman (*Deliverance*, 1972) was once offered a project by Grade and was told: "Let me tell you how I work. I don't want to read the script—haven't got time. I don't see rushes. Don't show me a rough cut....I don't even want to see the picture when it's finished!" However, Grade did instruct his filmmakers to avoid visuals and language that could result in an R rating in the States or an X certificate in England. He wanted all of his movies to be (mostly) safe for the lucrative general audience and clashed strongly with director Franklin J. Schaffner over the amount of blood in *The Boys from Brazil* (1978).

Wendell Mayes' original draft was worked on by another (uncredited) writer before being turned over for polishing to John Melson—who, while living in Spain, had contributed to an eclectic group of pictures including the big-budget World War II epic *Battle of the Bulge* (1965) with Bronson in a featured role, the Spanish horror movie *Blind Man's Bluff* (1970) with Boris Karloff, and the odd Jules Verne adaptation *Where Time Began* (1977).

Agent Paul Kohner got one of his director clients signed to the film—the legendary John Huston, whose string of classics included *Treasure of the Sierra Madre* (1948), *Key Largo* (1948), *The African Queen* (1951), and *Fat City* (1972). Huston excelled at adventure pictures shot on location, and his then-recent hit *The Man Who Would Be King* (1975) had successfully returned him to the genre. Paul Kohner had been Huston's agent since 1938, and it was his negotiating that led to the young screenwriter's directorial debut on *The Maltese Falcon* (1941).

Pancho Kohner also had a long history with Huston. He was the director's godson, had been a gofer on Huston's *Freud* (1962), and had directed Huston in *The Bridge in the Jungle* (1971)—an obscure, unreleased sequel to *Treasure of the Sierra Madre*. Huston also occasionally picked up paychecks for small acting roles and had scenes with Ireland in Bronson's *Breakout* (1975).

Huston's signing for the new Bronson picture was announced to the industry with great fanfare, including a costly, three-page ad in *Hollywood Reporter* that read: "Sir Lew Grade proudly announces a new major motion picture by master filmmaker John Huston." At age seventy-one, the director was still full of creative energy and began several months of pre-production on *Love and Bullets, Charlie*. Huston hired his son, Tony, as assistant director. Longtime associate Stephen Grimes (*Reflections in a Golden Eye*, 1967) was assigned as art director.

The director's gambling habit would occasionally lead him to accept a subpar script for a quick paycheck, but Huston looked forward to the Bronson movie and once said, "Bronson reminds me of a hand grenade with the pin pulled. I saw that quality of impending explosion in him in an obscure picture called *Red Sun* (1971), which I list with *Stagecoach* (1939) and *Red River* (1948) as the three best Westerns ever made."

In late September 1977, Huston reported for the medical examination required by the financers. The X-rays showed that he was in danger of a fatal heart attack and required immediate surgery. He wasn't expected to live, but after four surgeries and two months in the hospital, he was released and went to recover at his retreat in Puerto Vallarta, Mexico.

When Huston left *Love and Bullets, Charlie*, art director Grimes quit (he called the script "pretty terrible, one of those cops and robbers, shoot-'em-out things") and turned the department over to his son, Colin Grimes. Tony Huston stayed on the film as an assistant to the publicist. Huston was out of the Bronson picture, but he soon came back with the brilliant *Wise Blood* (1979) and directed (often accompanied by an oxygen tank) another half-dozen features before his death in 1987.

Principal photography for *Love and Bullets, Charlie* was announced to begin on Monday, October 10, 1977. The start date was postponed until November 28 to give time to find a new director and get him up to speed on the project. Stuart Rosenberg was the last-minute replacement. While not a legend like Huston, Rosenberg was a pro who had helmed television for two decades before directing the classic *Cool Hand Luke* (1967) and solid pictures like *Pocket Money* (1972) and *The Laughing Policeman* (1973) as well as Grade's production *Voyage of the Damned* (1976), a personal favorite of the mogul. Previously, Rosenberg was a late replacement for director Richard Mulligan on *The Drowning Pool* (1975) and later took over *Brubaker* (1980) from Bob Rafelson.

A month before Bronson, Ireland and their six children were to leave for Switzerland, a disturbing incident took place near the shooting location. On October 4, five-year-old Graziella Ortiz was kidnapped at her family castle near Lake Geneva. The girl was the grand-niece of Antenor Patino, of the Patino family that had made a fortune in tin mining. After eleven days, the child's father was instructed to deliver $2 million to a masked man on a freeway. Twenty-four hours later, the drugged (but safe) girl was dropped off at a motel. The authorities suspected that the still-at-large kidnappers were Italian professionals.

Bronson feared for his own kids' safety—especially that of then-six-year-old Zuleika—but he knew that it was too late to change the filming site. Still, he insisted that no unauthorized personnel, including journalists, be allowed on the set; that no press announcements be made of his presence in Switzerland; and that his enormous salary not be revealed. Publicity director Ernie Anderson said it was "a traumatic experience" trying to keep the new Bronson movie a secret.

The European leg of the shoot began after Thanksgiving, 1977. In Geneva, the Bronson clan occupied the entire floor of the Hotel Des Bergues and were spread out in twenty rooms—at a cost to the production of $2,400 per day. One room was turned into a classroom headed by the family tutor. The company also financed a team of armed bodyguards to secure all family members at all times. Bronson said, "My six children are my friends. We all enjoy ourselves as if I were another kid. My kids and I do the kind of things together that other fathers talk about doing. The things other fathers would do if only they had the time—I really do them. If I sit down and play checkers with them, and they beat me, that's all right. If it's fair, it's fair. I play poker with them. First I give them their allowance. Then I win it off them. And I don't give it back, either."

To increase his stamina for the high-altitude location, Bronson ran for two miles each sunrise and sunset through the village of Zermatt on cobblestone roads. He also ended, for good, his lifelong battle with cigarette addiction and said, "To make sure I didn't backslide, I sat in the non-smoking section of the plane coming over. I tried chewing dried

LOVE AND BULLETS (1979)

Congers (Bronson) smuggles mob mistress Jackie Pruit (Jill Ireland) out of Switzerland.

apricots, raisins—all kinds of fruits—and finally settled for bubble gum. The only trouble was, once we got to Switzerland, where it was twenty below, I couldn't blow bubbles. The stuff froze."

Screenwriter John Crowther, who had a background in theater and independent film, says, "That film went through a number of writers. I came onto it when it was already shooting in Switzerland. Pancho flew me over to Switzerland to do rewrites on the set. I was living on my boat on Marina del Rey in L.A. Pancho called me and said, 'We need you. Are you available to fly over to Switzerland?' And I said, 'Yeah.' It was a nice gig. I was over there less than a month—two, three weeks—generally, just 'punching up' [and writing] additional dialogue. What often happens is: you get on location, and you add scenes, and they just need to be written. It was a pretty quiet shoot. Bronson loved working with Jill. He wanted her around every minute. That was one of the classic, great Hollywood marriages. This was the first time I worked with Bronson. I never had any direct contact with him, in terms of the script."

By some accounts, director Rosenberg could get easily irritated on a set and had conflicts with some crew members. Crowther: "There was some bad blood floating around. Nothing serious, nothing that halted the production and delayed it. I had no problems with him. I wasn't really answering to Stuart as much as I was to Pancho. I didn't really have any input from Stuart. [Bronson and Rosenberg] seemed to get along just fine."

Ireland's gun moll/prostitute character Jackie Pruitt was supposed to be from the Ozark Mountains in Arkansas. University of Southern California dialect coach Robert Easton (whose previous clients included Sean Connery, Laurence Olivier and Charlton Heston) worked with Ireland on the accent prior to shooting and told her that the original Ozarks were settlers from Ireland and Scotland. Ireland said, "To portray such a woman called for the changeability of a chameleon. Nothing could have been further from my own life. So I found myself trying to find attitudes we might have shared as we were growing up. Some ambition, some secret dream. Then I remembered how much I wanted to be twenty-one when I was still a teenager. I think Jackie Pruitt also wanted to grow up in a hurry. There is, however, a vulnerability there—a little girl quality. To make the transformation complete, I concentrated on the voice. That 'little girl' voice is found in many country women, especially the impoverished ones. They aren't dumbbells. They grow up, but they seem to retain the voice of a child. There's a bit of burr and brogue still present in their accent. When I recognized some of their old folk tunes as songs I'd heard as a child in Scotland and Ireland, I could finally identify with Jackie Pruitt's roots. It's a challenging part, but I know I can play it convincingly. I've really soaked up the role, and I feel now I know everything about this girl." Ireland's preparation included listening to Loretta Lynn, Tammy Wynette and Dolly Parton records.

Love and Bullets (1979)

Pruit (Jill Ireland) and Congers (Bronson) in hiding.

Henry Silva (*The Manchurian Candidate*, 1962) played a hit man but, unfortunately, had no scenes with Bronson. He said on the set: "Charlie managed to switch to heroes by going to France, where he became a movie good guy in *Farewell, Friend* [1968]. When he came back to Hollywood, he kept that image. I spent ten years in Italy making twenty-five movies. In almost all of them I played heroes. But when I returned to Hollywood, they automatically had me wearing black hats again."

Crowther: "I got to be good friends with Henry. We got to be buddies over in Switzerland. We hit it off really well. He's a great guy. Terrific. He's funny. We're both big joke tellers, and we would trade jokes back and forth, and we would keep topping each other. We had a lot of fun."

Playing a villain alongside Silva was Paul Koslo, who had previously been in Rosenberg's *The Laughing Policeman*, *The Drowning Pool*, and

Voyage of the Damned as well as in Bronson's *The Stone Killer* (1973) and *Mr. Majestyk* (1974). Koslo said, "We didn't get along at all on that first film, *The Stone Killer*. My first day on the set, I sat in his chair. The first joke I ever told him was 'Hey, Charlie, did you hear the one about the Polish actor?' He said, No, what?' I said, 'Charles Buchinsky!' [He said] 'Do you think that's funny?' [laughs] Being Polish myself, I thought it was hilarious, but it went over like a lead balloon with Charlie....I saw something that Bronson did that I thought was really despicable. Bronson doesn't like people, yet he sits in the middle of downtown intersections in his chair for everybody to see. And then people come and bother him, and he tells them to fuck off. Apparently there had been an elderly lady that was driving by, and she wanted to know what the hubbub was about, because they had traffic controlled. And they said, 'Oh, it's a Charles Bronson movie.' So she went home to change and get her autograph book because he was her favorite actor. She brought her camera with her, too. He told her to fuck off when she asked for an autograph. She was so shocked that she just took a picture of him, right there, while he was there when she was leaving. He had the cops take the camera from her, take the film out, and give her the camera back. That wasn't nice. These things affect you when you've seen guys all your life that you work with, like I've seen Bronson. And I've always respected his work. You respect the guy's talent. But that doesn't mean you necessarily have to like him." Koslo also clashed with Bronson on *Mr. Majestyk*. "But he apparently asked me back for the third movie, *Love and Bullets*. I saw him a few times after that—not by design, but by accident—and he was cordial."

Crew members contacted the Sion weather bureau several times a day for condition updates. Director of photography Anthony Richmond (*The Man who Fell to Earth*, 1976) said, "The mountain is covered in mist, but by the time the cameras are adjusted to mist, the sun comes out—brilliant, bright sun. Then it rains." To stay on schedule, Rosenberg asked that the Switzerland scenes be written to take place in both good and bad weather. An action sequence that was to take place at the Geneva airport

Love and Bullets (1979)

was deleted at the last minute when location permits fell through. The script was rewritten, and the location was changed to the famous Hotel Beau Ridge.

Hit man Farroni (Henry Silva) and his mistress (Lorraine Chase). At the time, Chase was a popular model in print and TV ads.

Bronson said, "A little cemetery we passed every morning turned out to be one devoted to climbers who fell off the Matterhorn. Eleven fell off so far this year. But if you include the other thirty-nine peaks in the vicinity, fifty-five have perished. We were shooting a fight scene in the highest aerial tram in the world. It's just a little cable car, suspended in space over drops thousands of feet down. It doesn't show in the picture, but lined up against the wall of the cable station were rescue sleds with a big red SOS on each one, and three Alsatian dogs. When we first got in the tram, a Swiss patrolman showed me the trapdoor in the bottom. 'If the car fails,' just open this trapdoor and slide down the cable. We'll catch you.' There were helicopters around, too. One little old Swiss guy has been flying them through these peaks for years. He can pluck anyone right off a mountainside. I was scared in the mines as a kid. I was scared in the war sometimes, too. But now? I've got the best job in the world—and I don't intend to be number fifty-six in Zermatt's 'boot hill.'"

For the sequence of Bronson jumping a red Peugeot sedan off of a train's flatcar and down a deep, snowy hill, Pancho Kohner hired French stunt driver Rémy Julienne (*The Italian Job*, 1969), who had worked with Bronson on *Cold Sweat* (1970). The stunt took a whole day to set up and was filmed with five cameras, including one hidden in the snow and operated by remote control. One image was filmed on the lower part of the hill with Bronson and Ireland actually in the car while a cameraman shot from the back seat.

Among the script alterations done in Switzerland were the deletions of chunks of dialogue between the Bronsons' characters. The screenplay had Bronson using his bare hands to break a henchman's neck. At the star's request, that villain was dispensed instead by a tossed axe. Bronson created the vignette where his character turns a paper cone into a lethal blowgun that ejects nails. (This sequence was censored in Britain, according to *Variety*, "for fear the device could easily be copied.") These makeshift devices were a real-life favorite of the star. Between takes on his movies, he would often wander off and use a cone to blow nails into trees.

The Switzerland shoot concluded just before Christmas—two days earlier than scheduled. When the Bronson brood arrived in New York City from Switzerland, they took a limousine to the family farm in Vermont, where they spent the holidays. Ireland later wrote, "Charlie *needs* the isolation of Vermont, almost to survive. With one step he finds himself alone in an environment that provides instant solitude, freedom from the noise, the distractions and superficiality of the city."

Bronson and Ireland were back on set in the second week of January 1978 for the American leg of the shoot beginning with exteriors in Scottsdale, Arizona, then to the MGM studio in Culver City, California, for interiors. For union reasons, Fred J. Koenekamp (*The Towering Inferno*, 1974) took over as cinematographer for the American sequences.

The scenes shot in the States included those with Rod Steiger as Joe Bomposa, the Mafioso main villain. Decades earlier, Bronson had featured roles in *Jubal* (1956) and *Run of the Arrow* (1957)—two widescreen, Technicolor Westerns starring Steiger. At one time, Steiger was one of the screen's greatest character actors. He gave brilliant, underplayed performances in classics like *On the Waterfront* (1954), *The Pawnbroker* (1965) and *In the Heat of the Night* (1967). The latter got him an Oscar. By the mid-1970s, health and psychological issues had taken their toll, and Steiger's work had become overblown and hammy. For some reason, he decided to give his *Love and Bullets* character a speech impediment. He said during this era, "I'm sixty-percent saint, and forty-percent whore. You have to be in this business. I've found that no matter what ideals a man has, he can't afford to start acting on them if his family is at stake or if he is hungry. Take *Love and Bullets*. That was a movie I did just after I got over open-heart surgery. It's something I had to do to show this town that I could still do it. If they think something is wrong with your health, you can be finished in this town." (A few months after shooting, Steiger reunited with director Rosenberg on *The Amityville Horror* [1979], which ended up getting released before the Bronson picture. Steiger would play another stuttering mob boss in *The Specialist* in 1994, where his character meets the same explosive fate as in *Love and Bullets*.)

Mob boss Joe Bomposa (Rod Steiger) is confronted by Congers (Bronson).

Also in the interiors sequences was Strother Martin, who had played his signature "jail boss" role in Rosenberg's *Cool Hand Luke* and had worked with Bronson in *Hard Times* (1975). During his college days, Martin was a champion springboard diver. In *Love and Bullets*, the Speedo-clad actor performs a dive into a pool.

Crowther: "After I had finished up in Switzerland and was back in the States, I did go out just to visit for a couple days in Phoenix. It was calm, quiet and nice, and everybody was getting along." Crowther didn't rewrite any Arizona sequences, but numerous script changes were made on that location, including an alteration to Martin's death scene. In the script, the character was beaten to death by Bronson—in the film, Bronson drowns him.

Grade expected *Love and Bullets, Charlie* to be huge in all markets. During the Arizona shoot, Pancho Kohner rewrote the script to conclude with the spectacular explosion of an entire mansion. (Originally, just a fireball was to be seen in the distance.) The necessary pyrotechnics added another $200,000 to the budget, but Grade agreed that the movie needed the strong climax and cut a check for the effects. Shortly after production, the ITC Entertainment publicity department designed and distributed a full-color, nine-page, photo-filled, fold-out pressbook to distributors throughout the globe ("Danger, excitement and entertainment").

During post-production, which ended in the early spring of 1978, the *Love and Bullets, Charlie* title was shortened to just *Love and Bullets*. The music was by Lalo Schifrin, noted for action scores for TV (*Mission: Impossible*) and movies (*Bullitt*, 1968; *Dirty Harry*, 1971). Schifrin had worked three times before with Rosenberg and would score the director's *The Amityville Horror*.

On the finished film, Wendell Mayes was credited with the "story." Mayes and John Melson shared the "screenplay" billing. Uncredited writer Crowther met Melson a few years after *Love and Bullets*. Crowther: "It turned out that John lived in the apartments right next to where my boat was moored. John and I got to be quite good friends. After the film had been out, John said to me, 'How come you didn't ever try to get the credit? You could have gone to arbitration and gotten that credit.' And I said, 'I didn't know anything about that.' I had gotten the usual notification from the Writers Guild showing me as a 'contributing' writer and John and Wendell Mayes getting 'credit.' But it was much later that John said to me, 'When you got that notice, you could have gone into arbitration and actually gotten the credit, and you would have demonstrated that you did more than me.' I had no idea. It actually winds up costing you money because the 'credited' writers get residuals, the 'contributing' writers do not. John Melson thought that I had contributed more to the script than he did." Crowther did receive credit when he worked with Bronson and Pancho Kohner later on *10 to Midnight* (1983) as casting director and on *The Evil That Men Do* (1984) as a screenwriter.

Melson got a writing credit on one more film, the odd French softcore *Aphrodite* (1982), before meeting a sad fate that could have been a subplot in a Bronson picture. Melson suffered with bipolar disorder and paranoia as well as alcoholism and spent time in a mental institution. There were long stretches where he would disappear and could not be reached by family, friends or industry contacts. In January of 1983, he was found dead in a Malibu hotel bathtub with his throat slit. The death was investigated by a Malibu police detective based on rumors that the writer had been killed by the henchmen of a once-incarcerated bank robber/jewel thief who was angry because Melson had been hired to pen the ex-con's memoir but never finished it. The death was ultimately ruled a suicide.

Bronson's next movie, and the second project in his three-picture deal with Grade, was going to be *Power*. The film was to be shot in April 1978 and would reunite the star with his frequent director Michael Winner (*Death Wish*). *Power* was based on a 1973 script by Bill Kerby (*Hooper*, 1978) that was originally intended for a Dirty Harry movie at Warner Bros. until Clint Eastwood rejected it. After Winner and Gerald Wilson were hired to extensively revise the screenplay, Warners dropped the project. The script and director ended up with Grade. An international press conference for *Power* was held—with Bronson, Sophia Loren, Grade, and Loren's producer-husband Carlo Ponti in attendance—but the film, retitled *Firepower*, was made with former Bronson co-star James Coburn in the lead. According to some accounts, Bronson dropped out because there was no role for Ireland. Winner recalled differently in his memoir and wrote: "Charlie never did a movie with a star leading lady. He liked to be the only star in the picture. He was insecure. He didn't want competition....Sophia had not wanted to act with Charlie Bronson. She thought he was inferior." Loren was the exact same height (5' 8") (1 m. 72 cm.) as Bronson when she was barefoot—and she always wore heels onscreen. That could be another reason why he was reluctant to appear with her.

"They're all my favorites," Grade said about the ten features he had in varying stages of production. "I believe in the laws of averages. One of these has to be a blockbuster." He did end up with exactly one blockbuster, and it wasn't the Bronson epic.

Newspaper ad.

Love and Bullets became an odd, disjointed, confusing picture. Ireland is doomed by the Southern accent and gives her worst performance. Steiger's bizarre turn is at least interesting, but character legends Martin, Silva, Koslo, and Michael V. Gazzo are all wasted. The editing is weak, and the film may hold the record for the most dissolves in a movie from this era. Bronson sports an awesome pea coat, there is a decent action scene set at a carnival, and the downbeat and bittersweet ending is somewhat compelling. Still, *Love and Bullets* is surpassed only by *Assassination* (1987) as the star's weakest vehicle.

It was rare that a Bronson picture opened in foreign territories prior to an American debut, but *Love and Bullets* had its initial release in Sweden in January 1979. In the following months it appeared in Denmark, the United Kingdom, Portugal, West Germany, France, the Netherlands, and Finland—all well before the stateside release.

The American release of *Love and Bullets* was ultimately handled by Grade himself.

He was unhappy when his *Movie Movie* was released during the 1978 holiday season. He said, "Warner Bros., who were distributing the film, had some important Christmas releases of their own and didn't give *Movie Movie* their best shot. It was then that I made a fatal mistake. I knew that EMI [another British production company] were also dissatisfied with the way the majors distributed their films [in America], so we got together and formed our own distribution company—Associated Film Distribution [AFD]." The mogul promised "a minimum of twelve major pictures a year for a minimum of four years."

Numerous offices for AFD were set up in the major North American territories. *Firepower* was the new distributor's first release. It opened in April 1979, followed by the war movie *Escape to Athena* in June. Both of those Grade productions were made after *Love and Bullets*, which had yet to be released in the States. *Firepower* and *Escape to Athena* performed poorly, but the third AFD release was *The Muppet Movie*, which opened in June and became one of the biggest hits of the year, grossing over

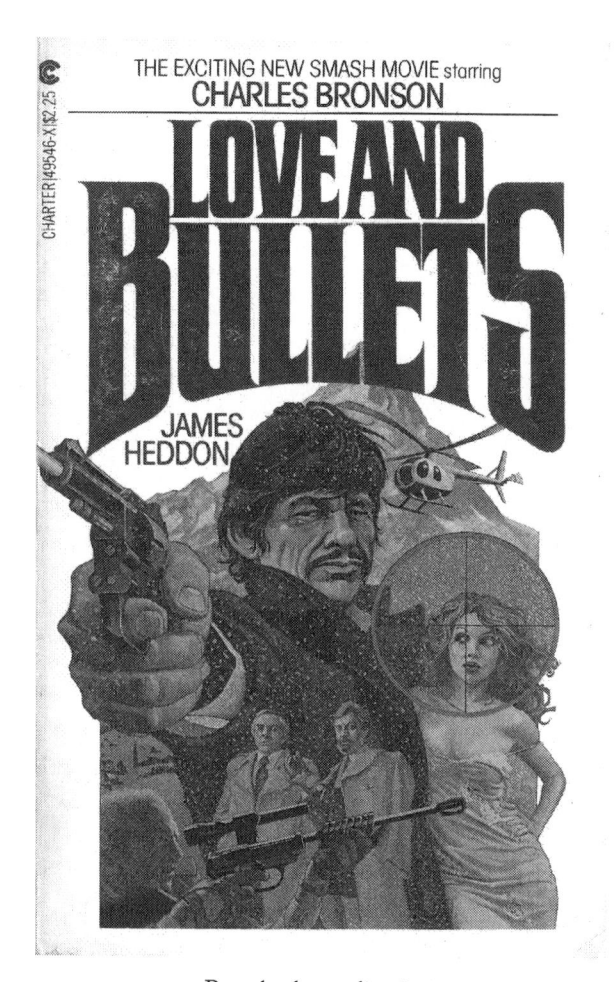

Paperback novelization.

$65 million. Grade said, "I have the biggest stars—Charles Bronson and Miss Piggy."

In July 1979, "to convince them we're here to stay," Grade spent $250,000 and travelled by Concorde to promote AFD's upcoming slate to the major theater chains in the States and Canada. The chains' executives were wined-and-dined while the jowly Grade's bombastic voice narrated a promo reel.

Love and Bullets became the fourth AFD release when it hit America on October 5, 1979—almost two years after the prior Bronson movie opened in the States. (*Telefon* was a major Christmas 1977 release.) Since 1968, at least two films starring Bronson had been released each year, but there was no Bronson picture in 1978.

The *Love and Bullets* pressbook promised: "Bronson's back…in action…in love…in trouble! Bronson leaves a trail of mangled hoods and colorful corpses across the scenic Alps. It's taunt, tense, bullet-spattered fun from start to finish, with Bronson at his bruising best." Promotional suggestions included: giving a red rose to the female patrons; awarding free passes to the winner of a radio-sponsored "Charles Bronson Sound-Alike Contest;" and a ticket-stub drawing for a free trip to Switzerland. A novelization by James Heddon was published by Charter Books. It was based on an early draft of the screenplay, and the story and action differed greatly from the final film. It also featured more graphic, gruesome depictions of violence than seen in the movie.

Janet Maslin, *The New York Times*: "[Bronson] spends most of his time escorting Miss Ireland onto trains, into hotels and across the snow. This is all very chivalrous, but it's also dull.…[Ireland] and Bronson approach each other with an appealing ease, which would be more appealing if it were not the movie's only selling point.…Rosenberg has had a long and successful career, and yet he still pays little heed to the most basic tricks of the trade, like establishing clear time sequences or letting the viewer know on which continent the action is taking place or even keeping his actors' faces out of the scenery.…[Steiger's] performance, which could seem restrained only in comparison with his *Amityville Horror* turn, would have been quite overwrought enough without the speech defect." *Variety*: "There are hints throughout of sharper characterizations and less superficial relationships, but these are hampered by unambitious dialogue and repeatedly trite situations.…Refreshing to report, this essentially family movie thriller refrains from gratuitous sadism and nudity, often seemingly employed to distract attention from a poor script, or regarded as the modern route to the public's wallet.…*Love and Bullets* is bland and fails to thrill.... The lingering pace and contrived backgrounds belong more to a travelogue than an adventure picture." Tom Allen, *The Village Voice*: "You can almost sense all the contracted, on-location luxuries that Bronson demanded before filming. *Love and Bullets* is a genre chase film with no rough edges, and a minimal sense of physical exertion on Bronson's part. Gone is the glowering that made Bronson the last mug you'd want to go against in a dark alley....More bullets and less love, Charlie." *Monthly Film Bulletin*: "*Love and Bullets* may not be the worst, but it is a relatively dismaying example of the Lew Grade entertainment formula: as locations, production values and clichéd set-pieces proliferate, scripts increasingly look like shaggy-dog stories desperately in search of a point, and actors are left to do their own thing as their characters disintegrate.... Bronson's persona just fades greyly into the wallpaper in those scenes where he is not called on for tight-lipped derring-do."

Los Angeles Herald-Examiner: "The one virtue of *Love and Bullets* is that, despite soupy direction, listless plotting, overscaled acting and blotchy cinematography, Bronson doesn't go soft on us." *Newark* (NJ) *Star-Ledger*: "For all its silliness, *Love and Bullets* has several virtues.... [Bronson] can get more mileage out of not showing any facial expression than any other actor around, with the possible exception of Clint Eastwood." *Spokane* (WA) *Daily Chronicle*: "When you go to a movie like this, it's to get a junk-movie high. And that's what you don't get from *Love and Bullets*. There's no fun in it. *Love and Bullets* is impersonal, perfunctory movie-making." *Miami News*: "Bronson's new one is nothing more than a blatant remake of Eastwood's *The Gauntlet*....[A]nother in that long line of films that seem made-for-TV. It's okay—not bad, not good, half interesting, half boring." *Sarasota* (FL) *Herald-Tribune*: "For those not devoted to [Bronson], I can't think of a single reason for sitting through this picture.... There is just about enough story material here for an hour segment of *Barnaby Jones* including commercials." (That review was headlined "*Love and Bullets* Should Be Shot.")

The final gross in America for *Love and Bullets* was less than $1.3

million, but like Grade's *The Eagle Has Landed* (1976) and *The Cassandra Crossing*, both of which flopped in the States, *Love and Bullets* did exceptionally well in foreign territories like Australia, Japan and the Far East—where Bronson's fan base remained huge.

The home video rental market had not yet exploded and Grade wasn't able to pre-sell to that medium as a financial cushion. *Love and Bullets* didn't appear on the American home video market until 1985 via Key Video (a division of CBS/Fox).

Grade said, "[In the late 1970s], if a movie wasn't a hit, you could kiss goodbye to most of your investment….In the movie business, blockbuster mega-hits are the exception rather than the rule. Having one is like winning the jackpot." *Love and Bullets* didn't hit the jackpot, creatively or financially, but the mogul still had Bronson signed for two more pictures, and they would turn out better.

Chapter 5
Cabo Blanco (1980)

"It was the biggest independent movie of the time," says producer Lance Hool about his *Cabo Blanco*. The $10 million film started out as one of the most ambitious, heavily promoted and highest-budgeted epics of Charles Bronson's career, but disputes between the producers and problems with distribution turned it into one of the more obscure of the star's vehicles.

Lance Hool was born and raised in Mexico and began his industry career in the 1970s with bit parts in locally shot films. After moving to California, he produced the low-budget, shot-in-Mexico action movies *Wolf Lake* (1977) and *Survival Run* (a.k.a. *Spree*, 1978). Hool recalls how *Cabo Blanco* was created: "It started about 1976. There was a writer, a Canadian fellow, his name was James Granby Hunter, who had a

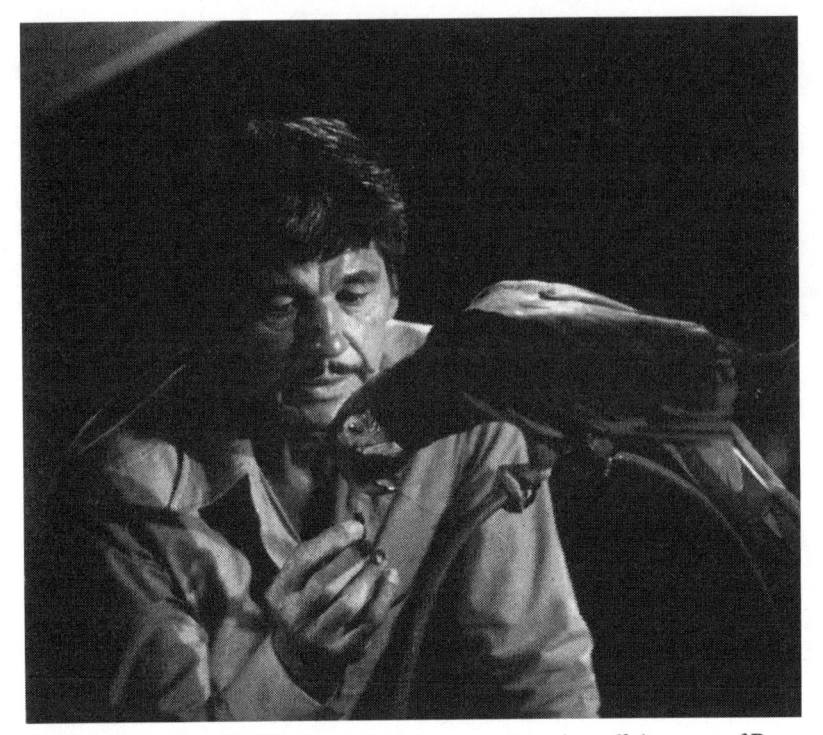

Charles Bronson as Giff Hoyt, an American running a bar off the coast of Peru, in *Cabo Blanco* (1980).

screenplay—which was more of an 'Indiana Jones' than what *Cabo Blanco* ended up being."

Hunter had read the true story of a ship filled with valuable European art that had sunk near Argentina during World War II. After the war, a German crew searched for the treasure, but the vessel wasn't found, and the men were never heard from again. Hunter's premise for *Cabo Blanco* was set in 1949 and centered on Gift Hoyt, a former American running a bar off the coast of Peru, who becomes involved with a sunken vessel loaded with solid gold religious items. Seeking the treasure (for various reasons) were: Ex-Nazi Gunther Beckdorff; local police chief Terredo; a young British Navy officer; and a mysterious and beautiful French woman.

Hool: "We worked on the screenplay, and it was a very cool idea, an adventure—which was what always attracted me, epic and adventure films. It was one man against a Nazi machine with a corrupt police force in this little town in Cabo Blanco. He's being chased, so he's gotta figure out what's going on. [The characters] were trying to get this sunken ship off the coast of Peru. This giant squid is messing around with them. There was a lot of comedy in it as well. It was very much *Raiders of the Lost Ark* [1981]. Somehow, that original script ended up over at [Spielberg's company] Amblin at one point or another. But that's just hearsay."

In 1977 Hool met Paul A. Joseph, an executive producer on the drive-in hits *Mako: The Jaws of Death* (1976) and *Moonshine County Express* (1977). Hool: "I had just finished doing a movie that starred Rod Steiger called *The Honor Guard* [a.k.a. *Wolf Lake*, 1977] that Burt Kennedy had directed. I had partnered with this company that was financing films called Creative Entertainment, [run by] a fellow called Paul A. Joseph and his partner, Malcolm Levinthal. I told them that I wanted to do [*Cabo Blanco*], but I wanted to do it totally independently. I grew up in Mexico, and I was involved in the film industry there, and we had quite a bit of success by getting our product out to the rest of the world. This was going to be a big-budget movie, and I thought that the way to cover it wasn't just to walk up to the studio and say, 'Here are all the rights, they're yours. Give us the money and we'll make the movie for you.' I wanted to have some control. My agreement with the Creative Entertainment guys was that they would put up enough money for me to test the waters and market the film. We had a budget of $300,000 to test.

"I put together a campaign with a marketing expert called Ira Teller starting with small ads in *Variety* questioning: 'What was *Cabo Blanco*?,' 'What was it all about?' And we put together a beautiful, big ad and had some great artists do renderings of our ideal cast. It was the five main characters. For 'Giff Hoyt' was a drawing that was almost the likeness of Paul Newman. We had a drawing that was almost the likeness of Orson Welles to play 'Terredo;' [an image like] Curt Jergens to play the German;

and the young British guy [looked like] Michael York. We wanted the people that were buying films for their different territories to get the idea that we were doing a real 'international' movie. Nobody had done an ad that size and that nice before, and it attracted a lot of attention from a lot of people. We ran it [in *Variety*] right before the Cannes Film Festival." The *Cabo Blanco* ad announced that filming would begin in the Caribbean in October 1978 for release in 1979. The female character was drawn to look like the French star who would actually get the role. Hool: "I always liked Dominique Sanda because I was enamored with her in De Sica's *The Garden of the Finzi-Continis* [1970]. She was just brilliant in it. At Cannes, we rented a very large, beautiful villa that was owned by the Prime Minister of France, and we did this huge party and invited all the people at the different studios to come. The party was a tremendous success. We invited, maybe, 150—we had to start turning them back at 300. All the big people in Hollywood were there.

Multi-page ad that ran in *Variety* in May, 1978—before a screenplay was written or any stars were cast. (Courtesy of Bryan Moose)

"On my way back to Los Angeles from Cannes, I got a call from the representatives of Paul Newman. I went to New York and met with him. He said, 'Look, I love the idea. I haven't had the chance to read the script.' [laughs] At the time, we really didn't have a script because we were still playing with that original concept, and I hadn't hired a script writer. It was an idea, a treatment. He didn't know that. Paul said, 'I can't do it because I just committed to Nissan to race for them for this year. You should go and meet with Steve [McQueen]. Let me set that up.' I went to [McQueen's] house in Malibu, and he was very sick. And he said, 'You know who should play this? Charlie Bronson.' Charlie, at the time, was number-one in the world, and I had not set my sights quite as high as *that*. McQueen and Newman would have been great, but Charlie was the man that I *really wanted*.

"On my way home from Malibu, I got a call from Charlie's agent, Paul Kohner, and I just about fainted. He said, 'We should get together. Charlie should be your man.' We had a lunch at the old Scandia. Now you gotta remember, I'm twenty-eight at the time. [laughs] And even though I had been in the business for quite some time, my biggest film to that point was a $1.5 million film with Rod Steiger. I was not exactly a household name for producers. We had the lunch, and Paul said, 'Look, Charlie wants to do this. He sees himself in the part.' [laughs] Keep in mind, at this point there's still not a script. [laughs] This is, basically, a great ad and the word that we had put out of what the movie was like. Nobody had seen a script. He said, 'When can we get a script? I also want to introduce you to my son [Pancho Kohner]. I'd like him to be a producer of some sort with you because he knows Charlie.' That was, sort of, the price. I said, 'Sure. Absolutely. I'd be happy to meet with him.'" The agent's son had already produced three Bronson movies.

Hool: "I hired Milton Gelman, a terrific writer who had done tons of TV [*Bonanza*, *Tales of Wells Fargo*] and was teaching at Loyola Marymount. While we were writing it, Paul got very involved and said, 'Who do you have to write the screenplay? I'd like you to meet some of *my* writers.' So Lukas Heller (*The Dirty Dozen*, 1967) was hired to do a pass on the treatment and see what he could come up with. Ultimately, the movie that I wanted to make was not what came out because of the influence on me to get these heavyweight writers on this screenplay. Everybody started pulling in different directions. Obviously, we needed a strong hand and a director. I had initially thought about, because I had worked with him before, John Huston. But he wasn't available. I thought about Burt Kennedy, but we had had a bit of a problem—he wouldn't shoot the alternate ending that the studio wanted for the Steiger film. I was told by Paul Kohner that J. Lee Thompson had worked successfully with Charlie. He was doing a movie in France at that time with Anthony Quinn, the Onassis film [*The Greek Tycoon*, 1978]."

The British J. Lee Thompson's long career began in the 1940s in England when he got involved in theater before breaking into the film business, where he became a writer, editor and director. His exceptional British films included the musical *The Good Companion* (1957), the action drama *Ice Cold in Alex* (a.k.a. *Desert Attack*, 1958), and the suspenseful *Tiger Bay* (1959). Thompson relocated to Hollywood in 1960, and the following year he helmed two action-suspense classics: *Guns of Navarone* (which earned him an Oscar nomination) and *Cape Fear*. His Hollywood output included more action pictures—plus excursions into dark comedy (*What a Way to Go!*, 1966), thrillers (*Eye of the Devil*, 1967; *Reincarnation of Peter Proud*, 1974), science fiction (*Conquest of the Planet of the Apes*, 1972), and musicals (*Huckleberry Finn*, 1974)—before he first teamed with Bronson and Pancho Kohner on *St. Ives* (1976) and *The White Buffalo* (1977).

Hool: "I flew over to France, and I met with J. Lee, and I liked him right way. A real 'shooter'—he 'gets' the movie, and he makes it. I wasn't so sure whether he had the same grasp of what I wanted to make—which was a real adventure, 'big' kind of film. I sensed that he was leaning towards, 'Wouldn't it be nice to remake *Casablanca* [1942] with Bronson?' [laughs] Which I didn't really want to do, because Charlie was known

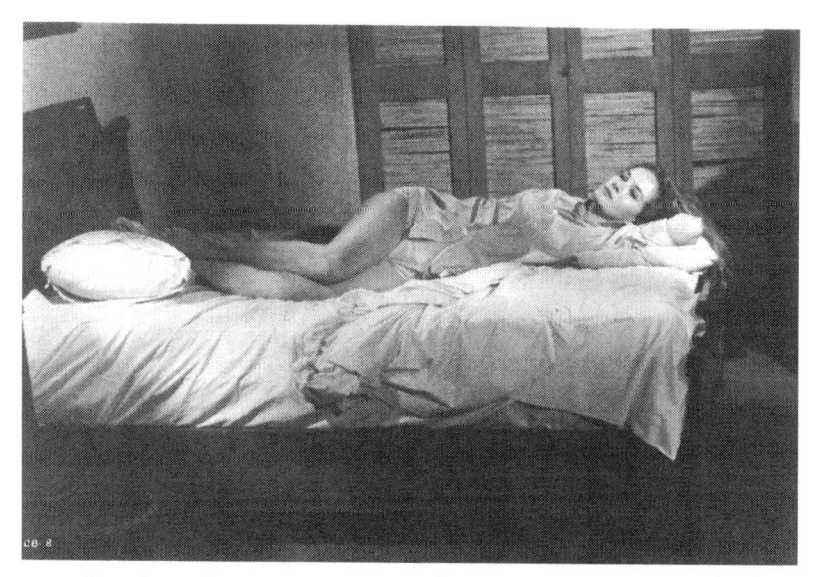

French star Dominique Sanda as the mysterious Marie Allesandri.

for action, and that's what people wanted to see. Ultimately, J. Lee came on [and] was involved in the process of writing the screenplay." Morton Fine (*The Pawnbroker*, 1964), who was then revising his *The Greek Tycoon* script on the set, began a draft of *Cabo Blanco* with Thompson.

Hool: "A lot of people claimed to be speaking for [Bronson], but they were speaking for themselves, not for him. There was a lot of jostling for power to be around Mr. Bronson. In later years, I found out that a lot of stuff never got to Charlie. I kept hearing: 'Charlie wouldn't do that. Charlie wouldn't jump in the ocean and swim. Charlie wouldn't be messing around with a giant squid.' So the movie started veering more and more towards a remake of *Casablanca*. It didn't have the sense of humor that I wanted in the movie—it diverted. I was the kid, and all of these grown-ups around me were saying, 'Let *them* do the job.'"

The young producer looked for more star names to embellish the international marquees. British actor Simon MacCorkindale (*Death on the Nile*; 1978) was cast as a Navy officer. American George Kennedy (*Cool Hand Luke*, 1967) was briefly considered for the head Nazi role until Jason Robards was signed. Robards had recently won back-to-back Oscars and had previously played opposite Bronson in *Once Upon a Time in the West* (1968) and starred in Pancho Kohner's offbeat *Mr. Sycamore* (1975). He had also been cast in Bronson's *Cold Sweat* (1970) before getting replaced by James Mason.

Hool: "I went after Jason Robards, and Jason accepted the part, which was great because I always loved the man and loved his work. [I cast] Fernando Ray (*The Discreet Charm of the Bourgeoisie*, 1972), another great actor and great guy. I flew to Paris and went to the office of [Dominque Sanda's agent] and told her how much of a fan [of Sanda] I was and that we wanted to write this [role] specifically for her. I was really tired and jetlagged, and I said, 'What's her price?' and she gave me this price. Clearly, she didn't want to work in an American movie unless they pay her a fortune. [laughs] And I started coughing. I couldn't stop. So [the agent] said, 'You think that's too much?' And I said, 'Yes. It is too much.' *Damnation Alley* [1977], which she had done before, was her only American movie and was not successful. Anyway, we came to terms. Bronson was the highest paid actor in the world at that time. He got his full ticket. And Jason Robards got a good, decent fee. They all got good fees.

"So they're all waiting for the screenplay. In the meantime, I was busy getting the movie financed. I interviewed a couple of young guys that were just in from Asia who were trying to set up a distribution company for foreign sales. They were very eager to get involved, and I liked them right away. It was Andy Vajna and Mario Kassar, whose company was called Carolco. So they came onboard, and we were expecting a certain amount of money to come from pre-sales." Carolco became the foreign sales agent and distributed a flyer to buyers announcing that *Cabo Blanco* would be available for delivery in December 1979. Carolco Pictures went on to produce blockbusters like the first three Sylvester Stallone "Rambo" movies (1982–1988) and *Terminator 2: Judgment Day* (1991).

Cabo Blanco (1980)

Nazi Gunther Beckdorff (Jason Robards) and police chief Terredo (Fernando Rey) are among those looking for the sunken treasure.

Hool: "I went to Warner Bros. and they loved the project so I made a deal with them for the United States and then with CBS for television. And I did a deal with Home Box Office for what was a very nascent thing back then—cable. We needed the other part, which was a bank to finance it. Creative Entertainment knew a fellow that had been a big guy at Union Bank, and he came on board to finance all these contracts. His name was Martin V. Smith, and he became the executive producer. He was an interesting guy. He was in shopping centers and commercial buildings and, basically, owned most of Oxnard [California]. He found out that the Navy was looking for a base, and he bought this swampland, which became Oxnard in Point Mugu. That's how he made his money. His daughter had worked for Paul Joseph, and that's how that connection came. We went off, made the movie."

Hool scouted numerous locations in South America and the Caribbean before finding Barra de Navidad, a small fishing and farming village in Mexico with a population of less than 1,000. During a month of pre-production at the location, the bar owned by Bronson's character was built from scratch.

As shooting got closer, the smaller roles were cast. Tall, blonde American ex-Tarzan Denny Miller (*Wagon Train*, 1961–1964) played Robard's henchman. He says, "My agent sent me the script, and I auditioned for the part. I read several times." Miller ended up staying ninety-two days on the location. The stunning Swedish actress Camilla Sparv was cast as an ex-lover of Bronson. Director Thompson had worked with her on *Mackenna's Gold* (1969) and *The Greek Tycoon* and insisted that she be cast in *Cabo Blanco*. Her role ended up being dramatically increased as the script was revised during the shoot.

Trade papers announced that the first day of filming on *Cabo Blanco* would be November 27, 1978. But by mid-December, the cast hadn't yet arrived on location, and press releases noted that the start date had been moved to January 2, 1979. Hool said at the time: "Working in Mexico has tremendous advantages. And you're so close to the United States that you can bring in things. There's daily flights. So in that sense, it's perfect and very convenient. The biggest difficulties in working on location are communication problems, and the fact that you have to set up offices in several different cities to be able to accomplish what you normally would do on the backstage or the lot." Hool's brother, Conrad Hool, was associate producer on the film.

Over one-hundred crew members were flown in from California. Hundreds of locals were used as extras, including a ninety-year-old woman, a two-month-old infant, and two goats. Hool said, "We are definitely not remaking *Casablanca*. What we're trying to do is make a film that has the gritty feel of a Warner Bros. movie of that era—a movie with a hero and a heroine, well-defined villains, pretty ladies." Producer Paul A. Joseph added, "The story takes place six years later, and it's a different area of the world. And nobody can put a copyright on people. We might end up shooting two different endings. We've been discussing it for three months, so we may have a *Return to Cabo Blanco* if things work out." Early in the shoot, Hollywood columnist Marilyn Beck reported that the script was "being changed daily and with neither cast nor producers yet sure how the adventure story will be resolved."

Hoyt (Bronson) battles Nazi henchman Horst (Denny Miller).

Thompson said, "How much of the film is as originally planned? None. Because the story used to be, so I understand, about a giant squid. It's no longer a story about a giant squid. Don't think I'm denigrating stories about giant squids or giant anythings. I'm not. It just happens that this story is about character. It's evolving as we go along. Naturally, most good actors are creative people. They take the scene, and they may not like a particular moment, and they may create a better one. On the other hand, they very often *don't* create a better one, and you have to talk them into remaining with what is written."

Dominic Sanda called the script, "a confusing story." Jason Robards said, "It's an entertainment, an adventure story. You can't start thinking about things like *The Iceman Cometh* while you're doing this. The thing to do is to just have fun with it. I used to let things like that bother me, used to rant and rave and scream about some of the movies I did that were being made just as entertainment. Not now."

Fernando Rey said, "It is practically a remake of *Casablanca*, but instead of taking place in North Africa, it is laid in Peru and actually filmed in Mexico. I play the Claude Rains role, the police chief, and when I first read the script I didn't like the part at all. I told the producers, 'It doesn't fit me.' After ten minutes on the phone, they were able to convince me I was wrong. I wasn't really wrong, but when J. Lee Thompson began shooting the picture, we kept making changes and building up the part until I felt comfortable with it." During the *Cabo Blanco* shoot, Rey—who had starred in Spanish-language films for decades—was considered by the locals to be a bigger star than Bronson.

Hool: "Charlie scared people because his persona was so strong. People wouldn't come up to him too much; they wouldn't talk to him too much. He liked to sit separately with a few of us, not many. He wasn't a guy that liked idle chat. But he was very interested in what was going on. He liked [his character]—he liked the adventure of it and that we were shooting in beautiful locations. He was there when he needed to be, exactly, and he left when he needed to leave, and he was always there for his fellow actors. Just a real professional. A tremendous human being and a real man's man. With Charlie, it was always 'less dialogue.' He would come to the set with whatever we were gonna shoot and say, 'I don't need to say all of this. I can just do it by looking.' He did his homework. And J. Lee listened very carefully and did what Charlie suggested."

Denny Miller: "Mr. Bronson and I did not socialize. He stayed to himself. Charles Bronson was not 'warm and fuzzy.' He and his wife stayed in another hotel than where the rest of the cast stayed. He was always making script changes so the producers had to have writers on the set at all times. The director was prepared and easy to work with. He got along with the cast and crew."

Hool: "We were shooting on this beach in the Pacific coast in Mexico—a very lonely sort of place. We had very little communication.

Hoyt (Bronson) is captured by Terredo (Fernando Rey)

And all of sudden, this big helicopter comes and starts going around the set on top of us and ruining our sound. Then a second one, and then a third one, and then a fourth one. We thought, 'What's going on? We've been invaded.' They landed about 500 yards away from the set. Then somebody came and said, 'The President of Mexico is here. He wants to say, 'Hello.' [laughs] He heard Dominique Sanda was there, and he wanted to meet her. So we cut for an early lunch, and he wanted to sit next to her, but Dominique didn't want that. [laughs] She sat me in between the two of them. His name was Portillo, and he was very proud that he was one-hundred-percent Spanish. I said, 'Don't you want to meet Charles Bronson?' He said, 'Is he *here?*' [laughs] I said, 'Yeah. He's the star.' [He said,] 'Oh, my God! Yes, of course! Of course, I want to meet Charles Bronson!' [laughs] So he did. Charlie was gracious. That day was ruined—there was no more shooting. [Portillo] heard me speak Spanish, and he said, 'You're Mexican?' I said, 'I was born in Mexico. My father is American.' [Portillo] had just become president of Mexico. His predecessor had nationalized the film industry, and that's why I had left Mexico to go to Hollywood. He said, 'I want you to go to Mexico City with me because I want to talk to you about this industry. I don't know anything about it, and I understand it's nationalized. What am I gonna do with it?' [laughs] So for the next four years of my life, I ran the [Mexican film] industry from L.A.

"Steve Peck, who is Gregory's son, did a 'making of' [documentary] which is pretty good [with] some good interviews, particularly with Charlie. The cameraman of that 'making of' was a young guy called Guillermo Navarro. He just won the Oscar a few years ago [for *Pan's Labyrinth*, 2006]. He was a good friend. A lot of people from that movie went on to do good things." In the documentary, Bronson comes off as relaxed, happy and charming. He is shown joking with Robards between takes and walking with his arm around Robards off set. Robards was one of the rare actors that Bronson felt chummy with. A still taken on the set of *Once Upon a Time in the West* shows the two actors smiling with their arms around each other.

Bronson said, "I never imagined that I'd be working down here in the tropics. It feels more like you're there in the location of the story. You don't have to try to capture the feeling from a fake atmosphere like a stage—here you have it. It's supposed to be tropical, and it *is* tropical. When I'm supposed to feel hot, I do feel hot, and I don't have to fake it. So it makes it so much easier." When asked to explain his popularity to the 16mm documentary camera, the star replied: "I don't even know if it's the screen character or the stories that I've been in or just pure luck. I have no idea. If I stopped to analyze it and if I could successfully analyze it, then maybe I'm in the wrong business and should be a psychoanalyst."

Bronson aggressively chewed gum between takes to reduce his constant craving for a cigarette. He told the press: "It's not the time you're getting paid for. It's the choice, like the choice between a brand. You're getting paid that amount of money because it's a short life, your professional life. You get the money while you can earn it, like a star athlete. You can never establish yourself at a certain price and expect

Cabo Blanco (1980)

Spanish poster.

the money to keep coming in. Most actors hit a peak and then go down the other side of the ladder. That's the way it's been from the beginning. No matter how much you're earning, you still have to worry about your health and welfare. You have to put money by for injuries and sickness and old age. And [actors] don't have the benefits some people have like pensions and that sort of thing. You have to make do with what you're earning now. That's why you ask for a lot of money, so that you can prepare for old age." He referred to himself as a "solitary man" during the interview and added, "If I have a problem, I go quietly and think it out. I don't discuss it with anybody. Not my wife, not anybody." As to his wife, Jill Ireland, he noted, "She thinks I'm the best looking man in the world, but I think I'm the ugliest."

Miller: "One of the local ranchers gave Mrs. Bronson a beautiful thoroughbred horse to use while we were shooting the film. She was a very good horseman."

Hool: "It was a long shoot. It was a very complicated shoot. But it wasn't difficult; it was pleasant. We stayed in very nice places, and everyone had a good time. Jill was there, always looking fantastic and being very supportive. Charlie and Jill had the penthouse of the nicest hotel in Puerto Vallarta. All of his family was there. [Bronson's stepson] Jason later became my assistant. A terrific guy. He died [young]. Very sad. There was no studio work. We built the [hotel] set in a place called Barra de Navidad, which is a sandbar. Many years later, I was producing *McHale's Navy* [1997], and we were scouting around to see where we were going to shoot it. It was supposed to be an island somewhere in the Caribbean. I said, 'Let's go back and see what's happened [to the *Cabo Blanco* set].' In the meantime, there had been a tidal wave that came and destroyed the whole little town except for the set. [laughs] So we used it again. It had not been damaged *at all*, and all of these other buildings were torn down by the tidal wave. Pretty amazing."

Miller recalled, "Charles would wait until it was time to shoot the scene and then suggest changes. This slowed down everything. I had a fight scene to do with Mr. Bronson. He was really good at stunt fighting. I wasn't bad at it myself. Two stuntmen had been flown down to double us in the dangerous parts of the fight. [Bronson] didn't like the looks of his double, so they flew another stuntman down. Charles wanted me to do the fight. He pointed to my double and said, 'You don't want to look like that on the screen. Look at the gut on the guy.'"

The stuntman was Tony Epper—who had been in the business for decades, was a frequent double for Burt Lancaster, and had once beaten a guy to death in a bar fight. To prevent the enraged, 6' 4" Epper from punching Bronson, the stunt coordinator sent Epper back to L.A. and Bronson blocked the fight, which involved Miller getting beaten with a dresser drawer and a metal canister. Miller: "He felt that we should not have breakaway furniture in the scene—that it was more realistic to use the regular drawer. He also did not want to use stunt men. So we actually did the entire scene ourselves." Miller left the set to stuff his Nazi uniform with pads to protect his arms. He recalled, "On the street, walking back to the set, I pass the Mexican cameraman. He'd been a treat to work with—creative, fast and a great sense of humor. Out from under his hat comes a whisper, 'Knock the head off the little S.O.B.'"

On one take, Bronson swung the drawer so hard that the handle broke off and the rest of the drawer went flying. On another, the star slashed three of his fingers on a sharp corner of the canister. After the blood was mopped up and his wound was wrapped with makeup-covered tape, Bronson continued the scene. He said during the shoot, "Most action and most body contact that you have is fierce in real life. It comes from an emotion first—except game sports, which this is not. This is trying to hurt somebody."

Miller recalled another anecdote: "Charles was sitting in a folding chair on the only cobblestone street in the fishing village we shot in. A shy barefoot kid loafed by. I could tell he wanted to talk but didn't know how to start. Mr. Bronson hadn't been friendly to the natives. Much to my surprise, he waved the kid over and motioned for him to sit down. He picked up a steel pipe and laid it across his lap. I couldn't hear them from where I was watching, but they seemed to understand each other. I'd guess the pipe was about four feet long and [had] a one-quarter inch to three-eighths inch hole in it. Charles took a nail out of his pocket and then tore a strip of paper from a page in his script. He wrapped the paper around the head of the nail and inserted the nail, point first, in the end of the pipe. Then they started pointing at a homemade wooden ladder on the flat roof of an adobe across the street. It was about thirty yards away. Charles held up two fingers. The kid shook his head 'no' and held up three. Charles nodded in agreement, put the pipe up to his mouth and that nail went zinging and zapped into the third rung of the ladder."

Bronson said "[*Cabo Blanco* is] a damned good movie. I think someday it's going to be a cult film, after it's a box office hit." When the *Cabo Blanco* shoot ended in mid-March 1979, Bronson did not have another project immediately lined up and took a rare, extended break at his farm in Vermont. He wouldn't be back on a film set until *Borderline* started shooting in mid-October 1979.

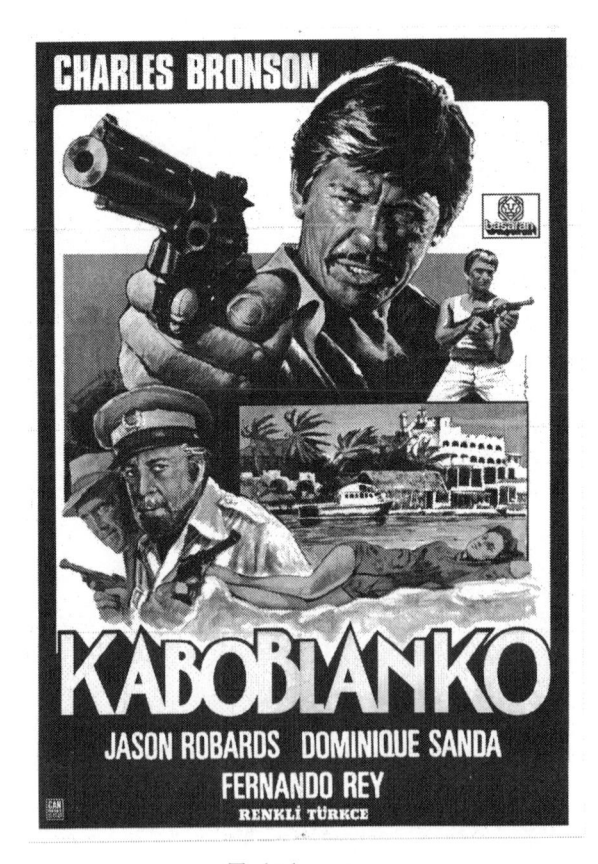

Turkish poster.

Hool had no break and had to concentrate on the post-production. He says, "The score is a tremendous score—Jerry Goldsmith. We went to London and did the whole thing." Goldsmith's previous scores included Bronson's *Breakout* and *Breakheart Pass* (both 1975) as well as Thompson's *The Chairman* (1969) and *The Reincarnation of Peter Proud* (1975). The *Cabo Blanco* score incorporated Roy Noble's song "The Very Thought of You," a 1934 composition that had been recorded numerous times as a vocal and instrumental track and was heard in Bogart's club in *Casablanca*. Goldsmith also wrote a song of his own for the film— "Heaven Knows," which was sung by his wife, Carol Heather. In March of 1981, the composer told *Soundtrack* magazine, "*Cabo Blanco* is one I'd like to forget—it hasn't come out anywhere, I think. There was a lot of source music of the 1930s in the picture. I don't think there will be much heard of the film."

Hool: "Years later, I was sitting in an office of a friend, and we could hear a mix coming through the walls. I said, 'I know this music.' Jerry had done *Under Fire* [1983], and he used part of the [*Cabo Blanco*] score in it. [laughs] I remember calling and going, 'Hey, Jerry, you're stealing.' [laughs] He said, 'Oh, no. It's just the inspiration.'"

Pancho Kohner was billed in the early publicity materials as an executive producer along with Martin A. Smith, but he ultimately decided to not take a credit on *Cabo Blanco*. Hool: "He felt that he was pushed on the production a bit, and he basically acquiesced his credit to Martin Smith. Pancho is a lovely man and a very good friend of mine. We subsequently did a couple of movies together." In the finished film, Milton Gelman and (original creator) James Granby Hunter received "story by" credit, while Gelman and Mort Fine got "screenplay by" credit. Lukas Heller was not billed.

Because of conflicts between Hool and Smith, Bronson's next two pictures—*Borderline* (1980) and *Death Hunt* (1981)—would be shot, completed, and released before *Cabo Blanco* was in American theaters. Hool: "Once we finished the movie, people thought that Martin Smith had put up all the money and was gonna therefore be a new source of funding. So they started filling his head with the idea that he was gonna be a big mogul in the film industry. Very much to my dismay, he announced that he was *not* going to take the Warner Bros. contract, *not* take the CBS contract, *not* take the Home Box Office [deal]. He was going to make a deal with Columbia Pictures for worldwide. The foreign contracts all stayed in place, which was good. I had to sue him. He played producer, as if he'd shot the film. He was leaning towards a more serious version of the movie than what we had actually shot. He monkeyed around with it."

In the spring of 1979, a two-hour cut of *Cabo Blanco* was released in Italy, France, Sweden, Portugal, Greece, Argentina, and Venezuela. Distribution for the United States and all other territories remained unsold.

Hool: "[Smith] never was able to conclude a deal with Columbia Pictures. Then he came back to me to ask me to help him get some contracts. So I did. Because he had not taken those [original] contracts, his bank would have to put up the money [if no distribution was found]. Warner Bros. wouldn't do it again because they were slighted. [laughs] This guy had painted us in a corner when all of his grandiose plans of taking over Columbia Pictures just didn't work for him."

In early 1980, Hool screened the film for the major American distributors and studios. They all passed except for 20th Century Fox, which stalled for six months before deciding against the film. *Cabo Blanco* was then chopped down to ninety-six minutes and then to eighty-seven minutes (including credits) to create a tighter-paced film that would appeal to American audiences. Thompson supervised all cuts of the film. Hool: "The original [cut] was two hours, and that's the movie that should be seen. There were long chases and a lot of action. The action in [the shortened cut] is: he takes out a guy underneath a tree and a couple of hammocks and that's it."

Among the trims was the first scene that introduced Bronson, depriving the star of a notable introduction in the picture. Clifton James' [*Live and Let Die*, 1973] comedic role as an American tourist was deleted entirely. (He was still billed in the credits and publicity materials.) A pre-credit action scene was chopped up and turned into a brief flashback for two scenes. Both scenes that featured Bronson's marketable bare torso were cut. Narration by supporting player Simon MacCorkindale was added to clarify the story.

Despite the sparse running time, the shorter *Cabo Blanco* still comes across as slow. The movie has a fantastic score, gorgeous locations and great photography with an interesting use of colored gels. Thompson is in good form. The film is filled with fine compositions, and the director's camera is constantly moving via dolly or handheld shots. Bronson is engaged and looks fantastic—it's apparent that time was spent on lighting him, but the story is confusing, and the final payoff is weak. Hool: "The [originally scripted] ending was much more powerful than the cyanide in the tooth."

The truncated version played the Netherlands, Finland and Turkey in mid-1980. Then *Cabo Blanco* was offered again to American distributors—this time in the short version. Hool: "It ended up going to Avco Embassy. That was where we could go, and they were happy to have it. Bob Rehme was the head of Avco—very nice guy, and later head of the Academy. Bob looked at the movie and said, 'This is fine. Let's go.' They did not have the money, obviously, that Warner Bros. would have had to release the movie. But [the Avco deal] saved the day for [Smith]. Ultimately, he was not able to cover the whole amount of the contracts, so he ended up with the rights, i.e. the bank ended up with the rights."

Avco Embassy was an independent distributor that released films on a slow, territory-by-territory basis with heavy TV advertising. They had recent hits with the cleverly marketed genre films *Murder by Decree* (1979), *Phantasm* (1979), *The Fog* (1980), and *Prom Night* (1980).

The Avco deal for *Cabo Blanco* North American rights (which involved an undisclosed cash advance plus percentage) was signed in

September 1980. The distributor told *Variety* that the plan was to open the movie in October in six "medium-sized markets" including Miami and Phoenix with an "action-oriented Charles Bronson campaign" and have the film in wide distribution by Thanksgiving.

Newspaper ad.

Bronson came close to starring in another action movie from Avco Embassy. The company was financing the futuristic *Escape from New York* (1981), which was then in pre-production. Director John Carpenter said, "Charles Bronson had expressed interest in playing Snake [Plissken], but I was afraid of working with him. He was a big star, and I was this little-shit nobody."

The violence and the abundance of topless Mexican women got *Cabo Blanco* an R rating. Avco Embassy played up the *Casablanca* connection: "*Cabo Blanco* starring Bronson in the kind of soldier-of-fortune role that was once the private province of Humphrey Bogart." The publicity claimed that the Mexican government had changed the name of the town of Barra de Navidad to Cabo Blanco in anticipation of the huge increase in tourist traffic expected to result from the movie's release. In reality, the town's name stayed the same.

Publicity gimmicks suggested for the American release included: Holding a "Cabo Blanco Treasure Hunt" wherein patrons would be given a treasure map and the map holder with the winning numbers would win "a fortune in prizes sponsored by the participating merchants"; a tie-in with a local travel agency with a drawing for "a trip to Cabo Blanco, Mexico's exotic new vacation resort named in honor of the picture"; and displaying posters around town asking "What is the secret of Cabo Blanco?" Local bars and restaurants were asked to participate by offering the "Cabo Blanco drink"—"Pour Kahlua over ice, add cream and Perrier water to suit your taste, and there you have it! A tasty toast that offers refreshing entertainment."

The first bookings for *Cabo Blanco* were on October 17, 1980, at thirteen Florida screens. The newspaper ads promised "An Epic Adventure at the Edge of the World." *Evening Independent* (St. Petersburg, FL): "It is neither epic or explosive....The people responsible for this movie presumably decided to vacation awhile and get away from the Hollywood rat race. They filmed *Cabo Blanco* while they were at it, but it's obvious they didn't do much work....Nothing much ever happens and what does is haphazard, insensible and unspectacular." The first week's gross was a mere $36,000. For the next ten months, the film slowly played the country.

Cabo Blanco got to New York on May 29, 1981—one week after Bronson's *Death Hunt* hit the area. At the same time, Thompson's modestly budgeted teen-slasher movie *Happy Birthday to Me*, which the director made after *Cabo Blanco*, was the number-one movie in America. *Cabo Blanco* played other major markets in July 1981.

Alternate newspaper ad.

People: "Even if Bronson is no Bogart, he does contribute a resigned dignity....The plot is light on plausibility, and Bronson has to finesse some dreadful lines....As movies go these days, this one is diverting and—nudity and violence aside—harmless enough." *Box Office*: "Since no one dared to remake *Casablanca*, the makers of *Cabo Blanco* have tried to evoke many of the same elements without actually copying. They would have done better to steal." *Variety*: "[a] tenuous leftover... [it] was perhaps begun as a tongue-in-cheek remake, but lost its way or lacked necessary dash to make it work. Result is particularly muddy, no matter how perceived." Kevin Thomas, the *Los Angeles Times*: "a feeble attempt to resurrect romantic '40s intrigue, but its script is too listless and uninspired to all its people to acquire any individuality or even come to life."

Cabo Blanco grossed less than $1 million in America. Hool: "Clearly, Avco didn't have the money to release it the way a big studio like Warners would have. We were all let down, but it was better than *not* a release. The place where they did spend a little money, in New York, we were number one. Charlie had a big following, obviously. It wasn't released wide. It did okay. There was never a Bronson movie that didn't do [at least] okay. It was not what it should have been. *Cabo Blanco* was to be released by Warner Bros. with a different tone to the film. It wasn't a remake of *Casablanca*; it was a movie with a lot more action. And if it had been released that way, that movie would have done very, very well. In some [foreign] territories it did very, very well."

Denny Miller: "*Cabo Blanco* was a very good script, a great cast, and sadly turned into a bomb of a movie. Show biz." Miller continued his long career as a character actor before passing away in 2014.

Avco Embassy paired *Cabo Blanco* with their surprise (*Death Wish*-inspired) hit *The Exterminator* (1980) for drive-ins and second-run theaters. *Cabo Blanco* didn't get released in Japan (one of Bronson's biggest markets), Norway or Australia until 1981. It played West Germany in 1983. Each of those territories played the shorter version.

Japanese poster.

The HBO deal for *Cabo Blanco* was lost, but the film did play on pay-TV via Channel Z in Los Angeles in December 1981. The station's printed schedule noted: "Prior to shooting, *Cabo Blanco* had a giant pre-production ad campaign.... The budget was enormous. An international cast was signed.... [The movie] had all the elements of an 'up-front, want-to-see' box office attraction. But the film opened this year in Los Angeles with a slim advertising campaign and almost no fanfare. More publicity surrounded the 'making of the deal' than the release of the picture!"

Paul A. Joseph went on to co-produce the teen comedy *Hot Moves* (1984) and the action programmer *Mission Kill* (1986). Martin V. Smith was never involved with any other films.

Hool: "Because of the lawsuit, I wasn't able to work for a couple of years. It tied me all up. It was a nightmare. I learned a lot. Then I came back with *Missing in Action* [1984], which was a big hit."

In the early 1980s, Hool arranged for the VHS and Beta distribution of (the short version of) *Cabo Blanco* and his *Survival Run* through Media Home Entertainment. *Cabo Blanco* has yet to be released on DVD or Blu-ray in the United States.

Hool: "Ultimately, in [Martin V. Smith's] dying days he called me up and said, 'I've done you a great injustice, and I'm going to get these movie rights back to you.' [laughs] I said, 'Well, that's very nice, but why don't you just give 'em to a place like a foundation or charity or something?' So he gave it to UCLA [University of California, Los Angeles]. All the elements were given over to UCLA, and UCLA actually has the rights to *Cabo Blanco*."

Never again would Bronson appear in a production of the magnitude of *Cabo Blanco*. J. Lee Thompson would direct six more Bronson films, but because of the diminished budgets and schedules, none of them would be as visually opulent as *Cabo Blanco*.

Hool: "Later, Charlie would talk about *Cabo Blanco* and said, 'You know, I really liked that movie.' I thought he was good in *Cabo Blanco*—very stoic. But I don't know that the chemistry between him and Dominique—that we all thought was gonna be incredible—ever really happened. It never really jumped at you from the screen. What was brilliant about the whole experience for me was that I got to make a terrific friend in Charles Bronson. And we were able to do a couple more good movies. We became best friends until the day he passed away. He was just a real man-of-the-earth and very principled and a terrific actor. He didn't get the credit that he deserved for being a great actor."

Japanese program.

Chapter 6
Borderline (1980)

In the late 1970s, Charles Bronson's name on an American marquee was no longer a box office guarantee. He had starred in several disappointments, and none of his post-*Death Wish* movies came close to the grosses of that 1974 blockbuster. During this commercial down period, Bronson made *Borderline*—an interesting drama and one of his more offbeat and atypical films.

Dino De Laurentiis' odd, big-budget Western *The White Buffalo* (1977)—with Bronson in one of his best roles—was intended as a major summer event, but distributor United Artists lost faith and dumped the movie into a "staggered," regional release with a misleading *Jaws*-like ad campaign. ("Now! The creators of *King Kong* bring another legendary

Charles Bronson as border patrolman Jeb Maynard in *Borderline* (1980).

creature to the screen!") It was the last film in a three-picture Bronson/De Laurentiis pact, and the Italian mogul didn't seek another contract with the star. MGM's Bronson thriller *Telefon* (1977) was widely distributed during the 1977 Christmas season to lackluster audience response. The costly independent Bronson movies *Love and Bullets* (1979) and *Cabo Blanco* (1980) were heavily promoted and anticipated during production, but distribution issues kept both films off American screens for over a year before they were sparsely released by underfinanced companies.

Bronson said in 1979, "Nobody stays on top forever. Nobody. It's impossible. I have a million people on my back, and one thing is for sure: when you're not at the pinnacle, you find out fast who's your friend and who isn't. I used to be uncomfortable because people said I was a star and not an actor; well, when you have enough money, labels don't matter much. Anyway, you get a different audience that goes to see my flicks than goes to see, say, Robert Redford or especially someone like Peter Sellers or Olivier. I'm not trying to be anything I'm not. I tell people to accept me or reject me—just don't try to change me. I'm not croaking out one flick after another now. "I've got enough [money] for the rest of my life and my kids' lives. But I'm a trouper, I like to get my hands dirty. Only I won't do it unless I'm fully satisfied about everything that's going on. Us legends tend to get picky in out twilight years."

Michael Douglas, the popular actor (*Coma*, 1978) and Oscar-winning producer (*One Flew Over the Cuckoo's Nest*, 1975), had produced and starred in *The China Syndrome* (1979), which dealt with the dangers of nuclear power. The film was a critical and financial success for Columbia Pictures. Douglas had an office at Columbia and was looking for another socially conscious script to produce.

Jerrold Freedman, director/co-writer of *Borderline*, says: "Michael Douglas had bought an original screenplay about the border from a reporter named Steve Kline. It was his first screenplay. He had covered the border as a reporter in San Diego and had become very friendly with a guy named Ab Taylor."

During the 1970s, Kline had gone undercover with members of the United States Border Patrol while researching articles about poverty-stricken Mexicans who would pay up to $300 to smugglers (i.e. "coyotes") who could get them across the border to work illegally in the States. Kline wrote, "One smuggling ring in Tijuana is a third-generation group. It now is estimated that ten percent of the population of Tijuana are intent upon getting across the border illegally—about 100,000 people. According to research, there are about 5,000 smuggling rings of various sizes operating in Tijuana." Among those that Kline worked with and interviewed was border patrolman Albert "Ab" Taylor, a legend in his field as the greatest foot-tracker in America.

Freedman had been an English major at the University of Pennsylvania. After a stint in the Army, he moved to Los Angeles in the late 1960s and broke into the TV industry as a writer, producer and director. His television directing credits included a half-dozen *Night Gallery* segments (1970 and 1971), the outstanding, fondly remembered science-fiction thriller *A Cold Night's Death* (1973), and *Lawman without a Gun* (1978) with Louis Gossett, Jr. Freedman's only theatrical feature prior to *Borderline* was the Raquel Welch roller-derby picture *Kansas City Bomber* (1972).

Freedman: "Michael [Douglas] and I had talked for years about working together. We had a few projects we tried to do that hadn't come together. He called me and asked if I wanted to read this [*Borderline*] script and get involved in it—both as a director and rewriting the script because Steve didn't really know that much about screenwriting. I came onboard and rewrote the script. Steve was okay with that. Michael had some kind of overall deal with Columbia. We were going to have Gene Hackman [*The French Connection*, 1971] play the boarder patrolman, Jeb. And about the time we got the screenplay ready to go, Gene decided that he wanted to retire. He's done that two or three times—retired and come back. At any rate, he didn't want to do it, so we didn't have a deal, we didn't have a picture.

"I had a friend named Harry Sherman, who had produced some films for me a few years earlier, and he was working at a company called Marble Arch, which was a British company owned by a wealthy man named Sir Lew Grade, and they were doing a lot of films in the United States." Marble Arch Productions was the Hollywood branch of Grade's ITC Entertainment—producer of *Love and Bullets* (1979), the first of a three-picture deal between Grade and Bronson. ITC had been around since 1954, and Marble Arch had opened in 1977.

Freedman: "I gave [the *Borderline* script] to Harry, and he said, 'Let me get it to these people.' They came back to me and said, 'We have a pay-or-play [deal] with Charlie Bronson. If we don't give him a picture within a certain amount of time, we have to pay him his fee. How do you feel about that?' I knew what Charlie's reputation was, both as an actor and as a person to work with. But I wanted to get the picture made. I said, 'Let's try it.' They gave it to him, and he wanted to meet me."

After finishing *Cabo Blanco* in early 1979, Bronson was on a rare, extended vacation from a movie set. Freedman: "[In August 1979,] I flew out to Vermont to meet with Charlie. He had this beautiful farm in Woodstock, Vermont. It was a pre-Revolutionary War farming house. It was absolutely gorgeous. For a guy who on the screen was brutish and not considered intellectual, he was very smart, and he had a real artistic side. He was an incredible antique collector and dealer. He also built the biggest indoor riding ring in New England. His wife was a fabulous woman, Jill Ireland. She was a horse person, and not only did she keep her horses there, but people all over kept their horses there and trained them there. So he and I spent a couple days together and walked. What he talked about was what he *didn't* want to do. For instance, I suggested that he shave his mustache. I thought that would be a good look, different from what people were used to, and he said, 'No, I'm not doing that.' He was very forceful about his image. He had done a film before [*Hard Times*, 1975], and he had shaved his mustache for it, and he got really good reviews, but he didn't feel it fit his image. His deal was: he was protecting his image, no matter what. He was Charlie Bronson, and that's what audiences wanted to see. But other than that he wasn't somebody who gave you extensive script notes or any of that stuff. He really didn't care about who I cast in the film."

Freedman recalls that Bronson liked that *Borderline* was less violent and more character-driven than his typical projects. Freedman: "He was happy to do something other than what his normal box was. He wanted to keep his image intact, but he was happy to try other things. I don't know if he would've done a comedy, for instance, but he was happy to do this. It still fit his image—it was a rugged guy going up against the system and righting some wrongs. We agreed that it would work out, so we started pre-production on the movie.

"Michael [Douglas] lost interest when Charlie came on. Michael really wasn't interested in doing a 'Charlie Bronson movie,' which is why his name is not on it. At the same time, they eased Harry out of the producing, and a partner of Michael's, Jim Nelson, came in and worked with me and produced it. Jim had set up all of Lucas' post-production during the first *Star Wars* [1977], and then he and Michael worked together for a long time. He really knew post-production better than production. But he was a real professional guy. Michael basically just said to me, 'Hey, it's your project now. Run with it, and if you get a deal set up, that'll be great. I'll take a fee.' The only thing he asked was that I use Jim as the producer, which was fine." (James Nelson had been associate producer on Douglas' *The China Syndrome*.)

Bronson's deal with Lew Grade paid the star $1 million for this second film in his three-picture pact. The *Borderline* budget was reportedly $8.5 million, but this was probably a typical exaggeration by Grade. The mogul presold the movie to network and pay-TV to protect part of his investment.

Borderline began shooting on October 15, 1979, in Los Angeles. Freedman: "We shot in Northern Los Angeles, Ventura County and the San Diego area, and we drove out every day. Part of the problem with this movie was our travel time. It was an hour to location and an hour back every day."

Bruno Kirby (*The Godfather Part II*, 1974; *Baby Blue Marine*, 1976) was cast as a rookie brought in to help Border Patrolman Bronson solve a pair of murders. The young actor had just been in Freedman's TV movie *Some Kind of Miracle* (1979).

Freedman: "Charlie was professional. He knew his part; he came to work; he was never late. If I wanted him to do something he felt was out of character, he'd say so. But ultimately, he didn't try to direct the movie. What he *would* do was talk to other actors and give them 'acting tips,' and some of them took it graciously, but others didn't take it so graciously. Most of the time it was Bruno Kirby, because they did all these scenes together. Bruno and I were exceptionally close. And I brought Bruno in specifically because I wanted somebody who would stand up to Charlie and not let him bully him and at the same time would let a lot of Charlie's stuff roll off his back. And Bruno was that guy. Charlie would give him pointers, and sometimes they were good. A lot of it was technical stuff. 'If your light is here, don't let this other actor block you.' He might reach his hand out to move an actor's head just an inch so his light wasn't impaired. He was old school. Bruno liked Charlie. Very different styles of acting, but they got along very well."

An eager, ill-fated alien (Panchito Gomez) crosses the border with an American "coyote" (Ed Harris).

Playing the villainous ex-Marine "coyote" Hotchkiss, who smuggles desperate Mexicans, was a young actor named Ed Harris, who had previously only done television and received "Introducing" billing in *Borderline*. Freedman: "It was Ed's first part of any consequence. I feel I broke Ed Harris out. My casting directors brought Ed to me and said, 'You really gotta meet this guy.' The character, as written, really wasn't somebody who looked like Ed Harris, but he walked in and was just powerful and very intense, so I cast him. He's turned out to be one of the greatest actors in the world. He probably was almost never on the set when Charlie was on the set. He didn't have any scenes with Charlie—just when he gets killed."

The supporting cast was loaded with exceptional character actors. Freedman: "They're all my people. I got Bert Remsen [*Nashville*, 1975], Michael Lerner [*St. Ives*, 1976], Kenneth McMillan [*Bloodbrothers*, 1978], Larry Casey [*The Gay Deceivers*, 1969]. Norm Alden I used in *Kansas City Bomber*. Jimmy Victor [*Rolling Thunder*, 1977] I had used many times. John Ashton [*Honky Tonk Freeway*, 1981] I've used many times. Karmin Murcelo [*Stir Crazy*, 1980] I used a million times. She's a spectacular Mexican actress. Everybody who's in it, in all the main parts, anyway, is somebody I've worked with before. I'm very open with actors. I talk about what we're doing and why we're doing it.

"[Wilford] Brimley [*The China Syndrome*] was a really special character. I had met him, and he had a great face; he was fresh. He's only in the film for the first fifteen minutes, but he left quite an impact. He and I are very close. He once said to me, 'There's only two directors in the world that I really respect—you and Sydney Pollack.' We were the guys that broke him out. He had been a stunt man and a horse shoe-er and a whole bunch of other things, and then we started using him as an actor. Brimley has a tough reputation; he's very hard on directors. I'm a professional director—I come on the set; I know what I want to do; I prepare. Actors tend to respond to that."

Brimley says, "I wasn't very busy in those years, and I was glad to get the work, and I was also glad to work with [Bronson] because he was a pretty reasonable kind of guy. Very professional. Well prepared. He and I became good friends right away. I did several pictures with him." Brimley was later in Bronson's *10 to Midnight* (1983) and *Act of Vengeance* (1986).

On the set every day were Steve Kline, author of the original script, and Ab Taylor, the real-life border patrol "tracker" who had inspired the Bronson role. Freedman said at the time, "They say that if a man can be traced by his footprints alone, Ab will find him." Producer Nelson added, "No movie has ever had a more dedicated technical advisor. He spent hours with Bronson, showing him the tricks of his trade, and the mistakes an officer can make which can get him killed. He kept watch over every technical detail, right down to uniform buttons and insignia on the patrol vehicles. All I can say is he is one stubborn cuss, and I'd hate to be in this country illegally—with Ab Taylor on my case." Taylor made sure that all of the tracking and electronic equipment seen in the film was accurate and that all of the terminology spoken by Bronson and the other actors was realistic.

Freedman: "Charlie really became close with and really admired Ab. If we were into something that had anything to do with 'tracking,' Charlie would turn to Ab and say, 'Okay, how would you do it, Ab?' I spent a lot of pre-production time with Ab. He was really great. We couldn't have done this film without the guy. It was kind of the story of his life. He actually played a part in the film. He's one of the border patrolman. And I think Charlie may have, even in the movie, called him Ab. You'll see him in the background. He probably had a line or two, not much."

The film's director of photography was Tak Fujimoto [*Melvin and Howard*, 1980], who shot *Borderline* with lightweight Panavision cameras. The excellent camerawork has many extended moving shots achieved via dollies or a Steadicam. Freedman: "He's one of the greatest cameramen in the world. He and I worked together many, many times. We had an extremely close relationship. We probably did six or seven films together. I always use Steadicam. I was one of the very early Steadicam people in the business. I was well-known for doing these incredible shots. It's a good way to get a lot of shots in a relatively short amount of time. Instead of doing forty set-ups or fifteen set-ups, you can do two set-ups if you have a really good Steadicam operator and know how to choreograph the stage. We did a ton of night shooting. Half of our picture was shot at night, which was a very challenging situation. We invented a whole series of lighting techniques that had never been used before. We got a lot of the ideas from Conrad Hall and Haskell Wexler, who had been experimenting with some of this lighting. We had banks of nine lights a mile away shooting across canyons—all soft and direct light. Those things had to be set up way in advance. We didn't use arcs. We couldn't afford arcs, and they would have been way too cumbersome. It was the longest shooting schedule I've ever had because of all that night shooting, which is extremely difficult. My recollection is fifty-five days, maybe fifty days. We were shooting in the wintertime. It was cold as hell. It was difficult, tough shooting. Our production company was very tough. The head of the Marble Arch production office was a guy I found very difficult to work with. He wanted to get blood out of a stone. He was very, very tight with money. He put the crew up in what I thought was really subpar housing."

Among the crewmembers was Bronson's twenty-year-old stepson Paul McCallum, who served as the star's stand-in. Freedman: "His stepson came to me one day and said, 'Charlie's never been happier on a movie.' [laughs] And I said, 'Shit, if he's happy here, I'd hate to see what some of his other sets were like.' Because Charlie was grouching all the time, 'Do I have to show up at this time?' He'd complain a lot. He and I would get into real arguments sometimes. When I'd want him to do a certain thing he felt was out of character, he'd say, 'Let's try this instead,' and 'No, I'm not doing that.' It was a real tug-of-war between him and me. Believe me, we had a lot of difficulties. [Bronson] didn't want to be called to the set, especially at night, then sit around. Let's say his call time was ten o'clock—he didn't want to be called and then not shoot until four o'clock. If we called him, he wanted to know that he was gonna come and shoot under a normal situation—you rehearse; you light; you shoot. Not, 'Okay, Charlie, we'll get to you in a couple hours.' That would have ticked him off, and we probably did that a few times. Circumstances change things—you have to change the location or the weather affects you.

"I felt, and so did my producer and other people, that if the film really was gonna work, [Bronson's] character should die in the end, and the young patrolman should pick up the mantel and carry it on, and I rewrote the script to reflect that. I gave Charlie the pages. The next day, we were shooting at the end of the day, and we had taken all day to prepare to shoot a half-an-hour at 'magic hour.' Charlie drives up all the way on the other side of this field, and the window of his limo rolls down, and he yells out, 'Fuck you, Jerry. I'm not doing it.' [laughs] Everybody heard it. Now, I could have finessed that. I could have said, 'Okay, Charlie, we won't do it,' and then shot around him and done it anyway. But I didn't want to go behind his back."

Some scenes were filmed in Northern Mexico, where 2,000 locals played immigrants. In late November, the unit shot for two weeks on a ranch near Oxnard, California. Production ended at the Baja California border station in San Diego at the end of December 1979.

After his traditional Christmas vacation in Vermont, Bronson headed to Canada in February 1980 to shoot *Arctic Rampage* (later retitled *Death Hunt*, 1981). At the time, the trades announced that Bronson and Toshiro Mifune would co-star in a follow-up to *Red Sun* (1971), but the sequel never happened.

Lew Grade was excited about *Borderline* and his other upcoming movies. He told the press that his goal was to be "the biggest film producer in the world." At the Cannes Film Festival in March 1980, he announced that ITC would be spending $120 million on eighteen more pictures. The mogul said, "The secret of filmmaking is you have to make enough films so you get a few hits. With the others you don't get hurt too much....You must make money unless it's a horrible, terrible, disastrous film."

The *Borderline* post-production took place in Los Angeles. Gil Mele, whose previous work included Freedman's *A Cold Night's Death*, composed the score. Freedman: "I worked with Gil on many things. I brought him into the film business. I knew him when he was a jazz musician, and I gave him his first television job back in the '60s, maybe 1970. I introduced him to Robert Wise, and he did *The Andromeda Strain* [1971] as a result of that. He worked with George C. Scott; he worked with a lot of people. He was one of the greatest electronic composers that ever lived. He probably did dozens of scores for me. When we were getting ready to do our [*Borderline*] score, the musicians in America went on strike, so we couldn't record the score in the United States. We flew to London and recorded the score with the London Philharmonic."

Jeb Maynard (Bronson) investigates the murders of a patrolman (A. Wilford Brimley) and a smuggled Mexican (Panchito Gomez).

Borderline was released on a regional basis in America (from September 1980 to February 1981) by Associated Film Distribution (AFD), ITC's distribution arm that had put out Bronson's *Love and Bullets* the previous fall. By this time, the "Sir Lew Grade Presents" credit on the mogul's movies was replaced with "Lord Grade Presents." The "lord" title had been granted in 1976, but Grade didn't use the rank in his film credits until 1980. The excellent *Borderline* poster art was airbrushed by Drew Struzan (*Star Wars*), who had also done the promo art for Grade's *The Muppet Movie* (1979). Spanish-speaking *Borderline* TV and radio spots were prepared for specific regions. A videotape with film clips and interviews with Ab Taylor was distributed to local news stations.

Although *Borderline* is less brutal than most previous Bronson pictures, there was still enough violence (including shotgun wounds) to warrant an R rating, and it is surprising that the film received a PG. (The PG-13 rating didn't exist then.) Freedman: "Today it would be PG-13, maybe even an R." Except for *Assassination* (1987), which was PG-13, all future Bronson pictures would be rated R.

The pressbook noted: "Bronson appears in a starring role that is unique even for his long and varied career. *Borderline* has little of the violence of some other films in which Bronson has starred. Bronson feels that now there is a trend away from very violent films and lauds the move." The actor described his previous roles: "They were characters of vengeance, more or less. I was usually the judge, jury and executioner. This film is not that way; it's a different approach to a dedicated human being. It is both controversial and dramatic. I believe that films can inform and still be entertaining, and *Borderline* does both." Suggested publicity gimmicks: Decorate the lobby with real newspaper clippings about human trafficking; Hold a special screening for law enforcement groups, border patrolmen and the press; Have a radio station's mobile unit—billed as the "Borderline Patrol"—announce random license numbers on the air and award the motorists with free passes.

Variety: "In welcome contrast to the several star-heavy feats of implausibility produced by ITC of late, this new Bronson vehicle works just fine. It tackles a serious subject with workmanlike dramatic skill and a notable preference for realism over hokum....Given the preponderance of night shooting and, in day sequences, cinematographer Tak Fujimoto's reliance on available light, Bronson's deep-lined face is mostly masked by heavy shadow. That hardly damages his enduring charisma, however, and the actor's apparent commitment to conveying the reality of the role is a definite plus." *San Francisco Voice*: "*Borderline* raises the consciousness for the plight of aliens, but more importantly, it's a well-crafted film that sustains interest and suspense....Bronson gives a nice low-key performance with overtones of compassion and warmth when allowed." *Miami News*: "You don't have to be a Mexican to hate *Borderline*—but I'm sure it helps.... This latest Charles Bronson snoozer treats Mexican aliens like rejects from *Night of the Living Dead*....*Borderline* is a pretty dismal failure, even when viewed as just an action movie." *Evening Standard* (St. Petersburg, FL): "If there's a major Hollywood star who can be singled out for undistinguished films, doubtless it's Charles Bronson. Not even Clint Eastwood's formula actioners are as devoid of character and contours as those of the Great Stone Face....It's as though Bronson's patented lack of expression is somehow infectious, condemning everything around it to the same monotony....Basically, all this film does is use the wetback issue as the backdrop for a typical exercise in Bronson vengeance." This reviewer also added that the killer was "played unexceptionally by newcomer Ed Harris."

Freedman: "It got decent reviews. It probably got as good of reviews as you're gonna get on a Charlie Bronson movie. A lot of critics are not gonna look beyond Charlie Bronson. It's probably a better movie than some critics gave it credit for, because they had a certain mindset about what a Charlie Bronson movie could deliver. I heard, second-hand, that

[Bronson] liked it, but Charlie was not the kind of guy that's gonna go around throwing bouquets, believe me."

Borderline did its best business in Arizona, California, New Mexico, Oklahoma and Texas. Within three weeks it collected $3 million on 317 screens in that handful of territories. (A *Variety* ad boasted: "*Borderline* Means Boxoffice!") The movie also did well in theaters close to the border that showed Spanish-subtitled prints. Freedman: "I saw one screening that was with a predominantly Latino audience, and they really liked it." AFD paired it with the previous ITC/Bronson picture *Love and Bullets* for double bills. *Borderline* ultimately collected almost $4 million in America, not bad for an atypical picture from a fading star but not enough to help the financers.

Things looked grim for Grade's ITC production company (where Bronson still had one movie left on his three-film deal) and the AFD distribution arm—which was burdened by high overhead, lack of product and, most notably, lack of product desired by the marketplace. Released earlier in 1980 by AFD were the costly science-fiction flop *Saturn 3* and the heavily-promoted Village People disco disaster *Can't Stop the Music*. Those two bombs were followed by Grade's *Raise the Titanic*, which cost a then-astounding $40 million to make (plus millions more to market) but returned less than $20 million during its entire global run. In this era, most blockbuster hits collected around fifty percent of their worldwide gross from American theaters—a market where most ITC releases fared poorly or dismally. *The Muppet Movie* was Grade's lone hit, and that film's $32 million domestic gross accounted for almost ninety-five percent of AFD's total income from American box offices in 1979–80.

In March of 1981, Grade shut down AFD. By that June, after the release of *The Legend of the Lone Ranger* (another big-budget flop), the mogul's films had lost $39.6 million for ITC. In June 1982, twenty-seven years after creating the company, Grade was forced to resign from

ITC. Bronson would make one more ITC production, but "Lord Grade Presents" would not appear on the credits of *The Evil That Men Do* (1984).

Borderline played HBO in March 1981. It was on *The CBS Saturday Night Movie* on September 4, 1983. The film wasn't released on home video until 1985 via CBS/Fox Video.

Borderline is a gripping, well-plotted drama and an interesting Bronson curio worth seeking out. The star gives an energetic performance

Italian poster.

and looks imposing in his rugged cowboy hat and brown leather Border Patrol jacket. The movie is far lower key (and lower budget) than earlier Lew Grade pictures—like the heavy-action epics *Love and Bullets* and *Firepower* (1979). Harsh reviews from critics who weren't willing to give *Borderline* a chance caused the picture to be ignored. It remains one of the lesser-known of the Bronson vehicles, and it is not held in high esteem by many of the star's fans, mainly because the action is sparse. (Bronson only kills one person in the entire film, but he does choke a "coyote" and stuffs his head into a filthy toilet.)

Freedman went on to direct more TV, including the rape/revenge movie *Victims* (1982), episodes of *The X-Files* (1993 and 1994), and the feature *Native Son* (1986). In 1991 (under the name J. F. Freedman) he published his acclaimed thriller *Against the Wind* and continues to write novels. He did encounter Bronson after *Borderline*. "We weren't social friends, but I saw him a few times." There was never talk of them doing another picture together. "For me, one Charlie Bronson film was enough. He was difficult to deal with, but I knew that going in. Look, Charlie was a good actor, but he had his range. If I had done this with an actor like Hackman, for instance, it would have been a different movie, let's face it. But it was a 'Charlie Bronson movie,' and it was, to me, a really good 'Charlie Bronson movie.'"

Chapter 7
Screenwriter David Engelbach on *Death Wish II*

A major gap in *Bronson's Loose!: The Making of the 'Death Wish' Films* was the omission of an interview with *Death Wish II* (1982) writer David Engelbach, who could not be located while that book was being researched. Fortunately, he can now tell his side of the story. It is important to note that Engelbach insists that the anecdote in the first *Bronson's Loose!* book that has him hand-delivering the *Death Wish II* script to Charles Bronson's home is completely false.

Engelbach studied fine arts at Fairleigh Dickinson University in New Jersey where he was involved with the theater department. In the mid-1970s, he graduated from the American Film Institute after making a series of short movies. As an AFI student, he got to be an "observer" on the set of *Jaws* (1975). After *Death Wish II* and other movies for Cannon Films, Engelbach wrote for TV shows like *Lottery!* (1983–1984) and *MacGyver* (1989) and penned the unsold Hulk Hogan pilot *Goldie and the Bears* (1984). He currently teaches screenwriting.

How did you get involved with Death Wish II?

It started with *Over the Top*. I have to go back a couple of years [before *Death Wish II*]. *Over the Top* was written as an independent project. Gary Conway and a producer had done a very low-budget movie [*The Farmer*, 1977] that they had raised money for independently and released through Columbia Pictures. I never saw it. If I did, I don't even remember. They had an idea. Gary and his dad had written a script called *American Dreamer* that they submitted to Columbia, claiming they had independent financing for it. It was about a truck driver and arm wrestling. An executive at Columbia, who was a friend of mine, called me up and said, "Look, these guys made some money on this little thing they made before. They've got a more ambitious project, but they don't have a director. Take a look at it because there might be a deal for you to rewrite it and direct it." So I read their script and it was dreadful. But there was an idea in it that they had neglected to develop, which was about the relationship between this truck driver character and his estranged son. So I went to Gary and I said, "Here's my terms. I want to direct it." I was looking to direct my first movie. I had to keep the arm wrestling, because that was the thing Columbia had to market. But everything else, I wanted to throw out. And they agreed, to my surprise. So I wrote *Over the Top*. And Columbia loved it. They gave [Conway] a fantastic "first-dollar deal," which is really unusual on an independent release. Generally, they take all these monies out and at the end of the day after you've sued them, there may be some money for the producers. [Columbia was] willing to split the first dollar after a cap on how much they could take out first for marketing costs. I got into pre-production on it and casting. I was gonna use Robert Young to play the grandfather. I loved the idea of

Father Knows Best giving the wrong advice. That was when it hit the fan that [Conway and his partner] really didn't have the financing to make the film. So the project went into Hollywood limbo.

But somebody had gotten involved with the project to try and save it with some German money. It was a guy named Andrew Gotti. Andrew was an Australian exhibitor and was in America trying to raise money to produce stuff and he really loved the script. Maybe a year or two after the project had went away—I think we're talking like 1980 or '81—he came to me and said, "I've shown the script to somebody and they want to meet cause they really want to make the film." He arranged a meeting and it was [with] Menahem Golan. I met Menahem and the first words out of his mouth were, "I love your script, but I have to direct it." [laughs] I said, "Well, I'm attached as the director." He said, "I know, I know. We will deal with that." [laughs] In the process of trying to get the movie made, I became "at odds" with Gary Conway, who was also supposed to star in the film. It was obvious that our working relationship was dismal by this point. [laughs] If we had moved forward, it would have been a very difficult relationship. I had a lot of time invested in the project and I wanted to be compensated, so I was looking to see it get made. Menahem had fallen in love with it. He said, "If we can make a deal to get the rights and make the film, we'll finance another film for you." As it turned out, they couldn't close a deal with Gary Conway because he insisted on starring in the movie. Yoram [Globus] said, "No way. We gotta get a star for this." And so the project didn't happen.

After a couple of months, I was developing a TV series called *Lottery!* for ABC and Menahem called me. I remember this conversation distinctly. He said, "David, I want you to write a movie for me." I said, "What is it, Menahem?" He said, "We are going to make a sequel to one of the great movies of the 1970s." I said, "Are you gonna do *Godfather III*?" He said, "Close. We're going to do *Death Wish II*. And I'd like you to write it for me." I said, "Well, I think not. It's not really what I want to do." He said, "I think you'd be great for it." I said, "Well, I don't think so. I don't do that." After a week or two, my agent called me and said, "I just heard from this guy Menahem Golan. Who are these people?" I said, "Well, they've got some money. Apparently, they're taking over Cannon Films"—which at this point was a moribund production and distribution company. He said, "Well, they'd really like you to do this thing. I think you should at least talk to Menahem again." When I had met with Menahem originally, he was a tough guy but I kind of liked him. He reminded me of a throwback to the guys who founded the business. They loved movies and to his credit, he loved movies. Unlike a lot of the suits who run the studios today, he really loved movies and he wanted to make good films. The fact that they *didn't*…[laughs] So I looked at the original [*Death Wish*, 1974] again.

What did you think of the first *Death Wish*?

I was always a fan of Charlie Bronson. I liked Bronson movies. I remember him back in *The Magnificent Seven* [1960], which I thought he was terrific in. I think [*Death Wish*] caught the temper at the time. And I liked the idea that the guy was an architect, he was a liberal. He wasn't a knuckle-walker that was forced to confront this level of violence. But that was '74. We're talking seven or eight years. There had been change and I didn't think the idea of doing the same vigilante again was appropriate. I wanted to make it more with heart. You want to root for this guy, we want to see him take down the bad guys—but not in the same manner. I said, "Well, if I'm gonna do this, what would I do? How do you get lightning to strike twice?" I thought about it and Menahem called and said, "Look, we'd still like to give you a project to direct. But first I have to hear you're gonna write *Death Wish II* for me." I said, "Well, do you have the rights to it?" He said, "Yes." And I had another question. I said, "Does Jill Ireland have to star in it?" He said, "Absolutely not." I said, "Okay, I'll consider it." So they cut a deal with my agent.

Did Golan make story suggestions? Did he ask for a certain amount of action or violence?

⊕ THE CANNON GROUP INC. Presents

From the Producers, Writer and Star of
DEATH WISH
Another Blockbuster

CHARLES BRONSON in
a MENAHEM GOLAN Film

DEATH SENTENCE

A Hal Landers - Bobby Roberts Production
Screenplay by David Engelbach Based on the novel by Brian Garfield
Executive Producer Yoram Globus   Produced by Hal Landers - Bobby Roberts   Directed by Menahem Golan

⊕ A Cannon Films Release

WORLD PREMIERE: CANNES 1981

World Sales: CANNON INTERNATIONAL INC. 6464 Sunset Boulevard · Suite 1150 · Hollywood, California 90028 · Telephone (213) 469-8124 · Telex: 18-1270
In Mifed: Old Center, Office 136 or Hotel Principe & Savoia   Y. Globus

Ad in the 1981 Cannes Film Festival issue of *Variety*.

No. In all honesty, they left me alone to do it. I went up to San Francisco and I said, "I want to set it in San Francisco." And Menahem said, "Great. Beautiful. Great-looking place." I thought, "Okay, in the first movie, [Paul Kersey] was an amateur. The second time, he transforms. He becomes something other than what he was before. You can't be touched by violence like that and not have it affect your life." That's why I created the idea of him having a relationship with this woman, which at the end of the movie goes away. She discovers what he really is and he's left as this shadow character, literally a shadow—which Michael Winner shot on the wall. I thought [that] was one of the better moments of the movie, that image of him on the side of the building. I wanted to say: being touched again, he's no longer an amateur. I felt this character may have been driven into crime by excess but I wanted to frame it in context. In my draft, set in San Francisco, he has an encounter with these thugs in a park and they take his wallet. They find out who he is. They beat him up, they try to rape the daughter—she was out for a day visit because she was still recovering in an institution—she goes into shock again, and she flings herself out the window and gets impaled on a wrought iron thing. The police won't call it homicide because of the circumstances and her mental instability. He struggles not to become the vigilante again. Winner kept him as an architect, I had changed his life entirely. I had him working as a manager at a radio station and the boss was really commiserate and said, "Look, I have a cabin in Big Sur. Go down there and spend some time on your own, work it through." I had a sequence in which he's chopping wood, trying to heal himself. The character's really struggling not to go back and become what he was. In the middle of the night, he's awakened by automatic weapon fire. He grabs the old Winchester and goes out and finds that near him is one of those survivalist encampments. They're out practicing and he's captured by these guys. They'd seen the newspaper [articles about the daughter] and they think he's a kindred spirit. They take him into their warehouse/supply room and they've got body armor, high-powered weapons and stuff like that. There's one sequence that Winner kept from that: he's chopping wood. When he comes back to San Francisco, he's changed. He's made that decision to become an avenging character and find the guys that were responsible.

What I was looking to do was make it a Western. If I could have had a gunfight in the dusty street at high noon, I would have. He was a different person, he wasn't using a little pistol. Apparently, some of the elements that were in that draft got put into some of the later [*Death Wish* sequels]. He went through the transformation process, transforming himself with the sailor's cap. He goes into the second-hand store and buys the stuff and gets the little hotel. I wrote the Chinese landlord: "Police come, you go. No trouble." [laughs] The first time he eclipses one of these guys, as he's driving back, there's a police blockade. But it's not about him, it's about some irate bus driver tried to kill the mayor. I had that sequence in there to try and get some reference point: he may have changed but the whole environment is quite crazy. The rest of the story thrust was pretty much the same [as the final movie].

In the process of writing it, Golan called me and said, "It's not a sequel anymore." They had run into a problem with getting the rights and also getting Bronson to commit. The guy who wrote the [*Death Wish*] book, Brian Garfield, had written a sequel [novel]—*Death Sentence*. So that was what the script was going to be called: *Death Sentence*. So I changed the character of "Paul Kersey" to another name, did *not* have the cop from New York [Vincent Gardenia] because it didn't need it, [and] made a couple of other adjustments to it. They actually made a poster up [for *Death Sentence*]. It was done in line and it was all high contrast—not very good-looking. They had it made up for Cannes and they took the script and they got enough presale on it to finance the movie. Golan was gonna direct it. They made the offer to Bronson. Bronson said, "I'll only do it if Michael Winner directs again." So everybody played musical chairs. Golan became a producer and Hal Landers and Bobby Roberts [producers of the first *Death Wish*] became executive producers. Bronson committed and the rest, as they say, is what it is.

Right before I was finishing the first draft, Menahem called and said, "It's a sequel again." [laughs] So I reintroduced the cop. I wanted to bring him back to the story because he was one of the few bits of humanity in it. I turned in the script, they liked it very much. And that was pretty much my relationship [with the film]. My agent would call me every week when I was writing *Death Wish II* and say, "What are you doing with your pages?" I said, "They're sitting in my desk." He said, "No they're not. Lock them away." I said, "Why?" He said, "It's cheaper for them to burglar them than it is for them to pay you for the rest of your contract!" [laughs] It wasn't true. They did actually pay on time—then. Later, I actually did have to go to the [Writers] Guild to collect monies from them. [laughs]

What were the Cannon facilities like at that time?

They had rented facilities in L.A. It was fairly modest with a couple offices. They had just taken over Cannon. It was before they were prosperous enough to create their own building.

In early Death Wish II *trade ads, the screenplay is credited to yourself and Michael Winner while Bobby Roberts and Menahem Golan have co-story credits. Do you recall Roberts and Golan working on the premise?*

They never touched a word. Menaham made *one* addition to my script. It was clearly written by someone to whom English was not the primary language. When [Kersey] first encounters the thugs, he had added an insertion: "Three men in different races." [laughs]

Once Winner came onboard, did you actually work on the script with him?

I was done. When he came in, I was prepping another movie for [Cannon]. It was originally called *Thunder Women*. The idiots changed the title to *America 3000* [1986]. But that's another story. When I read Winner's script, I was not happy. Not just because my script was rewritten—that's the game—but I think the things that made it interesting and made it stand on its own were deleted. I was disappointed by that because I thought it could be more. I liked the character of Kersey and I liked the fact that here's a character that really had to make a choice. Was he going to satisfy his vengeance, which would change him forever, or would he turn his back on it? I knew it was a sequel, but I was trying to give it some elements that would make it something new even though you were still dealing with the same Kersey character. I really wanted to challenge the character and make him really have to confront what he had become. Winner wanted to make the same movie again. It looked like it was photographed with a Xerox machine. Basically, Winner took everything out of my draft that was original. The scene where the maid is brutally raped was Michael Winner's invention. I didn't have that in there. Once the film goes into the director's hands, it's the director's movie. I was not "not a fan" of Winner's work. I think his opening of *The Mechanic* [1972]—that sequence with Bronson that's all done M.O.S. [silent]—is a *great* sequence.

Was the actual rape of the daughter in your script?

No. They *try* to rape the girl and she has a flashback to the original film, with "flashes" of what she had seen, with the original mugger. I wrote it in a way that they wouldn't have to use footage from [the first film]. And she breaks free and flings herself out the window to escape and ends up getting impaled. [Winner] had the more explicit rape and then there was the whole thing with the housekeeper. I was pretty appalled. From what I understand, some of the crew quit after [filming] that scene. The cameraman, I think. They felt that Winner was doing it for his own amusement, not for the benefit of the film.

The actress who played the maid [Silvana Gallardo] recalled that the original director of photography [Thomas Del Ruth] and his camera crew quit during that sequence.

Did she talk to you about her audition? That he had her screw a chair?

She said that in the audition, she had to sit in a chair while Winner walked around her, saying things to her.

She gave you the nice version. He had her, literally, hump a chair to see how far she would go.

Why was the location changed from San Francisco to Los Angeles?

It was a matter of money. Production reasons. Winner rewrote it and changed it. Personally, I liked the idea of the picture-postcard quality of San Francisco—which Los Angeles doesn't have—counterpointed by this dark violence. The story takes place at night—vampire time. In San Francisco, there's not as many places where you would find people hanging out the way you would in Los Angeles. I always had a problem with the logic of him connecting with these people when they set it in L.A.—it's huge. In San Francisco, there's only a few places—it made more logical sense.

Were you invited to the set?

I came to visit the set and watched the sequence where they did the line: "Do you believe in Jesus? You're going to meet him." [laughs]

Did you write that line?

Yeah. And there was one other sequence—that shootout sequence in the park where they drive the Cadillac off the cliff [and] that moment where he holds up the ghetto blaster and gets shot through the ghetto blaster. I've seen that moment with audiences and they always applaud.

That was in your script?

Yeah. I was living in Venice Beach at the time [where] people with their huge ghetto blasters go rolling past. That was my writer's revenge. [laughs] Almost all the gags given to those [villain] characters were in my script. Kevyn Major Howard told me he knew he was in character when he scared the LAPD. [laughs] Vincent Gardenia, very nice man, wanted some line changes. I went to Winner and said, "You want some changes here?" He said, "Go do what you want." I gave [Gardenia] a couple little things. I don't even remember what. But my working relation with Winner was limited. I do remember he had this poor assistant trail behind him with an ashtray. He'd smoke these cigars on the set and he had this assistant just holding the ashtray. And my relation with Bronson on the project was limited.

Did Bronson make any suggestions or changes regarding the script?

I don't think Bronson did anything much except show up, collect his paycheck, and leave. I was disappointed with his work in the film. It looked like he was just walking through. I didn't see the Bronson that I had seen in the first film. Or investing himself in it at all. I do remember Jill Ireland being on the set and being very nice and very warm and talking to me. It was like good cop, bad cop. I do remember some degree of amusement when Jill Ireland got cast as his girlfriend because that was one of the two things [I initially asked Golan]: "Does she have to be in the movie?" [laughs]

Do you recall any interactions you had with Bronson?

He came up to me and said, "Did you write this piece of crap?" And I said, "No. Michael Winner wrote this piece of crap. I wrote the original piece of crap. Would you like to read my original piece of crap?"

[laughs] And he said, "No. If it's any better I'll just feel bad that we're doing this one." That was pretty much the exchange. [laughs] He was not unpleasant when I talked to him. I asked him about some of his other roles when we talked informally while he was having a break. And it was fun because I was involved in doing a project that was supposed to star James Coburn. So I was talking to Bronson about Coburn cause Coburn had talked to me about Bronson. [Coburn] knew about *Death Wish II* and he talked a little bit about his relationship with Bronson when they were doing *Magnificent Seven* and the fact that nobody figured that they would be making their careers in that movie except Bronson. He said Bronson thought it would be a big break for him. And obviously it was.

Paul Kersey (Charles Bronson) is mugged by punks Stomper (Kevyn Major Howard) and Jiver (Stuart K. Robinson) in *Death Wish II* (1982).

Did you notice how Bronson interacted with Winner on the set?

Professional. I wouldn't say warm. I didn't see the long conversations. After Winner had finished it and they were in the editing stage he asked me to signoff as co-writer on it and I said, "No" and it automatically went into [Writers Guild] arbitration and he didn't get credited. It was ironic because at the time I kinda wanted him to because I wanted somebody to point the finger at. "Don't blame me for that junk." [laughs] I wanted my name taken off the film when I saw it. They were supposed to screen it for me before it was released and they didn't. I saw it three days before. And I was appalled. Particularly by the opening rape scene. I was *really* disturbed by that. I thought it was more of a turn-off to an audience than a turn-on. And I think it had more to do with Michael Winner's own predilection. I had read the script, so I knew it was in there. I just didn't know it would be as explicit and I really thought that was bordering on pornography. I thought, "My wife won't watch this. [laughs] I don't know *any* women who'll watch this." I knew women who had read the script and said, "Yeah, I'd see this. It's fun 'go get the bad guys' stuff." I got drunk afterwards. [laughs] I talked to my agent and said, "I want to have my name taken off this film." It was three days before it was to be released. He said, "That would be a *huge* problem." And he really strongly advised me to bite the bullet, hold my breath, and just let it happen. His line to me was: "You can either have your name on *no* film that's produced or your name on a film you're embarrassed by—which puts you in the company of pretty much every other writer in Hollywood. Your choice." [laughs]

The rape scenes had to be cut to get an R rating.

I'm sure they had to cut it down. I do remember somebody saying that the first rating was an X rating. But I never saw that cut.

Some foreign version are even more explicit than the R-rated cut.

I haven't seen those. I don't want to. I would be warped—even today, all these years later.

Other than the rape scenes, what did you think of the finished film?

I thought it was a disappointment. It seemed rush. It is what it is, what they did with it. I felt that Bronson didn't invest anything of himself into the film. I don't know whether he came up to speed on [the later sequels] or whether it was just, "Give me the paycheck, I'll go home now." I was really disappointed with the photography. When they told me they got Jimmy Page to do the music, I thought that was a plus and would be interesting. And I think his screeching guitar actually worked with it. I think the ad campaign was actually pretty good with "Bronson's Loose Again!" I thought their one-sheet was pretty good. It did well abroad. And it did finance Cannon's slate. Had it tanked, they probably wouldn't have been around much longer. They needed a hit. So they came out at least with a triple, if not a home run. They would sell the films by the kilo in the foreign festival, which is fine. It's a legitimate way to finance the movies.

Press kit cover.

Did you ever see **Death Wish II** ***with a general audience?***

I did. I dropped in a couple times. My folks were living in South Florida and I'd gone to visit them and it was the same time that the film was opening there. So [the distributor] asked if I'd be willing to meet with the press and do a little publicity since I happened to be going there at the same time it was opening there. I figured, "Sure, okay." I mean, you only go so far by saying, "I don't like it." It was in my interest to see it become commercially successful. It was playing in a theater in Miami Beach. I went with my folks to see it. When we left, my dad looked at me and said, "Well, I'm glad I spent all that money on your education so you could write dialogue like that." [laughs] I went when it opened on Hollywood Boulevard. I dropped in to see what the audience reaction was. I learned that when I was in [live] theater—at the intermission, you go down and listen to what the people were talking about. They seemed to like it. They responded. They did like the moments where the bad guys get killed—particularly in the big blowout, the shoot-out. The parts that they liked were the parts that I thought they would like: the revenge moments, the ghetto blaster. I'll tell you something I was really surprised and quite disturbed about: there was a large number of Hispanic families who had taken their kids to see that. If they wanted to go see the movie, that's fine—but don't take your seven-year-old kid into this movie.

What did you think of the critical response?

I wasn't surprised. I was disappointed. Even though I didn't like what [Winner] did, I was still hoping that they'd be a little kinder to it. [laughs] I knew they wouldn't be. As the writer, I got tarred and feathered for something that someone else had done. I remember Leonard Maltin, the critic, said it was "a film made by profiteers not filmmakers." It was painful to read that, but I felt he wasn't wrong. There was a director who was in the process of trying to do a sequel or a remake to a Hitchcock film. I don't remember what it was. It wasn't *Psycho* [1960], it might have been *The Birds* [1963]. He brought me in and asked me if I'd be interested in writing it and I said, "I don't think you'd want me to do that. I can just imagine the comments: 'The guy who ruined *Death Wish* has ruined Hitchcock now.'" [laughs]

Did you ever speak publicly about how unhappy you were with the film?

I did. I did an interview for CBS. They had a morning news show with one of the guys from *60 Minutes*. They were talking about violence in movies and they called me in. I remember that their lead-in was: "*Death Wish II* is even more violent than the writer wanted." I said I was upset by the specific gratuitous violence in it. I wasn't upset by shooting people—that was the catharsis that I had written into it—but I was upset by the rape and felt that it wasn't necessary to the success. [laughs] That tune hasn't changed in years.

Death Wish II *was a hit. What effect did it have on your career?*

I don't know, directly. I got good buzz on the script. I ended up doing a pilot for a TV series. The network executives who had recommended me to the producer had read my *Death Wish* script. I'm not sure the film made that much difference. If it had tanked, it probably would have hurt. In terms of a bump to my career, or in terms of suddenly the phone was ringing—no. I was a working writer at this point.

Were you ever approached to write any of the later Death Wish sequels?

Yeah. Menahem asked me if I wanted to do *Death Wish 3* [1985] and I said, "No." He didn't push me.

Over the Top *later became a big-budget Cannon movie starring Sylvester Stallone [1987]. Did you have any involvement with the project at that point?*

I didn't even know they were making it until I read it in the trades. I was actually in Israel making *Thunder Women/America 3000* at the time.

Over the Top *went through arbitration with the Writers Guild over the writing credits. Gary Conway and you ended up with "story by" credits.*

Everything goes through arbitration. Arbitration is almost always automatic. As a member of the Writers Guild, I've done probably two dozen arbitrations over the years as an arbitrator. I'm pretty familiar with the process. I know that Gary Conway felt he wasn't given the credit he deserved.

How much of your script is in that final film?

The story. The relationship with the son. From what I understand, Stallone read my original draft and liked it. It was very much in the *Rocky* [1976] vein. But *First Blood* [1982] had become a big hit and, I think, his agent and people around him were saying, "You can't have your nemesis be a fourteen-year-old kid." So they built up the part of the grandfather to the point where it was kind of stupid and they added where he drives up to the mansion and crashes into it. I wrote a character who was more of a bohemian character, it was a guy who knew what he didn't know. For example, he'd be driving in his truck and be listening to books-on-tape to try and improve himself.

What did you think of **Over the Top** *when you saw it?*

I've only seen it once and that was at the screening that Warner Bros. had. They had a barbeque out at the Warner ranch. I had tears in my eyes. Menahem came up to me and he saw and said, "I got you, didn't I?" I was crying because I thought my career was really over now and I was really screwed. My script had gotten a lot of good responses. People really loved my script. There was a certain anticipation about the movie. Cannon had done a lot of hype on Stallone, that he was the highest-paid actor. Cannon wanted to show that they were really on the map and a serious player and they were paying $12 million to Sylvester Stallone. But they forgot to mention [that] there was another movie slipped into that deal—*Cobra* [1986]. There was a twofer in there that they didn't talk about. [laughs]

Did you meet Stallone at any point?

I did. [silence]

Do you not want to talk about him?

[silence]

Did Over the Top *have any effect on your career when it was released?*

It didn't help it. I couldn't get anybody to read that script anymore. That piece of work as a writing sample wasn't something that I could actively use because people would say, "Nah, I've seen the movie." But for reasons that I don't understand, it seems to be better thought of now than when it came out. I don't know why.

Cannon has a large cult following.

I was curious as to why the sudden interest. They've basically been out of business for twenty-five years now. Why the interest in those guys? I did like Menahem. He said, "David, I will never stab you in the back. I will stab you in the front." [laughs] When I did *Thunder Women*, he was married but he had a girlfriend. We agreed on a handshake to do this film. By the time I left his office and got home, a messenger had already arrived at my apartment with a headshot and a bio of some busty blonde actress who, of course, was his girlfriend. [laughs] He was very much a throwback to the old school. I had to use her. I found a part for her. She had this West Virginia accent. She was a nice person. She helped get the movie made, in a way, because Menahem never read the script—she read it to him. I was trying to find a part for her where she wouldn't have to speak. I couldn't get away with it, so I ended up having to re-voice her. When I showed the rough cut to Golan, she was there in the screening room. He turned around and looked at her and said, "Victoria, take acting lessons!" He could be cruel. He could be crude.

Did you work on any other Cannon projects that never got produced?

There was *Déjà Vu*. Prior to *Thunder Women*—when the original deal for *Over the Top* went away and Menahem wanted me to do *Death Wish II*—there was a property that they had some relationship to with some French guy. Menahem said, "This might make a nice movie for your directing thing." It was going to be [with] Robert Mitchum and Yves Montand. The crumb that brought them together was a jewel theft. Mitchum was the cop who was supposed to find it. Yves Montand represented the insurance company. It was a mystery-comedy. Mitchum's manager didn't want to work with Cannon—which is funny because two years later, he did. He did *The Ambassador* [1984]. When Mitchum fell out, James Coburn was gonna do the Mitchum part. It was a good, fun script.

At one point, they had the rights to *Captain America*. When I was in post on *Thunder Women/America 3000*, Menahem offered it to me [to direct]. I remember when Winner was attached to that. They may have had everybody attached at one point. The script I read was set in the 1940s. I wasn't gonna rewrite it. I liked the comic book nature of it. I didn't think I wanted to do it as a Cannon film. I wasn't sure how financially stable they were at that point. There were "buzzes" going on. There were attorneys saying that [Golan and Globus] were taking money that was earmarked for marketing on one thing and dumping it into offers on another and trying to keep the boat afloat. They were burning the candle at both ends.

Are you frequently asked about **Death Wish II**?

I don't talk about it. But sometimes people bring it up. [laughs] It's online and it's on Netflix. I just got a residual check for it yesterday. [laughs] It still has some life.

Chapter 8
The Women of *Death Wish II*

In 1981 Charles Bronson and director Michael Winner reunited for *Death Wish II*, a follow-up to one of the highest grossing and most discussed films of 1974. In the sequel, vigilante Paul Kersey hits the streets to avenge the brutal assault and murder of his daughter (who had already been rendered comatose after an attack in the first movie) and his housekeeper. *Death Wish II* became not only another box-office hit, but the most-controversial film in the five-title series and the lone entry that alienates even the most diehard Bronson fans. *Death Wish II* owes most of its notoriety to two brutal and vicious rape scenes that were so grisly that they had to be extensively edited to achieve an R rating in the United States and were cut even further for other territories.

Robin Sherwood and Silvana Gallardo, who played the assault victims, both have strong memories of appearing in the film. Gallardo says with a laugh, "I remember everything about *Death Wish II*."

In the original *Death Wish*, the daughter, Carol, was played by Kathleen Tolan. For the sequel, Winner cast Sherwood as the mute girl. The actress and model's prior work included the horror flick *Tourist Trap* (1979) and Brian De Palma's *Blow Out* (1981). Sherwood recalls her *Death Wish II* audition: "I went in through the traditional casting system. I was submitted by my agent. I then went to the casting director and he said, 'I'd like you to meet Mr. Winner.' Charlie [Bronson] wasn't there and the producers weren't there. I didn't meet anyone else. It was all Michael Winner. We talked about the concept of the role. [Winner] kept calling me back and calling me back, but he wasn't saying that I had the part. So I just flew off the handle at him and I said, 'I don't want this part,' and I left and went to Miami Beach which is where I was from. I was sitting on the porch and I was crying, saying, 'It's over.' I really wanted this part. I got a telephone call from the casting director and he said, 'We want you to come back to New York. Mr. Winner has something to say to you.' So I immediately got back on the plane and I was hoping and I was praying. [Winner and] the producers were there and they were all smiling when I walked in and they said, 'Would you like the role of Charles Bronson's daughter in *Death Wish II*?' I said, 'Yes, yes!' [laughs] I was so happy. It was really a very intense auditioning process. They were very close to shooting [when I was cast]. Pre-production was going on."

Sherwood had already met *Death Wish II* producers Menahem Golan and Yoram Globus many years earlier at the Cannes Film Festival. Sherwood: "I was in Cannes when I was sixteen-years-old. I was already working as a professional model. The Cannes Film Festival is like a candy store of entertainment. [laughs] Golan and Globus, literally, had a booth that had a curtain and a chair and that was their production company."

The Women of *Death Wish II*

Paul Kersey (Charles Bronson) with daughter, Carol (Robin Sherwood), and girlfriend, Geri (Jill Ireland) in *Death Wish II* (1982).

Before Silvana Gallardo played the role of the *Death Wish II* housekeeper, Rosario, her credits included the television miniseries *Centennial* (1978), the feature *Windwalker* (1980) and two Broadway plays. She says, "I was working on [the TV series] *Falcon Crest* [1981] at the time. My agent called me and I went down to meet Michael Winner, who was a very nice man. He had me seated in a chair. I didn't read anything; he just walked around the chair. [laughs] And he asked me some questions and I guess he was seeing how I would react to different things that he was proposing. He talked to me and I listened. It was interesting. I had never had an audition like that. He's eccentric. I turned the part down several times because it was just too scary for me. I was terrified, so I turned it down. [Winner] called me up at home and I said, 'Just get another actress.' He said, 'I don't want another actress.' He was insistent. I said, 'I can't do it, I can't do it.' And everybody told me, 'You're crazy. You have to take this, you have to take this.' And I said, 'I *can't* do it.' When I had first come out to California, I did a television movie on

Inez Garcia [*The People vs. Inez Garcia*, 1977]. She had gone to jail for allegedly killing a man who had allegedly raped her. And one of the jurors, after the trial, said, 'I don't know why she killed him. He was just trying to show her a good time.' That stayed with me for quite a bit. I [thought], 'Well, no, it's not a good time. And if anybody can do this and show that it's not a good time, I can do it.' I went ahead."

Sherwood: "I had not seen [*Death Wish*]. Of course, I was familiar with it because it was a phenomenal success. I made a very deliberate choice not to see it because I did not want to be influenced by [Tolan's] performance. I loved creating a mute, which is why I took [the role]."

Gallardo: "I saw the first *Death Wish*. It was very good. As a matter of fact, I was an extra in the first *Death Wish*. [laughs] It was a scene when they were taking someone away in an ambulance. Michael Winner felt he had discovered me because I told him the story about the first *Death Wish*. He made a big deal about it. [laughs] He said 'Now you're playing a bigger role!'"

Both actresses had seen Bronson in person during their childhoods. Sherwood: "[My family] had gone to Las Vegas. I was about ten. They flew us in on some convention. It was pretty elaborate. It was probably a fundraiser. [My parents] saw Charles Bronson. They said, 'Oh, my God, that's Charles Bronson!' Of course, they sent me over because I'm the little girl. They said, 'Go over and ask him for his autograph.' So I did. He was charming, lovely, signed it, and smiled. I always remember that about him—his smile. I have always loved Charles Bronson since then. I didn't meet Charlie [again] until I went on the [*Death Wish II*] set. [Winner took me] over to Charlie's trailer. Charles Bronson's in there in a pair of jeans and a shirt. Now the man is sixty-six [and] he is in perfect condition. Perfect. And what is he doing? He's polishing his boots. Isn't that amazing? [Winner said,] 'This is your daughter.' And Charlie looks at me and he gets this huge smile and he said, 'She looks good.' [laughs]"

Gallardo: "When I was a kid, I grew up in a slum in New York. Charles Bronson came [to the area when] he was doing the series *Man with a*

The Women of *Death Wish II*

Stomper (Kevyn Major Howard) is about to assault the housekeeper, Rosario (Silvana Gillardo).

Camera [1958–1960]. I remember telling him on the [*Death Wish II*] set that I had seen him when I was a little girl and he thought that was cool. [laughs] So that was nice. It's such a circle."

Sherwood: "I adored Charles Bronson. He was delightful. He was just a phenomenal actor, a very well-trained actor. He picked up every little nuance. Everything. He was always present. I think he knew what his audience wanted from him. He certainly pleased his audience. He had this amazing presence. There were crowds always around. [He was] used to that."

Gallardo: "[Bronson] was wonderful. He was very real. I remember that he said something about rehearsing and I said, 'Sure,' and then he started talking to me and I didn't know that he had already started the scene. I thought he was just talking. [laughs] He was a very nice man and so was his wife. She was lovely." (Bronson's wife, Jill Ireland, co-starred in *Death Wish II*.)

Sherwood: "I loved Jill. She was breathtakingly beautiful. She looked like a porcelain doll. She was concerned that it was my first action film and she was very motherly to me. She said, 'Make sure that you protect yourself here.'"

Gallardo was a lovely young woman at the time of *Death Wish II*, but she was made to look much older for the film. She says, "They had me looking very non-attractive because they didn't want to make it seem like [my character] was bringing [the rape] on."

According to Sherwood, Winner supervised "every single detail" of her appearance in *Death Wish II* and she had no input into how she looked in the movie. She says, "I really did not. Maybe because I was fitting into a role that had been created in *Death Wish I* and I had to continue an image. They wouldn't let me wear any makeup. Michael didn't want any makeup on me and he designed my hair. He sent me to a person who could cut my hair the way he wanted it."

Gallardo: "[Winner] was very charming. He wasn't wishy-washy at all. He was very clear and very exact and very precise about what he wanted. He surely could not tell me anything about how to play the rape scene, because that was just real. I mean, it wasn't *real* real, but it was real for me, so I just responded."

Sherwood: "The part was very physical, very emotional. If you work with Charles Bronson, you have to be in very good shape. So I was dancing every morning for three hours and in the afternoon I would be walking miles. I would do this six days a week. I had to become very,

very thin because [my character had] been in an institution. I had to look frail. I did do some research. In the script [my character] actually screams. Loudly. They wanted me to scream at the rape. That character would have never reacted like that. She wouldn't have been strong enough to do that. That was something that I chose as an actress and, obviously, they liked it and they used it. [Winner] was detail oriented. He has a great eye. He never missed anything. He's very improvisational, so if you give him something, he'll pick up on it and he'll really elaborate on it. He really does use so much of what the talent brings. He's a perfectionist. What a character. He's hyper all over the place. The best way to be with Michael is real calm, because he'll be hyper for everybody. He's great to work with, but he has a temper. When Michael would be too much on me, Charlie would make some hysterical comment to Michael and Michael would just back off. If it was a confrontation between Michael Winner and Charlie, Charlie won."

Gallardo had spoken with rape victim Inez Garcia prior to playing her in the TV-movie and drew on that material while shooting her infamous violation scene in *Death Wish II*, which took six grueling days to get on camera. The gang members were played by young actors Thomas Duffy, Kevyn Major Howard, Stuart K. Robinson, Laurence Fishburne, and E. Lamont Johnson. Winner, who preferred actual locations, filmed the scene in an occupied neighborhood. Gallardo: "You could hear [my] screaming and I thought, 'Oh, the poor neighbors.' It was very difficult. [Winner] had to shoot like five different versions of it. It was pretty intense. [It was] mostly improvised. I had to get pushed and so forth. You're very vulnerable. I had a few 'black and blues.' I was tired. I had never done anything like that. [The other actors] were very careful to cover me up immediately after [a take]. I hated the still photographer. He kept taking pictures even after they had called, 'Cut.' I didn't like that. It was an experience to last a lifetime. It was good for me to do. I had to let go of a lot of fears. It was hard for the [other actors], too. I think one of them really got sick on the set. He threw up, or was going to, because it was so violent. [Laurence Fishburne] said it was the most horrible, awful scene he had to do." (*Death Wish II*'s original cinematographer, Thomas Del Ruth, was replaced early in the shooting. One rumor has it that Del Ruth and his crew left because they were offended by Winner's graphic staging of Gallardo's rape scene.)

Sherwood: "I didn't meet the actors [who played the gang] until they showed up on the set. They frightened me to death. I knew that they were actors, but they really did look like gang members. I was really frightened. They looked so realistic. [Kevyn Major Howard] looked disgusting. Laurence Fishburne never broke character. I really thought they had just found him in East L.A. They had whips—Laurence was smashing his against furniture all the time. We [were renting] somebody's location. I said, 'Laurence, you're destroying someone's furniture!' He said, 'That's too bad. I'm going to continue doing it.' I would watch them with their chains and stuff. They really were a sight. You couldn't have gotten better actors. Those [characters] have been copied so much. I remember Stuart Robinson being sort of calm and sweet. They ate lunch by themselves. I thought, 'I don't really want to associate with these people.' [laughs] 'I'll stick to Charlie and Jill. I'll put my chair over there.'"

Jiver (Stuart K. Robinson) and Stomper (Kevyn Major Howard) kidnap Carol (Robin Sherwood).

Like Gallardo, Sherwood wasn't expecting Winner to go as far as he did when shooting her rape scene. She says, "I knew from the script that it would have to be brutal. I didn't know it was going to be that graphic. I was rather upset about it. I wish there was [a body double]. I was far too young to insist upon that. And to make filming even more difficult, the *Los Angeles Times* was doing a series of articles on [the film] and one of the days they chose to interview everybody was the day of my rape scene. That was pretty intense. I think we were shooting for about a week in the warehouse in the middle of the night. There was running and all that kind of stuff. Of course, I didn't jump out the window—that's a stunt person. They really made her look like me. That was not a dummy. [The role] was very difficult and it was not so easy to jump back. I was trained by Lee Strasberg and was very much a method actress, so it was difficult to just go back. It took quite a while to gain back the weight and to get back my vitality."

Sherwood first saw *Death Wish II* at a pre-release screening. She says, "I knew that it was going to be a hit and was going to be very controversial. It was a very black and white film. But at that time, when everyone was so confused and things were so violent and people were so out of hand, I knew that it would strike a chord with a mass audience. As far as my performance goes, there was stuff that they did cut out. There was sweet stuff, [like] when Charlie took me to a Punch and Judy show. All of that was taken out. That was very upsetting to me because so much of my performance, and so much of our relationship, was not on the screen. Then there was beautiful footage on the boat. We had some wonderful, tender moments there. There was a beautiful little section with the glass menagerie, when we were selecting the little pieces. While it still is in there, it's cut really fast. There was more where I had the glass cat in my hand. When [Winner] came to my home, he saw that I had two cats and I had a little glass collection and that's how that ended up in the film. Let's face it, it's a very hard film to watch. There are some very dark sides to that film. Michael Winner made his point, and he did it well, and then he took it to this level that was very graphic. It just went too far, it was gratuitous. I really was upset about it and Charlie was pretty upset about it, too. [He felt] it was too graphic. We were at a restaurant and [the distributor was] saying that they wanted to really cut down the rape scene for an American audience and Michael Winner was very upset about it. He said [to me], 'This is really going to limit your role.' But, quite frankly, I could have done with much, much less. But as an actress, I had no control over that." She later watched the film with a general audience. "That was really fun, actually. It was a young audience and they would cheer and scream and yell and they were so happy when [Bronson was] going after the bad guys."

Gallardo: "I went into a really crowded movie theater on Hollywood Boulevard and when that [rape] scene came on, everybody was very still, so I thought, 'I did a good job. I did what I set out to accomplish.' I liked my work. It was interesting because I was afraid people would laugh. I got very angry at my manager because she went to see it and she said, 'How could you have been in such a horrible thing? How could you let yourself be seen that way?' And she had read the script. I was just mortified. I felt very alone. [A rape scene] was not something that I had ever done [before] or will ever do, probably, again. Everybody talked about my work. I got a lot of press on it [saying] it was the most violent rape scene ever. I got written up in the papers a lot. Michael Winner said, 'Who's your publicist? You're getting more publicity than me!' [laughs] I got a lot of e-mail [about *Death Wish II*]. Some really good, very perceptive ones. [Viewers] said that they were very moved; that they were affected; how hard it must have been. They were kind. Nobody said anything obscene, which was a fear." Until her death from cancer in 2012, Gallardo continued to work steadily in films and television and was a highly-respected acting instructor whose list of students included Angelina Jolie.

Sherwood: "[Winner and I] did start dating during the [*Death Wish II*] auditioning process, but nothing really serious happened. We really didn't return to dating until after everything was shot. I did visit him a couple of times in London. I went out for every female lead that I was right for, for every movie. I must have met every director that you could possibly imagine. People would ask for autographs. People wouldn't always know my name, but they'd say, 'You look familiar.' By that time, I had been working since I was fourteen-years-old and I said, 'I'm tired, I'm exhausted, I want to go to Paris.' It's a completely different world. So I went over to Paris and I fell in love and didn't want to go back to acting. I never went back. [*Death Wish II* was her last acting role. She is now a writer and an entrepreneur.] Believe it or not, I still get people asking for autographs, which I think is funny. Most people are very sweet. I get e-mails, quite a lot, about *Death Wish II*. I catch it on television when it's on. It definitely created a classic action hero. I look at it as a hero's journey. It's really a classic."

Chapter 9
Actor Robert F. Lyons
on *Death Wish II*

After appearing on and off-Broadway in the early 1960s, Robert F. Lyons went to Hollywood and appeared on TV episodes before become one of the most exciting young screen actors of the early 1970s. His performances in *Pendulum* (1969) as a psychopath; in Richard Rush's *Getting Straight* as a hippie college buddy of Elliott Gould; in *The Todd Killings* (1971) as a thrill-killer; and in *Dealing* (1972) as a weed-smuggling Harvard law student all earned him acclaim among counterculture film buffs and should have garnered him at least one Oscar nomination.

For the rest of his career, Lyons worked mostly as a television actor in episodes of shows like *Night Gallery* (1971); *The Rookies* (1972); *The Incredible Hulk* (1979 and 1981); *Magnum, P.I.* (1982); *Walker, Texas*

Ranger (1996); *Roswell* (1999 and 2000); *Cold Case* (2006); and *Criminal Minds* (2009 and 2011) plus small-screen movies like *The Disappearance of Flight 412* (1974), *Death Car on the Freeway* (1979) and *Dark Night of the Scarecrow* (1981).

Lyons first worked with Charles Bronson in *Death Wish II* (1982) (as the radio station manager) then worked with the star again on *10 to Midnight* (1983) and *Murphy's Law* (1986).

Did you ever encounter Charles Bronson before Death Wish II?

Prior to my working with him, he did a film called *The Mechanic* [1972]—a very famous film. I had loved Bronson. I always loved his work. He was a very unusual actor. He had seen my work, probably in a couple of films. He knew who I was. I was working around that time a lot. As a kid, I was putting out some pretty strong stuff. And he didn't know me at the time, but he had seen my work and he kept saying, "Get that guy. That's who should be playing the part."

You were up for the role of the apprentice in The Mechanic that ultimately was played by Jan-Michael Vincent?

Yeah, the kid. I knew Charlie had asked for me. We had the same public relations guy at that time. That's how I found out. Chartoff/Winkler were the producers on [*The Mechanic*] and I was brought in and we had a great meeting. I saw a flaw with the script and brought it up and they loved it because I knew how to fix it. My agent almost died that I even brought it up. [laughs] Chartoff/Winkler just flipped out and said, "Oh, God, you gotta meet Michael Winner. This is great, Bobby." I thought I was "in." I thought this would be a slam-dunk. So I set up an interview [with Winner] and I waited. He was over twenty minutes late. I got rave reviews on a film Winner didn't like, a film called *Pendulum*. I was just about to get up to leave and he came in the door and he went [blandly], "Oh, yeah. You're the one with the reviews." You don't say that to someone when you meet them for the first time. It was an invalidation and an insult to say that. My urge, and I usually follow them, was to say, "Thank you for the interview" and walk out. He spent forty minutes talking about himself. I left and, of course, I didn't get the part. But he got "a young Bobby Lyons." [laughs] Winner's a real winner, boy. That really pissed me off because that was a wonderful role and I'd have torn the thing apart because I was right in my prime, I knew just what to do. The thrill of working with Charlie. I worked with Gregory Peck and other wonderful actors and when you're working with that caliber of people, you come to the table loaded. You come to deliver. While they were shooting [*The Mechanic*] in Europe—I found this out through our PR guy—[Bronson] kept saying, "Michael, you were gonna show me your notes on Robert Lyons—why he didn't get the part."

You interviewed with Winner ten years later for Death Wish II.

I got a call: "Would I go out for *Death Wish II*? Would you go for this interview?" I said, "I don't wanna meet [with Winner]. He's obnoxious. I'll take the interview and if he gives me any of that crap, I'm gonna leave. I don't need that in my life." So I go in and meet him. Winner looked at me and he's like, "Who's this? Who's this?" We did the interview. He says, "How tall are you?" "Five-nine [1.75 m.]." "Good. No one working with Charlie can be higher than five-nine." And he's looking at me, I thought he was trying to get the color of my eyes. I said, "Green." He said, "Green? Green? What's green?" And I lost it. I said, "My hair!" And oddly enough, he cooled off. I thought he'd say, "Get the hell out of here" or something. He just relaxed and he gave me the part!

What was Bronson like to work with?

First day that I had to work, Bronson heard I was there and came right down to meet me and said, "Jesus, you haven't changed in ten years." And we had never met! I said, "I'm Bobby Lyons." He said, "I know who you are. Welcome. I'm so glad you're on the film." He was just a total gentleman. I was amazed. He had talked to my manager and said, "I'm so glad he's on here. I've wanted to work with this kid." He just liked me right off. And I liked him. What the hell is not to like? He's a quiet man. He doesn't say a lot. But what he says, it's Bronson. And we had a wonderful time. He was always well-prepared. A perfect gentleman doing business. He was very cool. He had no extra tinsel or "I'm a movie star." None of that shit. He was just a guy. He was crazy about [his wife] Jill [Ireland]. I loved watching the two of them together. There was a marked change that I would observe in Charlie Bronson when she was present. He was like a kid when she was around. I admired their camaraderie and their sharing of things and the way they looked at one another.

What was Winner like on the set?

He loved to smoke cigars. They were expensive cigars and he was always smoking. This kid had to walk behind him within three feet so there was always a cigar within his reach. [laughs] Winner was a very intelligent man and he could be very charming. Somebody like Charlie, he never spoke down to. But he would just blow up with people. There was another actor in that film and he kept screwing up his lines because Winner was all over him, a man by the name of [Michael] Prince. We had a long shot in a parking lot and it was on a dolly track and we had to step over the track which can be kind of cumbersome to do. [Prince] kept screwing up his lines and Winner was just all over him, overwhelmed him. We're onto take six now and he's just pounding on him. I grabbed Prince and said, "Talk to me. Work with me. Ignore him. Just look at me." We got through it.

By the way, I was fired during the production of the film. [laughs] There was a graveyard scene and I was originally not written in it. And when I read the script, I said, "I should have been in that. I should have been there." And [Winner] came to me and said, "You know, Robert, I think you ought to be in that scene." The first shot of the day was at the marina, let's say seven o'clock. And even though you weren't due at the marina but you were due at the graveyard, [Winner] would have the actors show up at the second location at the same time he was at the marina. Meaning, you had two and a half hours of just sitting and waiting. These are the kinds of things he would do that were annoying. I parked in the graveyard. There was an assistant director there. He said, "They're still at the marina, they'll be there for a while." So I drove off and had breakfast. Came back, they still weren't there. So I drove up on a hill of this graveyard and fell asleep in the car while I was waiting. Next thing I know, an A.D. [Assistant Director] is knocking on my window saying, "Bobby, they're looking for you." And I could hear [Winner] on the walkie-talkie: "Have you found that actor? Where's that actor? I can't wait any longer. I'm not going to use him. Fire him and tell him I'm not paying him for the day." Well, I *flipped*. I drove down and I went right up to him and I said, "I was here since eight o'clock. You are gonna pay me. Get your A.D. over here. You're signing me out and you're paying me for the day." I cut loose. And then I went over to apologize to Charlie and Jill. Charlie said, "What's going on?" I told him. He said, "Oh, man. He'll never hire you again." I said, "Charlie, I will never work with that man again. I will not." And Jill said, "Good. He earned it." Many had gotten fired before. I was told I was number thirty-six to get fired. [laughs] And I did get paid for that day.

Then I had to work with Winner again because I had to do [voice] looping and I dreaded it. And when I came in, he was charming: "Robert, so good to see you." I'm waiting for the other shoe to drop, which never did. I said, "I'm not very good [at looping]." He said, "Oh, don't worry. We'll get it one way or another." And I'm going, "Why in the hell aren't you like this on the set?" He was genuinely charming and patient and he was as pleasant as you could possibly see somebody to be. He was just an enigma. I'm just glad Michael Winner didn't do *10 to Midnight*.

Charles Bronson as the law-bending Lieutenant Leo Kessler in *10 to Midnight* (1983).

Chapter 10
10 to Midnight (1983)

10 to Midnight is an outstanding Charles Bronson movie of the 1980s. This thriller with Bronson as a rule-breaking cop on the trail of a severely unstable, sexually disturbed maniac was one of the most profitable of the many team-ups between the star, director J. Lee Thompson, and Cannon Films. It was a huge renter on videotape and an extremely popular item on cable TV. Audiences were stunned by the insane, R-rated mix of traditional Bronson action, graphic violence, filthy language, pathology, bare breasts and buttocks—and a bizarre masturbation contraption. *10 to Midnight* still stands as one of the more beloved Bronson/Cannon pictures, and it is also well-regarded by fans of '80s-era slasher movies.

Producer Pancho Kohner—son of Bronson's longtime agent, Paul Kohner—was always looking for material that would suit the star. The younger Kohner had already produced Bronson's *St. Ives* (1976), *The White Buffalo* (1977) and *Love and Bullets* (1979) and was an uncredited executive producer on *Cabo Blanco* (1980). He says, "[Bronson] always liked to satisfy his audience. He knew what his audience expected of him. He didn't want to deviate too far. He did a couple of films that were different, but mostly he knew what his audience expected of him, and that's what he wanted to do."

Bronson said, "I look for material that will entertain. I've sustained because I'm sympatico with the material I do and the other way around. An actor shouldn't just think of doing things *he* might enjoy doing. I think first of the audience, not of myself, but of the movie fans all around the world who want to be entertained."

Pancho Kohner's search led to the 1978 action novel *The Evil That Men Do*, by R. Lance Hill. In 1980 the screen rights were purchased by a partnership consisting of Kohner, Bronson, Jill Ireland (Bronson's actress wife) and director J. Lee Thompson. Hill was commissioned to turn his novel into a script.

While Pancho Kohner shopped the *Evil That Men Do* package, Bronson starred in *Death Wish II* (1982) for the Israeli filmmaking cousins Menahem Golan and Yoram Globus, who had recently moved into the American movie market by purchasing the distribution/production sleaze outfit the Cannon Group. The *Death Wish* sequel went to number one at the American box office, was a huge international hit, revitalized the Bronson name, and gave a major boost to Cannon's image. Naturally, Golan and Globus wanted a follow-up.

Pancho Kohner: "Golan wanted to do Charlie's next picture, and [*The Evil That Men Do* was] the one that we were going to do next. We were going off to Cannes to pre-sell foreign territories. I explained to Menahem that the right to the book and the cost of the screenplay was $200,000. Menahem said, 'Well, as a producer, that's your contribution.' I said, 'Well, that's very nice, but I put up a third, Charlie put up a third, and J. Lee Thompson put up a third. We must certainly reimburse them, if not me.' He said, 'Oh, I can't do that.' Menahem and I liked each other, but he didn't want to back down. It became a matter of principle. We were leaving the next day for Cannes. [Golan] said, 'I'll tell you what. We'll go to Cannes anyway, and we'll pre-sell the next Bronson picture. When we come back in two weeks, we'll find another story, and we will not make *The Evil That Men Do*. What's a good title?' I always liked [the title] *10 to Midnight*. That's how we came to do *10 to Midnight*. It wasn't until later [1983] that we made *The Evil That Men Do*."

With nothing but the star and the title, Cannon pre-sold their Bronson epic.

At the 1982 Cannes Film Festival in May, Cannon announced *10 to Midnight* as "an international thriller" with hastily-made pamphlets and a full-page *Variety* ad featuring a rough pencil sketch of Bronson clutching a machine pistol. The tagline read: "In a world torn by terrorism the ultimate vigilante is out to get even...and he's running out of time."

Pancho Kohner: "We went over to Cannes, and I sat in this suite at the Carlton, and all the buyers came through. I explained that there was going to be great action and great danger and great revenge, and it was called *10 to Midnight*. Everyone was pleased. We didn't have a script yet."

Golan said at the time, "Cannes is our Christmas. It's where we meet distributors from all over the world who are our friends. And we know how to take care of them because we learned the hard way. What's the hard way? Selling a black-and-white Hebrew film to Japan. We continue to do bread-and-butter commercial pictures because we need the foundation they give us. For me, an artistic movie is a movie audiences want to see. There is a great hunger for American motion pictures. And there are thousands of independent distributors who can't satisfy that need in their countries because they're cut off from the American product by the major studios who have their own worldwide networks. So we're here to make American movies to take care of those distributors.

"Look, we're movie-makers, not heads of studios who come to their plush offices from law firms or talent agencies or business schools. Our school was the school of smacks in the face and getting up to make more films. When we first came to Hollywood, we found a closed society in which deal-making is more important than movie-making. For them, it's ten percent making movies and ninety percent talk—on the tennis courts, in the Polo Lounge and at parties where a certain kind of cigarette is smoked. We had nothing to do with that, and we are buying no tennis rackets. What we are doing is going to the top—because we started at the bottom....We have only a hundred salaries to pay, which keeps our overheads extremely low....We don't know how to lose money. There is nearly $1 million profit on every film before we even open it in America."

Pancho Kohner: "We got back to Los Angeles, and I had to scramble to find a story that would be a Bronson project that Charlie would like. I called a friend of mine, Lance Hool, and I asked him if he had any stories."

Producer Lance Hool and director J. Lee Thompson had collaborated on *Cabo Blanco*. Hool says, "J. Lee and I were developing a movie called *Blood Bath,* and we were gonna do it at Paramount. He was a fanatic of the Richard Speck trial in Chicago—the guy that killed the nurses. We took offices together after *Cabo Blanco*."

Blood Bath was an original script by seventy-year-old William Roberts, whose previous screenplays included the Bronson hits *The Magnificent Seven* (1960) and *Red Sun* (1971). While creating *Blood Bath*, Roberts and Thompson emphasized the psycho-sexual aspects (i.e. as the killer dresses for his first kill, the script read: "Holding the knife against his abdomen, he presses the release. The shining blade springs forward, not unlike an erection.") The written description of the lead detective was perfectly suited for Bronson: "Kessler is solidly built, a strong man, not just bodily, but in resolute, unyielding durability. You hear it in his voice, see it in his face, toughened by years of exposure to the most elemental, least permissible kinds of human behavior."

Hool: "Charlie [Bronson] had been reading it as we went along. I got Charlie involved without the cadre that they put around him. Once we had it pretty far along, Kohner called and said that he had made a deal with these two guys from Israel for a movie with Charlie—but they didn't have a movie. [Kohner] said, 'Look. If you want to get this done quickly, Cannon wants to go right now.'" Pancho Kohner and Hool teamed up as producers. *Blood Bath* got financing (and a new moniker) while the *10 to Midnight* project found a script to accompany the title, the star and the money.

Variety ad, October 1982. (Courtesy of William Wilson).

The casting director for *10 to Midnight* was John Crowther, who had been an actor and director and had previously worked with Bronson and Pancho Kohner as an uncredited writer on *Love and Bullets*. Crowther says, "At that point, I was teaching acting. I started in this business as

10 to Midnight (1983)

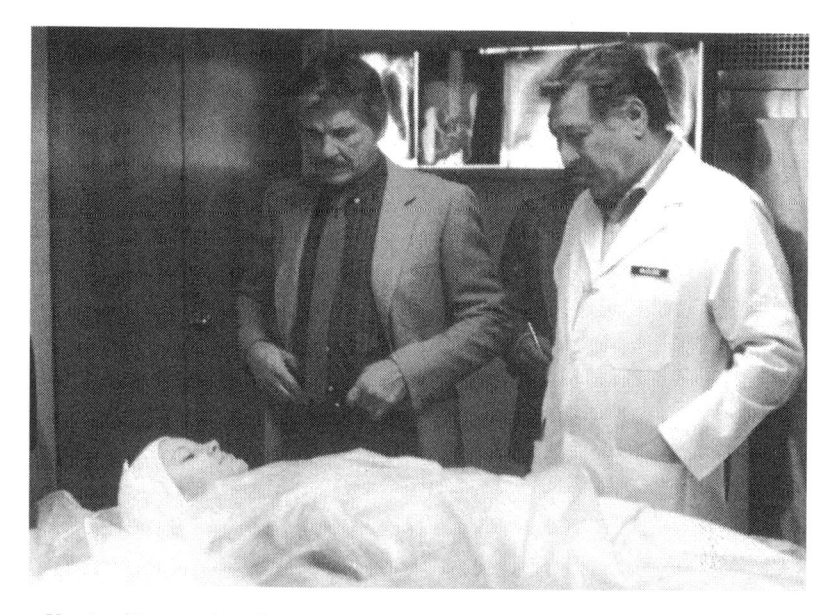

Kessler (Bronson) studies a corpse (June Gilbert) with the medical examiner (Jerome Thor). Thor was a longtime acquaintance of Bronson and had small roles in several of the star's movies including *Murphy's Law*, where he played the drowned judge.

an actor. I'd known Pancho Kohner for years. We got to be very good friends. Pancho called me and said that they had a casting director and it just wasn't working out. I think they were a week into pre-production. They had just opened their offices at Cannon. Pancho said, 'I know that you haven't been a casting director, but you know actors, you know acting. Would you be interested in doing it?' I said, 'Sure. Why not? I'll take it on.' And it was a bear because it was Cannon Films, and they didn't pay very much. They wouldn't even pay for an assistant. No one's ever cast a major movie in this town with no assistant. They gave us a suite at Cannon, but it didn't include an office for me. I was working out of the conference room at Cannon. I was working with people going in and out. It was crazy. It was lunacy.

"We cast almost entirely from agent submission. I would pre-read actors and make a cull, subsequently sending actors to what we call a 'producer's session,' even though it may exclusively be with the director. If they were right for the part, I'd bring them in to J. Lee. That is the industry-wide standard, if actors are being brought in that the casting director doesn't know in advance. The only other option in casting is 'direct offer,' without an audition, though occasionally a known actor will be brought in just to meet with the director, before a hard offer is made. Charlie was never in on a casting session. Nobody ever read for him. I don't think he ever really took a large role in the casting process. Pancho would run names by him of the major people. I got to know J. Lee, and we had a great working relationship casting that. It was very interesting working with him on the casting. He had a really phenomenal eye for actors, and he used to just pass on a lot of actors—he would say, 'Television actor.' We interviewed a lot of people who were 'known.'"

Sam Bottoms (*The Outlaw Josey Wales*, 1976), Parker Stevenson (TV's *The Hardy Boys/Nancy Drew Mysteries*, 1977–1979) and Frank Sinatra, Jr. were among those who lost the role of Bronson's partner to Andrew Stevens (*The Boys in Company C*, 1978; Bronson's *Death Hunt*, 1981). Crowther: "Andrew is one of the most underrated actors of his generation. Good actor. Solid. Professional. Everything about him was spot on. He really should have gone further." (1)

Lisa Eilbacher was cast as Bronson's student-nurse daughter. She had dozens of TV credits and had recently gotten attention for playing the candidate coached "over-the-wall" by Richard Gere in *An Officer and a Gentleman* (1982). Former Bronson co-star Wilford Brimley (*Borderline*, 1980) was rehired. New actresses Kelly Preston (*Christine*, 1983) and *Playboy* model Ola Ray (*Michael Jackson's Thriller*, 1983) played murdered nurses. Bronson's stepson Paul McCallum was cast as a weed-smoking lab technician. Cosie Costa, who was also in producer Hool's *Survival Run* (1979) and *Missing in Action 2: The Beginning* (1985), played a fornicating medical intern interrupted at a party by the gun-toting Stevens. In the screenplay, Costa's comic-relief role was a constant victim of mistaken identity and was always getting approached by gun-wielding cops, but only one of the character's scenes remained in the film.

Detective Paul McAnn (Andrew Stevens), Leo Kessler (Bronson) and Laurie Kessler (Lisa Eilbacher).

The most important piece of casting was the role of Warren Stacy, the sexually confused young psychopath. Crowther: "It was interesting casting that part. The description of the part that went out to agents by way of the breakdowns was for somebody who was anywhere from age eighteen to thirty. I thought with so many actors in L.A. we would be inundated with guys who might be terrific. As it happened, no one totally blew us away with his acting chops. We narrowed it down to about five or six that looked right and could play it, and these were the ones we screen-tested. In the end it was not an easy decision." Pop singer/teen idol Leif Garrett was one who unsuccessfully auditioned for the role.

Gene Davis, who had studied under Sanford Meisner and other noted acting coaches in New York City and was the younger brother of actor Brad Davis (*Midnight Express*, 1980), was among the many who read for the killer part. Davis says, "I had previously done *Cruising* [1980] with [William] Friedkin. David Chase wrote a pilot specifically for [the] character I had done on *The Rockford Files* [1978 and 1979]. I also worked with Roger Vadim on *Night Games* [1980]. They actually offered the [*10 to Midnight*] role to Bobby Di Cicco. He was in *The Big Red One* [1980]. He was 'hot' for a while out here. He turned it down. My agent submitted the picture, and Lance [Hool] and J. Lee had me come in for an interview. J. Lee and I hit it off incredibly, and he said to me after the interview, 'You are Warren.' And that was a wonderful thing to hear as an actor. The first meeting was just a general meeting, and the second was the actual audition, where they put me on tape. I don't think I came back for a second audition. I think they saw what they wanted on the first audition. It was Jill Ireland, Charlie's wife, who took to me when she saw the audition. J. Lee told me that she sort of influenced Charlie to go ahead and 'okay' me. After I met Jill on the set, I fell in love with her. Quite a woman.

"The elements of the character were real elements. That scene that took place in the dorm room where he killed all of the nurses was a replica of the Richard Speck murders. And there was a serial killer in London—Scotland Yard had a hard time catching the guy because he killed in the nude, and there was no evidence of his clothes or fibers. (2) [The script] put the two together. J. Lee's vision was that [Warren] would not be the normal sort of creepy guy, but that he was clean-cut. Remember how clean-cut Ted Bundy was? J. Lee had written this role. The reason the character's name was 'Warren' is because he envisioned Warren Beatty. Those are the elements that all worked into it. I didn't want to fashion my performance after some creepy guy. I didn't need to be over the top with it, at least I tried not to be. I knew who Richard Speck was. I knew who Ted Bundy was because I grew up in Florida. I remember seeing pictures of Ted Bundy and seeing how clean-cut and handsome he was. But that really doesn't factor into an actor's performance. An actor has to

10 TO MIDNIGHT (1983)

work from the inside out. So there was nothing for me, physically, to do to myself. I did *Cruising* and played a transvestite, so there was a physical transformation in that. But as far as [*10 to Midnight*], there was none. I had to remain as close to myself as possible. I was already going to the gym to stay in shape. I had a trainer; his name was Vince Gironda. He was a legend in the bodybuilding world."

Psychopath Warren Stacy (Gene Davis) stalks Karen (Jeana Tomasino).

There was no rehearsal process for *10 to Midnight*. Davis: "Nope. Jump into the deep end and swim like a madman. That was it. [laughs] [Thompson] left me alone, pretty much. I gave him everything that was humanly possible for the role, and he was happy with what I was giving him. The only thing he ever said to me is: 'We don't want the role to be sympathetic. I know you have the ability to do that, but please don't do that.' [laughs] That was about it. I loved J. Lee. He was a wonderful director. Absolutely. And his career was just amazing. He was the kindest human being I've ever met."

Davis was excited to be working with Bronson. "As a kid, I grew up in the '60s. I remember *The Great Escape* [1963]. I think I saw it ten times when I was a kid. It was one of my favorite movies of all time, and he was a stud in it. I was as taken with Charlie as everybody was. When you meet the people that you liked in junior high and high school, you're awestruck."

Shortly after acting in *Death Wish II* and clashing with director Michael Winner, Robert F. Lyons got cast in the next Bronson movie (as the assistant district attorney) and had a better experience. Lyons says, "Next thing I know, I got the part in *10 to Midnight*. J. Lee Thompson was a wonderful man. He did one of my favorite war films, *Guns of Navarone* [1961]. I heard some personal things about him that were just terrific. During the Second World War, because of his size—he was not a big man, he was a slight man—he was a gunner in one of those ball turrets under the plane. [laughs] You had to be a small guy to get in there. That's a terrifying job to have when fighter planes are trying to shoot your ass out of the air. He was a survivor. And a very funny man. He had this habit that was very unusual. He liked to take a sheet of paper and strip it in two. It was a little nervous thing. The strips would be about an inch, maybe a half-inch wide. It was just something J. Lee did while he was waiting. You can get awfully bored on a set. In fact, one time Charlie stood alongside him with a sheet of paper and was mimicking him while he was tearing. [laughs] He just stood there and did it alongside of him, and it was hysterical to see Charles Bronson just shredding a piece of paper. And Lee got a kick out of it. [laughs] It was just a warm, fun thing."

Warren (Gene Davis) makes an obscene call.

Davis: "It was an eight-week shoot. It was a very hard shoot. Very hard, physically. We were shooting in November–December [1982] down in Santa Monica during the rainy season. We pretty much stayed on script. There was a scene that I never shot that was in the script that I really thought was essential. It was sort of a creepy scene, but I knew how to turn it around. Remember the original *Frankenstein* [1931] and that scene where the little girl is down by the pond, and he walks up behind her and she gives him the flower? There was a scene in the park where Warren has an exchange with a young girl that age."

This vignette appeared in the screenplay after Warren is interrogated in his apartment by Leo Kessler (Bronson):

EXT. PARK – DAY
Warren, wearing a sweat suit, is jogging through the wooded park.
A STREAM runs along the trail. As Warren rounds a bend in the trail, his pace slows. Now he stops altogether, riveted by what he sees.

POV

Wading in the stream is a GIRL, a child of no more than ten, with only a suggestion of yet unformed breasts. On the bank of the stream are her dress and a pair of sandals. She wears nothing but underpants.

WARREN

He stands transfixed, no outward sign of unimaginable thoughts and impulses seizing hold of him. He moves forward silently. Reaches the bank of the stream. The girl senses his presence, turns around.

GIRL
Whew, you scared me!

10 to Midnight (1983)

The way Warren stares at her makes her uneasy.

> GIRL
>
> I forgot to bring my swim-suit
> or anything. (no reply) I think
> I'll get dressed now.

Which is by way of asking him to go away. Warren picks up her dress, holds it out to her, dangling it from one finger. The girl hesitates, then starts toward shore. When she is almost within reach of her dress –

> VOICE (O.S.)
>
> Susan!

Warren, startled, looks off.

WARREN'S POV

A woman (SUSAN'S MOTHER) emerges from the trees.

> MOTHER
>
> What are you doing?

REVERSE

Warren drops the dress, turns and trots off, into the woods. Eyes opaque, face a blank.

Davis says, "The point of the scene was that he *doesn't* kill her and that *he* becomes a child during the exchange. I talked to J. Lee, and I said, 'I can do this scene where Warren simply becomes a child as she is. And Warren's ability to relate to a child *as* a child would give me a chance to drop all of the issues that Warren was dealing with in the adult world which drove him to kill.' And J. Lee knew what I was talking about. I really wanted that scene because it would have given me a chance to give a window into Warren from a different point of view. But it would have probably generated sympathy for the character, and they didn't want that. J. Lee realized that it was too potent and would take attention away from Charlie. You have to remember it was supposed to be Charlie's film, not mine. They didn't want to take the chance of making Warren sympathetic, so that's why we just dumped it, and it wasn't shot."

That sequence was immediately followed in the script by another scene that was never filmed:

EXT. WARREN'S APARTMENT BUILDING – LATE DAY
Warren, still in jogging suit, parks his VW, gets out, locks the car, starts toward the apartment building.

A handsome YOUNG MAN is approaching, eyeing him in a speculative fashion. As the little girl in the park was made uneasy by Warren's staring at her, Warren reacts in much the same way. The young man smiles, takes out a cigarette. His voice is soft, insinuating.

          YOUNG MAN
        Hi. Got a match.

            WARREN
        I don't smoke.

          YOUNG MAN
      Oh? What do you do?

10 to Midnight (1983)

Laurie (Lisa Eilbacher) and McAnn (Andrew Stevens) record Warren's call.

> WARREN
> What's that to you?

> YOUNG MAN
> Just asking. No harm asking, is there?
> Is there? Hmm? Is there?

Warren is frustrated, as though these sly, probing questions had penetrated to a deeply hidden secret.

> WARREN
> Get away from me, faggot, or I'll smash
> your face!

> YOUNG MAN
> Sorry. My mistake.
> (faintly mocking)
> I guess.

He walks on. Warren glares at him then continues toward the entrance to the apartment building.

The double murder in the woods took one full day to shoot. Davis: "Out in the woods, it was rainy and cold. I was out in the weather with no clothes on. It was a very hard shoot. Very hard, physically." The actor had no protection on his soles while shooting the barefoot scenes.

The hospital segments were shot at the VA Hospital in Los Angeles, as was the nurse massacre, where Lisa Eilbacher hides under the bed. Davis: "It took all night to shoot that one scene. [The scenes] at the VA Hospital were done when it was like forty-eight degrees. I ended up getting sick after the film." During the nurse slaughter, the script reads: "CAMERA PANS to a large CLOCK over the desk. The time is TEN TO MIDNIGHT." If this image was shot, it did not end up in the film. Also in the screenplay during this scene is: "NOTE: The purpose here is to show the most repulsive side of Warren's nature, to turn the audience irrevocably against him."

Crowther: "Gene had a great quality. In terms of type, he was really spot on and worked very well in the film. Because he was such a tense actor, he couldn't control himself, and he went a little overboard. In the scene where he has to be strangling the girl, he put her in the hospital. He dislocated something. He hurt her, and she was incapacitated for a couple days." (Davis says that he was not told about any injury.)

Davis: "Charlie was very professional. He came in, did his work. He helped me stage the scene in the interrogation office where I flip out. It was his suggestion to pick up the chair and bash the door. It was not in the script. He pretty much staged that scene. He was always there to suggest things."

Crowther: "I didn't know Charlie very well. Whenever I was around him or talking to him, I probably came off as a little terrified of him. So he used to call me 'the koala.'"

10 TO MIDNIGHT (1983)

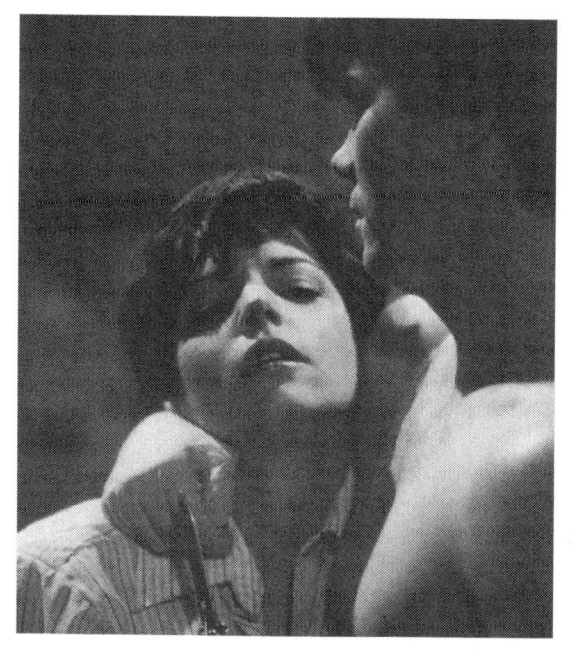

Warren (Gene Davis) chokes nursing student Bunny (Iva Lane).

Davis: "It was a really close set. Lisa, Andrew, and I spent a lot of time together on the set. Andrew was quite fun. He was a very lighthearted guy. We were all good friends. It was a tough shoot, and we all just buckled down and did our work. There were some funny things that I did when I had a light moment. [laughs] I know Lisa talked about it on *Johnny Carson* one time. [laughs] I tied a ribbon around 'it,' trying to make lighthearted of my life running around the set naked—which is not an easy thing to do." The character appears nude in the uncut version, but for publicity stills and the TV cut, Davis wore black undershorts. Davis: "You never saw any frontal nudity in the feature version, but you did see me from behind. I'd have to do [each] scene twice. They had to do the cable version. As far as the underwear/brief scenes, it was for television."

The movie's ending was altered during production. Davis: "Originally, in the script, Charlie was supposed to wrestle me down. But I was naked and he was not about to do that. [laughs] He didn't want that close physicality."

As written, the final confrontation between Leo Kessler (Bronson) and Warren (Davis) took place in an alley. As Detective McAnn (Stevens) and the police close in, Warren sliced Kessler's hand with the switchblade. From the screenplay:

> Again Warren slashes at him. This time Kessler is ready. One hand knocks Warren's arm upward, the other hand clamps hold of Warren's wrist. A powerful twist spins Warren around. Kessler's arm encircles Warren's neck from behind.
>
> MCANN
> Leo, no!
>
> Unheeded words. Gripping Warren's wrist, Kessler drives the knife into the killer's belly.
> As Warren did to his victims, Kessler wrenches the knife upward. Kessler lets go of him. Warren sinks to the ground. Everyone reacts in shock, everyone but Kessler, who shows no more feeling than if he had killed a mad dog. A moment passes. Then to McAnn—
>
> KESSLER
> You won't have to lie for me, I'll turn myself in.

Davis: "We shot the end scene twice. They rewrote it. We shot the end scene, but the following day when I came back to the set, J. Lee informed me that we were going to do it again. It was basically the same scene, but the dialogue was [added]. Where Warren says, 'You can't touch me. That's the law. You can't touch a sick person. You can put me away, but you can't kill me'—all that stuff was written on the second pass.

"Jill [Ireland] came to me after the movie was done. She gave me a book and said, 'This could be a wonderful role for you. I have six months left on the option, and I can't do it.' The book turned out to be the original version of 'Hannibal Lector.' It was *Red Dragon* [1981]. It eventually went to [Dino] De Laurentiis."

The editor on *10 to Midnight* was Peter-Lee Thompson, son of the director. The younger Thompson would go on to cut the remaining five Bronson movies that were directed by his father. Davis: "They ended

Laurie (Lisa Eilbacher) burns Warren (Gene Davis).

up restructuring the story in the editing room. [The script] opened on the office scene where I'm messing with the girl and I unzip the dress. Charlie actually didn't enter the picture until somewhere deep into the first act. The [final] film opens up with a scene that was mid-way through the script. When they got into the editing room, they had to rearrange things because it's 'a Charlie film.' It's not Warren's, it's Charlie's. They switched it around, which is fine. That's the way they do things."

A ninety-second scene of Bronson typing a report that originally took place twenty minutes into the movie was reedited to become the opening scene with the star bellowing: "I'm not a nice man. I'm a mean, selfish son-of-a-bitch. I know you want a story. But I want a killer, and what I want comes first."

Davis: "There wasn't a formal premiere. There was a screening at MGM. Some actors love watching themselves. I'm not one of those. I just find it hard to watch myself. I saw it, and there was nothing to be ashamed of, in my opinion. I gave it my all."

Hool: "*10 to Midnight* was originally going to be done for Paramount. *10 to Midnight*, with these guys at Cannon, was made for very little money. Yet, it's a very good movie. Charlie was great in that. I think he worked really well with Lisa Eilbacher. I thought he was great as the detective that Mark Fuhrman later confirmed—the detective from the LAPD that was busted for planting the [O. J. Simpson glove]. That was *after* our movie."

Andrew Stevens as Detective Paul McAnn.

The Cannon publicity team tried to justify the unrelated title in their *10 to Midnight* ad campaign. The tagline "A Cop...A Killer...A Deadline..." was accompanied by artwork of the psycho standing in front of a clock with his arms positioned at "10 to midnight."

Hool: "Cannon was not a distributor. They were experimenting with distribution. This was the first movie they distributed that was a mainline Hollywood movie." Golan and Globus opened the picture in the United States in 595 theaters on March 11, 1983. (Their previous Bronson movie, *Death Wish II*, was then playing on HBO.) *10 to Midnight* collected a little over $3 million in its first week. Cannon's release was "staggered," and the film played different areas of the country over a period of months. Among the first dates were Toledo, Ohio and Frankfort, Kentucky. In June, *10 to Midnight* was in Pittsburgh, where drive-ins paired it with Chuck Norris' *Forced Vengeance* (1982).

Richard F. Shepard, *The New York Times*: "If *10 to Midnight*...is not among the worst of its kind, then it is because its kind is among the worst of any kind....It is also a propaganda piece that argues against laws that let brutal slayers escape with insanity pleas." *Variety*: "William Roberts' screenplay, while it sags in the middle, is damnably clever at dropping in its vicious vigilante theme without being didactic, and J. Lee Thompson's direction...creates the full horror of blades thrusting into naked bellies without the viewer ever actually seeing it happen." *LA Weekly*: "a clichéd bloodbath full of gratuitous violence against women with a law-and-order sermon attached to it....Bronson has one of the most unique presences in film; he's neither articulate like Bogart nor obsessive like De Niro, but he projects more authenticity than either the true solitude of survival....Bronson virtually radiates what has been, for him, the high price of staying in the world at all. A pity movies sell this quality short—or don't pay him to reveal more of it." Linda Gross, *Los Angeles Times*: "a slickly made, suspenseful and scary movie, it is also inflammatory and extremely dangerous." *Toledo Blade*: "*10 to Midnight* is once again droningly devoted to the zombie-like, dial-tone approach to acting that has, for some unfathomable reason, served [Bronson] so well at the nation's box offices....The climactic, murderous scenes are indeed terrifying and suspenseful, although the very last action is at once as sickening as it is implausible. It might be more accurate to say that *10 to Midnight* is a good bad movie, the sort of thing that both Bronson and Clint Eastwood seem to come up with on a fairly regular basis."

Pittsburgh Press: "Something peculiar happened at Bank Cinema's matinee premiere of *10 to Midnight*, a very violent new movie: Almost every patron was between fifty-five and eighty. The rowdy action crowd that normally turns up to urge on the rapists and the slashers went instead to *Psycho II* and *Mausoleum*, forsaking *10 to Midnight* at least temporarily. *10 to Midnight*—a meaningless title, incidentally—varies only slightly a theme raised in Bronson's *Death Wish* and reiterated in his *Death Wish II*....[I]t worms its way through the route of all exploitation action movies, becoming unnecessarily explicit....Interestingly, the predominately older audience watched it in silence that is rare in any movie house today, much less Downtown. No cheering. No chattering. No epithets. Just an occasional groan at gruesome violence that was pitched at a more antisocial group the movie didn't draw anyway." *People*: "Surprisingly, this film creates a taut, suspenseful game of psychotic cat-and-mouse and even steps aside to comment on the loopholes in our legal system....Bronson skillfully underplays....Davis brings the countenance of a schoolboy to his vengeful character."

The final American gross for *10 to Midnight* was $7.2 million, less than half of what *Death Wish II* had collected the previous year, but that prior Cannon film had been distributed by the more-experienced marketing team at Filmways with a heavier advertising budget. *10 to Midnight* was yet another huge hit with Bronson's foreign fans, if not with the overseas critics. Eric Braun, *British Films:* "The film to me represents one more horror for the headman's axe....Never has Bronson's limitations as an actor been more apparent; a puffy scowl is all he can muster to cover every emotion." *Sydney* [Australia] *Morning Herald*: "*10 *to Midnight* offers the entertainment of ultra-violence....It's somewhat depressing to observe that these violent sagas are generally accompanied by whoops and cheers from the loyal Bronson audience, which obviously identifies with such blood-lusting solutions to life's injustices."

Golan and Globus tapped into the then-exploding cable TV and video rental markets. Cannon collected $12 million from MGM/UA Home Video in 1983 by selling home video rights to *10 to Midnight* and other titles. The Bronson film was sold to American pay-TV for $2.5 million. It was, by far, Cannon's biggest television sale of the year. *10 to Midnight* was ignored by most young males when the picture was in theaters and video shops, but once the movie hit HBO and other pay channels, teens caught the picture and rushed to rent the tape and rewatch the movie.

Spanish lobby card: Gene Davis wore briefs for promotional stills and the TV version.

Prior to producing and distributing Bronson films, Cannon mogul Menahem Golan had been a longtime fan of the star. Golan says,

"[Bronson] was a crowd puller and 'cool' in his action. He was cold like a fish. He would wait in his trailer or cabin until he was called to a scene, and then did his lines to perfection. He was a pleasure for any director to work with him. There were never any disagreements with him. He was an excellent listener, spoke very little, and I enjoyed his coolness. He was a friend." The relationship would continue for another seven movies.

Davis: "My wife and I went to Jill's birthday party after *10 to Midnight*. I was friends with Jill. We had something in common. I used to show 'hunters and jumpers,' and she was into horses. I was very, very close with J. Lee even after *10 to Midnight*. J. Lee became the godfather of my daughter." Davis would work with Thompson and Bronson again on Cannon's *Messenger of Death* (1988).

Lyons: "After *10 to Midnight*, Bronson had a Christmas party at his house, and I was invited. A very selective group of people were there. Bronson's house was beautiful. He knew who he was in this business. He knew he was 'Charles Bronson, film star.' He was just cool about it. J. Lee was at the party and treated me very nicely and said, 'You're part of the group now.' I took that as being very special." The actor was later in the Bronson/Thompson/Cannon movie *Murphy's Law* (1986).

Davis: "[*10 to Midnight*] was actually quite successful with the Bronson fans—that community loved it. I was recognized by people. I remember going to New York, and some guy walked up behind me and started quoting the lines. That was kind of creepy. Occasionally, I'll run into someone that will have seen [*10 to Midnight*]. It's usually someone that's older and was a Bronson fan. They show it on TV a lot. It's sort of a cult film."

---

(1) Stevens' recollections of working on *10 to Midnight* are in the foreword of *Bronson's Loose! The Making of the 'Death Wish' Films*.
(2) This London killer, nicknamed "Jack the Stripper," murdered six women from 1964–1965 and was never captured.

Chapter 11
The Evil That Men Do (1984)

The poster screamed: "Most criminals answer to the law. The world's most savage executioner must answer to Bronson." Charles Bronson's name on a marquee was always a guarantee of unchained action. When *The Evil That Men Do* opened, fans were hit with the expected violence—but this time they were also assaulted with thick layers of sadism, sleaze and depravity.

While looking for Bronson material, Pancho Kohner, producer of four of the star's previous movies, discovered an action novel called *The Evil That Men Do*. Published in November of 1978 by Times Books, *The Evil That Men Do* dealt with an assassin named Holland, who travels to Guatemala to take out Clement Moloch, a.k.a. "the Doctor"—a feared torturer described as "one of the most hideously depraved men

Charles Bronson as the sadistic assassin Holland in *The Evil That Men Do* (1984).

in all the darkest ranks of history...a man who stood in blood to the ankles." *Kirkus Reviews*: "A frightening, razor-slice thriller that holds the reader hostage until the last shuddering climax." Author R. Lance Hill's previous novel, *King of White Lady* (1975), which was about a cocaine dealer, was optioned several times by movie producers, but was never filmed. In 1980, a partnership made up of Kohner, Bronson, Jill Ireland (Bronson's actress wife), and director J. Lee Thompson was formed to purchase the screen rights. The cost of acquiring the book and a first draft screenplay by novelist Hill was $200,000.

Kohner presented the *Evil That Men Do* package to Menahem Golan and Yoram Globus at Cannon Films. The duo had just had their first big, international hit with *Death Wish II* (1982), and they wanted another Bronson picture immediately. When Kohner and Golan couldn't come to terms on *The Evil That Men Do*, that project was set aside while

Bronson, Kohner and Thompson made the thriller *10 to Midnight* (1983) for Cannon.

As *10 to Midnight* was being shot in late 1982, Kohner took *The Evil That Men Do* to the British-based ITC Entertainment where Bronson had one film left on a three-picture deal that had been set up when that company was run by mogul Lew Grade. *Love and Bullets* (1979) and *Borderline* (1980) were the earlier movies. Grade had recently been forced out of ITC after clashing with the new chairman, but he continued to produce films, television and stage shows until his death in 1998.

Bronson's ITC contract was a "pay-or-play" deal, meaning he would collect a fee by a certain date even if the third movie wasn't made. He had passed on numerous scripts presented by ITC, and the deadline for the "pay-or-play" was approaching fast. Bronson didn't want to take money without making a film, so ITC agreed that *The Evil That Men Do* could be the last movie in the deal and granted a budget of $4.6 million (which included the star's $1 million fee). Some earlier reports claimed that the Bronson contract was for four pictures, but he made no further movies for ITC. (In 1977 Grade had announced that he would finance Bronson's autobiographical *Dollar Ninety-Eight*—about life in a Depression-era mining town—but that film was never made by any company.) Lance Hool, who had already produced *Cabo Blanco* (1980) and *10 to Midnight* with Kohner, was brought on as executive producer of *The Evil That Men Do*.

R. Lance Hill's script was turned over for revisions to John Crowther, writer of the martial arts movie *Kill and Kill Again* (1981). Crowther says, "I had worked on another Bronson picture as a writer—I wasn't credited, but I was the final writer on location in Switzerland on *Love and Bullets*. I was casting director on *10 to Midnight*. Pancho had spoken with me a year earlier about planning [*The Evil That Men Do*] and said he would have me do the rewrite. It was fairly clear that [Hill] was not a screenwriter. He just made a screenplay out of a novel. There were things in [Hill's script] that weren't cinematic. It didn't make good action, it didn't make good visuals. It just didn't work as a movie. Pancho, Lance Hool, and I knew that this really needed a major, major rewrite—going back to the book and starting over. Pancho told [ITC] that they were bringing me on to rewrite [Hill's] script, which was really not true. [laughs] I wasn't really rewriting his script—I really went right back to the novel. They hired me on a weekly contract, thinking that it would take two or three weeks and I'd be finished. This all started in '82 in the fall. One of the things that I knew from the very beginning when I read the book was that there were holes of logic in it that you could drive trucks through. The premise is nonsense. It's ridiculous. 'The Doctor' has better security than the Israeli Mossad—it says so in the book. It's just impossible to get to 'the Doctor.' But the security for 'the Doctor' couldn't be more ridiculous. He's got these three 'lame-os' doing his security and this crappy video surveillance. [laughs] So the challenge was to just keep it going so fast that nobody would notice. I had to keep it moving and at such a fast pace that nobody would turn around and say, 'But wait a minute, that can't be.'"

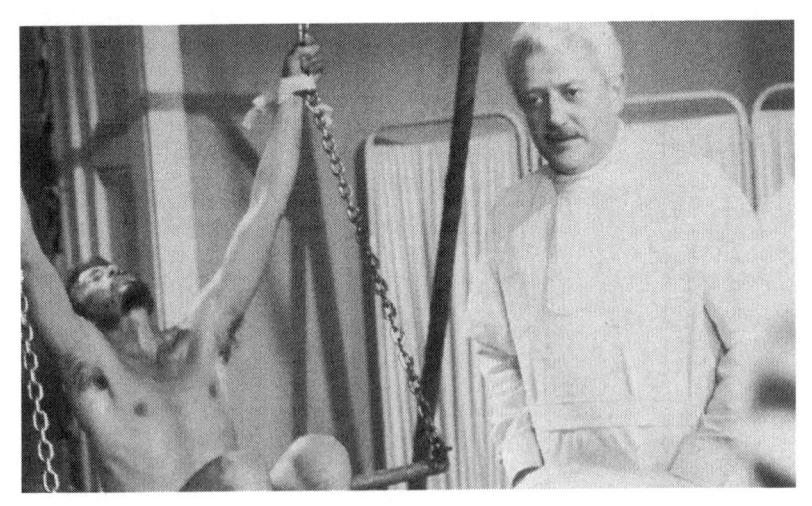

Journalist George Hidalgo (Jorge Zepeda) is fatally abused by Dr. Clement Molloch (Joseph Maher). This sequence was heavily-censored in England and other territories.

Several of the novel's minor characters, like Moloch's wife, were cut from the script. Also dropped were a number of vignettes, including: Moloch's surreal dream of being tortured in a concentration camp by Josef Mengele; the heroine disguising as a man; and Holland torturing the Doctor's sister to death.

J. Lee Thompson was originally attached as the director of *The Evil That Men Do*. Crowther: "J. Lee, at that point, couldn't do it because he was finishing up *10 to Midnight*—the editing and post-production." (*10 to Midnight* was to be released March 1983.)

Kohner turned to Fielder Cook, an Emmy-winning director of dozens of TV movies and episodes as well as a few small features, including *A Big Hand for the Little Lady* (1965). Crowther: "Pancho liked Fielder's work, and they talked about working together one day. It was a ridiculous choice. Fielder had absolutely zero experience with action. [On] Thanksgiving morning [1982], Pancho, Lance and myself met with Fielder Cook, and that was our first indication that things might be problematic because we were talking about the script, and it became painfully obvious that Fielder had not read the novel. [laughs] He had it with him, but he hadn't read it at all. He was really tap-dancing all over the place. He was winging that meeting, and we knew it. After he left, we all looked at each other and said, 'Oh, man. We're in trouble.' [laughs] Fielder had a [writer] friend, who had worked with him before, and he wanted me off the film and the friend on. I had an office at ITC. In the same building where I was working, they were interviewing [other] writers. It came time for Christmas break, and Fielder went home and, on his own, started working on a draft. And he made the huge mistake of turning that draft in to Pancho. We all looked at it and went, 'This is just *awful*.' It started off with pages of dialogue between 'the Doctor' and his sister talking about martinis. [laughs] It was impossible. I went to Pancho and said, 'You do what you want to do, but you're crazy if you don't get rid of him.' Pancho said, 'I'm not gonna get rid of him, but I'll tell him that he has absolutely nothing to do with the script.' Pancho thought that if he told him this, Fielder would quit—which any self-respecting director would do. But Fielder was desperate to do this movie. So he was cut out of the [writing] process from early on. Because it was a major rewrite, it just kept on and on and on, week-after-week."

The hooded Dr. Molloch (Joseph Maher) holds a torture seminar.

Jill Ireland served as the film's associate producer under her new production company, Zuleika Farms, named after the Vermont estate she shared with Bronson. (Zuleika was also the name of the couple's daughter.) Ireland said, "I found that after all my years in the business I knew what I was doing. It's exciting putting talent together and seeing it through. I like to be there and supervise every part of it. I took a different view about money and how it was spent. Also I was able to be helpful, because from the other side of the camera you see things that shouldn't go on, but you don't necessarily do anything about it. I had that experience of knowing where money had been spent when it shouldn't." Ireland's duties on *The Evil That Men Do* involved the casting. She wrote in a memoir: "As associate producer, I was introduced to Hilary Holden, an

Englishwoman who was the casting director. Hilary and I got along like a house afire. For two months we worked side by side, brown-bagging our lunches." (Holden had cast *Love and Bullets*.)

Early announcements for *The Evil That Men Do* reported that Ireland (who had already co-starred in many of her husband's films) would be playing the female lead, Rhiana—described in the book as half Swiss-Italian/half Latino, but Ireland decided that another actress was better-suited to the role. She wrote: "Theresa [Saldana] had been a special project of Hilary's and mine. We felt we had rediscovered her by fighting to have her cast in *The Evil That Men Do* after she had been brutally attacked and slashed on a Los Angeles street." On March 15, 1982, the young actress (*I Wanna Hold Your Hand*, 1978; *Raging Bull*, 1980) was stabbed ten times by a deranged stalker. She spent four months in a hospital and almost died. Ireland convinced Kohner to cast Saldana. Crowther: "That's consistent with Jill. She was such a nice lady."

Before accepting the role, Saldana discussed the brutally violent script with her support group. She said, "One of the saving graces is that the woman I portray is a nonviolent person." The actress did several of her own (minor) stunts in the film. "They thought I was too fragile," she said. "I'm feeling better than ever, and I desperately wanted to do my own stunts to show everyone I'm fine."

The cast and crew went to Mexico in early March, 1983. Crowther: "They saved a lot of money by shooting everything in Mexico. There was nothing on a sound stage; everything was actual location. Lance was experienced in Mexico." Hool was born in that country, and his previous productions *Survival Run* (1979) and *Cabo Blanco* were shot there. Producers Hool and Kohner were on set for the entire shoot. Ireland stayed on location for the whole production with Bronson and their six children. She got her good friend Alan Marshall a job as the makeup artist.

Crowther: "I, presumably, was finished [with the script] when everybody left for Mexico. Then they needed me in Mexico—the idea being that I would just do a little bit of rewriting down there and come back. That was actually the first film I worked on with a computer. We did take it to Mexico, [but] the power was just so [weak] down there, it just went out. In Mexico, it became painfully obvious after about a week or so that Fielder was really not up to this. Fielder was trying to get his [writer] friend on the movie again, and he was fiddling with the shooting schedule so that all of the action would be at the end of the shoot. He was terrified of it. We all got very nervous. He was spending a lot of time down there interviewing women to do his laundry. He had a huge trunk shipped down there filled with his cooking things. And any director who thinks he's gonna be cooking while he's shooting a Bronson picture really doesn't know what's going on. And Charlie would have just eaten him alive. Charlie had no patience for somebody who didn't know what they were doing. [laughs] He was a great guy, but he could be evil if you didn't know what you were doing. Pancho had come back up to L.A. and I went to Lance and said, 'Lance, you guys are crazy. You gotta get rid of him. Because if he stays on this picture, you're gonna get halfway into it and it's not gonna be working, and then you're gonna be really stuck.' So when Pancho got back, he and Lance and I sat down and we talked it through over a weekend. And at the end of it, Pancho called in Fielder and fired him. And in the meantime, had gotten in touch with J. Lee and said, 'J. Lee, we're in trouble down here. You gotta just drop everything and get down here and shoot the picture.'

"It was hysterical. We all met J. Lee at the airport with a mariachi band. [laughs] When he arrived, just three or four days before the shoot started, he said to me, 'John, you gotta stay here with me right through the thing. Because I'm gonna want changes regularly. And you gotta walk me through the script day-by-day and tell me what's going on.' [laughs] J. Lee was brilliant, and his ideas and his changes and where he wanted to go with it were just dead on. ITC were very antsy about my staying down in Mexico. They kept sending frantic messages saying, 'When is the writer coming home?' Not only was I still being paid by the week, but I was getting my hotel and expenses. But J. Lee put his foot down, and he said to me, 'You are not leaving here until the last day of shooting. You're not leaving the set until I do.' [laughs]" Thompson was seventy at the time. *The Evil That Men Do* was his forty-first film as a director and his fifth starring Bronson.

Bisexual henchman Whitley (Raymond St. Jacques).

Kohner says, "[Thompson] was so efficient that he would get twenty, twenty-five set-ups in a day. He started out as an editor. He knew exactly what he wanted. He knew exactly what angles, what shots. Lee knew exactly what shots he needed to put together the film. The whole crew appreciated when the director didn't make them work over and over getting the same shot from different angles. The crew and the actors know [when] the director is obviously going to direct the film in the editing room. Lee didn't need to do that at all. He was just a terrific filmmaker. So it all worked just fine, and Charlie mellowed out. [Bronson] had a lot of respect for Lee."

Bronson once said, "I avoid a director if he takes too long because I get paid the same if it takes ten weeks to make a picture as I do if it takes two years."

Crowther: "[Thompson] walked on a set very prepared. I don't know how he did on other movies, where he'd have more time to prepare, but on this one he didn't work from a storyboard. I sat down with him after shooting every day to go over the next day's shooting—not the shots, just the continuity. Because he came into it so fast, he had to be reminded what came before, what was going to come after, how things fit together. He had little pieces of paper, and he'd scribble things. He was such fun. I used to call him 'Lee T.' because he looked like 'E.T.' He looked like this little alien creature, and he had this very funny little English voice. Very prissy. [laughs] He was the total antithesis of Charlie, and they got along *famously*. They really worked well together.

"Charlie had a contract that said that he worked eight hours—period. He would not go overtime at all. He wanted to be with the family. He was such a professional that you got eight hours' *work* out of Charlie. He never had a problem with lines; he always was on his marks; he really knew what he was doing. Almost always on a set when you have a major star, and he has off-screen lines—in other words, it's somebody else's close-up—that star will just stand off-camera and just deliver the lines. Or they're in their trailer, and the continuity person will do the off-screen lines. Charlie always would be there right next to the camera, not only doing his lines but giving a performance. He never cheated a second. That was the coal miner ethos: You were paid for a day's work; you *did* a day's work. Early on, through the writing process [Bronson] didn't have anything to do with [the script] at all. [During production], he would come back with changes or he would have questions, little things. I had a thing in the script where he said, 'My name is Smith. Bart Smith,' and Charlie just guffawed and said, 'God, this isn't James Bond. What are you doing that for?' [laughs] He had an amazing ear for cliché. Charlie knew his stuff. He didn't want to do the car chase. He had grown to hate car chases, but he did it. When we shot the stuff at his [character's] home—

The Evil That Men Do (1984)

which was actually John Huston's place in Puerta Vallarta—it was the last thing we shot." (Huston once described the retreat: "The whales sail past, and the dolphins, and the manta rays leap out of the water, and I look on in fascination, just as a kid would.")

Holland (Bronson) kidnaps Claire Molloch (Antoinette Bower).

Crowther: "You could only reach it by pongas, these little open boats. That scene where he's looking at tapes, Charlie didn't like what was in the script, and he wanted it changed. J. Lee wanted it the original way, and I was in the middle of the two, trying to be a good craftsman. It was probably a half-hour discussion. Finally, because we were losing time, J. Lee said to Charlie, 'If John sits down and writes it right now, will you shoot it both ways?' And Charlie said, 'Yes.' And we shot it both ways. Most actors who didn't like one version would sabotage it. They wouldn't *act* it. But Charlie acted them both, full on. He was terrific in both of them. It just wasn't in his DNA to cheat. The version that J. Lee and I wanted, the original version, was the one that stayed in the movie."

Cast as "the Doctor" was the distinguished, Tony-nominated Irish actor Joseph Maher (*Time After Time*, 1979). Just as the character was described in the novel, Maher had pink skin and "a cradle of dense white hair." Crowther: "Interesting choice for the role. [His performance is] really over the top, but it works in the movie because everything has to be larger than life to sell that premise." Raymond St. Jacques (*Cotton Comes to Harlem*, 1970) played a bisexual henchman, described in the book as "a giant man…able to intimidate by sight alone." Crowther: "We did not hire Ray St. Jacques until we were down in Mexico and I suggested him. It wasn't written as an African American. I had known him a number of years before in New York. I thought he had the right kind of threat to him. When he got down there, he said to me, 'You wanna know something? It's the first time I've ever been hired to play a role that wasn't written as a black man.'" Oscar-winner Jose Ferrer (*Cyrano de Bergerac*, 1950) and then-popular TV actor René Enríquez (*Hill Street Blues*, 1981–1987) added prestige as good guys.

When Bronson's first two ITC movies were being made, then-head Lew Grade instructed the filmmakers to deliver a product suitable for a PG rating/family audience, but for *The Evil That Men Do* there were no restraints. Bronson may have been aging, but his movies definitely kept up with the trends in screen violence. Likewise, Thompson had no trouble with onscreen brutality—as he had demonstrated recently in his teen-slasher movie *Happy Birthday to Me* (1981) and in *10 to Midnight*. *The Evil That Men Do* is one of the more graphic and vicious films made by the star and director. Crowther: "Nobody ever asked for things to be toned down. When we were shooting the scene in the little Mexican village where the henchmen get blown away by Charlie in that little café, I remember J. Lee going, 'More blood, please. More blood.' [laughs] So [violence] wasn't a concern." Hool: "What I didn't like so much about *The Evil That Men Do* was that it was a little too bloody for me. But J. Lee loved blood. [laughs] He went around with a cup of 'blood' in his hand throwing more 'blood' at stuff. [laughs]"

The Evil That Men Do (1984)

The enormous, acromegaly-afflicted Mexican actor Miguel Angel Fuentes (*Fitzcarraldo*, 1979) was paired with Bronson for one of the more gripping fight scenes in the star's filmography. As described in the novel: "The fabric of the ladino's pants and the pouchy sac beneath were wrung through Holland's clamped fingers."

Holland (Bronson) and Rhiana (Theresa Saldana) flee.

The brutality of the action was matched by the sleaziness of the characters. At one point, Bronson's character passes himself off as a bisexual wife swapper. Crowther: "[That scene] was not in the version that we started shooting with. It's not in the book. I never in a million years expected Charlie to do it. I thought he would look at it and say, 'What? Are you crazy?' [laughs] But I wrote it because I thought that the idea of Charlie Bronson picking up a guy was too good to be true. And he loved it. He went for it with gusto. [laughs]" In the novel, Holland hides under a bed while the female villain has sex with a man. In the movie, the tryst is between two women. Crowther: "I changed it. I just thought it would be way more interesting. I just thought it somehow made more sense for her character, that really strange character. When I was coming up with stuff like that, nobody fought with me."

The film's sadistic climax, where "the Doctor" is attacked by a mob of his disfigured victims, is far more satisfying and effective than the ending in the book—where Moloch is blasted with a shotgun by Rhiana, shot in the chest by Holland's revolver, then hanged by his feet and bled. Crowther: "We didn't have an ending. That was troubling us all along—how to end it. I was the one who came up with the idea of having the natives, the miners, getting him. But it was out of desperation. It was like, 'We gotta go with this or we don't have an ending.' And it was a pretty radical idea because it's almost unheard of that an amazing, invulnerable hero has to be saved. And Charlie can't do it at the end of that movie—he has to be saved by the natives. I was on the set writing the ending. [laughs] I was sitting in Pancho's motor home writing the scene and handing [pages] out the window to the assistant director, in carbon copies. We shot that scene at a real mine outside Guadalajara, almost an hour's drive up in the hills—really remote."

The six-week production ended in mid-May 1983. Crowther: "It was a great shoot. It was a party the whole time. Sets generally are fun and happy, but you always have the tough times. There was never a tough time on this movie."

Ireland wrote: "When I returned, filming completed, Hilary and I decided to open a production office. We had dinner and spent the evening planning, designing our office, and discussing books that might make good film properties." The partnership ended suddenly when Hilary Holden died of a heart attack on May 13, 1983, at the age of forty-six. She was a single mother and left behind a fifteen-year-old daughter, Katrina. Hool: "It was four o'clock in the morning. [Bronson] and Jill were down there within an hour, and we asked, 'Well, what about Katrina?' Pancho said, 'Well, I'll take her home with me.' [Bronson] said, 'Oh, Pancho. You're just a bachelor.' I said, 'Charlie, I'll take her in.' He said, 'No, you've got your two little kids. We'll take her.' That's the way he was. She was a daughter to Charlie." Under the name Katrina Holden Bronson, she later became an actress and director.

The Evil That Men Do turned out to be a typically efficient action effort from Thompson, with extensive use of the Steadicam, a game (and well-dressed) Bronson, and no less than seventeen graphic onscreen deaths (the star kills eleven). Methods of destruction include: choking, knife-tossing, bullets in the head, shotgun blasts, hanging by fire hose, and testicular electrocution.

The screenplay was credited to David Lee Henry (the screen pseudonym of novelist R. Lance Hill) and John Crowther. The latter says, "My version was changed so much from [Hill's] draft that I felt that I did have a good case to have sole credit. It's helpful in terms of credit, but it's also helpful in terms of money. If you get sole credit, you get all of the residuals. It went to Writers Guild arbitration, and they ruled against me. That almost always happens when a novelist has adapted his own book for the first draft. The act of creating the original characters gives a lot of weight." Hill, as David Lee Henry, went on to rewrite Oliver Stone's draft for *8 Million Ways to Die* (1986). His original screenplays include the action classic *Road House* (1989) and the Steven Segal hit *Out for Justice* (1991).

Holland (Bronson) confronts some henchmen in a café.

By the time *The Evil That Men Do* was ready for release, Associated Film Distribution (AFD), the American distribution arm of ITC that had released the company's previous Bronson pictures, was defunct. In March of 1984, TriStar Pictures—a recently-formed subsidiary of Columbia Pictures—acquired North American distribution rights to *The Evil That Men Do*. (They also picked up ITC's *The Muppets Take Manhattan* and *Where the Boys Are*.) Hool: "*The Evil That Men Do* was one of the five original movies that TriStar was put together for." ITC handled distribution for the rest of the world. The new Bronson movie opened on March 15 in France, in other parts of Europe in the middle of the year, and in London in June.

Movie tie-in paperback.

TriStar released *The Evil That Men Do* in the United States on September 23, 1984, with a saturation run in 1,464 theaters. Never again would a Bronson picture open in so many venues at once. Surprisingly, the movie received an R-rating from the MPAA and wasn't threatened with an X. (The gore in Thompson's *Happy Birthday to Me* had to be trimmed for an R.) At the time, the MPAA was very strict on graphic violence and full-frontal nudity—and *The Evil That Men Do* contains both. The United States Catholic Conference gave the film an "O" (morally offensive) tag. TriStar's *The Evil That Men Do* trailer played like a promo for a *Death Wish* sequel. ("When the system of justice doesn't work, Bronson does! When the courts can't do what they must, Bronson will!") A month earlier, the novel was reprinted as a paperback tie-in with the star's image on the cover. The book had gained a cult following, and some readers were unhappy with the casting—Holland is thirty-three in the novel; Bronson was sixty-one when he played the character.

The New York Times: "audiences show up simply to watch [Bronson] kill.... There was plenty of audience participation at the theater. Crowd favorites, in addition to the electrode sequence, were a barroom scene in which Mr. Bronson inflicts an unspeakable form of pain on an enemy, and another scene in which he shoots off someone's head." *Variety*: "An assembly-line Charles Bronson pic." *Milwaukee Sentinel*: "just an excuse for Bronson to coolly go about blowing people's heads off...[b]ut if you like Bronson, and enjoy seeing people tortured with electrodes, this movie will probably please you." *Ottawa Citizen*: "Bronson still hasn't learned to act." *Evening Independent* (St. Petersburg, FL): "*The Evil That Men Do*, indeed is an ironic title, for Thompson's direction is so clumsy and false, Bronson's performance so mechanical and uneventful, they are the ones who stand guilty of evil—the evil of committing unforgiveable movie-making sins, one after another, for an odious hour and a half." *Montreal Gazette*: "This film glorifies in violence and gore. That automatically guarantees a huge audience full of the sort of people who get a kick out of picking wings off flies." *The Vindicator* (Youngstown, OH): "This film is for the sadistic at heart. It could well have been written by the Marquis de Sade himself." *Beaver County Times* (Beaver, PA): "*The Evil That Men Do* is a form of unbearable cinematic torture."

Naturally, this Bronson programmer was critic-proof. It opened at number two at the American box office and collected $4.5 million in its first week. (*Tightrope*, the latest from fellow action star Clint Eastwood, had opened at number one the previous week with $9.1 million.) The target audience apparently agreed with the underground fanzine *Gore Gazette*: "Bronson has always been revered by sleazemongers who can count on him to consistently deliver....[The movie has] some of the sickest killings and maiming depicted in a major Hollywood release to date....Gorehounds will howl with glee....A must-see for fans of truly depraved cinema."

While the film was in release in the States, the Bronson family vacationed in Hawaii. Then-waitress Christina Gere says, "In 1984, I was working at the Kapalua Bay hotel in Maui. That was the chic hotel where all the movie stars would stay. All the guys working at the hotel, from the busboys to the bellboys to the waiters, were *so* excited that Charles Bronson was there because he was such a tough guy. He was married to Jill Ireland. They had kids. It was like four, five, six kids altogether. Big family. I was the cocktail waitress for the lobby bar, and they'd come and have a drink in the afternoon. If he had one Coke, he'd give you a dollar. If he had twenty Cokes and twenty Mai Tais, he'd give you a dollar. No matter what the bill would come to, he would only give you a dollar tip. He was grumpy the whole time, and his wife couldn't have been sweeter, more wonderful, more gracious. She was the opposite of him. He was nothing like the persona. A lot of movie stars came to that hotel, and pretty much every single one of them was shorter than what you thought they were—by a landslide. These tiny little guys had these huge personalities on film as being big and tough, but they were wimpy.

"A couple of the hotels had their own private beach, and you'd push this little hot dog cart down to the beach [so] people could get sodas and snacks. I'm so excited 'cause I'm thinking, 'I'm gonna get to talk to all the movie stars that are hanging out at the beach.' And here comes Charles Bronson, and all he wants is an apple. So I said, 'The apple coasts a dollar if you pay me cash. If you want to charge it to your room, it costs $2 for the convenience.' He flew into this tirade; he's having a total meltdown, freaking out on me, making my life miserable—like I'm personally charging this poor sucker an extra dollar for this apple. Then finally, his wife comes up and rescues me. She starts screaming and yelling at him, telling him that she's had it, he does this every time they're on vacation, he always has to make a scene, and he's harassing this poor girl. She was a saint being married to him."

The final gross in the States for *The Evil That Men Do* was a respectable $13.1 million. The two previous Bronson/ITC pictures, *Love and Bullets* and *Borderline*, had each grossed less than a fourth of that total. *Death Wish II* and *Death Wish 3* (1985) were the only Bronson movies of the 1980s to make more money at American theaters than *The Evil That Men Do*. Hool: "A lot of people criticize this period of Charles Bronson and say that there were no good movies. I disagree. You gotta take it in the context of the budgets and how the movies were marketed. *The Evil That Men Do* was not an expensive movie. I thought [Bronson] was very good in *The Evil That Men Do*."

Prints of *The Evil That Men Do* that were released in some countries, like the United Kingdom and Germany, had less violence than the cut seen in the States. Stronger versions were released in Japan and Spain with: more blood spurting from Raymond St. Jacques's throat wound; an additional bodily shotgun blast in the café scene; and extra gore splashing on the faces of the miners at the climax.

The film was released on American VHS and Beta cassettes in April 1985 by Columbia Home Video. An *Evil That Men Do* "shelf talker" for video stores also promoted the trio of earlier Bronson movies available from Columbia. The movie played pay-TV later that year. Older Bronson followers had their interest in the star rekindled by seeing his current entries on the small screen. Younger viewers first became fans by watching the legend's new, ultra-violent pictures at home.

Promotional slick for the American home video release.

After *The Evil That Men Do,* John Crowther occasionally ran into Bronson, but he never wrote any other scripts for the star. He did work for producer Lance Hool again as a writer on the Cannon Films/Chuck Norris movie *Missing in Action* (1984). Crowther: "One of my favorite stories is about *Missing in Action*. I did my first outline of it and went in to pitch it to Menahem [Golan]. I started pitching it to him, and I said, 'He gets out of the prison camp and comes back to the United States, and this happens, this happens and this happens to him. And he goes into this bar and gets into this huge fight.' And Menahem stopped me at that point and says, 'What page?' And I said, 'This will be about page nine or ten.' He said, 'Make it page two.' And then he said, 'Okay, fine. The rest of it is fine.' He didn't even want to hear the rest of the story. All he wanted to know was what page the first fight was on. [laughs]" Crowther was casting director on the simultaneously shot *Missing in Action 2: The Beginning* (1985) and later wrote the action movies *The Wild Pair* (1987) and *The Damned River* (1989). Today, he devotes his time to painting, cartooning, and exhibiting his artwork. Looking back on *The Evil That Men Do*, he says, "I still get residuals. It continues to make money all over the world. I think most people like it better than I do. I think it's good because it accomplished what it needed to accomplish—it obscures the fact that it's a ridiculous premise. [laughs]"

Hool: "[Bronson and I] were able to do [three] good movies and would have done more if I hadn't had my Cannon fallout. [Bronson's agent], for whatever his reasons were, kept signing him to Cannon deals, and Cannon and I had a big falling out. I owned a big chunk of *Missing in Action,* and they wanted me to keep making movies, but they weren't paying me. [laughs] Then they stole credits and changed credits. I was the producer of *Missing in Action.* It was my story; it was my script. All of a sudden, [Golan and Globus] were the producers, and I was the executive producer and somebody else was the writer. It was discombobulated. So I had to sue them, and I didn't work with Cannon anymore. It was a lawsuit that took seven years. I finally beat 'em, but they were not good people, and I didn't want to work there. [Bronson] was in a contract to do movies for Cannon Films. He had to make movies for them. He never wanted to do *Death Wish II* or *3*. He really didn't want to do those movies. I think he was coerced, in a way. Charlie was not one of those stars—like we see more and more of today—who develop their own production company and their own films. He relied on his agents to bring things to him. I think it was a convenient move to sign him for a long-term contract. So they were always scrambling to find projects that would satisfy 'the model' rather than [asking] 'is the movie any good?' There's a big difference when you say, 'We gotta make this picture for "X," and you've got forty-days to shoot' versus 'This is a great story. We gotta make this happen.' There's a *huge* difference."

Hool developed a number of Bronson projects that were never made, including the star's pet project *Dollar Ninety-Eight*. "There was a bunch. I wanted to do Joseph Conrad's *Victory* [1915] with Charlie in space. [laughs] Perfect for Charlie. And he *loved* the idea. That's one that we were both very sorry that we didn't get to do. There was one that Pancho and I were working on—*Whistling Death*, which was a good one. There's a guy that takes an airplane, an old war bird, and he starts shooting people. He goes and hides in the desert, and Bronson has to get him. We were always looking at two-act plays for Charlie. Act one: they push him, push him, push him; Act two: he gets revenge. But they were fresh ideas, not the same tired *Death Wish 14*.

"Another one was *The Cowboy and the Cossack*. I still can't believe that I didn't get to make that movie with Charlie. It was written by Clair Huffaker. In the late 1870s, a cowboy's ranch is going under, and Russia is having a shortage of food, so they buy his whole heard of cattle. The cowboy puts the cattle on a ship and takes it to Vladivostock. Meeting him on the shore is the head of the Cossacks, and they are immediately at locks with each other. The cattle have to swim to the shore. [Then there is a] cattle drive to Moscow. It's a tremendous, tremendous screenplay that takes the two men all across Russia. Charlie wanted to do it. The concept, originally, was to have [Bronson] and Clint [Eastwood]—the two of them together. Cannon came to me and said, 'Why don't you make it with Charlie and Chuck Norris?' And I'm like, 'No. No.' [laughs]" Hool's later films included the excellent *Man on Fire* (2004), with Denzel Washington as a vengeful ex-assassin. "*Man on Fire* has a lot of *Evil That Men Do* in it—only a different star, different time. It has all of the elements that we had in *The Evil That Men Do*."

The Evil That Men Do turned out to be Bronson's only feature of the 1980s that was not made for Cannon Films. After his next film, Cannon's *Death Wish 3*, Bronson signed a consecutive pair of exclusive, lucrative, multi-picture contracts with Golan and Globus that forbade him to make movies for anyone else. The *Variety* review for *The Evil That Men Do* noted: "Only question that remains is how long Bronson can continue to milk this formula." The answer was: six more pictures in the next five years.

Kirk Taylor and Charles Bronson meet for the first time on the set of *Death Wish 3* (1985). (Photo courtesy of Kirk Taylor)

Chapter 12
The Giggler Lives:
Interview with actor Kirk Taylor
on *Death Wish 3*

The fast running, knife-wielding, purse-snatching creep "the Giggler" from *Death Wish 3* (1985) is one of the more-beloved screen villains of the 1980s. The wacky gang member has some hilarious bits in the first half of the surreal film and his death scene at the hands of Charles Bronson as vigilante Paul Kersey is a highlight—it always brings out delighted cheers and guffaws from the audience. Kirk Taylor's performance in the role coupled with the character's odd clothing and makeup have secured "the Giggler" a permanent place in cult/action cinema history.

Taylor was a young New York stage actor and student when he got his first movie gig (as a waiter) in Francis Coppola's *The Cotton Club* (1984). Featured roles in two other New York-shot features led to his

"Giggler" audition. His post-*Death Wish 3* movies include *School Daze* (1988) and *The Bonfire of the Vanities* (1990). Taylor continues to work on stage and screen in films like *The Sum of All Fears* (2002) and *The Angriest Man in Brooklyn* (2014).

***How did you get involved with* Death Wish 3?**

I was living in New York at the time. I had done a lot of stage work and studied with Strasberg and Stella Adler and some really good teachers in New York. I had done *The Last Dragon* [1985]. I had done *Streetwalkin'* [1985]—I had got a nice part in that. It was one of Roger Corman's productions. Interesting guy. I was building some momentum and I heard about *Death Wish 3*. I don't even remember how I got into the office with Michael Winner. I wore the shirt [from *Streetwalkin'*]—a black, sleeveless t-shirt that had silver studs all around the collar and around the arm—to my audition with Michael Winner when I went in to see and talk with him. I read through some things. It wasn't much of an audition, but he liked me right away for the part of "the Giggler" and he requested that I use that shirt. I thought, "I don't want to wear the shirt from *Streetwalkin'* in *Death Wish 3*. It's not good." He designed things that were *like* that, but we didn't use the exact shirt. It was a great, fun role to do and they were gonna shoot in England, which was really exciting because I had never been to Europe. Michael Winner told me to go get a passport.

***Were you a fan of Charles Bronson before you did* Death Wish 3?**

As a kid, I grew up seeing him. He was always an intriguing character. He had such an interesting quality to him. I was always fascinated by him. He was a real he-man. I'd seen him in *The Magnificent Seven* [1960]. He was such an interesting, charismatic, brooding character. So when I had a chance to actually work with him, it was pretty exciting.

Had you seen the first two* Death Wish *movies?

I had seen both of them. It was a fascinating idea about someone who, in his mind, is trying to make things right after the loss of his family. I knew what I was getting into.

Did you do any research to prepare for* Death Wish 3*?

Yeah. *Streetwalkin'* was shot in New York, too. For *Streetwalkin','* I had gone up and spent time in the Bronx. I came from a method acting background where you do a lot of research. So I went up to the Bronx and saw and heard some pretty harrowing things. It was really dangerous. It gave me a feel for things. I'm not from that area. I'm from Connecticut. My dad's a doctor. So it was totally a different vibe. I [met] this guy "Groovy D" who was a real tough guy from up in the area. I won't say he was a hit man, but he was somebody who had done "hits" and he had spent time in jail. He showed me a style of fighting that they do in prison—"jailhouse"—and I picked it up and I used it in the [*Streetwalkin'*] fight scene. I got word back from Roger Corman that he loved the fight scene. It was a good fight scene with me and Dale Midkiff. I used some of that preparation in *Death Wish 3*.

Did you work on coming up with a distinctive giggle?

I started playing around with it. I remember thinking this is someone who is disconnected from the real consequences of what violence does and what happens in life when people hurt one another. It's kind of a Three Stooges mentality. I grew up in a generation where we watched the Three Stooges and some families in our neighborhood didn't let them watch the Three Stooges because they felt it would inspire violence—and it really did. The Three Stooges would poke one another in the eyes. I did that to my little brother, I poked him in the eyes. I remember thinking about the Giggler as this guy whose laughter was his disconnection. Like this kid who grew up in front of a television set with no one guiding him—just getting his sensibility from watching the Three Stooges [and] watching the violence that was on television. His violence came out of that sensibility. It was not him really doing harm. It was him experimenting. It added an interesting, wacky dimension to the Giggler. The pathway to *Death Wish* was doing research for *Streetwalkin'* because I had to leave pretty quickly for England, so I didn't have the same kind of research time. So I used some of the same things and ideas I had come up with [for *Streetwalkin'*] and then added the Three Stooges thing for *Death Wish*.

Were you involved with what the Giggler wore?

Yeah. We were talking about what would make him look fast. The do-rag was something that I specifically asked for. For somebody who is running, it was a great thing. It had a back draft. In movies, I had never seen anybody wearing it. I remember seeing some films afterwards where they used that. I said, "Ah, they stole that from us."

Do you recall how many weeks you shot in New York?

It was two weeks in New York and five weeks in London. We went to London and they had made a city that looked like it connected to the New York stuff. When I do my first run, you see me running [in] New York and then you see me go into a parking garage that's [in] London. I did a transcontinental run in seconds. They were really surprised at how fast I was on my feet. I was really zipping around these corners. I was running full-pace. My body was definitely not used to running like that. We were running a lot and I start getting these cramps. I got "charley horses" in my calves and in my thighs. They were dastardly. I could hardly walk. This guy, I don't know what his position was, knew about acupressure and he would take a pen or his thumb and push it into the area. And it worked. Elephant and Castle was the area I stayed in. I thought that was a fascinating title. The area was outside of London. They were only paying the extras like forty pounds a day. I'm not sure what that equated to in U.S. dollars. It was a better exchange rate in U.S. dollars. I saved all my paychecks. They said, "You better cash those checks cause you'll get more money now." I had three months of checks that I had to cash. We were a pretty tight group—Alex Winter, Tony Spiridakis, Gavan O'Herlihy.

What was Bronson like to work with?

I really liked him. It was in London [and was] one of the bigger films I did. I was really "wowed" and "doe-eyed." And it's Charles Bronson. I said [to the still photographer], "I want to take a picture with Mr.

Bronson." He said, "Well, go ask him." I went up to talk to him and he made me feel very comfortable. I said, "Hi, Mr. Bronson. I'm Kirk Taylor. Do you mind if I take a picture with you?" He said, "No. Not at all." We took the picture. It's a beautiful shot. His wife [Jill Ireland] was nearby and he said, "Jill, come over here. I want you to meet Kirk Taylor, he's playing one of the heavies." I was like, "A heavy?" That's an old term. I was the new generation coming on and he brought his persona and his skill and very graciously put a hand of fellowship out to me. It was a good feeling, that moment. He welcomed me into the fold and gave me the official film noir name of "heavy." Very cool. He was very accommodating and very open in his own quiet way, because he was not a talkative guy. I heard stories about him. On one of his films, he would just sit in the corner, staring. He would not talk. So I was a little intimated by Bronson. But as opposed to the way Michael made us feel—like on pins and needles—Bronson on the other hand, was very gracious. He introduced me to his wife—that was very personal. The overall vibe was that he was really just very cool to be around. And fun.

But I found out the hard way that he was somewhat of a germaphobe. One day, I was going home a little early because I had a cold. I was losing my voice so they sent me home. He heard that something was wrong with my throat and as I walked back to Michael Winner—I was gonna say "Goodbye"—he screams across this big expanse, "Michael! Stay away from Kirk! He's sick!" Everybody heard it. I was *shocked* and I felt like a leper. Someone pulled me aside and said, "Don't take that personally. He's really weird about germs." I stayed away from everybody after that and I went home. I guess he'd dealt with stuff before when somebody was sick. He was not taking any chances on getting sick. Michael and he would eat separately. They wouldn't eat with us. The crew and all the actors would eat in the area that they had for us. Him and Michael would go away and eat on china. They had a special chef who was cooking.

Do you recall shooting your death scene?

It was shot in New York. I'm trying not to push [Bronson]. He was an old cat, right? I'm trying to make it *look* like I'm pushing him hard. And he said, "Kirk, push me hard." I said, "Really?" He said, "Hard." And I pushed him hard and he said, "No. Harder. Push me hard." I said, "Okay, old guy." I'm pretty strong and I didn't want to hurt him, but I pushed him way harder than I would have and he bounced into the fence. He was in really good shape. He wanted it to be realistically physical. He didn't want to have to act it. He wanted to get slammed so that he had an obstacle to work against.

The .475 Wildey, that's the gun. It had never been seen before. The guy that actually invented it was there. The guy showed me the gun and said, "This is being introduced in this film." Bronson had to get that long gun out of his coat. Have you ever seen a longer gun come from under a coat? It fires a modified rifle cartridge. It's got a piston action. This thing would have made a monster hole going in and then a bigger hole going out. One thing that comes to mind was how much that death scene affected me. They put the bulletproof vest on me. It made me a little suspicious. I was like, "Why do I need a bulletproof vest? Is this dangerous?" Then they put a metal plate on top of the vest. It was right on my spine. They put a plate, bulletproof vest, five blood packs, and five charges. They had a wire up my leg. When I ran, they touched the wire with a battery. It exploded and I did this tumble and then laid there still for a little while. When they took the vest off of me, it was shredded and the "blood" and "guts" were running out of it. And I got sick. I felt faint and said, "I need to sit down for a second." They had two or three vests to do it two or three times. I did a really good tumble but they had hired a stunt guy and he kicked his legs up a little higher. I liked my roll better but they ended up using his roll. Laying on that ground underneath that sheet, I *looked* dead. And I broke out so bad from that "blood" they splattered on my face. I had a bad rash after that. The woman who said, "He took my pocketbook last week" was the wife of [the New York Police Commissioner]. Her name was Olivia [Ward]. She was hilarious.

The gang-rape scene must have been difficult for the actors.

It was. I really liked Marina Sirtis. She was very skittish about doing it and she had all kinds of little things that she had to wear so certain parts wouldn't come uncovered. So I was sensitive to that. She went on to do *Star Trek* [1987–1994] and other things. I'm sure this is not a film that she's really gung-ho about remembering. [laughs] I was playing the Giggler like Baby Huey—this kid who doesn't really understand the ramifications and consequences of it. Just like kids who watch videogames, there's no connection to violence or hurting people and real pain—it's a game. I played it that way. I remember feeling bad that Marina had to go through that. It was cruel. I found a way to play it with him always laughing, always looking for the fun in it. I had one scene that was so intense that Michael Winner cut it out. We shot the scene where I broke her arm. They had the camera looking through the doorway, so you could see the faces of Gavan and Tony Spiridakis and you could see into the room as I was doing this. I went back in the room where Marina Sirtis' character is laying on the mattress after being raped. I grabbed her arm and I turned it so it looked like it broke. Her elbow suddenly went up, it looked like it snapped. And as I did it, I smacked her arm pretty hard so it actually sounded like I had broken it. It really sounded terrible. Gavan fumbled his cigarette and dropped it. And I came back out, smiling and giggling like this naïve kid, and we left. Everybody on the set was really affected by it because they didn't know what I was gonna do. I don't think Marina even knew exactly what I was gonna do. Gavan said, "That was freaky." It was a really gruesome scene. Michael Winner said that he wanted to put the scene in but they were threatening to give him an X rating just for the violence. He went up in arms and he said, "If they give us an X rating, I'm putting the scene back in." They cut it and, in a way, I felt it wasn't needed. I'm coming from the school where you don't have to show everything, you can let people use their imaginations.

Can you remember anything else that was cut out of the film?

In a sense, what got cut out of the film was me taking any real risks.

Personally, I liked Michael. He chose me for the role, so I'm very thankful to him for that. But he was a mean dude on set. He was not cool at all. I remember I was prepping, walking down the street just trying to get in the right frame of mind. We were still in New York. I had some creative things I wanted to do, with the Giggler running backwards. I wasn't sure what I was going to do but I was starting to formulate it. I was just thinking of different angles, different ways I could do things—stopping and then running. Basically, I was going to humiliate this guy Paul Kersey. "He's not gonna catch me." I could have stopped, jumped off a wall and gotten away. And [Winner] called me, I didn't hear him. He yelled at me for not hearing him. Finally, he just went, "Mr. Taylor! Your part is diminishing rapidly!" I was like, "Whoa." He screamed at me in front of the whole crew. It was loud and it was embarrassing. That's just the vibe that a director can set up on set. Some directors are "actor's directors" that make you want to do your best, they make you want to take chances. Sometimes that line between creative genius and going too far can be real close. If you go too far, you want the director to say, "Pull it back about fifty-percent." I didn't trust Michael Winner after that as a director. I liked him as a person but I didn't trust him as a director. I made a decision right then: "Okay, I won't be doing that backwards thing." I didn't want to make myself vulnerable. He was smoking cigars, he was yelling at people, he was really harsh. An overbearing parent—that's kind of like he was on set. At one point, somebody printed up a fake newspaper article saying, "Michael Winner Killed By Falling Scaffold. All 200 Crew Members Claim Responsibility"—which kind of summed up the vibe on set. He was okay but he was not someone that inspired you.

He directed [Marlon] Brando in [*The Nightcomers*, 1972]. He went to Brando and did the worst thing. He said, "Listen, you're a great actor, I'm not a great director. Let's just find a way to make this work." And Brando had no respect for him. There's a story about Michael Winner where he went into a bar and Brando was there with [Robert] Duvall and during the conversation, Brando pulled out his junk and peed on

Michael Winner. [laughs] Brando was peeing on him while they were talking and he didn't see it. I don't know if that's true or not, but that's the story I heard. Maybe that's what made him mean. I don't know.

Do you recall any other anecdotes about Winner?

Chomping on that cigar. It was hilarious because he wanted to look like the kingfish on-set. I saw a series of pictures that Michael had gone through and selected. Every shot made him look better than he really did or emphasized his control on-set. One picture was him smoking a cigar with Bronson walking behind him. It was subtle, but it was saying, "Yeah, I'm in charge on this set. Bronson walks behind me."

There was a girl on set named Sandy [Grizzle], this black girl you see in a couple scenes. Big-breasts, brown-skinned. That was Michael's girlfriend. There's a scene where you see Sandy smoking a cigarette and you see us standing behind her. She just had sex with the whole gang—that was the idea. He loved the scene. He made a big deal just laughing. And he said, "This is hilarious." At one point, I tried to talk to her. Interesting girl. I just loved that [British] accent. And she was very flirtatious. I'm sitting at a table and she's toying with me and I'm throwing it back at her. And she said, "My name is Sandy. Randy Sandy." I didn't know that in England, "randy" means "horny." I screamed, "Randy Sandy?! Your names actually match? That's amazing!" Not knowing that she meant "horny Sandy." [Winner] screamed from a window at me: "Mr. Taylor! Get back to your trailer!" After that, I left Sandy alone.

Your next movie was Full Metal Jacket [1987], which was also shot in England. Did you audition while shooting Death Wish 3?

Yeah. While I was doing *Death Wish 3* in London, I heard that Stanley Kubrick was casting *Full Metal Jacket*. I said, "That's not possible. He was casting that two years ago. I sent a tape in for it." It's been two years, but he's still casting. I called and did my best British accent. I said, "You *must* see Mr. Taylor. He's here from America. He's shooting *Death Wish 3*. You *must* see him." I convinced them that they should see Kirk Taylor. I show up and Kubrick wasn't there—it was his right hand man. They put a tape in and put a camera on me and I told a joke to Mr. Kubrick. And I read. The next day [Kubrick's assistant] says, "Stanley really likes you for the role of Alice, the main black character." I auditioned [again] for at least two roles. [The assistant] called and said, "Stanley, loved what you did. And he wants to give you the role of Alice." And Alice was this guy from New Orleans. I went to [New Orleans], took my tape recorder, was learning the accent, had some great stuff I came up with. Then a week or two before I was going to London to shoot *Full Metal Jacket*, [Kubrick's assistant] calls and says, "Stanley read over the script. He doesn't think it's going to work because he doesn't think you're black enough." I said, "No, no, no. He's Creole. I have the same mixture. I have the Indian, the black, and the European." He said, "No, I'm sorry. It's not going to work." I collapsed on my floor and wept for twenty minutes. [Later the assistant called back and] said, "Stanley loved your audition. He wants you on the film. We're letting the guy that was playing Sgt. Payback go and we're bringing you in." I felt bad about this. *Full Metal Jacket* put me in a different category as an actor because it was a pretty big deal to get into a Kubrick film. And *Death Wish* was the pathway to that.

Where did you first see Death Wish 3 and what did you think of it?

It was in New York City. When I saw it, I thought it was excessively violent—just too nutty with that level of depravity that we had as gang members. Knowing that some of that [violence] does actually exist, I felt saddened by it. Just the idea of this [Kersey] character—every time something good happens for him, something comes and takes it away. I remember being affected by that and being shocked. I thought some of it was comical, like when he was protecting that Jewish couple downstairs—he put up that board that had the spring in it and took the guy's teeth out. I was waiting and looking forward to my own death. [After] Martin Balsam said some stuff about the Giggler stabbing some girl in the skull, I remember thinking, "It's painting such a picture, man. I seriously deserve to be taken out. This guy has to die." And I was relieved when they killed him. I was like, "I really deserved that." I heard stories afterwards that Bronson was not happy about how much of a war it turned into. It was almost hyper-real. It looked like we were fighting in Beirut. I heard that Bronson didn't want Michael Winner to direct anymore of them.

Did you ever see Death Wish 3 *in a crowded theater when it first came out?*

I did. I would go sit in the back of the theater and see how people reacted to it. Even though it may not have been realistic, people really did enjoy it and there was a payoff. I made a lot of money on *Death Wish*. When I got my first residual check for *Death Wish*—it had to be, like, 1987—I hadn't gotten any real residuals. I was a pretty young actor. I didn't even understand the power of residuals. I got all this SAG [Screen Actors Guild] mail. I'm throwing stuff out and I said, "Just open it. Maybe it's something that you need to look at." I opened it up and it was a check for $5,000. *Five grand!* I almost lost my mind. I went through all my garbage. Of course, I didn't throw away any SAG mail after that.

Did you ever see Bronson again after Death Wish 3?

I never did. I regretted that. I wished I had seen him. But I had no way to directly get to him. It was hard to believe that Charles Bronson, who conquered all these criminals on screen, finally had to meet his death. My overall feeling of him is very positive and warm.

Were you ever recognized on the street for playing the Giggler?

One time, a guy on the street was staring at me. This was in the 90s. This guy's eyeballing me and I don't like it. I'm like, "Oh, man. Am I gonna have to fight with this guy?" And he walks up to me and says, "Did you play the Giggler?" I said, "What?" He says, "The Giggler, man! I just saw *Death Wish 3*! It was awesome!" It's funny and nice when someone remembers something that you've done and I had that with *Death Wish* a lot. I think the Giggler really did stand out. People really remember that character. It was pretty iconic. People still joke with me about that scene with Tony Spiradakis, where he says, "They killed the Giggler, man. They killed the Giggler!" My wife and I were sitting in *church* in Van Nuys and somebody comes up behind me and says, "They killed the Giggler, man. They killed the Giggler!" and ran out. We didn't see him. This was like in 2011. Isn't that crazy? And my friends still joke about doing a film called *The Son of the Giggler*—the Giggler's son is gonna get revenge on the Kersey family.

Chapter 13
Act of Vengeance (1986)

Sandwiched between the traditional Charles Bronson action vehicles *Death Wish 3* (1985) and *Murphy's Law* (1986) was *Act of Vengeance*. This 1986 made-for-cable-television movie was Bronson's most unusual project of the period, and it gave him a meaty, atypical dramatic role.

On New Year's Eve 1969, United Mine Workers union leader Joseph "Jock" Yablonski was gunned down in his home by a trio of killers hired by rival union head Tony Boyle. Shortly after publication, *Act of Vengeance*—Trevor Armbrister's 1975 book about the Yablonski saga—was purchased and put into development by Warner Bros. as a major theatrical feature.

Charles Bronson as ill-fated union crusader Jock Yablonski with Wilford Brimley as corrupt union leader Tony Boyle and Ellen Burstyn as Yablonski's wife in *Act of Vengeance* (1986).

In May 1978, Warners announced that *Act of Vengeance* would be directed by William Friedkin (*The French Connection*, 1971) from a screenplay by fellow Oscar-winner Abby Mann (*Judgment at Nuremburg*, 1961). By October 1981, *Act of Vengeance* was at Paramount Pictures, with Brian De Palma (*Dressed to Kill*, 1980) attached as director. De Palma scouted coal mines while novelist Scott Spencer (*Endless Love*, 1979) worked on a new draft of the script.

ACT OF VENGEANCE (1986)

Paramount finally dropped *Act of Vengeance,* and the project (and Spencer's script) was later picked up by Telepictures Productions. Best known for the popular syndicated show *The People's Court* (1981–1993), Telepictures had recently produced several acclaimed "based on a true story" TV-movies, such as *Crime of Innocence* (1985) and *Right to Kill* (1985). Telepictures president Frank Konigsberg set up *Act of Vengeance* at the pay-TV giant Home Box Office (HBO) and went after Bronson for the lead. Konigsberg said of the star, "He has a mystic American quality that somehow shines through. He's a working class hero."

Bronson loved the script and the Yablonski character and had a "window" in his schedule that made him available for *Act of Vengeance*'s fall 1985 shoot. The star had just finished *Death Wish 3* in June 1985 and wasn't scheduled to begin *Murphy's Law* until November. Bronson had disliked the screenplay for *Death Wish 3*, had been ill during the production, and was vocally unhappy about the final film. He saw *Act of Vengeance* as a chance to play a different type of character in good material.

One executive called the star's signing "a very fortuitous piece of casting," since the cable film was intended as a theatrical release in foreign territories where the Bronson name was still a guaranteed ticket-seller. Lorimar Motion Pictures International signed on as the overseas distributor.

For his previous television film *Raid on Entebbe* (1977), Bronson had a supporting role and received a record salary for only ten days of shooting. His drastically reduced, undisclosed fee for playing the lead in *Act of Vengeance* set no records. In addition to the pay cut, Bronson also agreed to work the exceptionally long hours required by a TV-movie schedule. The $4 million allotted to *Act of Vengeance* was about equal to what was being spent on Bronson's current theatrical features for Cannon Films (for each of which he received a $1 million fee). The cable budget wasn't high enough to afford a major theatrical director like Friedkin or De Palma, but the material was strong enough to attract Scottish director

John Mackenzie—whose previous work included the brilliant features *Unman, Wittering and Zigo* (1971) and *The Long Good Friday* (1980).

Bronson said at the time, "I gave it a lot of thought because I hadn't done television in years." (He had recently declined to reunite with Lee Marvin, Ernest Borgnine and Richard Jaeckel for the 1985 TV-movie sequel *The Dirty Dozen: Next Mission*.) "But I was glad to do the story of Yablonski. Having grown up in a coal mining town in Pennsylvania, I felt sympatico with the role. I had known and read a lot about the conflicts in the coal miners' union. I felt at the time like Yablonski did: that it was time for a change. I'm just hoping that this will take me out of the rut that I've been in and get me more supporting roles. It's also a hell of a story. Most of my movies are action movies, and you don't dare act too much because the audience goes to see the action."

In September 1985, exteriors (with Bronson) were filmed in Pennsylvania at the Tour-Ed Mine in Tarentum and in West Brownsville. The production company added $120,000 to the local economy during that leg of the shoot. The team then moved on to the small town of Lloydtown in Ontario, Canada, for interiors and more exteriors.

Wilford Brimley (from Bronson's *Borderline,* 1980, and *10 to Midnight*, 1983) played Tony Boyle, the union president who orders the hit on Yablonski. Brimley remembers that Bronson enjoyed the change-of-pace role: "He said he did. It was different for both of us. We went and had meals together, and I met his wife and kids and he met my wife and kids. I didn't keep in touch with him very often. He was a very private guy, and so am I. He was a good man. Totally devoted to his family. In an industry where there is so little of that, it was kind of refreshing to see."

Ellen Burstyn (*The Exorcist*, 1973) was cast as Yablonski's wife. Future star Keanu Reeves (*The Matrix*, 1999) had an early role as one of the killers. Bronson's stepson Paul McCallum played a member of Yablonski's staff. Another stepson, Jason McCallum, was given a job in the on-location editing room.

Bronson had refused requests to trim his famous mustache for

Telefon (1977) and *Borderline*, but he did shave his lip for *Act of Vengeance* to (slightly) match Yablonski's look. He said, "Neither Brimley nor I look like the characters we're playing. [Yablonski] was bald and had a thin pompadour. With his big shoulders, he had an aggressive look. So I tried to play the essence of the man." (The real-life Tony Boyle had a slighter build than Brimley.)

Yablonski (Bronson) is assaulted while campaigning with his son (Alf Humphreys). (Photo courtesy of Alf Humphreys)

Alf Humphreys played Yablonski's son, Ken. The young Canadian actor's many previous roles included the hanging/decapitation victim in *My Bloody Valentine* (1981) and one of the deputies chasing Rambo in *First Blood* (1982). Humphreys says, "I auditioned [for *Act of Vengeance*] with the director. I remember sitting across from the director while the 'reader' was reading the other lines, and it was just a very small cubbyhole. The director made me feel very comfortable. It was the scene where most of the family had been killed, and I was doing the eulogy, and I think the lines were: 'My father never spoke of death, nor did my mother. But if they were here today, they would say that the time for mourning is over.' As I was going into the scene, I was trying to hold back the tears because that's more effective. When I finished doing that, they thanked me. At the time, I didn't know it was going to be with Charles Bronson. I got the call, and my agent informed me that I was cast in that role of his son. My first introduction to Charles was when I was a young boy and I watched him in *The Great Escape* [1963]. Charles Bronson was my favorite character in that movie. And I never forgot that movie. Then I was cast to be in *Act of Vengeance*. The first day I was on set, there was Charles Bronson, and I'm going, 'Oh, my gosh. There he is standing in front of me!' [laughs] And it was a wonderful, wonderful experience. He was such a kind man. I really enjoyed him. It was just a great experience. And to work with him on set—that was terrific."

Between takes, Bronson would keep to himself and whistle George Gershwin tunes or play "catch" with a local kid. Director John Mackenzie said of Bronson, "He works hard, he's dedicated, and he's not an egoist. He's a professional."

Humphreys: "The director was so kind. He came up to me and said, 'When you did that audition where you were giving the eulogy, you almost had me in tears. I have to tell you, there are only two actors I've worked with who could do that. One is yourself, and one is Bob Hoskins.' It was such a wonderful compliment from this director. He said he was doing a movie, and [an] actor said, 'Whenever you want me to cry or be more emotional, press on my toes. On my right toe it would be more, and left it would be less.' When I [filmed] the eulogy the first time, it was a little 'big.' So after we did it, he said, 'Okay, let's do it again. But this time I want you to bring it down, and then I want you to bring it up.' I said, 'I'll tell you what, I can see you from the corner of my eye. So if you raise your [right] hand, I'll get more emotional. I'll do the same with the opposite hand—I'll bring it back down again.' He was so easy and comfortable to work with, and I think that's very important when you're on a set like that and you've got almost 100 extras."

Teleplay writer Scott Spencer says, "I played a scene with Bronson when I visited the set, but we had very little contact and did not interact during the scene itself. He spoke of his Victorian house in Woodstock, Vermont, and how his historically correct, preservationist neighbors were horrified that he had it painted purple. He seemed utterly unfazed by their horror." (Spencer can be spotted in the film as a minister.)

Ellen Burstyn, Charles Bronson, Caroline Kava, and Alf Humphreys on the set of *Act of Vengeance*. (Photo courtesy of Alf Humphreys)

Humphreys: "We were doing the scene in the house where [the family is] singing in their native language. After a few times, we had a little break so we'd be just standing around, and I was watching Charles. He was walking around very slowly, and he was clapping his hands in the air. And I realized that he was trying to kill the flies in the room. He said, 'You know, Alf, I believe that flies know that you're trying to kill them, so they try to antagonize you.' He was very relaxed on the set. I never saw him get anxious about anything. We were having lunch one afternoon, it was a very warm fall, and we were eating under the canopy of a barn. And I was sitting next to Charles, and we were having these nice little chit-chats, and it felt very comfortable, and it stood out that he was real.

"When we were having the wrap party, Keanu [Reeves] walked in. He had this long hair and this long Army jacket with big Army boots and blue jeans, and he came walking into this beautiful hotel, and he turned and looked at me and this other actor, and he said, 'Hey, guys. What's happening?' And I said, 'How you doing, Keanu?' 'Oh, cool, man. Cool.' And we had a little chit-chat, and he says, 'So like, where's the food?' I said, 'It's right down there.' He said, 'Okay, man. Chow.' And he starts walking away. And I looked at the other actor beside me, and I said, 'Man, if Keanu Reeves doesn't get his act together, he's not gonna go very far.' [laughs] He blew me out of the water!"

With much fanfare (including a *TV Guide* profile on the star), HBO premiered *Act of Vengeance* on the night of Sunday, April 20, 1986. *Murphy's Law*, the latest Bronson action offering from Cannon, had opened in theaters on Friday. Bronson was in a New York hotel suite a few days earlier to promote both movies. The jean-clad star told the press, "Frankly, I prefer that the films come out at different times. Violence is against my nature. Once you're typecast in this business and you want to go on earning a living, you take the roles that come your way. My wife and I did *From Noon Till Three* [1976], a light comedy, but it wasn't considered violent enough. I look mean. I have a permanent frown, and the ends of this mustache turn downward. I suggest an attitude in the characters I play. Every script that comes my way is violent. I don't know what to do except go for the ones that have something to say, like the Yablonski. I get murdered in that one."

Variety: "Powerful, suspenseful, even obscene, *Act of Vengeance* shows how strong a telefilm based on fact can be; it's compelling....Bronson's strengths are manifest throughout the vidpick." Vernon Scott, UPI:

"[Bronson's] warm qualities surface in the role of the union leader and family man." *TV Guide*: "Bronson as Yablonski; Ellen Burstyn, as his wife; and, above all, Wilford Brimley, as Boyle, are impressive. We could do without the explicit detail of the killer's sex life; this excellent real-life melodrama carries sufficient in-cold-blood passion of its own."

USA Today: "Despite the title, this dour and sour HBO movie isn't another Charles Bronson *Death Wish Fantasy*....This is a disturbing look at the 1969 murders....Frank in depicting violence and sex in the underworld, it would get an R rating in theaters....As the gregarious Yablonski, Bronson is cast against type. He's verbal. And effective." *People*: "*Vengeance* sheds as much light on its subject as a mine shaft would.... *Vengeance* has no feel for its people and no more for its story....Bronson is as animated as a lump of coal, and Burstyn as his wife comes off like some blue-collar Donna Reed. A good story wasted on a bad movie."

The New York Times: "The Yablonski story is, or at least should be, a moving chronicle of conscience rising up in opposition to unquestioned power and the inescapable lesson that absolute arrogance corrupts absolutely. This HBO presentation makes perfunctory gestures in that direction but the movie is clearly more fascinated with the violence and kinky sex habits of the misfits hired to kill the Yablonskis....Mr. Bronson is about as interesting as a sack of bituminous coal, which becomes painfully evident as, without mustache, he goes through the noble-victim motions." *Los Angeles Times*: "[This] Hollywood version of Yablonski's crusade gives the viewer virtually no hint of how his death effected sweeping changes within the UMW (United Mine Workers)."

Reportedly, Yablonski's surviving family and UMW leaders were unhappy with the depictions in the film.

While promoting *Act of Vengeance*, Bronson said, "I don't act for myself or I'd do theatre for the gratification of rehearsing for weeks, improving in every performance. But that's self-indulgent. I want to reach the widest audience and give them maximum entertainment. My appearance works against me now. I can't play just any man or wimps. It's a problem because I'm thought of as strong-faced and aggressive. Writers think of me in terms of being insensitive....[In] *Once Upon A Time in the West* [1968]...I was able to play a vulnerable and sensitive character, but you don't see those kinds of scripts anymore. I saw it again not long ago and it holds up. Slow but good. The Westerns were popular until they got comic-booked out of existence. So I searched for scripts that paid the most money....What I do is hard—two or three pictures a year with the possibility of a burn-out at the box office—being an advocate for non-achievers. You could say I've fallen into the success trap. I either stay in the violence-action area or fall back into supporting roles. I really do prefer a human kind of role to the hardened superhero. A sensitive man is easier to make believable. The characters I play are not for me. I'm an advocate for the audience, doing things the audience can't do for themselves. I'd like to satisfy this segment of the public while also serving a larger audience that prefers less violence and more sensitivity in the leading characters. I would like to star in *Liliom* [a classic 1909 Hungarian play]. I'd like to play a role with no sweat or profanity, something with fine dialogue, retorts and quick wit. I've done Shakespeare and enjoyed it. But I'm afraid people like to see me with a gun in my hand."

One month after the press conference, Bronson had a gun in his hand once again on the set of Cannon's *Assassination* (1987), where he played a Secret Service agent. *Act of Vengeance* did not lead to more offbeat, dramatic roles for Bronson. It would be a half-decade before he took on another non-traditional character.

Act of Vengeance opened theatrically in Canada on October 17, 1986, via the distributor/theater chain Cineplex Odeon Films. The ad campaign had a painting of the star's face (sans mustache) surrounded by an explosion and a trio of goons firing handguns, with the tagline: "His was an act of defiance. Theirs was an act of vengeance. BRONSON— ACT OF VENGEANCE." The violence and adult content earned the film a "Restricted" classification.

ACT OF VENGEANCE (1986)

Humphreys: "I only saw it when I went to the movies. I was watching it for the first time, and what really stood out was the scene where Keanu Reeves and Maury Chaykin blew open the bedroom doors and the shotgun fired, killing the whole family. And I thought, 'Jeez, I didn't realize it was that brutal.' I didn't think it was gonna be like that. I wish I had the film; I wish I could see it again."

Ad in the 1985 MIFED Film Market issue of *Variety*.
(Courtesy of William Wilson)

In November 1986, Lorimar Motion Pictures had foreign rights to *Act of Vengeance* up for sale at the American Film Market in Santa Monica, California. The movie was released theatrically in many territories. A soundtrack album with Frankie Miller's score was issued in Germany. The title was changed to *Local 323* for some European markets.

When *Act of Vengeance* hit the American home video market, the moniker and the action-oriented cover art insured that shop managers and Bronson's diehard followers would buy and rent the VHS tapes. Most Bronson addicts were confused and disappointed by the dramatic film, while non-fans of the star's traditional, brutal movies wouldn't even think of watching it, but for fans of "Bronson: the actor," *Act of Vengeance* is well worth seeking out.

Chapter 14
Murphy's Law (1986)

When Charles Bronson finished shooting Cannon Films' *Death Wish 3* (1985) in the spring of 1985, moguls Menahem Golan and Yoram Globus wanted Bronson's next picture to be *The Delta Force* (1986), which would team him with Chuck Norris (Cannon's other under-contract action superstar) as leaders of an anti-terrorist military group. The Bronson/Norris team-up was announced via trade ads, but the combo didn't attract enough presales to justify paying both stars' salaries. Norris ended up with top billing and the role intended for Bronson was reduced and given to the ailing (and soon to pass away) Lee Marvin (*The Dirty Dozen*, 1967), who was paid a mere fraction of the $1 million salary that Cannon was to pay Bronson.

Charles Bronson as the burnt-out, alcoholic police detective Jack Murphy in *Murphy's Law* (1986).

After the *Delta Force* plans changed, Golan and Globus claimed that Bronson's next Cannon movie would be an American remake of *Rider on the Rain*, the 1970 French thriller that was one of the star's biggest international hits and one of his personal favorites. The remake never happened. Bronson's camp looked for another suitable script.

Gail Morgan Hickman was a young action scribe who had first tried to break into the business by writing TV scripts in the late 1960s and early '70s. He recalls, "When I was a drama student at UC-Berkeley, this friend of mine, Scott Schurr, and I wrote a bunch of spec scripts. We wrote scripts for *Mission: Impossible*, *Ironside*, *Mod Squad*, *M*A*S*H*, the Bill Cosby sitcom. That was how we learned how to write, but none of them ever got sold. We were sitting around one day, and Scott said, 'You know what happened after the end of *Dirty Harry* [1971]? Harry got himself some scuba gear and went looking for that star that he threw in the water because nobody was gonna give him another job.' And then out of this joke, we started talking about the possibility of a sequel. Then *Magnum Force* [1973] was announced, and I thought, 'Oh, well.' But it just stuck in my head, and then I came up with this idea about this group of militants that would get weapons and terrorize San Francisco and kidnap the mayor. So Scott and I started to talk about ideas, and then I actually sat down and wrote the script."

With no contacts, Hickman tried to sell the Dirty Harry script, called *Moving Target*, on his own. He says, "I was a grad student in film at San Francisco State, and I sent it to a couple of agents. One agent said it was too much like *Serpico* [1973]—and there was nothing in it that was remotely like *Serpico*, so I knew he hadn't read it. One agent said she was gonna read it, and I must have called her five or six times, and the next thing I knew, she wasn't an agent anymore. I had a friend who was living in the Monterey area, and I was down visiting him, and I knew that Clint had a little restaurant down there. I said, 'You know where Eastwood's place is?' He said, 'Yeah. It's a place called the Hog's Breath Inn.' I had the script in the truck of my car, and on impulse I went down there. Clint wasn't there, but I said, 'Who's the manager?' They sent me to the office, and there was this guy there, and he was Clint's partner in the restaurant. I said, 'Look, I'm a young writer and I've got this script and I'm trying to get it to Clint.' And he said, 'I can't do anything like that. You've got to send it to an agent.' I said, 'Look, I understand. But I'm trying to get my break and I'm not connected with anybody.' He was a really nice guy, and he said, 'Do you have a synopsis?' I said, 'No, I don't. I've got the script.' He said, 'Send me a synopsis and I'll give it to Clint and we'll see what happens. But I cannot promise anything.' So I went back to the Bay area that night, I wrote up a synopsis, I sent it off to him the next day. And then I proceeded to call him once a month for the next nine months. He kept saying, 'I forgot to give it to him.' And I was thinking, 'This guy's gonna get sick of me.' After nine months he said, 'Look, I don't even know where [the synopsis] is anymore. Just send me the script.' I sent him the script, and three weeks later they optioned it. It was very crazy—completely the way you're not supposed to do things, but it opened the door for me." *Moving Target* was rewritten by veterans Stirling Silliphant (*In the Heat of the Night*, 1967) and Dean Riesner (*Dirty Harry*) and became the 1976 hit *The Enforcer* with Hickman and Schurr receiving "story by" credit.

Murphy (Bronson) with his estranged wife, Jan (Angel Tompkins).

Soon after, Hickman wrote another Dirty Harry script called *Chain Reaction*, which was optioned then discarded by Eastwood, and later wrote the Fred Williamson vehicle *The Big Score* (1983), which, contrary to most reports, was *not* recycled from the unused Dirty Harry screenplay.

Hickman: "That wasn't true at all. There was actually an article in *Jet* magazine where Fred said, 'It's a little known fact that *Dirty Harry* was created by black writer Gail Morgan Hickman.' Well, I'm white. I don't know if it was Fred's marketing ploy or if he just remembered it wrong. My career had been doing well, and then it plateaued, and I didn't work for about a year and a half. I had an agent, but we ended up parting ways. Then I sold this little script, *Number One with a Bullet*, which was a cop-comedy/drama, to Cannon but then it looked like nothing was happening with that. [The script was sold in 1984 but wasn't shot until 1987.] They bought it, and it wasn't for very much money." Hickman was then hired by Cannon's story department to write a trio of potential treatments for *Death Wish 3*, but his Paul Kersey premises went unfilmed.

Hickman: "I thought, 'I really gotta do something to jump start my career. I gotta write something really commercial.' So I had this idea that ended up being *Murphy's Law*. I thought it would be interesting to have a cop and a tough, bad-ass, girl car thief handcuffed together and on the run. It was actually inspired by *I Spy* [TV, 1965–1968]. There was an *I Spy* episode with Robert Culp and a Mexican car thief. Culp is on the run, he's been framed for something, and he meets this Mexican car thief, and they're on the run together. It was an interesting relationship, and it just somehow stuck in my mind. So I spun it around. I started to play around with that script. I was imagining, initially, of giving it to Clint because Clint had done the Dirty Harry movies, but he had also done *The Gauntlet* [1977], so I knew he was willing to do a cop story that wasn't necessarily Dirty Harry if it was a really different character. I wrote this guy as a self-destructive alcoholic. Several months went by, and I finally finished the script."

On the cover page of his *Murphy's Law* script, Hickman added a silhouette of a running, pistol-toting man handcuffed to a woman he pulls along. The first pages contained a logline as well as a description of the two lead characters:

He's a cop.
She's a thief.
They hate each other's guts.
But they have one thing in common:
They're both running for their lives.

JACK MURPHY
Homicide detective.
Tough as they come.
Getting old and doesn't like to think about it.
Used to be the hotdog of the force.
But sixteen years of being a cop burned him out.
So he started drinking.
Now when he looks in the mirror, it scares him.
A man precariously close to the edge.

ARABELLA McGEE
Thief.
Young, street-wise and bad-ass.
Mouth like a sewer.
Ran away from home at fifteen, been running ever since.
The way she sees it, life is a scam nobody wins.
Does what she has to to get over.
Angry at everything and going nowhere fast.

Hickman: "I gave it to a couple of friends to read, and they really liked it. I thought, 'I'm gonna use this script to try and get a new agent.'

Murphy's Law (1986)

Angel Tompkins as Jan Murphy.

Then I decided I was gonna send it out on my own. The idea of giving things to an agent and letting them do something with it had always bothered me. I've sold as many of my own scripts as my agent has. I knew Clint, so I sent it to Fritz Manes, who was his producer then. I knew Bob Daley, who had been Clint's producer on *The Enforcer* and had now gone off on his own and had just done a movie with Burt Reynolds—*Stick* [1985]. I knew Walter Hill [*Hard Times*, 1975] because I was Walter's first fan, and I knew somebody who knew him and I had a couple of meetings with Walter. And then I thought I wouldn't go to Cannon with this. I thought I had a better shot if I went directly to Bronson. I didn't know anybody in Bronson's camp, but I found out that Bronson's agent was Paul Kohner, and I called up Paul, and he took my call. He said, 'Yeah, you're the guy that wrote the three *Death Wish* stories.' I said, 'I've got a script called *Murphy's Law*. I think it would be good for Bronson. Would you be willing to read it?' He said, 'Absolutely.' I Fed Ex-ed it out to all of them on a Thursday. I had just finished it the week before. And the following Tuesday, I got a call from Paul Kohner saying, 'I like your script. Pancho, my son, likes your script. Charlie likes your script.' A week later, they bought it."

In early 1985, Paul Kohner shopped the *Murphy's Law* package, which included J. Lee Thompson as director, Pancho Kohner as producer, and Jill Ireland (Bronson's wife) as co-producer—the team that had recently made Bronson's *The Evil That Men Do* (1984). Paul Kohner offered *Murphy's Law* to Cannon but ultimately took the financing deal presented by Hemdale Film Corporation, a small outfit that had recently had a hit with *The Terminator* (1984). Hemdale then presold the *Murphy's Law* international home video rights to the hugely successful Vestron Video.

Enraged, Golan and Globus sued the Kohners, Hemdale, Vestron, Bronson, Hickman, and Ireland for over $55 million. Golan and Globus' complaint alleged that Paul Kohner had firmly committed *Murphy's Law* to Cannon and that they had already made presales to several territories and had spent over $30,000 marketing and promoting the new Bronson epic. Paul Kohner said, "We were in negotiations with Cannon and hopeful to conclude them, but Cannon's terms were unacceptable to us. They had no right to announce or sell the movie at Cannes—but Golan, in his customary way, went about and started selling the film." Hemdale filed a countersuit against Cannon for $65 million for trying to remove the movie from their production slate. When the suits were settled out of court, *Murphy's Law* became a Golan-Globus production, Paul Kohner negotiated a lucrative multi-pic Bronson/Cannon pact, and Hemdale was allowed to keep the presale money collected by Vestron Video for German video rights.

Hickman: "[Bronson] loved the script, initially. [laughs] Then I had this meeting with him and J. Lee at Pancho's house. Charlie was moody. I think what had happened was that Charlie really liked the script, but then as he *reread* the script, he realized that most of the good lines were the girl's and that he was kind of the straight man. He didn't like that. And Charlie started to complain. The script that three weeks earlier he had really liked, he now was ripping apart. I was just devastated. And then Jill showed up, and Charlie continued. Jill said, 'Oh, Charlie.' Then he kinda quieted down and then they left and there was just dead silence. At that point, they'd given me the first check for $100,000. I'd never seen a check so big. And that was just the down payment on the script, and I was gonna get more when it got shot and then more when it was in the can. All I kept thinking was, 'I know I've cashed the check, but I think I've only spent about $5,000 of it. I can give them their check back.' I just felt awful, and then J. Lee smiled and said, 'Well, that wasn't so bad. Charlie was in a good mood.' [laughs] And he sort of made light of it. Then they said, 'That's the way he is. He's very critical.'"

Hickman was involved with *Murphy's Law* for the entire production and received an "Associate Producer" credit. He had written the script to take place in his hometown of San Francisco, with specific locations like the Golden Gate Bridge, the financial district, Hunter's Point, and North Beach. To cut costs, *Murphy's Law* ended up being shot around Los Angeles. The earlier Bronson/Cannon vehicle *Death Wish II* (1982) was also written for San Francisco but was relocated to Los Angeles to save money.

Cannon's budget for *Murphy's Law* required that the script's action be pared down. Among the trims were: The airport shootout extending into an underground parking garage; Murphy riding on the hood of his stolen car as Arabella drives off; Arabella dangling out of the helicopter; and Murphy taking Vincenzo (Richard Romanus) to the penthouse roof and threatening to toss him off. The scene where the handcuffed pair encounter the pot-farming bikers was to begin with the helicopter exploding in the woods, followed by Murphy and Arabella getting trapped in a pit. The script also had Bronson attacking one of the bikers with a pitchfork. A vignette of Arabella taking Murphy to a warehouse full of stolen cars—where a thief attacks Murphy with a tire iron and a switchblade—was dropped entirely.

Art Penney (Robert F. Lyons) looks on as Murphy (Bronson) belts Reineke (James Luisi).

The climax was heavily rewritten to suit the available funds. Originally, Murphy was captured by Vincenzo's men and taken to a basement, where Vincenzo threatens him with a chainsaw. ("I'm gonna take you apart a piece at a time. First a hand. Then a foot. Then an arm.

Then a leg. I'm gonna cut you up into so many pieces you'll look like dog meat.") During the melee, one henchman's arm is dismembered by the chainsaw, a dozen flammable metal containers explode, and Vincenzo is impaled by a runaway forklift. Then Murphy pursues the psychotic Joan (Carrie Snodgress) into a church and uses his gun to blow her out of the bell tower. (The psycho toting a crossbow was added during shooting.) The ending as filmed all took place in one location: the famous Bradbury Building in downtown Los Angeles.

Comic moments cut from the script included: two thugs watching a Bronson movie on TV ("I love it when Charles Bronson kicks butt.") and Vincenzo receiving oral sex from a prostitute while watching TV where Shirley Temple sings "On the Good Ship Lollipop."

The screenplay had one final character moment for Murphy that wasn't shot:

> Murphy reaches into his pocket, takes out a bottle,
> opens it for a drink. He stops. Looks at the bottle.
> Drops it into a nearby trashcan.

A number of actresses were considered for the role of car thief Arabella. Hickman: "Initially, they were talking about Rae Dawn Chong, and I thought she would be terrific. Pancho didn't like her because he had seen her in *Commando* [1985] and felt that her performance wasn't strong. There was talk about Madonna, and I just thought it was great. Then Madonna wanted a million dollars or something like that, and Cannon just wasn't willing to pay it. I remember going into see Chris Peerce. He was the head of production. Golan and Globus were really just the guys sitting up there smoking their cigars having a good time, and Chris was really the guy who was at the controls of the train. I remember saying to Chris, 'Really, a million dollars for Madonna is [not bad], 'cause she's a big star. You're gonna get an audience there.' And they just weren't willing to pay it. She ended up doing *Shanghai Surprise* [1986] instead."

Rock star Joan Jett auditioned for the part, as did two of music icon Prince's protégés: Apollonia Kotero (*Purple Rain*, 1984) and Vanity (*The Last Dragon*, 1985), who would soon be cast in Cannon's *52 Pick-Up* (1986).

The actress/singer who finally got the Arabella role was twenty-one-year-old Kathleen Wilhoite. Although she received "Introducing" billing in *Murphy's Law*, Wilhoite had already played supporting roles in the teen comedy *Private School* (1983) and on a number of TV episodes. She was a frequent performer at Los Angeles music clubs. Wilhoite later said, "I seem to recall that ultimately it came down between me and Apollonia. Jill [Ireland] was a producer on the film, and she was extremely supportive of me. She was English and funny and smart. I kept getting called back. I must have gone in four or five times."

Cast as Art Penney, Murphy's partner, was Robert F. Lyons. The actor was making his third Bronson film in five years and had a bigger role than in *Death Wish II* or *10 to Midnight* [1983]. Lyons says, "I didn't audition for any of them. On the third film, I got a call that [Bronson] wanted me. And it caused some upset. I don't know the whole scene. I can only tell you that the casting people wanted someone [else]. But Charlie said, 'Bobby gets the part and that's it. That's who I want.'"

Angel Tompkins played Jan, the estranged, stripper wife of Murphy. The script noted: "She's got a great body and really knows how to move it." The tall, blonde, blue-eyed Tomkins was one of the more unforgettable actresses of the 1960s and '70s, with appearances in the cult features *Prime Cut* (1972), *Little Cigars* (1973), *The Teacher* (1974), *Part 2: Walking Tall* (1975), and *The Farmer* (1977), as well as in dozens of TV episodes. She says, "During that time, it was very difficult for actors to be submitted on projects if you didn't have what they call a 'top agent.' I hand-walked my submission over to the casting office, and I was called in by Jill Ireland. She was just as beautiful as she was onscreen. She was just as slim and, in her English accent, just as gracious and lovely. She was just an exquisite woman. She said, 'The reason I called you in is that I know your work.

I've seen your films. I will read the part with you.' I said, 'I'll be thrilled. Are you kidding? What a fabulous moment whether I get the job or not.' She said, 'That was just lovely. I really appreciate the fact that you came in.' I got called six hours later, and I was the one that got it.

"I took this film very seriously. This wasn't 'just a part.' I did not want this dancer/stripper to come off as 'flabby.' I had been working out at the gym for three months doing free weights, toning the muscles. I liked to bench-press. I wanted my body to be 'cut' in the abdomen just as if she were an athlete. I've had years and years of dance experience. I'm old school. The old school was that you studied, you trained, you did dance, you did everything. Your body is the only thing that you have to work with. I went to the producer, and I said, 'This striptease is a dance. It must be choreographed to really come off. This is not a five-second strip on a college beach bar outing. This needs and requires a choreographer.' [Pancho Kohner] said, 'Well, we don't have the budget.' I said, 'This *has* to have a dance choreographer, somebody who really knows what they're doing.' He said, 'Do you have someone in mind?' I said, 'Yes, I do.' I had met this woman who loved dragon sculptures. I met her in a shop with antiques. Some people like pigs, some people like frogs—she liked dragons. I was looking at this one exquisite dragon, and she said, 'I was thinking of buying it.' And we just struck up a conversation. That's what I do. I really love people. I love to talk to them, and I introduce myself at all times, and I very seldom hesitate. I had gotten her card, and I called her, and she said 'Yes.' And she did the choreography. [Kohner] said, 'All right, all right. You have two days, and you can rehearse in the warehouse next door.' The warehouse next door had a concrete floor; it had very little space. It had nails, dust, dirt. It was absolutely impossible. She said, 'We can't do this here, Angel.' I said, 'We can't do it in two days.' She said, 'I know of a place, but they're gonna' have to rent it.' So we went [to production] and said, 'Look, you cannot dance. You cannot get on your knees. You cannot walk barefoot. You cannot do any of that in this space.' They said, 'Well, let's go see the space.' [Kohner] looked at me and said,

'You're right. Go.' And she had a place. So we went and we worked on it for two weeks, and that's what you see on the screen.

"The costume/wardrobe person [Shelley Komarov] was a wonderful woman. She was Russian. She worked at the theater in Moscow and at the Bolshoi ballet. The [stripper] dress had to be made. We worked very closely to make sure that everything fits. I've done that since I began modeling in 1966 in Chicago. Every detail, every color scheme, I approve. They don't need that in the contract because most wardrobe persons who are really brilliant at their craft want the actress to feel good. Generally, my taste has always been right on the money for the character."

Murphy (Bronson) escapes from jail while handcuffed to car thief Arabella (Kathleen Wilhoite).

Wilhoite said, "The day before I went to work, J. Lee had a meeting with me and told me not to expect too much from Charlie—that he was a quiet man, and just because he didn't say much didn't mean he was thinking there was anything wrong. He said a lot of the actresses Charlie had worked with in the past would get progressively more paranoid as the filming went along. He told me that it was important I was made aware of that. My father's a lot like that. So when Charles and I had a long car scene, or when we were handcuffed together for long period of time, I just sat there quietly and let him steer the chit-chat.

The seventy-one-year-old J. Lee Thompson directing *Murphy's Law*, his sixth of nine Bronson films.

"The original script was written for an actual potty-mouth, someone who had dialogue that resembled something a person would actually say, a street person, a person who swears a lot. I have always talked like a sailor, so the words tripped off my tongue easily. They had rethought the swearing and turned her 'potty' mouth into what it is today—a bunch of odd phrases no one but a mentally ill person might say. My challenge then became: How to make this strange dialogue believable? I did the best I could. I didn't improvise. I had some resistance to the dialogue, actually. I thought it was silly. I come from a method acting school, a school that teaches its students to create real people, to connect to everything you say, to honor the playwright. So when they were wracking their brains trying to think of the weirdest and goofiest insults possible, it felt super cheesy to me. I did it because I was happy to have a job, and acrimony in the work place is not something I think is conducive to a creative environment. I like having fun when I work. I am a better actress if I feel supported and peaceful at work. If that means I have to say a bunch of silly shit that no one would ever say unless, as I've said before, they've got emotional trouble, then I'll say it. Once I got that rewrite, I knew that I'd have a mountain to climb if I wanted to get it changed back to the way it was. I had never had such a big part before. I was unwilling to make that climb. I'm positive I would have gotten fired. So I made the best of it."

Among the colorful insults spouted in the movie by Wilhoite were: animal crotch; snot-licking donkey fart; scrotum cheeks; bug-sucking booger; dinosaur dork; monkey vomit; dick brain; and butt crust. The script called for Arabella to be topless in the scene where the character seduces a security guard, but the vignette was shot with Wilhoite wearing a bra.

Cannon had announced a November 1985 start date for *Murphy's Law,* but production didn't begin until January of 1986. Lyons: "I'm on the set for the first day of work, which was in the original subway tunnel downtown in L.A. I had never been there. I was fascinated by shooting down there. [My role] was written for a different ethnic." Lyon's character was described in the script as "a tall, well-dressed black man in his late thirties" with dialogue like, "Yo, my man"; "You got it Whitebread"; "Say, hey, Mr. Cool"; and "I can't stand it when white folks talk like brothers." At one point in the original script, the drunk Murphy loses his temper and calls his partner a "spearchucker."

Lyons: "The writing was very good; I could use most of it with just a change here and there. Then the writer, Gail—he's a nice guy—went and changed it. And I said to Gail, 'Why? It was so good. Leave it alone. It was perfect.' Charlie said to Gail, 'This writing. I've seen every one of these scenes on TV. This is not good. C'mon, you can do better.' Gail said, 'Charlie, what do you want me to do? That's what they want.' Next thing I know, I get a call by J. Lee Thompson to go to his trailer. I go in the trailer, and he says, 'There's not gonna be any changes here!' He just started right in on me. 'This is the part. This is the part the way it is, and you're gonna play it.' Lee just went up one side of me and down the other. And that was my first main meeting with J. Lee. So Lee tattoos me before we even start the scene entering the subway. That was the first scene I shot, and it might have been the first scene of the film that was shot. We're talking, Charlie and I, and we walk down the staircase, and there's a girl in a red dress lying in front of the subway entrance, dead. It was a long scene walking down stairways [with] dialogue, and we got it in one or two takes. Then Lee came to me and said, 'You're gonna be fine. You're fine.' [laughs] In other words, the minute he saw me acting, he went, 'What is all the problem? The guy's good.' I think he wanted someone else [for the role]. And somebody else wanted somebody else. Everybody has their 'somebody else.' But fortunately for me, the power was with Charlie."

Murphy (Bronson) crashes a helicopter while fleeing with Arabella (Kathleen Wilhoite).

Hickman: "During the entire production of *Murphy's Law*, Charlie would show up on the set, literally every day, and say, 'This sucks'; 'This is stupid'; 'I don't like this'; 'I hate this line here'; 'Why can't he say this?' Then I would go back to the production trailer and rewrite the afternoon's pages and then give them to Pancho's assistant, and she would put out the pages for the afternoon shoot. I don't think that on most Bronson movies they had the writer on the set all the time. I think Pancho tried to have a writer around. Pancho and J. Lee were both writers themselves, so they were certainly perfectly capable of fixing scenes on the set. Pancho and J. Lee were really good collaborators."

Wilhoite said, "I remember doing scenes with [Bronson] in the car where it was just the two of us, and we had long periods of time together, and he would, out of the blue, ask me a question, to start up some kind of chit-chat. He was funny and smart. I was careful not to speak to him unless spoken to. They had told me not to 'try too hard' with him before shooting started. We formed a sweet working relationship. I remember when he felt the production was lagging, he'd say, 'Let's shoooooooooooot.' It was funny. Charles Bronson used to tease me and tell me that the guy I was dating looked like a chicken. 'He looks like a chicken, your boyfriend. He's a chicken, right? He's a chicken.' But he was just being a goof."

Hickman: "I think that Charlie was, emotionally, a somewhat closed-off guy. Jill told me that when she wrote *Life Wish* [1987], she gave the manuscript to Charlie. Jill made it clear that she was going to be honest about their relationship. Charlie said that he wasn't gonna read it, because he wanted her to be honest, and he knew that he could be a gruff and grumpy guy, and he didn't want to read things about himself or his relationship with Jill in any kind of a light that might bother him. I didn't know Charlie really well. But from what I knew of him, he did keep emotional things very much under control and very much to himself."

At the time, Bronson's ex-wife, Harriett Bronson, was dating actor James Luisi (TV's *The Rockford Files*, 1976–1979) who played a fellow cop in *Murphy's Law*. She recalled in her memoir: "As luck would have it, he and Charlie ended up being in a movie together. In the movie, my actor friend had a line where his character had to say to Charlie's character, 'I saw your ex-wife last night at the club she works in. She has great tits,' at which point Charlie's character socks him in the ribs. During the filming of this scene, Charlie actually broke one of my actor friend's ribs. When I asked him if he'd told Charlie he knew me, he said, 'Are you kidding?'"

Tompkins had first met Bronson briefly a dozen years before *Murphy's Law*. She says, "Charles Bronson was doing a film just off of the Sunset Strip called *The Mechanic* [1972], and I wanted to meet the director because I had heard that he had three other films that he was going to do. I found the set, and they were breaking for lunch. I met the director, and he said, 'Can you wait ten minutes and I'll take you over to the Cock n' Bull and we'll have lunch?' I said, 'Certainly.' So as I was looking around, I saw Charles Bronson. I went over to him and I introduced myself. He's not a cautious man, he's a quiet man. I said, 'I just wanted to let you know that I really admire your work and the films that you've done.' He said, 'Oh, really.' I said, 'Yes.' And he didn't say anything. I kept thinking to myself that I had the wrong actor. I said, 'Over the years, you've done a lot of Westerns and a lot of Army pictures.' And he looked at me. I said, 'I really enjoyed them.' He looked at me and said, 'Really?' I said, 'Yes.' And he said, 'I have never done a Western or an Army film in my life.' [laughs] I just looked at him and I said, 'Oh.' And I let it go at that. I knew that he was funning me, but at the same time, he said it so well and so authentically, I almost believed him. The first day that I shot anything [on *Murphy's Law*], we did the 'man/wife' photograph that is in his apartment. I told him that story after we shot the photograph, and he just looked at me and said, 'I said that?'

"The production level [on *Murphy's Law*] was superb; everybody worked in harmony. J. Lee Thompson was endless energy. He was in his seventies at the time. Very frugal, great filmmaker, got the stuff. Gee, what a pleasure. While we were shooting the strip scene, J. Lee was kind of embarrassed. He said, 'Okay, Angel. Just go and do your little wiggle-walk.' That's what he said, 'the wiggle-walk.' He wouldn't say, 'It's a striptease, and we come up to the part where you unzip the dress.' [He said,] 'Okay, continue wiggle-walk.' It was late in the evening, but he did not quit until he got every angle. He spent time with it. He was very funny, very British. I couldn't be more thrilled. Everyone was quiet and respectful. I had never done nudity in a film like that. I may have stepped out of a shower or something, but never like that. I came off the stage once—we had been shooting two nights in a row—and in the back of the room was Charles Bronson. He had been watching the filming the entire time. And as I walked by, he said, 'You did good, Angel. You did good.' And I looked at him and thought, 'What a terrific person.' Normally, he played [in films] with his wife, [and] it was easy to appear to have fallen in love. When he was supposed to still be in love with me as his wife, it absolutely helped his character to have an appreciation and not be just a stranger. Charles Bronson was a consummate actor. I found him to be very warm, kind and dedicated to what he was doing in terms of acting. Very serious about it. He had a funny sense of humor, and he liked to throw people off-guard. He was quiet; he was cordial. It was my dream to work with Charles [and other] respected actors. And I did that."

In the small role of Tompkins' lover was Joe Roman, a husky Italian whom Bronson had first met shortly after World War II when Bronson was working a night shift as a baker. Bronson said, "If it weren't for Joe, I'd never had been an actor. I had $10 and caught a bus to New York. But I ran out of money, and Philadelphia was as far as I got. I found a $5-a-week room and went to a gym to work out. That's where I met Joe. I decided to become an actor when Joe told me they made $42.50 a week in plays. In 1947, I thought that was a lot of money for two hours' work a night. So I went to the same drama school with Joe." Bronson got his old friend bit parts in *St. Ives* (1976), *The White Buffalo* (1977) and *Love and*

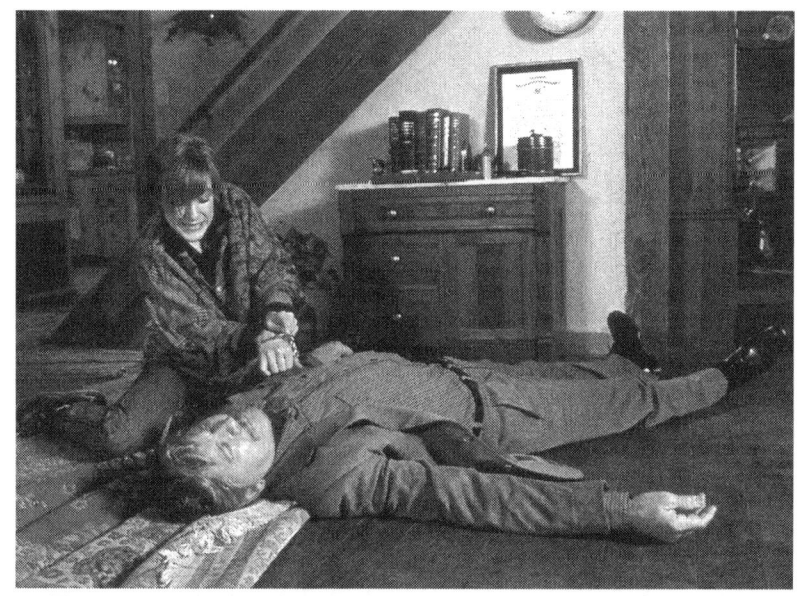

The wounded Murphy (Bronson) passes out while still cuffed to Arabella (Kathleen Wilhoite).

Bullets (1979). Whenever Roman had a role in a Bronson movie, he was one of the few people allowed into the star's dressing room during the lunch break.

Tompkins: "Charles Bronson picked the character to play my boyfriend. He had been a bodybuilder friend of his for decades. Charles' friend had a hairpiece, and he was always licking his lips and flexing his muscles. He was totally into himself and self-conscious. By that time, I was an old pro at looking like I was really shot and dead. [laughs] My 'boyfriend' was stiff and nervous about being 'killed.' In doing the scene [with] the breakaway glass, I knew what to do, but he came off stiff. They called us back about four weeks later, and they reshot the scene because they didn't get what they wanted. I was probably on that shoot maybe a total of two weeks, and it was a third week when they had to do the reshoot. I've been 'killed' so many times, it's kind of like second nature. No problem. In my one *Mannix* [1969] show, they had me in a closet, and they opened the door, and I fell out dead. [laughs] I 'died' so many times. I loved 'dying.'"

Wilhoite said, "J. Lee was hilarious, talented, kind, and ran a tight set. I loved the cast and crew. I adored them. I was in Heaven doing that shoot. The gory stuff was a blast. I'm a tomboy, so running around with guns and getting 'squibbed' was an extension of a good old-fashioned 'cops and robbers' game. I loved it. Getting 'squibbed' is when they put a small explosive device on you that, when detonated, blood spurts out and a bullet hole appears."

Lyons' character in *Murphy's Law* was his favorite of the three roles he played opposite Bronson, but there was one bit in the script that he was not happy about. "I've got a certain principle about certain things, and I was able to get something *out* of that film. There was a scene when [Bronson is] on the run, and he turns to me for help. Charlie opens a drawer and goes, 'What the hell's this, Art?' And here's this machine—they had one in *10 to Midnight*, too—it was a male masturbation thing. I was like, 'How am I gonna get this out of the movie?' I went about it very deliberate, and I put it on Charlie. [laughs] And here's what I said: 'You know, guys, I gotta tell you something. Not only is it gratuitous and has nothing progressing the story, [but] Charles Bronson depends on me, his partner. He's trusting *one* guy. It's gonna make him look like he doesn't know what he's doing. He didn't perceive that my character was a little bit *strange*? And I don't look like the kind of guy that needs to jerk off. If anyone wants my resume on women, I can come up with one.' [laughs] That's how I presented it—it would make Charlie look bad if he would trust a guy that has some *stupid* thing like that. And they went, 'Yeah, okay. Yeah, take it out. We'll drop it.' And I was thrilled that I got it out. That had nothing to do with anything except shock value. They already had it in *10 to Midnight*. Charlie had to pull it out in a scene with [the killer] while he was interrogating him. With that character, I can understand it because that guy was such a sicko. That actually had a little bit of theme in it."

Murphy (Bronson) confronts mobster Vincenzo (Richard Romanus).

Carrie Snodgress played the first (and only) female psychopath ever battled by Bronson. She had gotten an Oscar nomination for her first feature, *Diary of a Mad Housewife* (1970), then left the business in 1971 to live with rock icon Neil Young and their son. Snodgress returned to acting in 1978 and, just prior to *Murphy's Law*, played the female lead in Eastwood's *Pale Rider* (1985). Shortly after working with Bronson, she said, "I'm starting to play strong, determined women with a real opinion about life and how to live. Most of my characters have tended to be victims."

Wilhoite said, "I remember Carrie Snodgrass. She was my friend. She was an amazing actress. She taught me how to break down my script and organize my scenes. She was extremely generous with me."

Tompkins: "Carrie Snodgress and I were both under contract at Universal Studios. I was signed because of the picture *I Love My Wife* [1970] and that year Carrie Snodgress did *Diary of a Mad Housewife*.

We were both nominated for the Golden Globe as Most Promising Newcomer. She won the second round, there was a tie on the first one."

Lyons: "I adored [Snodgress]. She was a good gal. She had been away from acting, she came back. We had some talks. She was energetic and friendly. That was a tough part. She died young." (Snodgress passed away in 2004 at age fifty-nine.)

Carrie Snodgress as psychopath Joan Freeman.

Hickman recalls having a "little bit" of trouble getting paid on time by the Cannon moguls: "There was a check that I was supposed to get [for] *Murphy's Law* that they delayed on. I was supposed to get this big check on the first day of principal photography. I think we were down to the last week of shooting, and this check had still not cleared. It was clear that Cannon was having financial problems or trying to collect interest on the money. Cannon was notorious for paying as absolutely late as they could."

Murphy's Law completed filming in early February 1986. The picture was edited (by the director's son, Peter Lee-Thompson, and Charles Simmons) as it was being shot in order to meet the United States release date that was only ten weeks away. At this time, all Golan-Globus movies had extremely accelerated post-production schedules. Thompson's next film was Cannon's *Firewalker* (1986), which would be rushed to theaters ten weeks after production ended.

The screenplay and the first cut of *Murphy's Law* opened with a hungover, burnt-out Murphy (Bronson) being awakened by a phone call, then going to the location of the call-girl murder. During editing, the movie was restructured to open with Murphy's first encounter with car thief Arabella—a scene that was originally ten minutes into the film. This gave the movie an exciting opening and presented the standard image of a tough and energetic Bronson.

Dropped from the final cut was a monologue by Wilhoite:

> Look. You want my life story? Okay.
> I'll give it to you. (beat) I grew up in
> L.A. My dad split when I was ten, which
> was fine, because he used to beat my
> mom to a pulp every Friday night. And
> when he wasn't hitting on her, he'd have
> a go at me. My mom wasn't real thrilled
> having a kid and no old man, so she sent

me to live with my aunt in Fresno. We
didn't exactly get along. I ran away when
I was fifteen. Ended up in San Francisco.
No money, no job. I tried turning tricks
for awhile. Got tired of getting beat up by
the customers and the pimps. One day I met
Julio and he showed me how to steal cars.

The score was written by buddies Marc Donahue and Valentine McCallum (Bronson's stepson). Valentine's brother, Paul McCallum (who played one of the biker pot growers), wrote the closing song "Murphy's Law" with John Bisharat and the movie's lead actress. Wilhoite says, "Paul and Val grew up with John. I had pitched the idea of me singing the end credit song to Jill Ireland, and I guess she liked the idea. I pretty much forced their hand in working with me. Neither Paul nor John were thrilled about writing lyrics, and I loved writing lyrics. And neither of those guys were very interested in singing. So I guess by process of elimination, those areas became mine to cover. John and Paul are heavily influenced by jazz. I am more of an Americana style of writer. They came up with the track, and I wove a melody and lyric on it. The song took us a couple of days to write and rewrite. We'd written it to be a verse, chorus, verse, chorus, musical interlude, bridge, chorus deal, and the editors said that all of the vocals needed to be upfront. I hated that. I thought the compromise ruined it. There was a lot of drama around that. I think I was cruel to Paul about it. He's a sweet guy and didn't deserve my wrath. The night we recorded the song, we were working in Cloris Leachman's son's [George Englund Jr.] studio. The saxophone player was amazing. Val ended up playing in my band for the next few years after that. Val is an insanely talented singer, guitar player and song writer. I never performed the song live because there would be no way in a million years I'd ever be able to play it. The musicians they used on it were all super top-notch jazzbo guys. I think the lyrics might be a tad on the lame side."

Arabella (Kathleen Wilhoite) is kidnapped and gagged to lure Murphy.

Murphy's Law turned out to be an excellent action movie, with a great script, good set pieces, and a fine cast with nice chemistry between Bronson and Wilhoite. It is the second-best of the Bronson/Cannon epics, surpassed only by *10 to Midnight*.

Hickman: "I always thought that *Murphy's Law* was *okay*. But part of the problem was that our budget was a little bit limited. I think if we had another million dollars, we could have done pretty amazing action sequences that would have probably made a much more commercial film. The original script of *Murphy's Law* was this big, *big* action story with lots of action. It was really *Lethal Weapon*-like. And Charlie had a problem with action that he felt got too big or too cartoonish. Charlie kept reining in the action scenes. You'd have five explosions, and he'd make it one explosion because he was looking for movies that were in a more gritty reality, and I was a younger guy who would be looking for James Bond. I was never fully satisfied with the film."

After the theatrical release of *10 to Midnight*, which Cannon (sparsely) handled themselves, Golan and Globus set up a lucrative deal with MGM to distribute their films in the States. However, when Cannon's two most-anticipated movies of 1983 were either shelved after test screenings (*Sahara* with Brooke Shields) or deemed unreleasable (*Bolero* with Bo Derek) by MGM, Golan and Globus were back to handling their own distribution by the time of *Death Wish 3*.

Cannon opened *Murphy's Law* on 1,260 American screens on Friday, April 18, 1986. (The following Sunday, Bronson's cable movie *Act of Vengeance* premiered.) Cannon invested $4.5 million on the prints and advertising. The only picture that Golan/Globus spent more money on promotion that year was *The Delta Force*, which had opened in February. The *Murphy's Law* trailer and TV spots (and the cut version later released to TV) had alternate footage of Bronson spouting, "Don't *mess* with Jack Murphy," instead of "Don't *fuck* with Jack Murphy."

The New York Times: "*Murphy's Law* is not tough....it's sleazy....[The story] is just a pretext for stock scenes." *Variety*: "a very violent urban crime meller...tiresome but too filled with extreme incidents to be tiring....[This] nasty smeller for Bronson fans should score well in quick, wide release, but fall off quickly." *Los Angeles Times/Washington Post New Service*: "Occasionally here, Bronson shows what an excellent actor he can be. Bronson uses all of his sixty-four years to good advantage. In a way, it is an old man's movie; director Thompson is seventy-one, and it is best when you feel the years, feel a little palpable weariness, weathered toughness." *Pittsburgh Press*: "Arabella invents and spews about three revolting nicknames per man per minute....One person at Bank Cinema's first showing yesterday laughed at several of Arabella's witticisms, repeating each to try it out in person, then laughing again." New York *Daily News*: "Standard Lesser Bronson. Not one of his greatest hits perhaps, but a perfectly serviceable vehicle for a player of perfectly serviceable, albeit specific talents....Much of the dialogue elicits, to put it kindly, chortles, but you don't go to a Bronson picture for its brilliant Joycean wordplay. Bronson, a man who wears the accumulating years very well indeed, seems rather looser in this film than his Wooden Man popular image has permitted him to be in the past." *Palm Beach* (FL) *Post*: "Certain elements remain constant in Bronson's movies....There are few exceptions in *Murphy's Law*—only the violence, language and circumstances are more twisted and revolting than usual...a particularly disturbing and violent mess."

Cox News Service: "Bronson's answer to Eastwood's much-praised *Tightrope*, and a darn good reply it is. This is the usual Bronson bloodbath, but done with unusual attention to character and style....The film has freshness and flair and a genuine vitality that has been missing from the star's more recent efforts....Bronson seems thrilled to be playing a real character instead of a gun-toting cliché. Bronson fans, our boy is back in form." Rex Reed: "This new Charles Bronson movie stinks of sewage and stale ideas, recycled for the millionth time. Call it *Death Wish 90*....The movie is a gnat-brained farrago of requisite Bronson ingredients—guns, mayhem, violence and splattered ketchup....Bronson stomps through the noise and body odor with one expression—terminal boredom. I know how he feels." *Nevada Daily Mail*: "Although it is a violent action film, it has a charming vein of self-deprecating humor....Director Thompson manages to pull off a couple of surprises that show even formula movies can have their creative moments." Los Angeles *Herald-Examiner*: "Bronson doesn't really make movies anymore, he allows other people to make movies around him. *Murphy's Law* is the snappiest recent Bronson picture by a wide margin, but it still isn't much....If you like your burgers rare with ketchup, you could do a lot worse." Rick Sullivan, *Gore Gazette*: "Sleaze fans should give a special commendation to Charles Bronson who over the past three years has consistently shirked artistic merit of any degree in an attempt to bring us the most base, violent exploitation potboilers around....One can always count on Charlie to deliver something to offend everyone. *Murphy's Law* continues this trend....J. Lee Thompson packs the flick with non-stop action, gobs of gratuitous violence and even a dash of nudity....A must-see for fans of relentless action and excessive bloodshed."

Japanese program.

Wilhoite said, "It got a little weird when after the film came out, I was doing a play in New York, and a homeless guy followed me down 8th Avenue, saying, 'Hey, donkey dork. Hey, hey, donkey dork.'"

The newest Cannon/Bronson film grossed $3.4 million in its first week. Nationwide, it was the second-highest-grossing movie after the fantasy *Legend*, which collected $4.3 million. In New York City, the Bronson picture beat *Legend* and was number-one for the week. *Murphy's Law* played drive-ins on a triple-bill with Cannon's *Runaway Train and The Delta Force*.

The final American theatrical gross for *Murphy's Law* was $9.9 million. Cannon's cut of the net rentals came to $4 million. *Murphy's Law* was Cannon's third-highest grosser of the year after *The Delta Force* and J. Lee Thompson's *King Solomon's Mines* (1985). By this point, Golan and Globus were lucky to just break even at American box offices. The profits came via foreign, videocassette and TV sales.

In the spring of 1986, Golan and Globus signed an exclusive, three-year pact with Showtime/The Movie Channel and Viacom Enterprises to have sixty Cannon movies shown on pay-TV, pay-per-view and syndicated television. *Death Wish 3*, *Murphy's Law* and the remaining, upcoming Bronson/Cannon pics were included in the deal.

At that year's Cannes Film Festival in May, Cannon screened *Murphy's Law* for the smaller film buyers that had not pre-bought the film. Golan said, "Cannon is doing movies non-stop. We don't take too long to give answers on proposals and generate many of the scripts ourselves. We are also signing actors and filmmakers to multiple-picture deals, such as a recent exclusive pact with Charles Bronson for six pictures in three years following the current *Murphy's Law*....We spread the risk and protect our downside by financing films with pre-buys. Also, instead of setting up our own home video distribution operation, we prefer to make deals for home video rights which bring in production coin.... Overall, this allows Cannon's yearly production schedule to have its total costs covered before the films go into theatrical release."

Golan wasn't exaggerating about the money that could be made from home video sales. That same month, after turning down several lesser bids, Cannon signed again with Media Home Entertainment when that company advanced $50 million for the North American video rights to twenty-three upcoming Golan/Globus productions. (The previous year, Media paid Cannon the same price for thirty-two films.) In addition to the advance, Cannon—which promised to (but obviously didn't) spend $5 million to $5.5 million on each of the films—would collect twenty percent of anything Media collected after the advance was recouped. The deal stipulated that each movie had to have (at least brief) theatrical exposure. To meet this requirement, several rock-bottom titles—such as the trucker/action pick-up *Thunder Run* (1986)—were offered to theaters in the New York City area at the flat rental rate of $100 per week, with Cannon providing no TV or newspaper advertising.

Tompkins: "I thought [*Murphy's Law*] was excellent. It was because of *Murphy's Law* that I did more pictures at Cannon." She later did *The Naked Cage* (1986), *Dangerously Close* (1986) and *Crack House* (1989) for the studio and recalls Golan and Globus fondly. "How missed they are. They were delightful. They were just glorious filmmakers that loved to make movies. You could walk the halls, you could talk to them, you could be in the screening room—they would invite you in. What a sad state of affairs when they lost their studio."

After *Murphy's Law*, Pancho Kohner and Thompson hired Hickman as the writer of *Death Wish 4: The Crackdown* (1987). At thirty-three, he was atypically young to be writing for Bronson at that time. The four other writers of Cannon/Kohner productions were between sixty-five and seventy-five when they penned a Bronson movie. Hickman: "What was nice about *Murphy's Law* and *Death Wish 4* was that I was the sole writer and was allowed by Pancho and J. Lee to ride the movie all the way through from beginning to end. I was enormously grateful because it honestly doesn't happen that way very much anymore. More and more, even if you see a solo credit on a movie, there are going to be other writers involved. It's really kind of a revolving door. I did this other film for Cannon—*Number One with a Bullet*. I was the original writer. At one point, Jim Belushi was going to be in it, and then Belushi and two friends of his—they were writers from *Saturday Night Live*—came in and rewrote it. Then Belushi moved on, and Cannon decided the script was too jokey. So I went back and I rewrote that. And then I was going to do the final production rewrites, but I was too busy doing *Death Wish 4*. So then they brought in another writer after me."

After his three Bronson movies, Lyons acted again for Cannon. He says, "For a while there, they were making more films than anyone in this town. I knew Menahem because I did another film called *Platoon Leader* [1988]. He had three guys under contract. He had Bronson, Michael Dudikoff and Chuck Norris. And I worked with all three of them. They were doing another thing having to do with Navy seals, and Menaham said, 'Get me Bobby Lyons. Now.' He loved my work in *Platoon Leader*. Oddly enough, the Israeli director was already sold on Jan-Michael Vincent. [laughs] Funny how it comes around." Lyons had auditioned for the role that Vincent won in Bronson's *The Mechanic*. Golan's 1992 Navy Seals epic, *The Finest Hour*, ended up without Lyons or Vincent.

Lyons didn't make any further films with Bronson, but the two actors stayed in touch. Jason McCallum Bronson, the adopted son of Jill Ireland and David McCallum, briefly studied with Lyons. "[Bronson] knew I taught acting as well. Charlie sent him to me. He came over to my class, we talked, this and that. But I don't know that he was as deep into [acting] as his parents or Charlie. I think Charlie was just trying to be a father and was concerned. I remember how devastating it was when this young guy died." Jason McCallum Bronson died in 1989 after many years of struggling with drug addiction. Lyons continues to act and teach. "I work with a lot of 'name' actors that I teach and prepare for roles. I've done it for years. I'm very good at it because I really care. At one time, I had twelve different people on [TV] series, as regulars, that had either studied with me or come through me on a private lesson. Kind of a nice stat."

Tompkins: "Jill Ireland and Charles Bronson made you a part of their family. Their appreciation went beyond just doing the job and saying, 'Goodbye. Next,'—which happens a lot of times. [After] making that movie with them, my husband and I were invited to their annual Christmas party every year before her death. And that came out of trust, appreciation. They embraced you. We'd sit at the table with them at their party. This was an open, joyous, loving group of people. They gave everybody gifts when they came to their Christmas party. One of my gifts was a little Tiffany silver bookmarker, engraved with the date of their party and their names. It was exquisite. From the day Jill Ireland died, I've missed [her]."

Spanish lobby card.

Cannon Films' American box office results for 1986 were weak. Their high-budgeted epics *Runaway Train* (which made $7.7 million) and *The*

Delta Force (which had been expected to gross $100 million in the States but only collected $17 million) had been especially disappointing.

Hickman: "Cannon was like this bubble. It got bigger and bigger and bigger, and then it collapsed. I got in at the beginning when it was getting bigger and bigger and bigger. *Murphy* and *Death Wish 4* came along right when the bubble was expanding—the fabric had been stretched about as far as it could go. Overall, the coffers at Cannon really seemed to be overflowing, and they were developing a lot of stuff. They had a bunch of big projects, but they were doing more and more sort-of arty projects that I don't think they had any business doing. They were wasting money on movies that they shouldn't have been wasting money on, and they were trimming the budget on movies like *Murphy* and *Death Wish 4*. They were being economically frugal in places that they shouldn't have been and spendthrift in places that they shouldn't have been."

But Golan and Golan still had some steam left after *Murphy's Law*, which was their fourth Bronson epic—and there would be another quartet of Charles Bronson movies still to come from Cannon Films.

Secret Service agents Jay "Killey" Killion (Charles Bronson) and Charlotte "Charlie" Chong (Jan Gan Boyd).

Chapter 15
Assassination (1987)

Death Wish II (1982) and *Death Wish 3* (1985) were huge international hits for Cannon Films. Naturally, studio moguls Menahem Golan and Yoram Globus wanted Bronson in a fourth vigilante adventure, but the star refused to sign for *Death Wish 4* unless Cannon included that sequel as part of a six-film deal, with each picture paying Bronson a $1 million fee. The final arrangement called for *My Affair with the President's Wife* (ultimately called *Assassination*) to be the first picture in the pact, followed by *Death Wish 4*, then by three non-sequel cop movies in the traditional Bronson action mold, and, finally, by a fifth vigilante follow-up. Bronson said at the time, "I was very pleased with the arrangements."

My Affair with the President's Wife was a screenplay by Richard Sale, based on his unpublished novel about a Secret Service agent assigned to protect the targeted First Lady—and the romance that develops. Sale had been in the business since 1937 and had writing credits on over twenty-five features, including *Suddenly* (1954) and Bronson's *The White Buffalo* (1977), as well as TV episodes, novels and short stories. He had also directed a dozen films. Sale got his *My Affair with the President's Wife* script to Cannon via his longtime agent Paul Kohner, who had set up Bronson's multi-pic package with Golan and Globus.

In early April 1986, Pancho Kohner (the son of Bronson's agent and a producer on seven prior Bronson epics, including two with Cannon) asked Bronson's wife, Jill Ireland, to be his co-producer on *My Affair with the President's Wife*, which was about to begin pre-production. Ireland, who had already worked with Pancho Kohner as a producer on *The Evil That Men Do* (1984) and *Murphy's Law* (1986), wrote, "I doubted I would be healthy in time for the film, but I punted and told Pancho to send me the script." She had just had a lumpectomy, was suffering from pneumonia, and was heavily involved with the writing of her memoir *Life Wish* (1987). Ireland read the script and suggested Jaclyn Smith (TV's *Charlie's Angels*, 1976–1981) for the First Lady role. (Smith had done the 1985 Cannon artsploitation film *Déjà Vu*.)

At Ireland's fiftieth-birthday party in April 1986, Golan and Globus personally asked her to star with her husband in *My Affair with the President's Wife*. She agreed to co-star instead of co-produce, and Golan searched the crowd for her agent. Ireland said, "I thought, how terrific, because my book would come out at the same time with the message, hang in there with your chemotherapy; don't feel that your life is over. With my book coming out, it seemed good to be visible at the same time. It seemed fate that I should do it."

Sale continued to revise his script throughout April and May 1986. Bronson's favored director J. Lee Thompson was busy at the time with the Cannon/Chuck Norris picture *Firewalker* (1986), so the new Bronson project was assigned to British director Peter Hunt, editor and second-unit director on the James Bond films *Thunderball* (1965) and *You Only*

Live Twice (1967) and director of *On Her Majesty's Secret Service* (1969), one of the best films in that series. Hunt had previously directed Bronson on *Death Hunt* (1981) after taking over that film late in pre-production when Robert Aldrich (*The Dirty Dozen*, 1967) dropped out.

Cast in *The President's Wife* as Secret Service agent (and Bronson love interest) Charlotte "Charlie" Chong was Jan Gan Boyd—a young, adorable Asian-American actress/dancer who had been in Yul Brynner's final *The King and I* tour in the early 1980s. She was introduced to Hunt shortly after starring in Richard Attenborough's film *A Chorus Line* (1985). Boyd says, "Peter Hunt was a friend of Dickie Attenborough, they're both from England. I was going to do a James Bond film with [Hunt]. They were about to film *A View to a Kill* [1985]. He had a part written in there for me. I took promo pictures. The costumers put me in this red, rubber dress. And then he got sick, and then they turned it over. [John Glen ended up directing *A View to a Kill*.] He was lovely, just a lovely man. He was light-hearted, and he was an English gentleman. He became a good friend of mine.

"When [the Bronson film] came up, Peter wanted me to meet Charlie Bronson to see what kind of 'action-film star' I'd be. They were looking for an Asian actress. I wasn't a huge 'action-star fan,' so I had never really watched a lot of his work. I saw *Death Wish* [1974] when I was young, and it frightened me. I'm not a real big fan of violent movies, but before I auditioned, I prepared for the role, and I watched a lot of his films. I started watching some of his *amazing* work like *The Magnificent Seven* [1960] and *The Great Escape* [1963] and this one where he's in the wilderness running from Lee Marvin [*Death Hunt*.] It was tremendous. They had me talk to Charlie for a while and then do a chemistry test to see how compatible we were. I immediately took to Charlie. He's so much more endearing and warm in person than he comes across on screen. On screen, his demeanor is tough and gritty. But he's actually very, very gentle and very kind. [laughs] And when I said to him, 'Gosh, you're so much more gentle in person,' he said, 'Shh. Don't tell anybody that, Jan.' [laughs] He loved my name. He'd always go, 'Jan Gan Boyd. Jan Gan Boyd. I love to say Jan Gan Boyd.' [laughs] He was very cute. When I first met him, there was this chemistry between us as if we'd been friends for a long time. It was very interesting. I was so comfortable around him and so at ease, and he made me giggle and he made me feel comfortable. It wasn't difficult. I had a wonderful time at the audition, which doesn't normally happen. [laughs] The script was really good. Peter Hunt really loved the script."

Killey (Bronson) guards the First Lady, Lara Craig (Jill Ireland), at the inauguration parade.

During pre-production, Pancho Kohner and Hunt went to Washington, D.C. to shoot stills of the White House. The art department used the photos to recreate the White House interiors on soundstages in Marina del Rey, California. Hunt said, "I think we might have been allowed to actually shoot inside the White House under different circumstances. But there's a great fear of terrorism today, and they were concerned that the noise and clutter of a movie crew might compromise their security blanket." A portion of the White House's North Portico exterior, including the black iron gates, was built at West Los Angeles' Veteran's Administration.

Under the shortened title *The President's Wife*, the film began shooting on May 20, 1986. Golan said at the time that Cannon was spending an average of $5 million per movie, but it is more likely that the Bronson programmers were capped at around $2.5 million (plus the star's $1 million salary).

Among the cast was Bronson's long-time friend Michael Ansara (*Broken Arrow*, TV 1956–1958) as a shady senator. The two had known each other since the late 1950s. When Bronson was starring on *Man with a Camera* (1958–1960), he would hold parties with other young TV actors, including Ansara, Steve McQueen (*Wanted: Dead or Alive*, 1958–1961) and Chuck Connors (*The Rifleman*, 1958–1963). An odd casting choice was William "Billy" Hayes, the young American who spent time in a Turkish prison in the 1970s for smuggling hashish and later wrote the book *Midnight Express* (1977) about his ordeal. Hayes got into performing on the lecture circuit for his book and made his movie debut in the low-budget *Scorpion* (1986). Ireland was a fan of Hayes' book and was instrumental in getting him in the Bronson film, where he plays a curly blonde-mulleted, missile-launching bad guy (with no dialogue). The *President's Wife* script called for a cameo by real-life CBS news reporter Connie Chung, but this didn't happen.

Boyd: "Both Charlie and Jill were amazing. I loved her. The two of them actually did take me under their wing as if they were my mentors. Prior to *A Chorus Line*, I was primarily a dancer, so I was still getting my feet planted in the acting world. I was always choreographed to be on camera. Not being choreographed, I was kind of stiff and uncomfortable on how to move my body. They talked to me about how to look more natural on film. He gave me a lot of pointers on that. I remember he was going over a telephone scene I had—how to relax and talk like there's somebody actually on the other side. He said, 'Give it time as if you're listening to somebody and as if you're having an actual phone call. I always hate people who look at the telephone before they hang it up. In natural life when you hang up the phone, you don't look at it before you hang up—you just hang it up.'

"We filmed in Washington, D.C. around the White House. And I had to drive, and I'm a terrible driver. I'm Chinese, I'm a woman—it's not in my gene pool to be able to drive. [laughs] Charlie and I are in the car, and I'm supposed to drive up to these gates where these guards are. It's a back gate, because we're supposed to be Secret Service. And I can't go too far, I can't go too close to the gate because we aren't 'cleared.' We were shooting it without the 'okay' of the White House. You're not allowed to film unless you get all these 'okays.' So we had a few cameras on the tops of buildings. And so I drive maybe a little too fast and maybe a little too close to the gate, and the guards start to move because they're staring at our car coming up towards the gate. And Charlie starts screaming at me, 'Jan, stop! Slow down! They're gonna shoot us!' [laughs] He was so frightened. That was the only time I've ever seen Charlie lose his cool. [laughs] He wasn't too happy with me.

"Another time, I was supposed to drive Charlie screeching around this monument. So they teach me the route, and I got it. They say, 'Jan, we have to wait for it to be dark.' We had to wait a long time. We had the walkie-talkie inside the car, and they said, 'Okay, it's dark.' And it starts to rain. They yell, 'Okay, we're ready on the set. All clear. And action.' I hit the gas, and I'm going down the street, and I turn one street too early, and [laughs] we end up on the freeway heading into Virginia. [laughs] And they're going, 'Jan, where are you?' Charlie picks up the walkie-talkie and goes 'Yup, we're heading towards Virginia.' And I'm speeding. I don't know where we are. I don't drive very much, and I certainly don't drive well at night when it's raining in Washington, D.C. So we pull over, but I have no idea where we are. They send a Teamster over to drive us back. They set us back onto the street, and they go, 'Jan, remember *not* the first street, the *second* street you turn right.' I go, 'Okay.' They go, 'And action.' And I do the *same* thing. I turn down the wrong street [laughs], and we're heading into Virginia again. And they're going, 'Where are you?' And Charlie's getting really angry now, and he goes, 'We are heading into Virginia again.' So they come and get us. And this is taking up time, so everyone's pissed at me. I'm even pissed at me. They go, 'Jan, *please* remember. Do not turn on the first street, turn on the second street, where the monument is.' I go, 'Okay.' I turn down the [right] street, I go around the monument, and they go, 'Cut! Okay we got the shot, we don't want another one.' [laughs] So I pull over, and Charlie jumps out of the car and he goes, 'You cannot drive!' And I go, 'Charlie, I think we established that the *first* time I was driving.' [laughs] Charlie was *furious* at me. He gets out, and they go, 'Okay, Jan, just drive up to your trailer.' And I'm furious at this point because Charlie yelled at me, the director yelled at me. So I was yelling at the P.A. [production assistant]: 'You know I can't drive! I don't know where I am! You get somebody in here and have them drive me to my trailer because I am *not* driving anymore!' I get in the passenger side, and I'm steaming. Then one of the P.A.s gets in, and he drives straight maybe 300 feet, and there were the trailers. [laughs] And I just went, 'Oh. Thank you.' We shot all of the scenes in Washington, D.C. first and then all the scenes on the set in L.A."

Killey (Bronson) and Lara (Jill Ireland) board a train to hide from the posse of assassins.

The script originally had Ireland's character disappear from the story deep in the third act and not reappear. A final meeting between the Bronsons' characters was added and filmed during the Los Angeles interiors portion of the schedule. The Inauguration Day parade was filmed during two Sundays on Colorado Boulevard in Pasadena, where the Rose Bowl Parade takes place.

Sale's script included this moment:

> [Charlotte] is dressed (if you can call it that) with two daisy-type pasties over her nipples, her breast bare. She is wearing a delicate lace maid's cap on her jet-black hair. Around her hips is a delicate lace apron, a tiny thing, completely sheer except for a black panel, completely opaque which covers her pube. The fact is, she is thoroughly covered from the front. But as she walks away, we see that although covered everywhere else, her pretty buns are naked as a hairless bustard. (This is a shot for humor, not sex.)

Boyd: "I was supposed to do a nude scene, and I said, 'Charlie, I am so uncomfortable with the nude scene.' So he talked to the producers and the director, and he said, 'Okay, we're going to allow you to not do a nude scene.' And that rarely happens. If you sign a contract and it says that you have to do a nude scene, you have to do the nude scene or you could be sued for not fulfilling your obligation. I knew he really cared about me because if he didn't care about me, he wouldn't go up to bat for me. He had the costumer come up with a way of me not having to be nude in two scenes. In one I had a little nightie, and in the other one I had a turquoise cheongsam, a Chinese dress. It was because of Charlie that I didn't have to be naked.

"One time, Charlie and I were sitting in our chairs on the side, and he's fanning through the *National Enquirer* or one of those rags. I'm like,

'Charlie, I didn't know you read the rags.' He goes—he had this really cute inflection—'Yes. I gotta' keep an eye to see if my picture's in here or if my wife's is in here.' And I was laughing, and I go, 'Really?' And he goes, 'Yeah. See that guy behind the tree?' And there was a guy taking pictures of us, trying to hide behind a tree. He was just a fan. And [Bronson] goes, 'That's what I don't like.' And he called one of the production assistants to make the guy leave. And he goes, 'If that man asked me if he could have a picture with me, I'd have no problem with that whatsoever. But that guy is being sneaky and creepy about it. And I don't like that at all. Have enough courage to come up to me and ask for my autograph or ask for a picture. I don't like weasels trying to take a picture whenever they can.' That's how he was. He was actually very, very shy. And people took that as him being standoffish and guarded. But him being guarded was because he's very private and didn't like to share his personal life with people. He respected people who respected his privacy—his and Jill's.

"He would tell me stories of filming *The Great Escape* or of times when he was hanging out with the guys. I was telling a story, and after I was done, he said, 'Jan Gan. Jan Gan Boyd. Jan Gan. You tell the most boring stories I've ever heard. Do you ever tell funny stories or interesting stories or stories that don't make a person fall asleep?' [laughs] He was really endearing with me."

Because of her dance and gymnastics background, the flexible Boyd was able to do many of her own stunts. "I did most of them. I was able to run and duck and cover. [laughs] But where we're in the house and a boat blows up and the glass shatters, they had stunt doubles because of insurance reasons." The exploding yacht sequence was shot at Newport Beach harbor.

Boyd: "We were supposed to film in Tahoe [Nevada] for a month. We were in Lake Tahoe, and they said, 'We are out of money, so we only have two weeks left to finish the movie.' The scenes that we were supposed to do in Lake Tahoe got cut way down [by] basically ripping sheets out of the script. I remember Peter Hunt being very upset. The action scenes near the end of the movie were really cut short."

Among the casualties of the budget cuts was an outrageous action sequence where Bronson and Ireland crash their small plane into the snowy Rocky Mountains and encounter a mountain lion in a cave. Reno Bracken (the lead villain played by Erik Stern) parachutes down after them, gets attacked by the lion, falls off a cliff, and is buried in an avalanche. Bronson and Ireland then use all-terrain tricycles to travel up Donner Pass. Also deleted was when Bracken turns up later to assault Charlotte (Boyd) and taunt Bronson over the phone.

From Sale's screenplay:

> Bracken has tied off her ankles on the bottom stays of the bed so that she is now spread-eagled, wide-eyed and totally conscious. He sits on the bed (still in the dark) and leans toward Charlotte as he brandishes a knife and flicks out a nine inch blade.
>
> BRACKEN
> You get your hotshot ass over
> here in ten minutes flat, or
> your Oriental yingyang is going
> to get fucked by a nine-inch
> switchblade!
>
> He hangs up and taps her pantied pube with the flat blade as he smiles at her.

In the scripted climax, Bronson's character pointed his bare finger at Bracken's chest and said "Bang!" just as a hidden Secret Service agent showed up to blow the villain open with a .44 Magnum. The hastily-rewritten ending in the finished movie has Bronson's stunt double chase

Bracken via Jet Ski to an island, where the villain is dispatched with a handgun. Bronson then tosses a (dummy of) the evil senator out of a glass elevator. (The on-the-water shots were quickly filmed in Orlando, Florida.)

This was one of the few Bronson/Cannon vehicles where Golan and Globus actually visited the set. Boyd: "Charlie would have talks with them, and they'd be very cordial with Charlie, at least on the set. I don't know what it was like behind the office door. I was always very impressed with how polite they were to me. I had dinner with Menahem Golan and Yoram Globus one time. We had dinner at Charlie's house—the two of them, Jill, Charlie and me. I heard that they're not that easy to get along with, but they were super nice to me, and maybe that was because Jill and Charlie were with me. They were not mean at all."

The final day of shooting was July 21, 1986. After the diminished shooting schedule, Boyd stayed close to Bronson and Ireland. "I went to

The Secret Service agent (Bronson) spends the night with the First Lady (Jill Ireland).

their home several times for dinner, and I got to know their family. They would be immersing me into the group. I don't know if they did this for a lot of people, but it would be just me and a couple of other people. We had dinner with Billy Hayes one night. He was talking about *Midnight Express*."

Ireland wrote, "The proceeds of my participation in *My Affair with the President's Wife* helped to buy a beach cottage in Malibu."

In *Variety*'s special issue for the May 1986 Cannes Film Festival, Golan and Globus had a forty-five-page ad including a full page billing their new Bronson movie as *Assassin*, a title that Cannon had trademarked earlier as a generic, potential moniker. The ad read: "screenplay by Richard Sale, based on his novel," although the book was actually titled *My Affair with the President's Wife*. An unnamed Cannon spokesman told *Variety* in July 1986 that when applying for filming permits in Washington, D.C. the title *The President's Wife* was used only because "There was some concern that *Assassin* might have a negative connotation and the crew might not get cooperation; people in Washington are worried about terrorism." Pancho Kohner responded, "It's called *The President's Wife*, based on Richard Sale's novel *My Affair with the President's Wife*, and as far as we are concerned it's not going to be called anything else." The book was never published, and the final screen credit was "Written by Richard Sale" with no mention of a novel.

At the MIFED Film Market in October, Golan and Globus announced that forty new Cannon movies would be made and/or released the following year. Among them would be sixteen in the "medium range budget" including their new, completed Bronson movie and the upcoming *Death Wish 4*. *Variety*'s special MIFED issue featured Golan and Globus's costly, thirty-six-page ad including a whole page touting the Bronson epic with its final title of *Assassination*.

Cannon continued to economize on *Assassination* during post-production. Most of the *Assassination* score was new pieces written by Robert O. Ragland (*10 to Midnight*, 1983) or (Ireland's son) Valentine McCallum (*Murphy's Law*), but the *Assassination* opening credits played over composer Jay Chattaway's (uncredited) theme for the Cannon/

Assassination (1987)

Variety ad, May 1986. (Courtesy of Bryan Moose)

Chuck Norris picture *Invasion USA* (1985)—whose weak box-office was one reason for Golan and Globus' penny-pinching.

Boyd went to Bronson's birthday party that November and to his Christmas party the following month. "What do you buy Charlie

Bronson for his birthday? I gave him a t-shirt with a shark on it. I think it had something to do about being 'bull-headed.' I just thought it was kind of cool. And he opened it up, and he laughed and said, 'This is a great gift. No one's ever given me something like this, and I really thank you, Jan. And I'm gonna cherish this.' And then he threw the shirt over his shoulder like the shirt was trash. [laughs] But that was his humor, that dry wit. At a Christmas party, George C. Scott was there and Lee Marvin and a bunch of people. It was people that I had seen growing up that I recognized from cowboy movies. I was in awe of how many people he was close to. I was shocked at the camaraderie and the friendship that these guys had. It was really exciting to see him horse around with his old acting buddies.

"We didn't have a premiere [for *Assassination*], but we had a private showing in Hollywood. I saw it in a screening room with Charlie and Jill, the producers, the cast members, and some of the crew members that were close to Jill, like the makeup artist and the costumer. I thought that you could tell when we ran out of money. [laughs] We had this really nice movie up until the ending. It was really interesting and well-thought out, and then it just ended abruptly."

By late 1986, when *Assassination* was ready for release, Cannon was on shaky ground due to angry stockholders and (mostly) unimpressed moviegoers. Responding to reports that his company might be going under, Golan said, "They'll keep saying what they want, but we'll go forward. We've never been in better shape!"

Assassination turned out to be the weakest of Bronson's Cannon pictures and the poorest, by far, of all of the star's leading vehicles. The movie has shoddy production values, awful optical effects, and laughably obvious stunt doubles for Bronson and Ireland. It's a cookie-cutter Golan/Globus programmer with no outstanding action set pieces. Ireland is better than she was in 1979's *Love and Bullets* (the second-worst Bronson film) but *Assassination* does not put her to good use (though she does wear a number of attractive outfits). Bronson is required to carry the entire film on his shoulders via his effortless charisma.

Billing their star for the first time by surname only in ads touting "BRONSON ASSASSINATION," Cannon opened the movie in the United States on January 9, 1987. The studio's press release boasted: "[Bronson's] character in *Assassination* is an affable, more diplomatic type than the taciturn lone wolves he's played in his previous films. Put this down to the romantic chemistry between himself and Ireland, and the fact that *Assassination* has a somewhat lighter, Hitchcockian touch, alternating between light-humor and rapid-fire thrills." Despite Cannon's last-minute budget cuts that drastically compromised his movie, director Hunt said, "I'm very pleased with how the film turned out. It's my sort of film: a romantic thriller, with a healthy dose of paranoia and suspense, and lots of magnificent American geography. I can't image a better way to spend two hours in a darkened theatre."

During the promotion, Bronson said, "Jill's role dominates *Assassination*....I like working with my wife. She's easy to work with. Sometimes we get into a conflict over her suggestions, but we work them out. Often her ideas are great, and I tell her so. Jill turns down a lot of pictures, including some with me. She only accepts scripts she thinks are absolutely right for her. Not that I get many opportunities to play love scenes with anybody, but it is easier to work scenes with Jill because we both know how to draw the best reaction from each other....Jill plays different characters from what she is in real life. My roles are close to myself. They're not way out. You don't see me wearing eyeglasses or different hairstyles. I don't play extreme characters. And there isn't much opportunity to express humor. For years I've had to play characters with minimum dialogue, and that makes it tough. Dialogue helps develop the character, allowing him to express himself. I have to express my character through attitudes and body language. It's been a long time since I played a villain or comedy role. I have some light moments in *Assassination,* and

I enjoyed playing them. I'd like to do a comedy if it was well-written. But producers don't think of me in those terms."

Assassination was given a PG-13 rating from the MPAA. The brutal violence, sleaze and nudity seen in Bronson's *Death Wish* sequels, *10 to Midnight*, *The Evil That Men Do* and *Murphy's Law* had pushed the R rating to its limits. *Assassination* was far too tame for what fans expected from a Bronson movie at this point in his career. The next four (final) Bronson features would all return him to an R rating.

Vincent Canby, *The New York Times*: "*Assassination* has a majestic, slightly arthritic pace that's almost soothing....The story makes no sense whatsoever and most of the performances are awful, but that's not important in a Bronson vehicle. He is an implacable movie presence, quite unlike any other. It's good to know he's still in there squinting at the bad guys and occasionally dispatching them with as little effort as possible." *People*: "Maybe this sorry Bronson vehicle won't hurt his future as a box office draw, but it won't help. Bronson simply goes through the motions… with quick reflexes and a tired stare." *Variety*: "[a] fun Bronson vehicle…. What makes the film watchable anyway is Bronson's self-assured charm. No matter that he's reaching retirement age for a Secret Service man and has no business chasing young hippies, Bronson has by now mastered a low-key but menacing presence that's simply fun to watch and rarely has he been better." *Los Angeles Times*: "a floundering enterprise, almost like a hit squad that's lost its bullets.…[Bronson] remains, as always, cool, adroitly understated, the very picture of no-nonsense professionalism. Bronson clips off his lines with the battle-weary disgust of a tough-shell veteran." *Milwaukee Sentinel*: "Making a stupid movie becomes more difficult when you are stuck with an interesting premise and an actor with the strong screen presence of Bronson. The makers of *Assassination*, however, have gone that extra mile.…Even the romantic sparks between Ireland and Bronson, which should look natural, come across as forced. Bronson will survive this fiasco on the sheer force of his personality but with films like *Assassination* and *Murphy's Law* it seems like he has a death wish against his career." *Reading Eagle* (Reading, PA): "another dumb, near-generic action film which wastes the underrated (and no wonder!) talents of [Bronson]. Charlie keeps crankin' 'em out, his only concern apparently to make a pile of money, and to provide an occupation for his wife, an actress who is not in much demand....It gets so preposterous even the Bronson fans in the audience started to groan. Only diehard Bronsonites will go for *Assassination*. Others will just call it asinine."

Pittsburgh Post-Gazette: "[The film is] strapped with what must have been a tight budget. The crowds that turn out for the inauguration motorcade are embarrassingly paltry....[Ireland] looks like Barbara Walters and acts like Alexis Colby and turns in a lively performance." Calkins Newspapers (PA and NJ): "One of the softest and silliest action pictures ever put on celluloid....Since *Assassination* has the ugly look of a Z-grade effort, it's safe to assume that Bronson's fee practically bankrupted the production....For some reason, Bronson's followers still believe in the star. His movies, no matter how bad (and *Assassination* ranks near the bottom), turn a tidy profit without the star ever stretching himself in any way." *Moscow-Pullman Daily News* (Moscow, ID): "Bronson and Ireland rarely have been good together on film. This time is no exception." *Michigan Daily*: "[Bronson] consistently looks puffy and acts senile....Admirers of Bronson may want to refrain from watching a usually well-rounded actor deflate into a mindless cartoon." *Miami News*: "It's been a long time since the last great popcorn drama hit the big screen. Now, Charles Bronson returns with a fast-paced action adventure...an entertaining movie, well written and executed." *Star-Ledger* (Newark, NJ): "Bronson never looked better on screen....[B]y far the blithest and best movie of his career."

Boyd: "When I went to the [public] theater to watch that movie, people were catcalling me when I was in the nightgown, and I thought, 'Oh, my God. I'm so glad I wore a negligee. [laughs] I can't even imagine if I was naked.' [laughs] People were whistling. A few people came up and asked me if that was me, and they asked if I could sign their movie ticket."

Assassination opened as the sixth-highest-grossing movie of the week, with a paltry $2.8 million. The final gross was just over $6 million at the American box office. Boyd: "Movies were changing at that time. VHS had come on the market. It really killed the low-budget movies because people decided, 'I'll just see it when it comes out on VHS instead of going to a theater.'"

As *Assassination* was in release, producer Pancho Kohner was already in pre-production on *Death Wish 4* for a spring 1987 shoot and was also prepping Cannon's "Untitled Charles Bronson Film" for the fall. The latter movie became *Messenger of Death* (1988).

Assassination came out on VHS and Beta in June 1987 via Media Home Entertainment and was announced with full-page ads in the video trade magazines. Slick, color sell-sheets and promo buttons with Bronson and Ireland (for staff members to wear) were distributed to the stores. The video's cover art (with Ireland clutching Bronson) and the love story premise attracted female viewers, and *Assassination* became, surprisingly, one of the best-renting Bronson titles of the era.

The VSDA (Video Software Dealers Association) Convention was held every July in Las Vegas. At the 1987 event, Bronson was at the Media booth on one day (for an hour only) to greet attendees and sign *Assassination* stills. He would return the following two years to promote *Death Wish IV: The Crackdown* (1987) and *Messenger of Death*. Bronson titles were perpetual moneymakers during the VHS heyday, and his tapes kept renting until they got chewed up in someone's VCR. Within a few years of its tape release, *Murphy's Law* generated $8.4 million in video rental fees in the States, while *Assassination* collected $11.3 million in American rental fees.

Millions of Bronson fans saw Boyd in *Assassination*. She says, "It was really weird because not as many people saw *A Chorus Line*. I'd be walking down the grocery store aisle, and I would see what Charlie was talking about—people walking a few feet behind me, looking at me and then looking away as I looked at them or them running and getting a disposable camera and then I'd hear clicking. [laughs] People would come up to me and go, 'Where do I know you?' And I'd go, 'Well, I'm an actress.' They'd go, 'Well, what have you done?' And I'd say, 'Well, I was in *A Chorus Line.*' They go, 'No. I didn't see that.' And I'd be like, 'I was in a movie with Charlie Bronson.' 'That's it!' It's *always* Charlie's movie; it's always *Assassination*. I don't know why that movie and not others. I had quite a few fan mails from that movie. I had people asking me for locks of my hair, asking me for my underwear. People wanted my shoes. I had semen sent to me in a vial. Let me tell you, it was vile. [laughs] Very creepy."

VHS cover. Besides the *Death Wish* sequels, *Assassination* was the best-renting of the Bronson/Cannon films.

Assassination turned out to be Ireland's final film and the last of the sixteen pictures she did with her husband. Bronson later said, "Working with her was terrific. There was a communication that you have all your life, so why not in the work? We had our arguments, but they never affected our relationship. I wish we could have collaborated on everything."

Boyd: "Charlie and I were talking about a sequel to our movie. He was trying to put out a bunch of movies at that time. We were going to do another *Assassination*, but then Jill passed away. I was debating whether to have children or pursue my career. Charlie and Jill said, 'You should have children. They are the most precious thing.' She said, 'I was able to do motherhood and acting, but it's hard.' Charlie said [their children were] the best production of their life. So I did have a child, and then I had another child, and then I was pregnant with my third child at her funeral. At Jill's funeral [1990], I spoke a little bit about Jill. I thought her funeral was really difficult. Jill's whole outlook was, 'I want people to celebrate my life rather than mourn over me.' She wanted a party, so she had music and a banquet, and there was alcohol served. And she wanted people not to wear black; she wanted them to wear colors. But I was grieving. I was very sad. And Charlie and his family were extremely sad. I saw a table of people—some of her doctors, neighbors and friends—and they were getting drunk and dancing and celebrating, which was what Jill wanted. But I'd look over at Charlie, and we'd make eye contact, and I could see that he was so sad. He was mourning and had to be around people that were coming up to him and chatting and laughing. I was trying to allow him to have his grief.

"I stayed in touch with Charlie when he remarried—Kim [Weeks]. And I would go to his house and have lunch with them or we'd go to Duke's, after hours when the restaurant was kind of closed. I think Duke's was his favorite place. [It was near Bronson's home in Malibu]. It was interesting how close we became. He was always very blunt with me—like, 'This is what it is, and this is what I see.' He never was judgmental with me, he was just more like 'guiding.' He was always 'protecting.' He wouldn't include me as close to his family as he did if he didn't care about me, if he didn't trust me. I would talk to him numerous times on the phone about how he had helped me and just what he was going through. And when he got sick, we talked on the phone."

After *Assassination* was completed in 1986, Bronson was still in good health. There would be eleven more years and eleven more movies before illness took him permanently off the screen.

Charles Bronson as Colorado newspaper reporter Garrett "Garr" Smith in *Messenger of Death* (1988).]

Chapter 16
Messenger of Death (1988)

Charles Bronson's post-*Assassination* (1987) movie for Cannon Films was *Death Wish 4: The Crackdown*, which grossed just under $7 million at American theaters in November 1987 and then sold over 100,000 cassettes when it was released to domestic video stores in April 1988. But even Bronson wasn't tough enough to save Cannon.

In February 1987, Cannon moguls Menahem Golan and Yoram Globus had announced that their annual output would be slashed from forty films a year to fifteen. Golan said, "Fifteen is a very big number for a small company. Look at Warner Bros., Fox and the other majors. About fifteen is normal." He noted that Cannon would be producing movies "chosen more carefully" and that each budget would be "no higher than $6 million." Cannon had been slapped with numerous lawsuits, and many of the company's employees were cleaning out their desks. Despite the heavy promotion given to highly commercial movies like *The Delta Force* (1986) with Chuck Norris and *Over the Top* (1987) with Sylvester Stallone (both of which Golan himself directed), Cannon was never able to produce a box office blockbuster. The dance-fad gimmick movie *Breakin'* (1984) (which grossed $38 million in America) and the Norris epic *Missing in Action* (1984) (which collected $28 million in the States) were Cannon's only big hits. The "artsploitation" endeavors earned little acclaim and even less money. The Cannon acquisition *Roman Polanski's Pirates*, which was released in the summer of 1986, became one of the biggest flops of all time. Hence, Golan and Globus decided to focus on the genre where they had the most success: modestly budget action. Their Bronson, Norris, and *American Ninja* (1985–1989) franchises had collected only minor grosses at American box offices but went deep into profit via foreign, video, and cable TV deals.

Pancho Kohner, who had already produced nine Bronson movies (including four for Cannon), says, "When you're making pictures with Charles Bronson, people would send scripts. And all of a sudden, a good script would come." Among the many properties submitted to Kohner and Cannon was *The Avenging Angel*—a 1983 mystery novel by Rex Burns, an author based in Boulder, Colorado. *The Avenging Angel* was the fifth entry in Burns' hardboiled series (begun in 1975) featuring "Gabe Wager"—a Hispanic, ex-Marine, rule-breaking homicide detective with the Denver Police Department. In the slim, tight book, Wager (and partner Max Alton) investigate a series of murdered corpses found clutching a sketch of a sword-wielding angel. The hardcore Mormons in the area believe the killer to be an "avenging angel" (i.e. a Mormon vigilante that murders infidels). The novel climaxes with a brutal gun battle between two rival Mormon clans (including the mud-caked, long-bearded "avenging angels").

Burns says, "The story idea for *Avenging Angel* came out of newspapers plus the need to come up with something new for my protagonist to face." *The New York Times*: "Mr. Burns is a skillful and sensitive writer, and *The Avenging Angel* moves in a big, logical curve up to its wingding ending." *Publishers Weekly*: "The writing is taunt and stylish; the landscape 'painting' graphic, evocative, finely rendered; the narrative momentum unremitting."

Burns: "The film rights were sold after publication by my agent. My agent wisely told me to take the up-front money and run. My agent was adamant that the movie should in no way reflect my protagonist—no police background, no automobile or sartorial similarities, no Hispanic touches. In short, Golan-Globus bought the story only and nothing else. [The casting of] Bronson was something of a surprise. Bronson was apparently filling out his obligation to complete films for Golan-Globus, and there were no more overtures for future films based on my books." After *The Avenging Angel*, Burns wrote six more Gabe Wager novels, the last in 1997. No others were filmed.

Mormon leader Willis Beecham (Jeff Corey) evades Smith's (Bronson) questions.

Other than not being Hispanic, Bronson physically resembled the character as described in the book. One passage read: "Wager's triangular shadow, disproportionally wide at the shoulders and tapering quickly to his feet," and another character calls Wager "nasty, brutish and short."

Gail Morgan Hickman, who had written the Bronson/Cannon movies *Murphy's Law* (1986) and *Death Wish 4*, was approached to turn *The Avenging Angel* into a screenplay. He says, "I had actually talked to Pancho about possibly writing that, [but] then I was hired onto my first TV show. I was going off and working on *Crime Story* [1986–1988]."

Richard Sale, writer of Bronson's *The White Buffalo* (1977) and *Assassination*, was rehired by Pancho Kohner for *Avenging Angel* and turned out a solid script that would have made a fine, brutal, traditional Bronson/Cannon picture. Sale's draft began with homicide detective Garrett "Garr" Smith (Bronson) and partner Max "Max-the-Axe" Alton in a classic warehouse shoot-out. It was a faithful adaptation and included most of the novel's characters (albeit some with name changes). Sale embellished the story with gory images of corpses with severed hands and a dead guy hanging from a Ferris wheel with barbed wire digging into his neck. Alterations from the book included portraying the "avenging angels" as ski-masked non-Mormons and having the detective's girlfriend (Jo, a recurring character in the novels) as a female cop who dies at the ending.

This screenplay also included a gruesome massacre that appeared halfway through the novel, but Sale's depiction was far more explicit than that of Burns. Sale wrote: "On the parlor floor, three dead women can be seen, lying in grotesque positions, mouths open in horror, bullet wounds in each heart and forehead. Flies surround them, buzzing gruesomely.... There are five dead children piled up in the corner all clinging to each other. Three girls from eleven to fourteen, two boys from eight to ten. All have been brutally shot in the head and the heart, their eyes wide open, blood covering their dead faces.... A DOG. Just a big yellow-haired mutt with a bullet hole in his head lying in a corner. A little baby, two months old, is in the crib shot through the head.... The playpen has a one year old toddler sprawled on his back, shot through heart and head. The small bed holds the corpse of a young girl...perhaps four-years-old, shot through heart and head, flies crawling around her bloody mouth."

The draft concluded with a fiery, epic war between rival Mormon gangs, with one of the clans led by Bronson's Uzi-toting character. Dozens of men get roasted alive by a gasoline fire, heads are blown off by rifle shots, and the main villain's body is riddled with the bullets from an entire magazine.

Sale finished his adaptation in mid-August 1987. The title *Avenging Angel* had already been used for a 1985 hooker/vigilante movie, so the new Bronson project was given the tentative moniker of *Messenger of Death*—and this would be the name it kept. Pancho Kohner made a number of suggestions and asked for another draft, but the seventy-six-year-old Sale's eyesight had become extremely poor by this time, and he was not up to doing any more writing.

In November 1987, at a press conference in Golan's office to promote *Death Wish 4: The Crackdown*, Bronson picked up a promo image of himself and asked the Cannon press agent, "Who picks the photographs for those trade-paper ads? Tell them to stop all that retouching. You can't see my wrinkles. The kind of movies I do, you expect wrinkles." When asked if he would consider writing a memoir of his own, as wife Jill Ireland had recently, Bronson replied, "Never! I just couldn't do that. Some of the things I did in my life I wouldn't want anyone to know, not even my wife." He explained how he spent his rare time off: "I'm playing golf. I have a house on the L.A. Country Club, and I used to watch the golfers go by. I said to myself, 'What a silly game.' Now I'm playing it myself. What a frustrating game it is, fighting that little ball. [Golan and Globus have] been good to me, and I think they've been healthy for the film business. I hope they can continue." The star had another three movies left on his multi-picture Cannon deal and noted, "The scripts for the next three pictures are very good." Next up was *Messenger of Death*.

Smith (Bronson) beats up then demands answers from a child murderer (John Solari).

Paul Kohner, father of Pancho and agent of Bronson, suggested that his ex-client Paul Jarrico be brought on for the *Messenger of Death* revisions. Jarrico had written B movies for Columbia Pictures in the 1930s, including *I Am the Law* (1938) with Edward G. Robinson, and got an Oscar nomination for writing the comedy *Tom, Dick and Harry* (1941). After getting blackballed in the early 1950s for not testifying before the House Un-American Activities Committee, Jarrico produced the independent political film *Salt of the Earth* (1954), then relocated to Europe for two decades writing screenplays uncredited or under a pseudonym. When he was hired for the Bronson project in early 1988, Jarrico was seventy-two years old and was teaching screenwriting at the University of California, Santa Barbara. Instead of just polishing Sale's *Messenger of Death* script, Jarrico restructured the entire story and altered the screenplay completely. No other Bronson/Cannon movie had gone through as many extensive story/premise/script revisions as *Messenger of Death* would.

J. Lee Thompson was signed to direct his eighth Bronson movie. Cannon had originally announced that *Messenger of Death* would begin shooting in October 1987, but filming didn't start until January 6, 1988. Shortly before production, Jarrico changed Bronson's role from a police detective to an investigative reporter for the fictitious *Denver Tribune*. The main female character was changed from a cop to a fellow reporter. The romance angle was dropped.

Bronson got his Malibu neighbor Trish Van Devere (*Where's Poppa?*, 1970) a role in *Messenger of Death* as a newspaper editor. The actress and her husband, George C. Scott (*Patton*, 1970), were regular guests at the Bronson Christmas parties. In the novel and original screenplay, her character was male and was one of the murdered victims. In the final movie, Van Devere just disappears from the story at the midway point.

Five days of Colorado exteriors were shot first, including scenes at the Colorado National Monument and the Brown Palace Hotel. Bronson and Van Devere were at the Colorado shoot, as was Bert Williams, an old acquaintance of Bronson's who had small roles in four of the star's previous movies. William's lawman role was the surprise villain in the novel and first script draft, but in the final film, the character is just a bit part in one scene. (Bronson often insisted that older actors be cast in bit roles so that they could earn much-needed credits towards their Screen Actors Guild health insurance and retirement plans.)

Novelist Burns stopped by briefly during the Colorado shoot. He says, "The only contact I had with the filmmaking team was a polite invitation to visit the shooting location in Glenwood Springs. I had a good talk with J. Lee Thompson. Bronson came out of his trailer for a pro forma handshake. He was immediately surrounded by a couple of young women who 'ahh'd' and 'oo'd' over my six-month-old daughter and turned to the more important business of impressing Bronson—who obviously preferred his women older than my daughter. I found it rather comical."

After the week in Colorado, the majority of the exteriors and all of the interiors were shot in California. Piles of salt were spread on the California grounds to match snowy Colorado.

Lawrence Luckinbill (*The Boys in the Band*, 1970) played Homer Foxx, a shady politician created for the final draft by Jarrico. Luckinbill says: "I loved Bronson. Great to work with, accessible, very intelligent, kind, responsive—all the things the best actors, and the ones that make it, are. He talked to me openly and extensively about his worries about Jill and actually cried—so genuine a man. [Bronson's wife had cancer.] We were talking about alcoholism for some reason, and he told me about his brother, who ended up on 5th Street in downtown L.A.—skid row. Bronson was a coal miner, hard blue-collar. My family were all blue-collar, too, so it was another point of contact. The movie we were doing was poorly written and not really much good, but it was still done in a first-class manner. That was Charlie—first class. I am sorry I did not stay in contact with him. I think of that film and miss my talks with Bronson. It is rare to meet a man like him, and I was mentored by his calm fortitude and deep feelings. I remember J. Lee being a fine, patient man, and Charlie seemed to love him from other experiences."

The Mormon leaders were played by character actor legends John Ireland (*All the King's Men*, 1949), Jeff Corey (*True Grit*, 1969) and Charles Dierkop (TV's *Police Woman*, 1974–1978). Dierkop says, "When I first met [Bronson] on the set, we discussed the fact that he didn't kill anyone for the first time in a movie. He said that he now had grandchildren and didn't want them to see that anymore. He had been known to be very difficult to work with. I found it the opposite. At this time in his life, he was mellow. We worked very well together, and there was talk that he wanted me to be in his next movie. When they wanted Bronson on the set, they would call, 'Charlie,' and we both answered. They said to me, 'We are going to find a different way to call you.' I kiddingly said, 'Well, you can call me Mr. Dierkop.'"

Crooked politician Homer Foxx (Laurence Luckinbill) threatens Police Chief Doyle (Daniel Benzali).

Screenwriter Jarrico was on the set for the entire shoot and showed up each morning with fresh pages he had composed the night before. His extensive, ongoing overhaul included moving the massacre of the women and children from the middle of the script to the very beginning and dropping all of the other "avenging angel" murders from the story.

Kimberly Beck, a young actress who had been working for three decades and had lead roles in dozens of TV episodes and in cult movies like *Massacre at Central High* (1976) and *Friday the 13th: The Final Chapter* (1984), played one of the young wives killed in the opening slaughter in *Messenger of Death*. She says, "I was asked to do that part. I think that they knew me from other work. And I never read the script. They just said to me that it was a little independent that was shooting for, like, four weeks, and I had a full week. So I assumed that I had a really big part. [laughs] I remember getting the script the day before I started working, and I saw that I got killed in the first two pages. I was disappointed. *But*, I was a working actor that had a mortgage to pay, and I wasn't going to not do it. We were doing it in Malibu Canyon. I was there a whole week. When they couldn't do [another] scene, they'd come back to my scene. I was embarrassed, a little bit, that I had such a small part. [laughs] I was a little upset, not mad. It was not a hard shoot at all. It was very calm. To be honest, I never really was a Charles Bronson fan. I knew he was a big star. But I wasn't giddy. I wasn't like, 'Oh, my gosh!' I was just meeting another actor. Charles Bronson was such a nice man. He did talk to me a lot in between takes. I had to be in a real body bag, and that was scary. I remember being really upset about having to be in a bag that gets closed. It was a little claustrophobic. And he was really nice and comforting about that. I've never even seen this movie. I have no idea what I look like in it or anything. [laughs]"

Gene Davis, who starred as the psychopath in *10 to Midnight* (1983), was hired back by the Bronson/Cannon unit for a small role in *Messenger of Death*. He says, "I was out of work, and I had two kids. I went to J. Lee and said, 'I need a job.' And he said, 'I'll find something for you.' He actually wrote that part for me. J. Lee was the kindest human being I have ever met since I've been out here. We did [my scene] up in Canyon Country. [Jill Ireland] fell ill during *Messenger of Death*. Charlie was having a hard time. I never saw Charlie after that."

The Rex Burns novel and the Richard Sale draft ended with a nighttime battle and numerous casualties. Not surprisingly, Cannon could not afford to finance a climax of that magnitude. Burns: "I was asked to come up with an ending for the script, which had an amazing range of colored [revised] pages. [My suggestion was to] set it in the Union Station building in Denver—at the time dark and atmospheric at night because that area of town had been neglected. I can't remember the action but believe it included a shoot-out with the bad guy and a resolution of the puzzle. But the ending I submitted was not approved by Charles."

The huge conflict between dozens of men was rewritten into a lackluster one-on-one fist fight between a tux-clad Bronson and the film's assassin. In the book and the early screenplay, Bronson's character kills the main villain. In the final film, the villain (a newly created character not in the novel or original script) commits suicide. To compensate for the loss of the climactic massacre, a mid-film stunt sequence with Bronson in an SUV being pursued by a series of tanker trunks was added as the major action set piece.

During the shoot, Bronson told the press, "I try to base my movies on realism. Things that happen in everyday life. I don't even carry a gun in this picture. I don't know if I'd print that. My fans might be disappointed. I don't think they will be, though. This story has plenty of action and suspense, and that's what I'm looking for in a script—entertainment. I've been stuck in action stuff for quite a long while now. Nobody pays any attention to the titles of the pictures anymore. They just put 'Bronson' up there. It's a Bronson picture, the way the critics write it, as though one is the same as the other—and probably to them they are."

By the end of production, Jarrico had collected $45,000 for his complete rewrite of *Messenger of Death*. He was awarded sole "screenplay by" credit by the Writers Guild—since the final film contained absolutely no story elements, action or dialogue created by Sale. (Two early *Variety* ads for *Messenger of Death* had billed Sale as the lone screenwriter.)

During the *Messenger of Death* post-production, Pancho Kohner was already putting together *Kinjite: Forbidden Subjects* (1989), the next Bronson/Cannon epic—which would turn out to be the last. *Messenger of Death* was Kohner's personal favorite of the half-dozen Bronson movies that he produced for Golan and Globus. (1)

Messenger of Death is an offbeat, unusual Bronson picture and is the most curious of the star's 1980s vehicles. The movie lacks the hardcore, constant brutality of the other Bronson/Cannon productions, but the film has a compelling, suspenseful atmosphere. Director Thompson is in good form during the effective, disturbing first scene. The vignettes with the religious zealots are intriguing and well-acted. The spooky images of angel ornaments and the score by Robert O. Ragland (*10 to Midnight*)—with its eerie, chanting choir—are assets. Bronson's exceptional wardrobe includes several dark, tailored suits with colorful ties; a maroon, paisley-print robe; and a brown, military-style parka with a fur collar.

The movie was as tame as the PG-13-rated *Assassination*, but the opening massacre (involving children) and one utterance of "fuck" got *Messenger of Death* an R rating. *Messenger of Death* opened in New York City and other major markets on September 16, 1988. At one brief point in the film, Bronson fires a shotgun at an empty coffin—the one time in the entire movie where he holds a weapon. This gun-toting moment was the main image used by Cannon to (misleadingly) promote the movie. By this point, Golan and Globus were spending almost nothing on theatrical marketing. Cannon's poster artwork was subpar, press kits were pared down to a bare minimum, and TV promotional was almost nonexistent.

Kevin Thomas, *Los Angeles Times*: "A solid, efficient mystery, crisply directed....A genre piece from start to finish, nothing more, nothing less." *Variety*: "In the old days, this would have been regarded as a routine programmer, but in these days of mindless mayhem and random plotting, Paul Jarrico's script at least offers some substance....It takes the sleuthing Bronson a reasonably engaging ninety minutes to put all the pieces together, and he manages to do so without shooting anybody." *LA Weekly*: "A very odd Charles Bronson movie, one seemingly calculated to disappoint fans and detractors alike. True believers are sure to be frustrated by the fact that Bronson not only doesn't kill anybody, but he doesn't even get into a fistfight until the last fifteen minutes." *Seattle Herald*: "Bronson varies his formula ever so slightly in *Messenger of Death*....The fact that the movie is set outside of the big bad city is one step away from Bronson's *Death Wish* routine, and the fact that he's not playing a retired hit man lured out of retirement is another....The film degenerates into the same old Bronson shoot-'em-up, with our man exhibiting his usual invincibility....J. Lee Thompson, a regular collaborator in Bronson's last, sleepwalking decade, directs." Knight-Ridder Newspapers: "A standard movie-of the-week plot....Though cliché, it's well executed by Thompson....The opening scene is a surprisingly engaging one."

McClatchy News Service: "Such a silly, entertaining movie that it's hard to dislike. This is strictly a Saturday matinee adventure, closer in atmosphere to [an] old TV serial than to any movie....One chase scene is genuinely exciting." Rick Sullivan, *Gore Gazette*: "Exploitation stalwart Charles Bronson should be led out to pasture gracefully lest he tarnish his fine exploitation reputation by making any more of these low-key, second-rate whodunnits that seem as if they're made for the safer parameters of TV rather than the ultraviolence demands of sleaze mavens....Director Thompson starts *Messenger* off in grand style with a grisly graphic depiction of [a] slaughter, but then [cops] out completely by leaving the balance of the flick devoid of any bloodspewing as Bronson limps his way through this agonizingly dull, convoluted mystery. In fact, Charlie doesn't shoot or kill *anyone* in the *entire* picture....A succinct, accurate review of *Messenger of Death* was yelled at the screen by an angry member of one of 42nd St.'s ethnic minions during a lengthy, talky sequence where Bronson is attending a church service: 'What the fuck is Bronson doin' in Colorado? He should get his tough ass back to da city!' Our sentiments exactly."

The final American box office gross for *Messenger of Death* was barely over $3 million. It was the last of the Bronson/Cannon films to be distributed on video by Media Home Entertainment. The video release was accompanied by a standee of the shotgun-toting Bronson. Close to 100,000 cassettes were sold to video stores, but *Messenger of Death* was the least rented of the Bronson/Cannon titles and remains the least popular of the star's Cannon output.

Promotional slick for the American home video release.

On March 16, 1988, shortly after *Messenger of Death* was filmed, Paul Kohner died at age eighty-five. He had been Bronson's agent for twenty-five years, and his guidance and negotiations had helped turn a minor, supporting character actor into a highly-paid, international screen icon. Bronson didn't immediately seek other representation, as his exclusive contract with Golan and Globus still had three more pictures to go.

Messenger of Death (1988)

At the end of the *Messenger of Death* shoot, the sixty-six-year-old Cannon contract star said, "I keep the same pace I always have. I don't strain. It's not so bad, getting older—so far. Audiences know when you have it and when you don't. When I don't have it anymore, I'll be forced to move aside and let the younger ones step in. But not yet."

---

(1) A "trivia" note on the Internet Movie Database (IMBb) states: "Director J. Lee Thompson fell ill during the making of this film, the picture was finished by the 2nd unit director." This was not confirmed by any of the interviews or research done for this book.

Charles Bronson as the anti-Asian Lieutenant Crowe in *Kinjite: Forbidden Subjects* (1989).

Chapter 17
Kinjite: Forbidden Subjects (1989)

Kinjite: Forbidden Subjects, with Charles Bronson as a detective searching for a Japanese girl who has been kidnapped by a sadistic pimp, is tied with *10 to Midnight* (1983) and *The Evil That Men Do* (1984) as the sleaziest, most shocking and most lurid of the star's films. *Kinjite* is so depraved that it begins and ends with male-on-male rape scenes, but the script gave Bronson a much-deeper cop character than usual, and the picture was an excellent, unforgettable closure to his 1980s output and to his Cannon Films era.

Kinjite: Forbidden Subjects began as an original screenplay by Harold Nebenzal, a longtime producer (*Cabaret*, 1972) and screenwriter (*The Wilby Conspiracy*, 1975). He says, "I'm a little bit of an Orientalist. I was a captain in the Marines [during World War II], and I spent a lot of time interrogating Japanese prisoners. I speak Japanese fairly well, and I'm interested in Japan. I kept reading about women being molested in the trains and being helpless on two scores. Number one: they were jabbed by men; and number two: there was the shame element that stopped them from reporting it. I thought this was an interesting premise, and I developed that a little bit, and it resulted in a screenplay. I write very quickly. Knowing the material, I wrote a draft, probably did one or two rewrites. I don't think the whole thing took more than three months." He completed his script in early March of 1987.

Nebenzal: "I knew Paul Kohner, who was the dean of all the film agents in this town. He was a powerful, wonderful figure. He put me in touch with his son, Pancho Kohner, who was interested in the screenplay. I guess there was a part in there for Charles Bronson. They made a deal to make the picture. It was not one of those things that was 'on fire' or negotiated for a long time. It went relatively quickly. Once I delivered the script, it was pretty much out of my hands."

The Kohners set the project up at Cannon Films, where Bronson was contracted to make features for the studio heads Menahem Golan and Yoram Globus.

Nebenzal's screenplay was originally called *So Sorry (Gomen Nasai)*, but some dialogue in the first scene inspired a new title for the film: "Things that occur below the belt, or below the obi for that matter, and are perfectly natural in Japan, are Kinjite, forbidden subjects in the West." The script originally opened with this scene, which showed the Japanese protagonist Hiroshi Hada in a class where American customs were taught.

Bronson called the *Kinjite* script, "a little more interesting than most I've been offered. It's from the point of view of a policeman who never read a business page in his life, but he can see what's happening and he's not sure he likes it or understands it. I keep looking desperately for scripts that haven't been done dozens of times before. I think guys

340

keep writing from what they see on TV, copying what's already there. Plenty of scripts come in, but they're all the same. I can tell within forty pages—fewer than that, sometimes—whether it's anything worth doing. Few scripts have good endings any more. I don't know why that is."

Crowe (Bronson) rescues teenage prostitute Dee Dee (Nicole Eggert) from a john (Sam Chew, Jr.).

In late March of 1988, almost immediately after *Messenger of Death* (the previous Bronson/Cannon movie) finished shooting, *Kinjite* went into pre-production. The Writers Guild of America had gone on strike on March 7. Nebenzal: "What happened was not to my liking. My guild, the screenwriters, went on strike—which meant that we could not be called in for polishes or for rewrites. So the producer, Pancho Kohner, and the director, J. Lee Thompson, sat down and rewrote the script." The screenplay was restructured into a more traditional Bronson/Cannon picture. A scene where the lead character saves a teen prostitute was taken from late in the first act and moved to the script's beginning— enabling the movie to open with a brutal Bronson fight. (In the original draft, the Bronson character didn't assault the "john" with a dildo as in the movie, but with a broken broom handle.) Four other action scenes for the star were written: a scuffle at a snack bar; a gunfight in a delicatessen; the busting of a porn shoot; and a climax where the star has to deal with a runaway crane. Overall, the rewritten script followed the original and retained a good deal of Nebenzal's dialogue, although, as always, the dialogue for Bronson was shortened considerably at the actor's request.

This Bronson role was more complex than his standard police detective role. There was a great deal of depth to the character's conflicted feelings towards his teen daughter and to his growing rage towards Asians. The character was initially an Irish/Catholic (named Dwyer), and there was emphasis on his heritage. In the final draft, the character (renamed Crowe) stayed Catholic, but the Irish was dropped. (Also gone was Marlene, a female cop character who worked with the detective.)

The American segments of the story had been written to take place in New York (partially at Christmastime), and the script called for specific sites of the city, including a scene set at the St. Patrick's Day Parade. To accommodate Cannon's slim budget, the New York location was changed to Los Angeles. (The interiors representing Japan were also shot in Los Angeles.)

Some provocative material in Nebenzal's draft was removed: a Japanese prostitute presenting Hada with a lock of her pubic hair; Hada's encounter with his first white prostitute and his disappointment that she does not have blonde pubic hair; and the pimp Duke having to get his Rolex surgically removed from his colon after being forced to swallow it.

Moments involving the Japanese culture and characters got lost during the rewrite, including a vignette where the mourning mother of the kidnapped girl visits a church and imagines the statues of Christ and the Virgin Mary with Japanese faces. Another cut scene had the mother seeing the missing girl's photo on a milk carton. Nebenzal's script read: "A legend: HAVE YOU SEEN ME? Underneath, Fumiko's picture fills the screen. She is smiling, carefree, even on the wax coated reproduction. And then, like a 'Miraculous Virgin' in a shrine in Naples, the condensation from the icy display case sends 'tears' coursing down Fumiko's cheeks."

Nebenzal recalls that his script was changed "a great deal. The end was different. The beginning was different. The emphasis was different. The basic story was the same: that little girls are shopped in the sex trade." He explains his original ending: "The daughter committed traditional Japanese suicide: tying her ankles to stay modest, even in death, and she shot up. The two detectives found out where the perpetrators were: at the New York Yacht Club. They saved two more girls, and they arrested these two perpetrators who say, 'I got to call my attorney.' [Bronson's character says,] 'No attorneys, no courts.' After the end title, we see a golf course and two canvas bags lying on the green. Between the two bloodstained bags, there's an old tire, like a funeral wreath, with a note pinned to it: 'United in Eternity. They loved little girls—too much.' For reasons of economy, [the filmmakers] did something totally different." In the finished movie, Crowe (Bronson) leads the villain into prison and says, "You know, Duke, it was my intention to leave you beside the road somewhere in a gunny sack. But I felt that justice would not have been served." Duke is then led past rows of jeering inmates, before being locked into a cell with an enormous rapist. Crowe listens to Duke's tortured screams then walks off smiling and says, "That's justice."

A number of the Japanese roles were cast with Chinese Americans, including James Pax (*Big Trouble in Little China*; 1986), who played Hiroshi Hada, the sexually obsessed father of the kidnapped girl; and Helen Lin, who played the young woman assaulted on the Japanese subway. Nebenzal: "This was a low-budget picture. Nothing is very accurate. They got extras who were not Japanese—they were Chinese and Tai. The American public doesn't know the difference, anyway. Anything that sociologically could have been accurate was in the script and they threw it out."

Sex-obsessed Japanese businessman Hiroshi Hada (James Pax) gropes a hostess (Veronica Carothers).

Perry Lopez, who had played one of Bronson's fellow Native Americans in *Drum Beat* (1954) and had recently been a villain in *Death Wish 4: The Crackdown* (1987), played Bronson's detective partner. Peggy Lipton (TV's *The Mod Squad*, 1968–1973) was cast as Bronson's wife.

Black actor Sy Richardson—whose eclectic resume includes *Petey Wheatstraw* (1977), *Nocturna* (1979), *Repo Man* (1984), and *They Live* (1988)—was cast in *Kinjite* as Lavonne, a member of the prostitution/drug ring. He says, "In those days, I worked a lot. In the '80s, I was always working. I would finish one and immediately go to another one. For some reason, I'm what they call a 'cult hero.' [For *Kinjite*,] I was sent to a general interview. When I got to the office, there were at least ten or twelve "TVQ" black actors. One I knew from 'black exploitation' [movies]. Even a 'Heavyweight Champion of the World' was there. They called me in first. The director looked at my resume and said, 'Oh, you were in *Sid and Nancy* [1986].' I said, 'Yes.' He said, 'Well, what did you do?' I said, 'Well, I was the methadone clinic guy.' He said, 'Oh, really?'

He took the script, threw one to the producer, threw one to me, and said, 'Turn to such-and-such a page and read.' So we read together, and he said, 'Thank you,' and I left. I'm at the elevator, waiting to go down, and a crew guy came up to me and said, 'You got that.' I said, 'Thank you. That's between your mouth and God's ear.' When I got to my car, my cell phone rang. I picked it up, and my agent said, 'Sy, I gotta meet your God.' I said, 'Why?' He said, 'You got the part.' I said, 'I did?' He said, 'Yeah. What happened?' I told him the story. He said, 'I'll be. You got it. It's yours.'"

Caribbean actor/model Juan Fernandez (*Crocodile Dundee II*, 1988) got the lead villain role of Duke, described in the script as "a handsome Caribbean type, about thirty, could pass for a Latin." Richardson: "He was really wonderful. We had a good time together. We immediately connected as if we had known each other a long time. We hung out together the whole time we worked. He was very talented."

Shooting started in Los Angeles on June 20, 1988. *Kinjite* would turn out to be the final film for the then-seventy-four-year-old director Thompson, who ended his career with seven Cannon programmers, four of which starred Bronson. The one-time Oscar nominee, who had once been compared to fellow British directors David Lean (*The Bridge on the River Kwai*, 1957) and Carol Reed (*The Third Man*, 1949), later said, "I've been accused of selling out, and when I look back, I really can't argue with that description of my career. I'm afraid I lost the individuality I had in my early British films....I blame myself for wanting to go to Hollywood and to stay in Hollywood....You're soon out of business if you don't produce something that's making money for them....In fact, I look upon my Hollywood career as being successful in Hollywood terms. I was perhaps one of the oldest directors working in Hollywood."

Richardson: "At first, [Bronson] was a little scary [laughs] because he didn't talk. Then someone said, 'You know, Bronson is a method actor.' I said, 'Oh, cool. Then I'm alright.' I understood what he was doing. He didn't want to talk to us because he didn't want to get to like us—because we were the bad guys. He stayed in character as long as we were on the set, and the minute we got through, he lost it. He walked right out of the character. We watched him on the set and off the set. You can learn just by looking at a man work—watching him do what he does. We were outside at lunch, and a lot of fans were coming over asking me to sign my autograph on a five-by-seven card. Charles called me over and said, 'Don't sign a five-by-seven card with just *your* name. Always put *their* name on it as well as yours. If you don't, they're gonna' sell it at an autograph fair. You don't give money away, Sy.' I said, 'Okay. Thank you.' [laughs] I had a good time working with him.

"[Thompson] was an 'old-time director.' He would tell you lines he wanted a certain way. He would tell you how he wanted you to hold something or how to stand. He wasn't as free as the young [directors] today are. I had to do a scene where they were going to drop me from the second floor. I wasn't that nervous. When you're young, you don't think of dying—you're just having fun. I figured, 'It's not that far,' and there was a big mat down there. [Bronson] came over to me and said, 'Sy, if the director asks you to do anything that you're a little nervous about doing or skeptical of doing, you come and tell me.' I said, 'Okay,' and he walked away. They dropped me two stories; they dropped the stuntman nine stories; and they dropped the dummy all the way from the top of the building."

The kidnapped girl, Fumiko, was played by American Japanese actress Kumiko Hayakawa. Richardson: "She was sweet, she was a Catholic, and she was very nervous. I told her a story that I tell all young people. When I was in college, I was a music major. My professor was the first trumpet player for Sammy Davis, Jr., and he told me: 'Sy, every time Sammy or Frank Sinatra got ready to go on stage, they would regurgitate. They were so nervous, they had to regurgitate. That nervousness was not about being afraid of going out there and working, it's more or less being worried that you won't be able to do the best job that you can. So allow the nervousness to ride with you.' And I told her the same thing so she

Crowe (Bronson) burns the Cadillac of Duke (Juan Fernandez).

would be comfortable. It definitely worked." (The actress was dubbed by a voice artist in post-production.)

Nebenzal: "We were on the set a few times, my wife and I. Pancho invited us to come to the set. We went there to be sociable and have dinner when they had some night photography. They were shooting on the hillside, overlooking the city of Los Angeles, and they were blowing up a Cadillac. And I met Charlie Bronson a few times. It was a pleasure to know him. I got in trouble with the guild because somebody reported that I was on the set. And the Writers' Guild gave me a bad time. I said, 'I didn't write anything. I went there to have dinner.'"

Robert Axelrod played a sleazy security guard in *Kinjite*—after already playing shady characters in the Bronson/Cannon movies *Murphy's Law* (1986), *Assassination* (1987) and *Death Wish 4: The Crackdown* (1987). He recalled Bronson in an interview with historian Mike Malloy: "Very nice guy. Kept to himself. He ran a little nickel-and-dime poker game with the makeup girls and the hair girls. I walked in once, and I said, 'How do I get a seat?' He turned to me and said, 'You don't.' He was nice about it, but he made it clear that he wanted just him and the girls."

Among those playing inmates in the final prison scene ("Hey, sweet thing, I got something big and long for you!") was Mexican American Danny Trejo—an ex-convict with a creviced, memorable face and an imposing physique. He had gotten into acting with small roles in Cannon's *Runaway Train* (1985), *Penitentiary III* (1987) and *Death Wish 4: The Crackdown*. Prior to working with Bronson, Trejo was a longtime fan. "Always," he says. "Before *Death Wish* [1974], there was *Chato's Land* [1972] and there was *Once Upon a Time in the West* [1969]—great, great movies. His acting goes all the way back to *House of Wax* [1953]. I loved him. [*Death Wish 4*] was where I first met Charles Bronson. I [auditioned] for it, and he liked the way I looked. I played one of the bad guys. He was supposed to throw a glass of water in my face. And he came up to the table, and he goes, 'Hey, wait a minute, take these out.' He noticed that the glass had ice in it, and he didn't want to throw the ice in my face. Then we became friends, and he called me up about six months later because he did another film called [*Kinjite:*] *Forbidden Subjects*, and he put me and my friend George Perry in that because he liked us. [Perry was another ex-con with an interesting look who was an extra in *Runaway Train* and other films.]

"[Bronson] was a great guy. He was unbelievably nice to everybody. He would say, 'Hello,' to all the extras and talk to everybody. He was just a sweetheart. He looked like he wasn't approachable, but he was. He was cool. I couldn't ask for a better role model. I loved J. Lee. He was amazing. He wasn't one of those directors that yelled a lot. And he was very conscious of his actors. Most directors are, 'Hurry, hurry. I gotta get this done.' He was very, very conscious of everybody on the set."

Trejo would occasionally run into the Bronson in later years. "I used to see him. He used to go to a public golf course on Rose Avenue [in Venice, California] in the morning. And I happened to live close to there. So I would see him when I was jogging." Trejo went on to a long career in cult films like *Spy Kids* (2001) and *Machete* (2010).

Kinjite: Forbidden Subjects (1989)

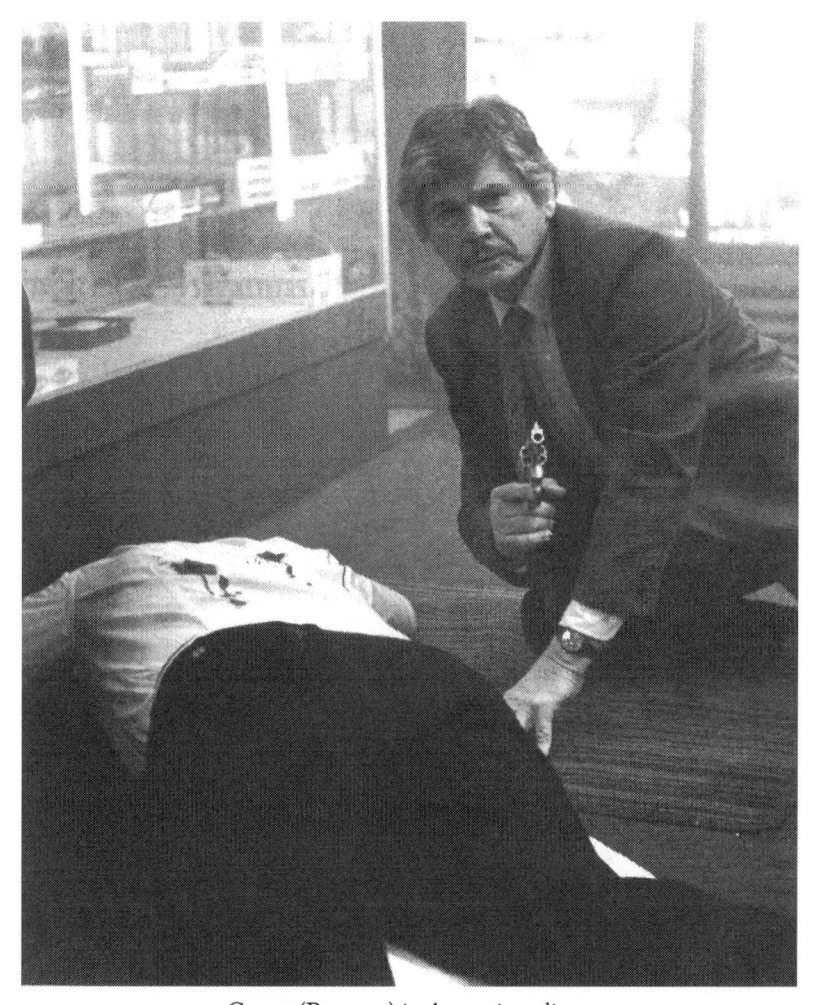

Crowe (Bronson) is shot at in a diner.

After *Kinjite* wrapped in Los Angeles in late July 1988, a skeleton crew was sent to Japan to shoot some exteriors. The sixty-seven-year-old Bronson wouldn't be on another movie set for almost two years, and it would be five years before he did another action picture.

Kinjite: Forbidden Subjects had a "staggered" release in the States beginning on February 3, 1989. Cannon's publicity campaigns for their movies at this time were extremely frugal. The sparse presskits contained only a few pages. Previously, the bios for Golan and Globus alone would take up six pages of a thick promo packet. Cannon was struggling and was giving only limited, token theatrical distribution to their small action pictures—like the Bronson movies, *Penitentiary III* and *American Ninja 3* (1989)—before sending them to the more lucrative home video and foreign markets.

Nebenzal: "The first time I saw the picture, to my horror, I saw an open suitcase with 'marital aids' and sexual accoutrements and heavy emphasis on what happens to you as a man if you go to jail. The [original script's] ending wasn't with the malefactor being incarcerated and the people in jail yelling, 'You'll walk out of here on high heels!' [laughs] The original script, although it was racy and provocative, was not indecent. On the other hand, I've been in this picture business my entire life, so I've been around the block a few times. I know it is so difficult to make a picture, and that it's the producer's job to produce a product which will have maximum financial appeal, so I don't bear any grudges to Mr. Kohner and Mr. Thompson. I realize they couldn't avail themselves of the services of a writer, so they went ahead and they did what they did. The only things I resented were the smutty, sexual things at the end and at the beginning, which were really not necessary. I think the production values are good. Charlie Bronson was Charlie Bronson; that's what you want him to be. Charlie Bronson was a journeyman actor who made his whole career going from picture to picture. He's no Marlon Brando. That doesn't detract from him. He is what he is." Nebenzal's later work included the acclaimed novel *Café Berlin* (1992).

Richardson: "The first time I saw it, the only thing I really saw was me. I have to go through that to see what I did right, what I did wrong, what I could have done better. The second time, I actually saw the film and the story, and I really enjoyed it. It was sad what happened to the little girl—to know that things like that really go on. Being in this little circle of ours, you don't really think about things like that. And what happened when [the girl] was on the bus when this guy put his hand underneath her dress—those kind of things really bothered me. But it was a good film."

Partners Eddie Rios (Perry Lopez) and Crowe (Bronson) examine bullets.

Variety: "Pic unravels at tortuously slow pace, with poor dialog and several howler scenes that ultimately turn it into low camp." *Seattle Herald*: "The new Charles Bronson movie is called *Kinjite: Forbidden Subjects*, and the title is only the first weird thing about it....Some of this falls into the so-bad-it's-unintentionally-funny category, but quite a bit of the film is creepy and ugly....It's an unpleasant movie. I'm guessing that at some point, the complicated screenplay may have been a serious look at a policeman who, dehumanized by his job, begins to crack up. Something along the lines of Clint Eastwood's *Tightrope*, for instance. But in the hands of Bronson, everything gets trivialized. This badger-faced, beef-fisted actor can still mix it up." *People*: "Bronson has let too many formula action flicks drain the life out of him. His acting style is now limited to two expressions: combative and comatose." Janet Maslin, *The New York Times*: "one of Mr. Bronson's better-made if more rabidly xenophobic efforts....Mr. Bronson seems to require a little more editing help to get through the action sequences than he has before. But in fight scenes he can still manage quite a nice high kick." *Washington Post*: "could be the worst Charles Bronson film ever, and that's saying something. If it were any slower, it would be running backwards....Bronson seldom acts these days; he simply endures, sleepwalking through his lines."

Los Angeles Daily News: "Lurid, violent and racist, *Kinjite* is, nonetheless, an exploitation movie with something on its mind....The concept admittedly sounds ridiculous: a Bronson flick with a brain. However, *Kinjite* actually attempts to make some statements about sexuality and the dangers of racism before it lobotomizes itself.... Screenwriter Nebenzal and director Thompson obviously are groping toward some sort of psychosexual catharsis. The problem is, *Kinjite* drops this potent subject matter as quickly as it picks it up—in favor of extended and racist violence. So what do we make of this? Did *Kinjite*'s makers decide that an 'intelligent Bronson flick' is an oxymoron? Who knows? Still, this picture, which starts out as something a bit different, ends up as more of the same old trasheroo." *News Tribune* (LaSalle, IL): "*Kinjite* has some original ideas mixed in with its numerous action picture clichés. The element that comes to the forefront, however, is its overall sleaziness. It ends up being more disgusting than thrilling....*Kinjite* is actually well crafted and Bronson seems more alive here than he has been in a long time."

Roger Ebert, *Chicago Sun-Times*: "an odd, well-made and thoroughly unpleasant thriller....Charles Bronson has played so many avenging fathers in so many different movies in the past fifteen years that he seems almost to have settled into the role, as William Boyd eventually became Hopalong Cassidy....Bronson's most polished movie in a long time; it's slimy, but slick." Michael Wilmington, *Los Angeles Times*: "just another Charles Bronson thriller—a bit sleazier and more repellant than most—in which Bronson is put through his patented paces and car chases by director J. Lee Thompson, a brazen old pro who apparently doesn't care anymore who he offends....[A] pretty odd, murky stew. If you think you might be offended by it, don't go. You will be." Rick Sullivan, *Gore Gazette*: "In an apparent attempt to atone for last fall's dismal *Messenger of Death*, the indefatigable Charles Bronson returns in this sordid, violent, lewd actioner....Along the way, veteran Bronson sleazemeister director J. Lee Thompson packs the flick with first-rate graphic violence, surprisingly kinky sex and nudity....As such, *Kinjite* emerges as one of the best and most depraved Bronson exploitationers released in years."

Kinjite's brief American theatrical run grossed a total of $3.4 million. The film was released to American video stores in June of 1989, only a few weeks after it played theaters in some markets. Cannon's deal with Media Home Entertainment had ended and *Kinjite: Forbidden Subjects* was distributed on home video by the studio's own Cannon Video. Posters were supplied to the video rental shops but Cannon provided no buttons, standees or special marketing items.

Duke (Juan Fernandez) grooms the kidnapped Fumiko (Kumiko Hayakawa).

Golan and Globus's financial troubles caught up with them in 1989, and their unstable company went under. Cannon faced Chapter 11 bankruptcy and were investigated by the Securities and Exchange Commission regarding the company's financial records. During the meltdown, Golan and Globus had a falling out. They stopped making movies together and refused to speak to each other. Reportedly, Golan painted out his cousin's name on the Cannon movie posters that hung in his office.

Prior to *Kinjite*'s theatrical release, Bronson allowed a UPI reporter into his Malibu home and said, "I still have a couple of films to do for Cannon, and my agents are trying to get them to increase the budgets for better productions. I look for pictures that I think will entertain audiences all over the world, audiences who like the kind of pictures I do. I want to get away from the violence and into stories that are different from what you see on TV. I would like to work with another star. It makes for better box office. But Cannon believes my name is enough. I'm not afraid to work with another star. I would welcome with open arms having another star in one of my pictures. I read a book or a script and think of a star who might be very good in a role with myself in another part, but the scripts that are sent to me only have one starring role in them. I get about five or six scripts a week. I read twenty or thirty pages and realize they aren't any different from pictures I've already made. I look for stories that will turn on an audience's emotions. Most scripts don't include strong roles for women, as if women aren't needed in violent, action stories. Before I think about my co-stars, my first consideration is a good script, especially if it's something different. Sometimes things change. Because of costs, what you read in a script cannot always be done on film. I have script approval, but you get into production and realize that compromises have to be made whether you like it or not. It's always disappointing when that happens. If I wanted a script to reach the screen as I'd like, I'd have to produce, direct, and edit it myself. I certainly don't want to do that."

Unfortunately, Bronson had to stop thinking about better scripts.

He had to focus on taking care of his all-time favorite co-star. His wife, Jill Ireland, was once again going through extensive, painful treatments for cancer. In early 1989, her doctors said that she'd be dead within three years. That November, Ireland's twenty-seven-year-old adopted son Jason McCallum Bronson, who was part of the extended Bronson family for two decades, died after a long battle with drug addiction. Bronson's favorite brother (and long-time personal assistant) Dempsey also passed away suddenly during this era. In 1990, Ireland said, "Charlie can't just whip out a machine gun and mow down the cancer cells. Charlie had always been able to protect me and the family from everything. This was something he couldn't do anything about. I think that was very hard on him." She passed away on May 18, 1990.

Bronson said, "I didn't do anything for the last two years [of Ireland's life]. I didn't want to be away from Jill. I couldn't take her along because she needed to be where she was at the moment. When you love someone you feel their pain. It's why some husbands go through morning sickness when their wives are pregnant. But to talk about it is difficult. I wouldn't tell Jill how I felt. I behaved in such a way that was opposite to how I felt. I must have seemed strong to her. I didn't want to bring her down. It was like keeping the stiff upper lip, of being British about it. Of course, she understood that. The fear really hits you. That's what you feel first. And then it's the anger and frustration. Part of the problem is how little we understand about the ultimate betrayal of the body when it rebels against itself. You always worry about charlatans. We found that specialists did not know as much as we thought. So, you think maybe there are other answers. There are not, but if you believe something will help you it probably will: it will help, not cure.

"What kind of man would I have been if I had not been there to help her? I felt along with her—not the physical pain, of course, but all her mental anguish. You can't be detached. She needed to have someone who understood what was happening in her mind. That was what I was for. I don't have friends, I have thousands of acquaintances. No friends.

I figured I had a wife and children. They took up all the personal time I had. My children are my friends. My wife was my friend. We were opposite, but I figured it made for a better relationship that way. One of the difficult parts of being a public person married to someone who was seriously ill is that people asked, 'So how's your wife?' I found it difficult. They were strangers."

After *Kinjite: Forbidden Subjects*, there would be no more Cannon films for Bronson (although he would reunite with Golan for *Death Wish V: The Face of Death* in 1994) and no further collaborations between the star and Pancho Kohner (who had produced eleven Bronson movies) or director J. Lee Thompson (who had directed ten of the star's films). Kohner says, "Jill died, and Charlie didn't want to work. He sort of retired at that point. He was just reluctant to work. It sort of took the wind out of his sails when Jill died. He would rather play golf and be with the kids." Thompson passed away in 2002. Pancho Kohner went on to produce the live-action feature *Madeline* (1998) and a series of animated TV shows (1989–2000) based on the classic *Madeline* children's books.

After taking a hiatus from acting to care and mourn for Ireland, Bronson would be back in eight more movies. Several of those projects would provide him with some of his more interesting roles.

Chapter 18
Yes Virginia,
There Is a Santa Claus (1991)

After the 1988 production of *Kinjite: Forbidden Subjects* (1989), Charles Bronson had dropped off the screen to care for his ill wife, Jill Ireland. His acting hiatus continued as he mourned not only Ireland's death but also the recent passing of his troubled stepson, Jason McCallum Bronson, and his favorite brother, Dempsey.

Lance Hool, who had produced three Bronson films and was close to the star, says, "Jill died and Charlie was not doing too well. Sean Penn, whose father [Leo Penn] had been very nice to Jill and cast her in a couple of his films, asked Charlie if he would play a part in his film *The Indian Runner* [1991]. It was hard for Charlie to say, 'No.' But the part, a man who had lost his wife, was going to be difficult. He went ahead and gave a terrific performance. The film was submitted to the Cannes Film Festival, and they took it with the promise that Charlie would show up. My wife and I went with Charlie. The screening was at the prime time; a black-tie full house at the Palais. When Charlie was introduced, he got a twelve-minute standing ovation. Unheard of in those days."

Bronson put himself back on the acting market and signed with the William Morris Agency. New promo portraits of the well-groomed, dapper-looking legend were taken by noted photographer Blake Little. Bronson had no trouble getting offers. His first lead role since the sleazy *Kinjite: Forbidden Subjects* turned out to be a complete change of pace for the action star. The film was also a departure for the project's writer/executive producer, Andrew J. Fenady.

Fenady says, "I was not noted for doing 'bedroom farce' and that kind of thing. I worked with Duke [John Wayne]—on *Chisum* [1970] and on *Hondo*, the series [1967]—and with Robert Mitchum and a lot of heavyweights, and I was pretty damn good, I think, as far as characterization goes and as far as production goes." Fenady's long career included creating and producing the Western TV series *The Rebel* (1959–1961) plus writing and producing features like *Stakeout on Dope Street* (1958), *Ride Beyond Vengeance* (1966), *Terror in the Wax Museum* (1973), *The Man with Bogart's Face* (1980), as well as TV-movies like *Black Noon* (1971), *Mayday at 40,000 Feet* (1976), and *Jake Spanner, Private Eye* with Mitchum (1989).

Fenady: "My son, Duke, who is also my partner, and I had a deal to do movies and television. One of my favorite movies was *Miracle on 34th Street* [1947]. I said, 'You know, Duke, if we could come up with a Christmas show, that's something that could last for a long, long time—so long as there is Christmas. It's an evergreen. So I called a friend of mine, Hank [Henry] Grant, who had the column 'The Rambling Reporter' in the *Hollywood Reporter*. And I said, 'Listen, Hank, will you put an item in the paper saying that the Fenadys are looking for a Christmas yarn?' He did, and he said, 'Don't call me, call them.' And I got a call from a young lady named Val De Crowl. Duke took the call and said, 'Dad, I think you outta talk to this lady.' She introduced herself and said, 'I got an idea and some pages on a Christmas show. It's called *Yes Virginia, There Is a Santa Claus.*' I smacked myself in the head and said, 'That editorial is one of my favorite literary pieces. Why the hell didn't *I* think of that?' [laughs]"

In the fall of 1897, Virginia O'Hanlon, the daughter of a Manhattan surgeon, sent a handwritten letter to the New York paper *The Sun*: "Dear Editor: I am 8 years old. Some of my little friends say there is no Santa Claus. Papa says, 'If you see it in The Sun it's so.' Please tell me the truth; is there a Santa Claus?" A few weeks later, in the paper's September 21 issue, an unsigned editorial responded (in part): "Yes, Virginia, there is a Santa Claus. He exists as certainly as love and generosity and devotion exist, and you know that they abound and give to your life its highest beauty and joy. Alas! how dreary would be the world if there were no Santa Claus! It would be as dreary as if there were no Virginias. There would be no childlike faith then, no poetry, no romance to make tolerable this existence....Not believe in Santa Claus! You might as well not believe in fairies. You might get your papa to hire men to watch in all the chimneys on Christmas eve to catch Santa Claus, but even if you did not see Santa Claus coming down, what would that prove? Nobody sees Santa Claus, but that is no sign that there is no Santa Claus....Thank God! he lives and lives forever. A thousand years from now, Virginia, nay 10 times 10,000 years from now, he will continue to make glad the heart of childhood." Years later, *The Sun* staff writer/ former Civil War correspondent Francis P. Church was identified as the author of the response, which continues as a classic, constantly reprinted Christmas piece.

Fenady: "[Val De Crowl's script] was a good first effort, but she concentrated everything on the family's perspective—never mentioned the newspaper aspect of it. And it was pretty skimpy, but I said, 'You know what? I know what this needs. You wanna collaborate on this?' And she said, 'Sure, sure.' So I did all the stuff from the newspaper's point of view. I figured there had to be a conflict. So that's how the character of Frank Church became instrumental. [The script] started with him in the cemetery. His wife had just died a year ago on Christmas Eve. He had become a drunk instead of the great reporter that he was, and he's handed this assignment."

When working on the teleplay, the two writers used some dramatic license. The real Francis Church never had a spouse or children, but the script had him suicidal over the recent death of his wife and child. The "Is There a Santa Claus?" letter motivates him to write again. Virginia's wealthy medical doctor father was rewritten as a hot-tempered, unemployed Irish immigrant who can't buy food or Christmas gifts for his impoverished family.

In early 1991, Television veteran Bob Banner (*The Carol Burnett Show*; 1967–1978) joined *Yes Virginia, There is a Santa Claus* as co-executive producer. Financing for the TV-movie came from the American production company Paradigm Entertainment, the Paris, France-based Quinta Communications, and the Italian company Silvio Berlusconi Communications. American broadcast rights were licensed to ABC-TV, who scheduled the film to air during that year's Christmas season.

To save costs, Fenady planned to shoot in Vancouver, Canada. This meant that the crew and most of the actors had to be locals—with the exception of a few American-based "name" stars. Richard Thomas was cast as Virginia's father. Thomas had become a television icon after playing "John Boy" on the classic series *The Waltons* (1971–1977) and starring in a long string of acclaimed TV-movies. A trainer was hired to teach the actor the Irish street-fighting style that was required for several scenes in *Yes Virginia*.

A number of girls in Los Angeles were auditioned to play "Virginia." After Fenady watched a videotape provided by a Vancouver casting director, he decided on eleven-year-old Canadian actress Katherine Isobel. Years later, with the new surname "Isabelle," the actress went on to a long career in movies and TV and a cult following among horror fans for starring in the *Ginger Snaps* movies (2000–2004) and *American Mary* (2012).

Fenady met with reps at the William Morris Agency to find a star to play reporter Frank Church. Fenady: "William Morris, when they read the script, they went nuts. They had a whole bunch of very good clients. I had the client list, and when I saw his name on the client list, I said, 'Wait a minute. There's no chance of getting Charles Bronson in this is there?' And they started looking at each other and looked at me and said, 'You know what? We're gonna give him the script. We think that it would be great for him.' And they called me back and said, 'He loves it. He's waiting for your call.' He had been away from acting. His wife suffered from cancer, and she had died not too long before this came about. And when he read the script, I think that it hit home."

Bronson may have seemed an unlikely choice to star in a Christmas movie, but Jill Ireland wrote in a memoir that he had always loved the holiday: "[He] had been in charge of buying the Christmas tree. It was always his job; he liked doing it. In Vermont, he took the snowmobile and chopped down a tree and hauled it back....As a child the only gift he ever received was a cellophane-wrapped popcorn ball that the mining town's company store gave to each child in the family. These were hung on the family Christmas tree. Perhaps that was why our tree always gave Charlie so much pleasure. I watched him climb the ladder, painstakingly winding tinsel garlands around the tree, completely absorbed in his job, singing once in a while in his funny, slightly off-tune voice. Charlie Buchinsky, the little boy who once had such belief and faith in Santa Claus that he hung up his little black sock for Santa in a house that was too poor to fill it or even to notice that he did it. In the morning when he got up eagerly to see what Santa had brought for him, it was empty."

Yes Virginia was the first time that Bronson and the film's writer-producer had met. Fenady: "Didn't know him. I used to see him around, particularly when we were doing *Hondo* and he was doing *Jaimie McPheeters* [1963–1964] over at MGM. But I can't say that we had more than a nodding acquaintance, if that. We started from scratch. Charlie Bronson was a suspicious sort of a fellow if he didn't know you. He was a very private guy, and he was not the kind of a fellow who, when you first met, would say, 'Hey, let's have a beer together.' But once we started *Virginia*, we really became fast friends. It didn't take long. We really became strong friends up in Vancouver while we were preparing and while we were shooting. He hadn't done this kind of a thing before. He was a damn good actor and a fine, decent human being, and this touched him. It's something different, and it's something that he could grab a hold of and relate to."

Edward Asner and Charles Bronson as real-life newspapermen Edward P. Mitchell and Francis P. Church.

The director was Charles Jarrott, whose eclectic resume included *Anne of the Thousand Days* (1969), the musical version of *Lost Horizon* (1973), *The Other Side of Midnight* (1977), and the Disney comedy *Condorman* (1981). Fenady: "He was a fine gentleman. The below-the-line of *Virginia* was just a little over a million. We shot *Yes Virginia* in twenty days. *Yes Virginia* was really two pictures. It was the story of the family, but just as important—and as far as the marquee goes, more important—it was the story of Frank Church and Ed Mitchell. So I shot that [part] first in two weeks and then shot the other part in two weeks." Fenady put in a cameo as a reporter.

Edward Mitchell was the real-life editor of *The Sun* at the time of the "Yes Virginia" editorial. TV legend Edward Asner (*The Mary Tyler Moore Show*; 1970–1977) played the part. Asner, who had briefly worked with Bronson decades earlier on the Elvis Presley vehicle *Kid Galahad* (1962), recalls working with the star on *Yes Virginia*: "He belied any of the volatile images I had ever heard about him. I kept staring in surprise: When does he erupt? When does he trash the set? And of course, it never happened. He was unbelievably quiet, patient, very unassuming. He was just a very sweet man to be around. He seemed quietly pleased to be there and to be doing what he was doing."

Asner said at the time, "I find myself doing quite a few Christmas tales. I suppose this will have a generous amount of schmaltz, but I thought it was a good story." He said that he played the Ed Mitchell role as "rough, gruff and bombastic. I'm certainly drawn to [journalistic roles] because they are the spires of the world."

The real life Church had a bushy, droopy mustache that covered a good bit of his lower face, but Bronson sported his trademark, thin mustache for the film. Unlike Asner in the movie, the real Mitchell was trim with a Van Dyke beard.

Yes Virginia was shot from mid-June until early-July of 1991, with the Vancouver temperature often reaching ninety-five degrees. For many of the exteriors, Gastown, a waterfront town established in 1867, stood in for turn-of-the-century New York City. Horse-drawn sleighs and $40,000 worth of crushed ice was brought into Stanley Park to create a Christmas atmosphere. Interior sets were built and filmed at North Shore Studios.

On Christmas morning, Church (Bronson) hears his editorial read by O'Hanlon (Richard Thomas) to Virginia (Katherine Isobel).

Fenady: "When we shot that opening scene in Vancouver in a cemetery, there wasn't a dry eye on location—including Charlie. Our eyes glistened." Asner: "He had been visited by tragedy—his wife's death. Maybe he had an inkling of his own fatality."

When a *TV Guide* interviewer asked Bronson if he identified with the character, he said, "You don't think I'm going to answer that, do you? You don't think I'm going to talk about how I dealt with my wife's death? That has nothing to do with this movie! The character's wife and child die suddenly. With me it was years. Years of dying. A strong man doesn't *allow* himself to break down! If a man can't withstand what's happened to his life in a strong way, if he breaks down, that to me, is a little wimpy.... Look, I don't mind talking about professional things—but not personal things. I don't want anybody to know too much about me. The face I present is the one I want to be known for. Nothing else.... There's no end to the mourning, it's everlasting—if you are aware. It's very nice, of course, not to be aware. That's what my character, Frank Church, was trying to do with his life—to drink himself into unawareness. But that will never, ever be me. That's just not part of my nature."

Foreign sales flyer.

The movie had its world premiere in October at the MIPCOM trade show in Cannes, France where it was screened for international television buyers. Italian actor Massimo Bonetti (*The Night of the Shooting Stars*, 1982), who played an immigrant dock worker in the film and who had name value in Europe, was prominently billed with Bronson, Thomas and Asner on the sales fliers. Unlike Bronson's previous American TV-movies *Raid on Entebbe* (1977) and *Act of Vengeance* (1986), *Yes Virginia* did not play theatrically in the foreign market. By this point, movies made for American television were still (mostly) being shot on 35mm motion picture film, but the post-production was being done on videotape, making it costly to produce acceptable film prints that could be run thru a movie house projector.

Yes Virginia, There Is a Santa Claus was first broadcast on ABC-TV on Sunday, December 8, 1991 at 9:00 p.m. The promotion included a full-page ad in *TV Guide*. Retail giant K-Mart co-sponsored the broadcast. (Five other new Christmas-themed TV movies also debuted that month.) *Yes Virginia* turned out to be a charming Yuletide drama with good production values and fine performances. Fans were glad to see Bronson back on the screen (albeit small). The movie saw him in one of the better and more unusual roles of his latter-day career.

Hollywood Reporter: "You will be charmed by this wonderfully sentimental telefilm....For a telefilm, the production values are exceptional....Bronson, in a rare television appearance, and cast totally against type, is thoroughly convincing as the distraught newspaper man." *Variety*: "The pace is refreshingly unhurried. But while this provides ample time for rich characterizations, the clichéd script results merely in stick figures and stilted dialogue....The warm and happy ending is appropriate both to the season and the movie's consistently amiable if bland tone....Bronson's economic gestures convey great pain and warmth." Knight-Ridder Newspapers: "[The] big finish had me casting about for a Kleenex."

Yes Virginia, There Is a Santa Claus (1991)

The movie was seen internationally on television and was re-run by ABC-TV two years later. It has a strong cult following, mostly among women who have never seen any other Bronson films, but it was never released on VHS or DVD in North America. Fenady: "One of these days, *Yes Virginia* will be discovered. I'm still paying storage on the negative. We've had offers, but we're very jealous of the possession of that. I know that the right DVD [offer] will come along, and it will be re-released, and people will say, 'Wait a minute. Where the hell has this thing been?'"

Charles Bronson as Wolf Larsen in *The Sea Wolf* (1993).

Chapter 19
The Sea Wolf (1993)

The relationship between Charles Bronson and writer/producer Andrew J. Fenady that started on *Yes Virginia, There Is a Santa Claus* (1991) led to the duo making a second TV movie. It was another project that had Bronson giving a fine performance in an atypical role—this time as one of the great villains of American literature.

For years, Fenady had been developing an adaptation of Jack London's classic novel *The Sea Wolf*—which dealt with shipwreck victim Humphrey Van Weyden and his psychological battles with sadistic sea captain Wolf Larsen, who was based on real seamen the author had met or heard about. Like all of London's work, *The Sea Wolf* was immensely popular with working class readers when first published in 1904. London once said, "In writing a story I always keep in mind these two motives: First, I want to make the tale so plain that he who runs may read and then there is the deeper underlying psychological motive."

Fenady says, "I loved Jack London. He's my favorite writer in the whole damn world. The first half of [the *Sea Wolf* novel] is *great*—the characterization, the action, everything. But the truth is, the second half was overly sentimental. The book should have ended when Wolf Larsen died. That's the way the Warner Bros. movie [1941] ended, and that's the way that mine ended, too. I said to my son, Duke, when he was starting to write: 'If you're gonna ever get a collaborator, get a dead one. They don't give you much trouble.' I've had the privilege of collaborating with a lot of great authors who didn't voice much objection to what I was doing. [laughs]" For his adaptation, Fenady streamlined the story, created some characters, combined others, and retained a good bit of London's dialogue, especially that spoken in the book by Wolf Larsen.

Fenady: "We were already talking about *The Sea Wolf* while we were doing *Yes Virginia*. Up there in Vancouver, I had the script of *The Sea Wolf*, and I said, 'Charlie, do you know Jack London? Have you read his stuff?' He said, 'Yeah, sure.' And I said, 'How is it that you've read Jack London?' He said, 'Well, when I was working in the mines down there in the fields in Pennsylvania, and I had some time to read, I read Jack London.' I said, 'You ever read *The Sea Wolf*? How would you like to play Wolf Larsen?' And he said, 'Would I. Let me see the script.' So I handed him the script, and he said, 'Yup. Let's go. Let's do it.' The movie with [Edward G.] Robinson was one of my favorite movies of all time. I thought he was great in it. He was even shorter than Charlie Bronson. Bronson wasn't short, but on the other hand, he wasn't tall. I think I had that [script] for five years. But we were busy all that time. It's not as if we were sitting idly. There were other projects that were easier to get made. That was not an easy one to cast, and it was not what you would call a low-budget picture. It took quite a bit of doing. But once we got Charlie, it got made."

Earlier in the development, Fenady had considered two other stars for the Wolf Larsen role. Fenady: "One was Sean Connery [*Dr. No*, 1962]. I had a very good meeting with him, and he read the script and he loved it. He said, 'The only thing is, you never see the battle between Wolf Larsen and his brother, Death Larsen.' And I said, 'Sean, that's a cinch. I can take care of that.' He was very receptive to it. But he had such a heavy schedule that it was impossible to line him up. The other fella that I thought of was another good friend of mine, Telly Savalas [TV's *Kojak*, 1973–1978]. But once Charlie came into the picture, it was no contest as far as I was concerned."

Bronson was a perfect choice for Wolf Larsen and matched London's physical depiction of the character: "he was of massive build, with broad shoulders and deep chest.... And while the whole face was the incarnation of fierceness and strength, the primal melancholy from which he suffered seemed to greaten the lines of mouth and eye and brow, seemed to give a largeness and completeness which otherwise the face would have lacked." Bronson also strongly resembled a 1904 illustration of the character seen in the *Sea Wolf* serialization in *The Century Magazine*. One exception: The star sported his traditional mustache for the role and was not "clean-shaven" as described by London. (1)

An ideal actor was also found to play the other lead. Fenady: "I had always pictured Pierce Brosnan as Van Weyden. [The William Morris Agency] offered me John Travolta, and I said, 'No, thanks.' Then they said, 'Look, Christopher Reeve is looking for something different. He wants to lose that Superman business and start playing some human beings.' And he read the script and, boy, he loved that part, Van Weyden."

Reeve's fine performance in the title role of the blockbuster *Superman* (1978) made him a major screen star, but his non-superhero films had all performed poorly at the box-office, and after the failure of Cannon Films' hopelessly-underfinanced *Superman IV: The Quest for Peace* (1986), he was no longer considered a bankable big-screen star. The actor explained in his memoir, *Still Me*: "Many times my agents would submit me for a part only to be told that even though I was right for the role, the producers wanted a 'fresher face.' But I was always able to find some kind of work, though I have to admit I thought it was ironic that my film career had bottomed out just as I was making real progress in my development as an actor. Sometimes I did a TV movie-of-the-week to pay the bills, but even then I worked diligently with Harold Guskin, my extraordinary acting coach, to make the most of it. Some projects, like *The Sea Wolf*, were pieces I really believed in and still think of as some of my best work."

The Sea Wolf was shot in Vancouver in July and August of 1992 with a (mostly) Canadian cast and crew. Bob Banner served as co-executive producer, as he had on *Yes Virginia*, with Fenady. Financing came from the American sources Primedia Productions and Turner Pictures, the production company owned by media mogul Ted Turner.

Fenady: "We did some [pre-production in California], of course—the casting and as much as we could. But once we got up to Vancouver, we didn't have a hell of a lot of time to do the preparation. We took a couple of trips up there with the art director and laid things out. I think we were only up there a week before we started shooting. *The Sea Wolf*, of course, was more expensive [than *Yes Virginia*]; it was a couple of million dollars."

Michael Anderson (*Logan's Run*, 1976) was chosen as director. Fenady: "First of all, he's a real gentleman. He was lovely. He was great. He had done some pretty good things. He had done *Around the World in 80 Days* [1959] when he was little more than a kid. He did *The Wreck of Mary Deare* [1959], which was not an easy picture to make. He was Canadian, too, so that worked out beautifully."

Cast in the lone female role was Catherine Mary Stewart, a young actress known for video and cable-TV cult favorites like *The Last Starfighter* and *Night of the Comet* (both 1984). In his adaptation, Fenady changed the character's name from "Maude" to "Flaxen." Fenady: "'Maude' reminds me of my grandmother. I never liked that. It was popular for the time, but I thought that 'Flaxen' was a more suitable name. Catherine Mary Stewart was great. She's lovely. And she was not a 'Maude,' she was more of a 'Flaxen.' We saw *Weekend at Bernie's* [1989] and a few of the other things that she did, and I thought she'd be fine. And also, we did [*Sea Wolf*] with 'Canadian content,' so we got a break if we used people [from] Canada. She was one of 'em, and so was Len Cariou [*A Little Night Music*, 1977]—he was Canadian, and Mark Singer [*The Beastmaster*, 1982], too. We didn't do that 'Canadian content' on *Yes Virginia*, but we did do it to get a tax break on *The Sea Wolf*."

The production also had to cast another important role: Wolf Larsen's ominous ship, the *Ghost*. A 126-foot-long (38.4 meters) schooner built in 1924 called the *Zodiac* was used. Fenady: "I found this sailing vessel up in Washington. I looked at a lot of 'em, and this one was fine, except it had some modern stuff on it like radar and all that. So we took all of that frou-frou off of it and sailed the son-of-a-bitch to Vancouver. We also replicated practically the whole damn ship on a tank that they had up there—the first part of the ship and practically the whole stern of the ship when we had to sink the damn thing because we weren't gonna sink the regular ship."

A recreation of the schooner's front half was built and filmed at the Ocean Engineering Centre at the University of British Columbia on a large (30.5 meter) wave basin. The shaking water was heated for the climax, where Bronson goes under. (Among the many other pictures filmed in this tank was *Friday the 13th: Jason Takes Manhattan*, 1989.)

Catherine Mary Stewart says, "There was a big dinner in Vancouver before we shot. I met [Bronson] there. I was warned about him. I think the warning was along the lines that he was 'standoffish' or intimidating or something like that. I wasn't bothered. I plopped myself right down next to him and started up a conversation. He was lovely. I didn't know what to expect. I knew his work. I remembered that in the TV show *The Golden Girls* [1985–1995], Estelle Getty's character was always talking about her crush on Charles Bronson. I expected to meet quite the stud!" (To prepare for her role, Stewart tried to rent the 1941 version, but it had not yet been released on videotape.)

Two weeks of the *Sea Wolf* shoot were spent filming exteriors on the *Zodiac*. The interiors of the *Ghost* were shot on studio sets. Fenady: "Mostly. There were a few interiors on the replica, but I didn't want to shoot on the tank any more than we had to. So the captain's cabin, and the lazarette, and all that kind of stuff, we built them. We shot *The Sea Wolf* in twenty-one days principal and two days second unit. [laughs] We didn't stand around and talk things over, I'll tell you that." (Fenady cameoed as a bartender in an early scene.)

On location with the seventy-one-year-old Bronson was his thirty-two-year-old assistant/girlfriend, Kim Weeks. Former Bronson director Michael Winner recalled in his memoir, *Winner Takes All*: "I spoke to Charlie regularly on the phone. He told me he'd met a girl, Kim Weeks, who was the first person since Jill [Ireland]'s death he felt really keen on. He met her because of me. I had an actress on *Death Wish 3* [1985] called Deborah Raffin. Her then-husband, Michael Viner, was a publisher and a manager. He befriended Jill, took her on, and represented her two books. Kim Weeks was his secretary. That's how Charlie met her." When Bronson's brother Dempsey, who worked as the star's personal assistant, died in the late 1980s, Ireland hired Weeks to be Bronson's secretary. Weeks married the star in 1998 and was with him until his death.

Fenady: "With Charlie—and I never called him 'Charlie,' I always called him 'Charles'—you went through phases. The first phase, he was kind of suspicious of everything and everybody. But when he saw what we were doing with both *Yes Virginia* and *The Sea Wolf*, there wasn't anything that you asked him to do that he wouldn't do. He was a real pro, and he was also a fella that would take chances. He did a lot of the stuff himself. He *loved* to do fights. [laughs] He was terrific. He was finished with *Yes Virginia* in a couple of weeks, but with *The Sea Wolf*, he was in *a lot* of the scenes. He was paid well for his time. There was a time when he was the highest paid actor, day-for-day, [of] anybody in the whole world. But when he did these, he knew damn well that that wasn't in the budget, and he certainly was not unreasonable as far as his money goes."

Christopher Reeve had a lifelong interest in boats and owned the *Sea Angel*, a forty-six-foot sailing yacht. He said during the *Sea Wolf* shoot: "I sail all over the East, Nova Scotia and Maine. My idea of a wonderful weekend is to be fifty miles offshore with people, if they are hardy types, or alone. I enjoy long-distance sailing alone. To work against fatigue is a real challenge. You have to rely on yourself. Your ingenuity is tested. If something breaks, things go wrong, you think, 'What do you do?' You just go out and test yourself as far as the conditions warrant. It's fun to go out there and tackle the elements. I have sailed to Bermuda a few times. I haven't done anything particularly dangerous. But it is a real challenge. [Making an adventure film is an opportunity] to borrow from the personae of people who are better than you, more intense, more interesting, because a movie has to have some kind of edge to it, like a fight for survival—a fight between good and evil, a fight between the rational man and the animal man. All of those kinds of topics are interesting. We can visit them for the length of a movie and then go back to comfort. It's a safe way to play."

Reeve, who at 6' 4" (1.93 m) was taller than any of the actors who played his *Sea Wolf* tormentors, said, "Just because you are a big person or have a large physique doesn't necessarily mean you know how to use it. So if you play it as a man who is an intellectual, a jaded sophisticate, he can still have an athletic frame and not be [athletic] because of his upbringing. Spoiled people come in all shapes and sizes. In between takes, I spent a lot of time working with the crew, sailing the boat or handling lines and stuff. Then I would have to step in front of the cameras and pretend to be absolutely sicker than a dog and disoriented. It was just kind of funny."

Fenady: "[Reeve and I] really got along. He was an extraordinary fellow. He was a hell of a Renaissance man. He could do everything. He was a jet pilot. He was a hell of a sailor. He took that damn ship that we had, and he brought her home one day. He said, 'Can I take her home?' We were way the hell out in the ocean, and I said, 'You're gonna have a very short turnover.' He said, 'I don't care. Let me take her.' I said, 'Go ahead.' So he did, and he was very competent. A happy ship was the *Ghost*. [Bronson and Reeve] were very compatible. There was no friction at all."

Reeve said, "It seemed like [Bronson] had to have control....He does things very technically. I read the script. I read the scene. My job, I felt, was just to listen [to Bronson] and see what would come out. I don't know what I am going to say next, so why should it be different when you are acting? I would see him orchestrating things and I thought, 'I am going to try to find a different technique because we have to try to find all the differences between us.' The movie is about the differences between us, so let's work a different way, too."

Stewart: "It was a thrill to have the opportunity to work with such luminaries as Charles Bronson and Christopher Reeve. Mr. Anderson was very British—no nonsense and very direct. Working with these kind of professionals is such an education. Charles was very unassuming. He was quiet and somewhat to himself, but totally professional. I think there was a lot of mutual respect between Christopher and Charles. Christopher was much more up front and opinionated. I learned a lot working with him. At that time, he was burning the candle at both ends. His wife, Dana, and newborn son, William, were on location with him. I think that little baby caused a few sleepless nights! I was a newlywed myself, and my husband was on location with me. He and Charlie would play golf together on our days off. We had some dinners together on location. I adored Charlie. I guess some people found him intimidating because he was quiet and maybe a little shy. But I found him to be a kind, gentle, generous man. His wife, Kim, is equally as kind."

Fenady: "We had terrible weather. There were times when everybody on the ship, including the cat, got seasick except Charlie and me. It was a rough, as they say nowadays, 'shoot.'"

Stewart: "I didn't find it a difficult shoot, in general. It was quite beautiful on the boat out in the Pacific. At one point, a pod of Orca started leaping out of the water not far from the boat. The shoot just spontaneously stopped as we all scrambled to get a closer look and to take photos. It was an incredible event to witness. For me, the most difficult [sequence] was in the huge wave tank. The scene where Christopher and I climb down to the little dingy and I have to hold on to the ship was pretty frightening. I was sure that I would be tossed into the water, or crushed, or something. It was terrifically, physically challenging. For me, it was a wonderful opportunity and experience. I feel like it was a highlight in my career. I made some lifelong friends, and I am very proud of *The Sea Wolf.* I think [Bronson] liked it. He wasn't one to talk about his work much."

Fenady: "For what we had and what we did, I think that it was a superior film. I think that the damn thing looked like it cost $10 million."

The Sea Wolf turned out to be an excellent movie with a fine script, good performances and attractive production values that make the film look far more expensive than it was. It is unfortunate that a bigger-budgeted, more sumptuous filming of *The Sea Wolf* had not been made in the 1970s, when Bronson was at his physical and box-office peak.

Ted Turner's TNT cable network premiered *The Sea Wolf* on April 18, 1993. A full-page *TV Guide* ad was part of the promotion.

Los Angeles Times: "a sturdy retelling of this dark, brutal 1904 tale of Darwinian survival at sea. The production rivals the classic Edward G. Robinson remake....[T]he success of this latest *Sea Wolf* probably rests with the aptness of bringing Jack London and Charles Bronson together. They seem made for each other. Bronson, playing what's probably his first thinking man's heavy, seems right at home as the power-maddened Wolf Larsen butting heads and spouting lines from Milton ('It's better to reign in hell than to serve in heaven'). The movie catches the roll and pitch of the ship, the mutinous, homicidal sailors and is essentially faithful to the novel." *Hollywood Reporter*: "In TNT's adaptation of this moody story of redemption and loss, we get something of what London put into his book, a novel about struggle and acceptance, of fate vs. freedom and the amount of control any one man or woman has over life in the larger play of events....Rendered with a discriminating eye by director of photography Glen Macpherson and fleshed out with telling sentiment by Reeve, Bronson and [Clive] Revill, TNT's *Sea Wolf* works best as large-stroke interpretation of the original. Yet still and all, this small-screen version does, at moments, suggest the mystery and mystique of London's adventure and its dark subtext, imparting at moments the quandary of life's uneasy sway."

Variety: "Barnacled story suffers from miscasting, loose direction and archaic dialogue; the meller founders....Though struggling manfully with the complex role of Wolf, Bronson, stuck with some of London's original lines, not only can't find the pattern but acts ill at ease." *TV Guide*: "with Bronson's zombified performance—he doesn't act like an old salt, he acts like a bored doorman—and a flat script, it should be called 'Sea Slug.'"

Promotional art.

The Sea Wolf later played theatrically in some foreign territories. Turner Home Entertainment released the movie on VHS in America on August 25, 1993, with the then-standard retail price of $89.98. Due to "mild language and violence," the film received a "PD-M" (Parental Discretion-Mature) rating from the Film Advisory Board Rating System—a cheaper alternative to the MPAA that was designed for shows that didn't play theaters. The sleeve's cover art (with Bronson and Reeve not in costume) and the back cover text gave no indication that the film was a period piece. Turner spent over $2 million promoting the cassette release with TV ads. Thousands of color flyers boasted that "Bronson Means Rental Action!" and reported that the star's previous cassettes had grossed over $150 million in video rental fees. A yellow "free rain slicker complete with Turner Pictures imprint and its own pouch" was given to stores that bought multiple copies. *The Sea Wolf* ended up in every Blockbuster Video in the country as well as in hundreds of other shops and was a steady renter among students wanting to avoid reading the ancient novel.

Fenady: "The damn thing was released by Ted Turner, and it seemed like just a few days went by and we got a profit participation check. Turner loved it. He was a sailor himself. After we did *The Sea Wolf*, I said, 'Charlie, it's too bad we didn't meet ten years ago; we could've done ten pictures together.' And his response was, 'We can still do 'em.' Unfortunately, we never did. We were gonna, but Charlie was over seventy years old, and he told me, 'You know, Andy, I just don't feel up to it.' And he wasn't. We more than stayed in touch. We did the town together. He was over at [my] house numerous times, and when he fell in love with Miss Weeks, they would come over; we would go out to dinner. We would go to Chasen's; we would go here; we would go there. We were good friends. He and my son, Duke, and also my other son, Andrew Francis—who is now the president of physical production at Universal—would go out and play golf together. It was a very intimate situation. We were at his engagement party out in Malibu. And I talked to him right up until almost the very end when I would call him. [Weeks] would say, 'You want to talk to Charlie? He's not in very good shape. Would you like to say hello to him?' I'd say, 'Oh, please. I'd love to.'"

Stewart: "When we returned to Los Angeles after the shoot, my husband and Charlie played golf regularly. After we moved to New York, we saw Kim and Charlie whenever they were in town and vice-versa. We even stayed in their Malibu beach house during a California stay. My husband and I were devastated when Charlie passed away. He was buried on a hillside in Vermont. We attended his funeral. Kim is still our friend to this day."

The Sea Wolf was Fenady's last movie, but the tireless novelist continues to write daily—in longhand. In 2006 the Western Writers of America presented him with the prestigious Owen Wister Award for his lifetime achievements and contributions to Westerns. His recent novels include *The Range Wolf*, published in 2014. Fenady: "Do you know what the hell *The Range Wolf* is about? It's *The Sea Wolf*—only instead of a sailing ship, it's a cattle drive. But the characters are basically the same. I changed the name of 'Wolf Larsen' to 'Wolf Riker' and 'Van Weyden' to 'Guthrie'—he's the dilettante from the East. He's going to go write about the West, but after an attack on a stagecoach, he finds himself part of this cattle drive along with the 'Flaxen' character, and we take it from there. Duke and I have also done [*Yes Virginia*] as a play—and very successfully. It not only plays at Christmas—I get fat royalty checks during the summer. It's been performed in every state in the union—and repeatedly. The same with *The Sea Wolf*. Both of those have been successfully done on the stage. *The Sea Wolf* is also a radio play. I am writing a book about all my years in Hollywood writing and producing projects with the likes of John Wayne, Robert Mitchum, Robert Taylor, and all the people that I've worked with. A lot of them should be on Mount Rushmore."

---

(1) Raymond Massey, Peter Graves and Chuck Connors were among the stars that had played Wolf Larsen in other movies.

Chapter 20
Donato and Daughter (1993)

Before Charles Bronson's cable-TV movie *The Sea Wolf* (1993) first aired in the spring of 1993, the star was already on the set of *Donato and Daughter*, his third consecutive television film. The *Donato and Daughter* material put a gun back in Bronson's hand in a lurid police detective story that would have been perfect for one of his programmers for Cannon Films in the 1980s. Bronson played Sgt. Mike Donato, a disgraced cop who teams up with his estranged daughter, Lt. Dina Donato, to track down a psychopath that rapes and murders Catholic nuns, then stores their severed ring-fingers in a jar.

Charles Bronson as the hardened Detective Sergeant Mike Donato in *Donato and Daughter* (1993).

Donato and Daughter was based on a 1988 novel of the same name published by E. P. Dutton. *Orlando Sentinel*: "A carefully crafted police procedural...a thriller that operates on several levels...a novel of family emotion...and a good portrayal of a woman who has come up through the ranks of the NYPD by her own merit." (At one point in the book, two characters go to Times Square to see *Death Wish 4*.) It was the third (and last) detective novel by Jack Early, who consulted with former and current cops from the New York Police Department's Fifth Precinct while writing.

"Jack Early" was later revealed to be a pseudonym for New York-based Sandra Scoppettone, who said, "I'd been writing for years as Sandra Scoppettone, both YAs [young adult] and adult novels. My career had come to a standstill. As they say, I couldn't get arrested. So I went into a funk and lay on the couch reading one crime novel after another, mostly PIs [private investigator novels]. After about a month of this, a male voice started talking in my head. I thought that either I was going crazy or he was my next protagonist. I decided on the latter. Since I found myself writing in the first-person voice of a man, I felt I should change my writing name and came up with Jack Early. The Early books got great reviews, and I was compared to some of the best male crime writers. That hadn't happened to [me] before, and it hasn't since. Can't prove a thing, but I'll never be dissuaded that using a man's name on the book at that time accounted for its reception. I let [the pseudonym] go because another voice came to me. This was a woman's voice, again in the first person. Also, the book was about a lesbian detective, and I didn't think a man's name on it would be very politic." Scoppettone went on to write five novels with her female detective protagonist, Lauren Laurano.

The movie rights to *Donato and Daughter* were purchased by Multimedia Motion Pictures, a production company that had recently been formed to make network television films. Multimedia's first movies included *Deadly Matrimony* (1992) with Brian Dennehy and *Torch Song* (1993) with Raquel Welch. Part of the budget for *Donato and Daughter* came from ARD Degeto Film, a German TV distributor, and CBS-TV, who advanced a considerable sum for the right to broadcast the movie twice in America.

Scoppettone was not asked to adapt her book. She said, "I got the check and saw the finished movie on TV with everyone else." The *Donato and Daughter* teleplay was by Robert Roy Pool, writer of *The Big Town* (1987) and the later big-budget epics *Outbreak* (1995) and *Armageddon* (1998).

Naturally, many of the 341-page novel's colorful vignettes and red herrings had to be trimmed, including: Donato's affair with a much-younger assault victim; a nun's ill-fated lesbian encounter; a little girl getting dragged by a drug dealer's BMW; the interrogation of Sister Bang Bang, a 6' 4" (1.93 meters) roller-skating butch-queen; and Donato going to a rough-trade gay bar in Manhattan's meat-packing district and then to a drag joint where all of the patrons look like classic movie actresses. For budgetary reasons, the locale was changed from New York City to Los Angeles.

The novel described Donato as fifty-five years old and "almost six-two and weighing 185…Donato felt he was in as good shape as he'd been thirty-three years before when he'd graduated from the Academy. And women told him he was just as handsome, maybe more. The gray temples and salt-and-pepper widow's peak did the trick." Bronson was seventy-one at the time, but he was still a good fit for the role, and he was the first choice of the producers, the financiers and the network. *Donato and Daughter* director Rod Holcomb says, "It was written with him in mind to play the part."

Holcomb had directed fifteen television movies and dozens of TV shows, including episodes of *Quincy M.E.* (1979), *Hill Street Blues* (1981), *The Equalizer* (1985), and *Wiseguy* (1987). He had never met Bronson prior to *Donato and Daughter*. "But I was a huge fan," he says.

Cast in the other title role was Dana Delany, best known for the Vietnam War-set TV series *China Beach* (1988–1991), which earned her four Emmy nominations and two wins. Just before *Donato and Daughter*, she shot a supporting role in the major feature *Tombstone* (1993). Delany said at the time, "Television has been very good to me, and I'm not a snob. And the roles are better for women than they are in film." She researched her *Donato and Daughter* part by hanging out with members of the LAPD. Delany had worked before with Holcomb, who won an Emmy for directing the *China Beach* pilot.

Donato (Bronson) and (estranged) daughter, Dena (Dana Delany).

Donato and Daughter was shot entirely in Los Angeles in the spring of 1993. It was the only Bronson TV-movie of the 1990s that was not filmed in Canada. Holcomb: "I usually ignore what other people say about actors until I have had a chance to meet them myself. I found

Charles to be a quiet man. When, or if, he got frustrated, it was because he was a professional trying to do his very best. Charles knew his limitations as an actor. He was very comfortable. He surprised me at how he dealt with the personal and emotional issues in his character. He was very convincing. He was always prepared. He came from a period where actors were required to know their lines when they hit the stage. He was a very private man, but he did talk to the crew. When he was on stage, he tried to stay in character. I think that was his work ethic. However, he was very approachable. He made some suggestions because he knew his character, and he knew what his character would say or not say in given situations. I think some of those choices were based on what he knew Charles Bronson would be able to say that was true to character and story. He was very smart when it came to his character." As usual, Bronson's contract stipulated that he would only shoot for eight hours a day. Holcomb: "It never was a problem for us. We had a lot of other scenes without him, which gave us the necessary flexibility."

Xander Berkeley (*Candyman*, 1992) played the disturbed killer. Bronson's assistant/companion Kim Weeks, who had bits in a handful of previous TV movies, had a small role as the murderer's unsuspecting wife. Holcomb: "I liked Kim. Always pleasant. It was a great cast. Dana was really into her character. She worked very hard, and [she and Bronson] were both very giving as professionals. I think we all had a good time doing the film together."

Delany said, "I wanted to work with Charles Bronson because he's kind of an icon. You watch Charlie with a gun in his hand, and you know he's done it so many times, it's so natural to him. I couldn't believe though that I was a part of it. I mean, he's an absolute icon in this genre—no one is superior to Charles Bronson. It was fun, but he's a tough nut to crack, not easy to get to know. But underneath it all, he's a very sweet man and quite funny. This is probably the most talking he's done in a while. He got down. There's an emotional confrontation between us. I find that I have nightmares when I do comedy. But with something like this, where there's so much action, it's very cathartic. It's almost like a heavy duty workout—at the end of the day, I feel relaxed."

Holcomb: "Because it was on television, the network was very careful that we did not show any actual violence. Everything was after the fact: a body, a finger in a jar—all very disturbing images, but the actual violence was not acceptable to the network, the producers, the cast, and especially me. It was a very good-looking film photographed by Tom Del Ruth, an amazing cameraman." Del Ruth had been the original cameraman on *Death Wish II* (1982) until he and his crew walked off that picture in disgust during the multi-day filming of a graphic rape scene.

Delany said, "We see so many movies now about serial killers, it's really being overdone, so I wanted to emphasize the relationship between father and daughter. I believe there is a place for violence in films and television. Yes, the problem is that a child could be watching unmonitored. But violence is also an outlet for those fears and nightmares we have, and it's better to watch it than do it. I don't think television is the source of violence. That's about gun control and other things."

Holcomb: "It had the makings of a pilot. I would be surprised if Charlie would have done a series. But it was a good part for Dana. It had a *Law and Order: SVU* feel to it." Delany said at the time, "I don't think either Charlie or I would want to do [a weekly series] right now. But there's always wishful thinking. What was discussed was doing one of those 'wheel' things, and that would be fine." (A "wheel" is a recurring series of TV movies with established characters.)

Donato and Daughter turned out to be a fine, suspenseful movie with excellent performances by Bronson and Delany. The photography is exceptional for TV, with great lighting design and effective use of the Steadicam. The murder scenes and the snippets of gore are quite disturbing.

In June 1993, the four networks—ABC, CBS, NBC, and Fox— plus Ted Turner's cable channels decided to start airing a warning on programming with violent subjects and images. The television industry had been under pressure from the public and some members of Congress, including Representative Charles Schumer (D-NY), who said, "Under the guise of 'empowering' parents, the industry is avoiding its own responsibility for the violent content of the image it produces. The networks, cable and film industry efforts should be focused on lowering the amount of violence on TV and reducing children's exposure to it."

TV Guide ad.

Donato and Daughter was the first made-for-TV movie stamped with a "content disclaimer" when it aired as a "World Premiere Movie" on *The CBS Tuesday Night Movie* on September 21, 1993. Prior to the opening scene and after each commercial break, a "violence advisory warning" appeared: "Due to some violent content, parental discretion is advised." The disclaimer was also noted on promo spots, print ads and press releases.

VHS cover.

Variety: "formulaic suspense thriller...Bronson may be a step slower, but his screen presence remains textured....[he] delivers his customary spare and sinewy style, tailored for TV."

The movie came in second place for the timeslot, after ABC's powerhouse sitcom block of *Roseanne* (1988–1997) and *Coach* (1989–

1997). Despite the high ratings, there would be no further *Donato and Daughter* entries, but CBS-TV would star Bronson in their *Family of Cops* 'wheel' a few years later.

Two years after the initial broadcast, Vidmark Entertainment released *Donato and Daughter* on American home video with the new title *Dead to Rights*—an old phrase (not heard in the movie) for "caught red-handed while committing a crime." The tape release inexplicably received an R rating despite not containing any more violence than was seen on TV.

In the late fall of 1993, a few months after shooting *Donato and Daughter*, Bronson went to Toronto to reprise his most famous role in *Death Wish V: The Face of Death* (1994) for producer Menahem Golan, who had recently formed 21st Century Pictures after his split with cousin Yoram Globus and the fall of their Cannon Films. After a two-year hiatus from in front of the cameras, Bronson shot *The Sea Wolf* (1993), *Donato and Daughter*, and the fifth *Death Wish* all within a sixteen month period. *Death Wish V* would be Bronson's last theatrical feature, but he would soon be back on CBS-TV for his final trio of movies.

Chapter 21
Actor Robert Joy on *Death Wish V: The Face of Death*

All five of the *Death Wish* movies have unforgettable villains. One of the strangest and most bizarre bad guys in the entire series—which is no small feat—is the dandruff-afflicted, oddly-coifed, nattily-dressed, security-obsessed Freddie "Flakes" Fiskes from *Death Wish V: The Face of Death* (1994). Freddie Flakes is a character held in high esteem by fans. Actor Robert Joy played the role after having supporting parts in movies like *Atlantic City* (1980), *Ragtime* (1981), *Desperately Seeking Susan* (1985), and *The Dark Half* (1993). His many post-*Death Wish V* credits include an eight-year gig on the TV series *CSI: NY* (2005–2013).

Pre-production sales flyer for *Death Wish V* (1994).

Before you were cast in Death Wish V, had you seen the previous films in the series?

I'd seen the first *Death Wish* [1974], which I thought was very compelling. I liked that. I'd always been an admirer of Charles Bronson since he was a supporting actor in a lot of earlier movies—*Dirty Dozen* [1967] and all that.

Do you remember how you developed the Freddie Flakes character?

It had a lot to do with [director] Allan [Goldstein] and a lot to do with the script. Allan had this real sense of Freddie being kind of obsessive and that his strength came out of his weaknesses. He was a security expert because he was paranoid, so his neurosis would develop his strength and his neurosis would generate interesting behavior. The fact that you see him in the bath says something about how concerned he was about cleanliness and his hair and the idea of the dandruff bothering him. For someone who was such a heinous villain, he had comical weaknesses. He would overcompensate for those weaknesses. He had a sense of style. I remember the fittings were very strange. As I recall, when they fitted me for one of the jackets he wore, they wanted it to be too tight. It wasn't the right size for me at all but it created this look of someone who wanted to be not just tailored but extra-tailored. [laughs] They had some really good ideas. I went with their ideas as far as the physical look was concerned. I remember the hair design, too, was fantastic. It seemed to me that they were totally on the right track—the wardrobe people and the hair people and Allan had really cool ideas.

Director Allan Goldstein said that he was going for a dark comedy approach. Was that discussed beforehand?

I don't remember it being discussed beforehand because it would have been maybe a little dangerous for the actor to go into it thinking in terms of it being a comedy. But what Allan was very smart to do was to give me a lot of leeway as far as how concerned I could be by the dandruff or by something else. I could show something beyond a cold, heartless villain so he let me show these other colors. The sense of freedom I had with the character led to whatever dark comedy was there. I had a great time working with Allan—very smart. It was a lot of fun to work with him. He was inventive and had a wit about him. He was a really easy guy to talk to and he had a great attitude about the work. He seemed to want to make something special out of this particular film even though, of course, it was number-five in a franchise. But he thought there was room for us all to be creative and not just put out a cookie-cutter sequel.

Within one character you almost play multiple parts. Was that interesting?

Oh, very much. You get to be in drag, you get to be in a bubble bath with a beautiful girl, and you get to wear all these flashy outfits and driving gloves. [laughs] It was a real egomaniacal character, which is always fun to play and it makes for a multidimensional character instead of [just] the guy who shoots the gun.

Charles Bronson in his final performance as vigilante Paul Kersey.

What was it like shooting the scene where you beat up and kill Lesley-Anne Down while dressed as a woman?

It was a hard scene and it was technically-difficult, too. As I recall, shooting into the mirror was hard for the crew. Anytime you use mirrors, it's a big problem. And we were also under scheduling restrictions. We were *really* running out of time and there was one last take and I asked Allan if I could just improvise my way through it and [then] they could figure it out in the editing. I remember getting that green light from him and being able to really go for something beyond just sadism. It was an extraordinary little improv session for me. We only had time for one take and we only had one mirror left to break and we were right up against the wall, schedule-wise and technical-wise, and we just let the camera roll and I just went for something that I thought showed Freddie's weaknesses even more. So the cruelty that he inflicts on her ultimately becomes a pathological expression of his need to be loved. I remember letting it go to a place where I'm sniveling and being very tender with her hair. I get very moved by the whole experience which, of course, made it even sicker than it would have been otherwise. I remember finishing that day and thinking, "Whoa, how many times as an actor do you get the chance to create something under that kind of pressure and have a chance to pull off a little coupe?"

Was it a stuntwoman or a dummy that was used to break the mirror?

It was neither. It was the actress. Lesley-Anne Down was there. She was an incredible trooper through the whole thing. It was a stage-fighting technique. I had her head in my hand and I was pretending to be shoving it but she was, in fact, controlling it. That's a common stage-fighting technique. I was tensing up my arm and grimacing as if all the effort was coming from me. But, in fact, I just had my hand resting in a claw pattern in her hair and then *she* would bring her head to the mirror. And there was a guy on the other side of the mirror with a hammer. They could see on the monitor when I was doing it and they would break the mirror from the other side. When it works, it's fantastic. I timed it out with the dialogue. I made the dialogue rhythmic and said, "Away... from...you!" so that everyone can count or find a cue in the dialogue. When I hit that word, Lesley-Anne would bring her head to the mirror and the guy behind the mirror would break it. It was all orchestrated. I do remember that we seemed to have pulled victory from the jaws of defeat at the end of that day because we were thinking that we didn't quite get it and then just as we were about to go into triple overtime, we got it.

Paul Kersey (Bronson) with ill-fated girlfriend, Olivia (Lesley-Anne Down).

You don't have many scenes with Charles Bronson, but what do you remember about working with him?

I remember how private he was, mostly. And maybe it's because I played one of the villains and he played the hero, but he kept to himself. I don't think I spoke more than two words to him. A very brief conversation, maybe. He was very private. And I thought maybe there was something melancholy going on. He gave everything that the other actors needed. But in a movie like this, and in the scenes we had together, there wasn't that much we had to give to each other. He was a consummate professional and he was there and knew what was needed for the scenes and provided it. And he was very practical—"Let's get the footage that we need." When you're on a film set, that's what it's all about—you're trying to get the footage you need and not overextend the schedule.

Do you remember anything about Chuck Shamata, who played fellow villain Sal?

He's so much fun to hang out with on the set. He's a storyteller and just a good guy. There's so much waiting around on a movie set that it's always great when you have somebody around who is good at telling stories.

What about Kevin Lund? He played bad guy Chickie.

We'd, all three of us, stand around talking. I think I had more conversations with those two than with anyone else. It was a lot of fun working with them.

How about Sharolyn Sparrow, the blonde who shares the bathtub with you?

That was a fun day. We were in this amazing house. It wasn't a set that was built. We borrowed this house from some rich guy. And we just had a good time hanging around that house. I remember it was so opulent. And she had a really playful sense and was very smart and fun to work with. There were small bits, small instances of invention as we went along. When you're actually with the other cast members, you tend to find little opportunities—what to do with the bubbles. You figure little things out as you go along. You try to keep it playful so it seems like it's not something coming from a page, it's something coming from human beings.

Was it a short shooting schedule?

I recall it being, pretty much, average. It wasn't a big-budget schedule by any means. But it seemed like we had just enough time to do it. In difficult scenes, like the mirror scene in the bathroom, the tightness of the schedule revealed itself. But I remember when we did the soccer ball explosion, they left plenty of time for that. It was an extraordinary stunt.

I finished my work but I stayed around to see it happen. I couldn't believe it. They take such chances, these stuntmen. The stunt people often take themselves so close to the edge, always playing with that possibility of injuries.

Do you remember* Death Wish V *as a good experience?

It was wintertime in Toronto, so that part of it was sometimes a bit tough. But I recall having a good time working on it. I hadn't done that many action things, all these technical things. I was having to do all this action stuff, like banging Lesley-Anne Down's head into the mirror. I remember that driving scene, careening around. That was funny. For me, it had that novelty of having to convey the madness of somebody behind the wheel of a car. And all that is totally pretend. So that was a cool exercise for me cause I hadn't done those kind of action things very much. On those heavy action days, you try to stay stretched out, you try to stay rested enough so that you're mentally sharp. Because otherwise, you'd be getting tired when you're there for twelve hours and then you do something that's vaguely dangerous. Not only could you hurt yourself, but you could screw up the footage. [laughs] So you feel responsible to prepare properly to stay both loose and sharp.

Did you see the film when it first came out?

Yes. I think I probably saw it on videotape. I thought it was pretty good. I thought, "Well, it came together exactly as Allan wanted it to be."

Is* Death Wish V *a film that you're asked about or recognized for?

I was surprised. Because I'd done a couple of horror films, *Land of the Dead* [2005] and *The Hills Have Eyes* [2006], I was asked to go to some of the fan conventions for horror stuff. And I'd be surprised at how many people who would come up to the table where I was signing photos and say, "I remember you from *Death Wish V*" and "Wow! Freddie Flakes!" I was *really* surprised to hear so much about *Death Wish V*. More than any other of the films I'd done more than ten years ago, that was the one. One guy came up with a photo that he'd printed off from an online site. The scene in the church, I had the half-gloves on. He just got a really bad quality photo from somewhere and I signed that. It was very flattering to realize that that character had made such an impression over such a long time. There are a lot of fans of that series.

Kersey (Bronson) takes out one final bad guy: Tommy O'Shea (Michael Parks).

Charles Bronson as Detective Paul Fein, patriarch of a *Family of Cops* (1995).

Chapter 22
The *Family of Cops* Series (1995–1999)

When *Death Wish V: The Face of Death* was released in early 1994, Charles Bronson said, "The audience likes to see the heavies get their comeuppance. I think audiences liked the revenge motive of the character I played. They thought that was terrific, and it spoke for an awful lot of people, especially in big cities. [I] didn't think there was going to be more than one [*Death Wish*], but they came to me and pleaded and pleaded."

Producer Menahem Golan intended to continue the franchise. He says, "I had such a plan," but when the announced *Death Wish 6: The New Vigilante*, which was to feature a Bronson cameo, fell through, Golan never saw the star again. Golan: "Unfortunately, he disappeared to the west side of New York [Vermont] to take care of his stables." Regarding his nine Bronson productions, Golan says, "They are all my favorites because they all have the 'Bronson look.'" Golan never regained the glory of his Cannon years, but he continued to produce and develop features until his death in 2014.

Bronson was finished with Golan and *Death Wish*, but not with action movies. In January 1995, he signed a deal with CBS-TV for a pair of television films to be produced by the Canadian company Alliance Communications. The first movie in the deal was to be the cop drama *Breakwater*, written by T. S. Cook (*The China Syndrome*, 1979), and was to be shot that summer. *Breakwater* was cancelled, but CBS and Alliance immediately found another appropriate project.

Bronson was cast in *The Brewery* as Paul Fein, a Milwaukee police inspector and the patriarch of a large Jewish family, almost all of whom had gone into law enforcement. Television veteran Douglas S. Cramer (*Dawn: Portrait of a Teenage Runaway*, 1976; *Dynasty*, 1981–1989) was executive producer of the movie (and the two eventual sequels). The teleplay was by Joel Blasberg, who had written for the short-lived TV shows *Maximum Security* (1984) and *The Insiders* (1985). Blasberg was a native of Milwaukee, where "the brewery" was the nickname for the building that housed the police department.

The Brewery was scheduled to be filmed in September 1995, primarily in Toronto, Canada, after three days of exteriors in Milwaukee. Most of the cast and crew were Canadian, including director Ted Kotcheff, who had directed hit features like *North Dallas Forty* (1979) and *First Blood* (1982), but by this point was working almost exclusively in television. The Canadian actors included Barbara Williams (*Thief of Hearts*, 1984), John Vernon (*Point Blank*, 1967), Angela Featherstone (*Dark Angel: The Ascent*, 1994), and Sebastian Spence (*The Boys of St. Vincent*, 1992). The American-based cast members included Daniel Baldwin (TV's *Homicide: Life on the Street*, 1993–1995), Simon MacCorkindale (Bronson's *Cabo*

Blanco, 1980), and Lesley-Anne Down (*Death Wish V*). Bronson's assistant/companion, Kim Weeks, got a part as a detective.

The first day of the Milwaukee shoot was Thursday, September 7, 1995. Bronson and fellow actors Baldwin, Featherstone and Spence were flown in to film exteriors at the police station, Mitchell International Airport, the courthouse, and aboard the Iroquois boat on the Milwaukee River. Shot first was an exterior action sequence with Bronson leading a police posse into a downtown apartment building. When it started to rain, Kotcheff decided to set the action in wet weather, but the sky cleared before the scene was finished. Handheld rain machines had to be brought in to douse the actors and match the earlier-shot footage.

The local police provided technical advice and vehicles. A dozen off-duty cops wore their uniforms to serve as background extras. Among them was Bronson fan Philip Arreola, chief of the Milwaukee Police Depart, who told the local press, "[Bronson was] personable but quiet. He's always espoused a sincere character. I was kind of excited to be in a scene with him." A local woman watching the filming said, "I saw Charles Bronson. I think it's time for a star to come up here and make a movie in Milwaukee. This is a dream come true." Another lady added, "People have spoken to [Bronson], but he didn't speak back—just looked away. Maybe he was too busy. He could've waved back."

The company then headed to Toronto to shoot the rest of the exteriors and all of the interiors. Bronson had recently been in Canada for *Yes Virginia, There Is a Santa Claus* (1991), *The Sea Wolf* (1993) and the fifth *Death Wish*.

Barbara Williams, who played Bronson's public defender daughter, says, "I figured [Bronson and I] would have different politics. I am very left leaning, and I had heard he was conservative. He was conservative, but he was actually sympathetic to my activism to stop clear-cutting, and we bonded over being from large working-class families. He was sweet. I liked him a great deal. We talked a lot about our backgrounds and how we came to Hollywood, how he picked his name."

Angela Featherstone said during production, "Jackie is fun to play. She's on probation for ringing up her dad's credit card. She's like a surf punk, wears 'surfy' clothes. Jackie drinks and has sex a lot. I'm always getting offered movies-of-the-week like [with] Liz Taylor and Annette Funicello. Then I read this and I wanted to do it. The reconciliation 'father scene' attracted me. It's a girl's dream, working with Charles Bronson as your dad. When we do scenes together, he's there for me. In close-ups, it's all in his eyes. He'd smile for me, even when they were shooting my close-ups. He's in his mid-seventies but he was doing his own running in some scenes. From the back, he looks like he's in his fifties."

CBS-TV planned to premiere the film at the end of November, less than sixty-days after production ended. During the accelerated post-production, the title was changed to *Family of Cops*. (Promotional materials billed the movie as *A Family of Cops*, but the "*A*" does not appear over the title on the screen.)

The network had high hopes for their Bronson movie and scheduled it on *The CBS Sunday Movie* for November 26, 1995, at 9:00 p.m., during the November "sweeps" period. The director of media relations for rival ABC-TV said at the time, "[Sweeps months] are the most important of the TV season. Everyone brings out his best programs for the sweeps. It's ferocious, but that's the name of the game. When you're in a contest, you put your best foot forward."

At the beginning of 1995, CBS was the most watched of the three major networks, but had dropped almost immediately to third place. The rate for airing commercials on CBS was lowered drastically. The TV industry was referring to CBS as "the old network" because the majority of their viewers were well over fifty. The network's most popular shows at the time were *60 Minutes* (1968–present) and *Murder, She Wrote* (1984–1996) starring the aging Angela Lansbury.

CBS-TV gave *Family of Cops* a heavy promotion and arranged press interviews with Bronson. A full-page ad was in *TV Guide,* and the movie was the cover story of many local television papers. Bronson said, "[I

The *Family of Cops* Series (1995–1999)

TV Guide ad.

play] a cop with two sons who are policemen, and a daughter who's a wild party girl. It's a good, solid drama. I'd rather the other actors took more a part in the story, but being the father of the other characters gives you more power, or at least appears to. Usually, I play heroic anti-heroes. When I read a script, I decide whether I'm going to be comfortable in the part or not. I've done somewhere between ninety-five and one hundred films. Some of them good, some not so good. I don't see them anyway. The last time I saw one of my own pictures was *House of Wax* [1953], and I slumped down in my seat and left before anyone else. I thought, 'That's the last time I'm ever going to look at myself. I don't like myself on the screen. I'm one of the few actors who think they look better in person. I also think I have a good sense of humor, but no one's seen that side of me.

"[Television] involves more hours per day, and it's normally in my contract that I don't work more than a ten-hour day. Then, the director will come to you and say, 'You know, we have to finish this [scene]. Do you mind working a little longer?' If it starts out being a five-day-a-week shoot, that adds on virtually an extra day. With this one, I think the idea is there to turn it into a series, but I didn't sign for that. I don't want to do a series. I'm too old for that now, and it would take too many hours. Those offers keep coming in, and I keep turning them down."

Barbara Williams: "We knew it was part of a 'wheel.'" (A "wheel" is a recurring series of TV movies.)

TV Guide: "As the head of the family, Charles Bronson gives an understated (for him) performance. But the rest of the cast, especially Daniel Baldwin as an overweight detective, overdoes it, and the ends of the mystery are tied together a little too neatly. My score: 4 [out of 10]."

Eugene (OR) *Register-Guard*: "Routine cop drama that looks suspiciously like a pilot for a series. Bronson isn't bad, but the story is all too familiar."

Many Bronson fans tuned in to watch *Family of Cops*. The movie came in second place for its timeslot—after ABC's *Jurassic Park* (1993) rerun but before NBC's network debut of *Groundhog Day* (1993)—making it a very rare ratings hit for CBS that year. Naturally, the network wanted a follow-up.

In September 1996 it was announced that Bronson would star in

Family of Cops 2 for CBS. The teleplay by original creator Joel Blasberg involved a murdered priest and the Russian mafia.

The sequel began filming in October 1996. The new director was four-time Emmy-winner David Greene (*Roots*, 1977; *Rich Man, Poor Man*, 1976). The actors who played Bronson's kids in the first film returned except for Daniel Baldwin, whose role as the oldest son was taken over by Joe Penny (TV's *Jake and the Fatman*, 1987–1992). Kim Weeks' part was expanded, and her character became romantically involved with Bronson's. The movie was shot entirely in Toronto. This time, no cast members went to Milwaukee. A few exteriors of the police station (without any characters) comprise the only footage shot in Milwaukee.

Bronson personally chose Oscar-and Emmy-nominated Diane Ladd (*Alice Doesn't Live Here Anymore*, 1974) to play the new role of Aunt Shelly, sister to his character. Ladd says, "I'd met him when I was much younger. In fact, I went on a double date. He was another person's date—it wasn't Jill [Ireland]; it was somebody else. And he was a perfect gentleman and so gracious. Through the years, there were times we were at the same parties. I knew his wife, Jill Ireland, very well, too. He sure was a great actor, and I loved him. I saw nearly every movie that he did. I can never forget him standing in that phone booth quoting, 'Miles to go before I sleep' [in *Telefon*, 1977]. God, he was so good in that.

"Then when this role came up, he called and said, 'Diane, can you do a Jewish accent?' I said, 'Yeah, I think so. Because I may be Jewish.' He said, 'What do you mean?' I said, 'Well, my grandmother was named Schmidt. I think that's a Jewish name. She was from Germany, and her family was quite wealthy and aristocratic, and she went to a private girls school in Switzerland. The professor was a handsome, young ski champion, and his name was Anderson, and he was Catholic. The family said, if you marry him, you will be disinherited. So they ran off to Mobile, Alabama. Then she married him and wanted to get in touch with her family. And they were all dead; they had been killed by Hitler. Whether I am or not, Charles, I can certainly do a Jewish accent. I'm very good with accents, Hebrew, English, Irish, Italian—you name it.' He said, 'Well, I really want you to do this part. It's a very important part in the show. It's the key, it's the focal. You're younger than the part, but I know you can do it.' I said, 'I'll be glad to fulfill the part for you, whatever it is.' He said, 'Well, don't you have to read it?' I said, 'No. If you've asked me to do a part for you, I don't even have to read it. I'm yours.' I had a wonderful time doing it. He was one of the most gentle and ethical persons I've ever been privileged to meet. Everybody loved him. I wish there were more people like him. And I wish he was still around. He was so lovely."

Shortly after the second movie wrapped, producer Douglas S. Cramer hinted that the series would continue: "Charlie is amenable to doing them, as long as he likes the scripts. He's in great shape. He does everything."

TV Guide ad.

The *Family of Cops* Series (1995–1999)

As *Breach of Faith: Family of Cops II*, the sequel premiered on *The CBS Sunday Movie* on February 2, 1997. The TV industry had recently created its own rating code, and the Bronson movie was branded with a "TV-14" rating (not suitable for viewers under fourteen). It won the timeslot and was the sixteenth-most-viewed program of the week.

Foreign sales flyer with Bronson and Joe Penny.

TV Guide: "a tale much harder to swallow than the brew that made the town famous. Bronson does a fine job, adding a grandfatherly dimension to his usual stoic tough guy. Still, this sequel is populated with stock leather-clad gangsters who keep saying things like 'Chomsky ding?' into pay phones, while Bronson keeps shooting them. My score: 4 [out of 10]." *Hollywood Reporter*: "There are few suspenseful moments in this serviceable but somewhat predictable, well-photographed thriller.... Bronson's portrayal is understated but effective."

Breach of Faith: Family of Cops II had a better premise and more suspense than the original, and the staging and photography in the action scenes was superior. The sequel was nominated for two Gemini awards: Best Actress in a Supporting Role (Barbara Williams) and Best Photography (Ron Orieux) by the Academy of Canadian Cinema and Television.

Bronson signed for a third entry. It would turn out to be the seventy-five-year-old screen icon's last movie. Writer Noah Jubelirer replaced creator Joel Blasberg, who remained as "executive consultant." The premise had the Fein family investigating a money-laundering ring that involved drug dealers, corrupt cops, and a dirty politician.

Canadian-born Sheldon Larry, who had been helming TV movies like *Behind Enemy Lines* (1985) with Hal Holbrook and shows like *Remington Steele* (1983–1985) for twenty-six years, was hired as director. Larry says, "My background is all over the place. I worked in London for the BBC, but then I spent ten years working in the theater in New York. I've gone from comedy to drama, and I've done good chunks of action. The last movie I did was a musical [*Leave It on the Floor*, 2011], so that gives you the range. One of the reasons why I wanted to do [*Family of Cops III*] was to get an opportunity to be in a room with [Bronson] and [have] the thrill of being able to direct him. I was a kid when he started working and built his career. He's, obviously, a legend and had an extraordinary career. I grew up on him in all those amazing films. The first thing any of us in this business does before we take a job is due diligence—find out about the people we're working with. I thought, 'Is he doing this for the money? Is he slumming? Is he just going to show up and not do the work?' I heard nothing but good and pleasant stuff. I knew that he was getting older. I had heard that he was having a lot of difficulty remembering his lines. [I found out that] he was the son of a coal miner from Pennsylvania. Even though he had an extraordinary Hollywood career, he had been on stage. Theater actors take their craft a little more seriously and are interesting perfectionists. There was some record for [him being a] serious craftsman and a more thoughtful person than we knew about. Knowing where he'd come from and what his journey had been, I thought, 'This makes me what to do this even more.'

"I remember having a meeting with [Bronson] and Kim in a restaurant in Malibu. He certainly had director approval, but he trusted Doug Cramer, who had produced the other two. I wanted him to approve me. I knew that his partner had also been cast in the movie, and I had to make sure I was cool about that, and I was. When you hear the star's girlfriend is gonna be in the movie, you think, 'What am I getting in for?' She was really loving and very sweet with him and also very protective, and I really respected her for that. Because I didn't know Kim as an actress, I really wanted to get a sense of who she was and what specific energy she was going to bring. Putting a cast together is like doing an arrangement of flowers—how you put them together and what the mix is like. We had that meeting for my curiosity and for theirs as well. She was set; I was not. I was delighted with her. She was really good in the role."

The movie was shot in the fall of 1997, with Toronto once again standing in for Milwaukee. Larry: "I went to Toronto four or five weeks before principal photography, putting together crew, casting the other roles, picking out the schedule. I didn't regard it as a third film with a different director. I thought 'I'm gonna make the best movie I can.' That's what I worked towards. I'd seen one of [the *Family of Cops* movies] before, just to get a sense of the world. Doug [Cramer], the producer, let me get into the script and rework it and help shape it."

Angela Featherstone, who had played Bronson's youngest daughter in the first two entries, was replaced for this one by fellow Canadian

Nicole De Boer (TV's *Star Trek: Deep Space Nine*, 1998–1999). The Aunt Shelly character from the second movie had to be omitted. Diane Ladd: "[Bronson] wanted me to work with him, but I wasn't available. And I was very, very sorry that I wasn't."

Larry: "[Bronson] was a lovely, lovely man. You'd think he was gonna be this macho guy throwing his weight around, swinging his balls around. But that's not at all who he was. He was quiet; he was serious; he was very modest. I found him to be a very tender and thoughtful man. There was always a sweetness about him that really moved me. We ended up having a very meaningful working relationship on the film. He had done an endless number of lesser movies towards the end of his career. He had walked through a few films and not put in the energy or the effort. I think people didn't know how to respect him as an actor or how to get good work out of him. There are filmmakers who have greater or lesser abilities to work with actors, and I pride myself on the thought that I can. We had a trusting relationship. He knew I was looking out for him, and he therefore was willing to work hard and with as much focus and integrity as he could. Maybe I'm patting myself on the back, but I think his work in *Family of Cops III* is more focused than his work in the other two films. He showed up to work and respected the work and the process. For every actor, the role is like a coat—you wrap it around yourself and make sure it fits. That goes back to the theater actor he was years ago—you're there to make the lines work and the story work. I knew he was fading. When people get to middle age, memorizing lines sometimes becomes tougher. I know that's happened with many actors. That was a little bit of a thing with him. But we worked hard on it."

Barbara Williams: "I sensed [Bronson] would rather not be doing this. He didn't need it. The physical demands were difficult for him, and he struggled to remember his lines. At one point, he told me he was just doing it for Kim."

Larry: "He wasn't the kinetic, scene-stalking guy that he might have been. Although I do have to say that there was one scene where he was ambushed and had to shoot at a moving car—and someone else came out when the weapon was in his hand! It was 'old Bronson.' [laughs] You really saw an ease and comfort and sense of 'I know what I need to do, and I know who I am in this scene.' It's like putting on a jacket that fits so well. It was amazing. That was really cool to see. This was a very, very happy experience. It's a memory that I cherish. It's a special part of my life.

"The [Fein] family was supposed to be Jewish. I remember the scene of the Jewish Thanksgiving festival. There's a holiday for the Jewish religion in the autumn, and they build this temporary area outside, and they hang it with autumn fruits, gourds and pumpkins. For a week, you're supposed to eat out under the stars. I'm actually Jewish. Bronson, of course, wasn't Jewish. But that's one thing I remember talking about. A lot of Jewish-American families come from an Eastern European environment—they're from Poland, Russia or middle Europe. What I found interesting was that even though Bronson was not Jewish, he was very aware from his own father of what the life was like back there, and I think that made it easy for him to feel comfortable with that tradition.

"[Bronson and Joe Penny] seemed to have a good relationship. But Joe was from a different generation and a different world, so I don't think they ever became really good friends. But Joe is a good, solid and committed actor, and Bronson really appreciated that.

"Back then, we were doing stunts. There wasn't a lot of CGI work being done then. All of the shootout scenes were done with multiple cameras. That whole big explosion on the bridge [was] completely choreographed. It was an all-night shoot. Because it was autumn, it was getting cold. So I tried to get rid of [Bronson] as quickly as I could. There was respect in terms of his time and his age. It was a very ambitious sequence to do with the bridge going up, the explosives and flipping the car. We did that all in one night. I remember racing because the sun was coming up. And in some of the shots you can actually see the horizon getting a little lighter.

"[The schedule] was four weeks—standard. That was part of that really lovely era [when] television movies [were] being lavished with a bit of money and time. You would be expected to shoot a twelve-hour day, with an hour or forty minutes for lunch. You didn't continue to work as a television director if you couldn't make your schedule. There would be periodic days when you'd go over into a thirteenth or sometimes a fourteenth hour if it was a big, big thing, but not as a rule of thumb. Not only do you have to do it good, but you've got to be able to do it on time and on budget. I always likened making films to running a marathon. The minute the gun goes off, you run and start pre-production. As long as the clock is ticking, money is being spent. You don't know until you're completely finished that you've got something that makes coherent sense as a movie. It's hard work making a movie—long hours and total stress and dealing with a lot of money being spent in a short amount of time.

"[Post-production took] eight or nine weeks from the last day of principal photography. You're editing for five or six weeks and then getting network notes and doing sound work. Everybody in the process wants to give input. In the case of television, if the network is paying for it, you get notes from the executives at the network. I always liked to stay with the film through network notes and then be at the sound mix because that's so critical. I would make that part of my contract. Some other directors just wanted to jump from project to project. [TV movies] always had accelerated post schedules because of when they'd schedule them on the air."

On December 28, 1998, a year after the third *Family of Cops* was shot and before it aired, the seventy-seven-year-old Bronson married the thirty-six-year-old Kim Weeks.

The completed *Family of Cops III* was kept on the shelf for almost a year before it premiered as a *CBS Tuesday Movie Special* on January 12, 1999, two years after the previous installment had aired. CBS didn't take out a *TV Guide* print ad, nor did they make the third film available to critics. *Family of Cops III* was seen by fewer viewers than either of the first two entries and was barely beat in the ratings by new episodes of the NBC sitcoms *Just Shoot Me!* (1997–2003) and *Will and Grace* (1998–2006).

Variety: "He's very much the old-timer now. He's got a gut. His cheeks are puffy. But make no mistake, Charles Bronson is still Charles Bronson. That squinty-eyed glint that leaves strong men quaking is still there."

Larry: "A couple of critics have liked it the best of all three. The franchise was pretty successful for CBS. The movies always did really well for them. At that time, CBS was viewed by a slightly older audience. Their audience remembered [Bronson] as this kickass movie star, so the idea of him being the figurehead of this family suited the network. I don't think it was a distinctive highlight of his career. But it, sadly, turned out to be the last film he ever did."

Williams: "I think the films were quite decent. There is one scene in which I have a father-daughter conversation with Charlie that I found very moving. My on-set conversations with him were a highlight of the films for me. I invited Charlie to a concert I was having. He couldn't go, but he sent a 'good luck' note and a huge, beautiful bouquet of flowers. I still have the vase."

Despite his advanced age, Bronson still exercised as vigorously as he could. He took frequent, long walks and worked out regularly with a punching bag, but the inevitable aging process had slowed him down considerably, and in *Family of Cops III*, he was the heaviest that he ever appeared. His scenes account for only half of the movie's running time, and a double had to be used for some long shots, but Bronson could still command the screen and was still fast-moving with his distinctive panther-like swagger. The *Family of Cops* trio was a good close to the actor's extraordinary career. The material gave Bronson some good dramatic and light moments. He is impeccably groomed and dressed in all three movies with colorful shirts and ties and his eternally-thick mane of hair. Bronson's return to acting in the 1990s yielded some fine work from him. *Yes Virginia, There Is a Santa Claus*, *The Sea Wolf* and the first *Family of Cops* should have gotten him Emmy and/or Golden Globe Award nominations.

Williams: "I believe it was in my contract that we might continue with more sequels."

Unfortunately, Bronson's increasing health problems made a fourth *Family of Cops* movie impossible. He continued to get acting offers, including being asked to reunite with Robert Vaughn on an episode of *The Magnificent Seven* TV series (1998–2000).

The *Family of Cops* films were released theatrically in some foreign territories. In America, they came to VHS via Trimark, the video distributor of *Death Wish V*. The first two *Family of Cops* came out on tape just prior to the broadcast of the next. (The *Breach of Faith* subtitle was dropped from the second entry.) The movies' surprising amount of violence (by TV standards) earned each of them a PG-13 rating on the video sleeves. The sole image on each cover was a reliable piece of promotion: Bronson's mustached, creviced face holding a gun.

Larry: "After the film, [Bronson and Weeks] sent me a Christmas present, which I thought was remarkably sweet and kind. We did speak and exchange cards for a year or two, and then we lost touch. I [sent] him a note and didn't hear back, and then shortly afterwards I heard that he was pretty sick."

Williams: "[Around 2000] I saw him at a Malibu restaurant just after my son was born. I went over to say 'Hi.' Kim was preoccupied on the phone, having some real estate business conversation. I said 'Hey Charlie, this is Liam.' Charlie didn't say anything; he just started crying. I sat down and took Charlie's hand while I jostled my son in my arm. Charlie just sobbed and sobbed. Kim said something like, 'Oh, babies always make Charlie cry.' But it was more than that. There was some deep pain that he was trapped in. It was very disturbing. That was the last time I ever saw Charlie. I was very saddened by his passing."

The *Family of Cops* Series (1995–1999)

For the VHS cover of *Family of Cops*, the distributor reused a *Death Wish V* promo still.

In 2000, Bronson was diagnosed with Alzheimer's. In July 2003, his health declined drastically. Early the next month, he suffered organ failure and died of pneumonia on August 30, 2003, at age eighty-two. The screen icon was buried near his farm in Vermont and left an estate worth $48 million. His death received little fanfare in the press.

Lance Hool, producer of three Bronson films and friend of the star, says: "The Academy didn't do anything special. I was very troubled by that, because he deserved a lot more. He is one of the greatest stars we've had."

Today, Charles Bronson's astounding filmography is readily available on DVD, Blu-Ray, and online. The Bronson cult is larger than ever and continues to grow as more as young action movie fans discover the one-of-a-kind film legend. Bronson, who never watched his movies, would be amazed. "I dislike most things I do. I'm not a fan of myself. I wouldn't go to see me. I don't like the way I look and talk. I like the way I walk, but I don't like the way I stand. I hate the way I stand. There's something about the way I stand. I'm embarrassed at myself. I'm not embarrassed at what I'm doing. I'm just embarrassed at myself."

Bibliography

Interviews:

Edward Asner (phone: June 26, 2014)
Kimberly Beck (phone: July 28, 2014)
Maggie Blye (phone: July 18, 2015)
Jan Gan Boyd (phone: September 10, 2014)
Wilford Brimley (phone: July 17, 2014)
Rex Burns (email: March 3 and 4, 2014)
John Crowther (phone: October 16, 2013 and October 16, 2014; email: April 23, 2015)
Gene Davis (phone: June 29, 2014; email: May 11, 2015)
Charles Dierkop (email: July 1, 2014)
David C. Engelbach (in-person: March 18, 2014)

Andrew J. Fenady (phone: May 28, 2014)
Jerrold Freedman (phone: February 21, 2014)
Silvana Gallardo (phone: March 16, 2006)
Christina Gere (phone: January 20, 2015)
Frank D. Gilroy (phone: June 20, 2014)
Bruce Glover (phone: June 13, 2014)
Menahem Golan (email: June 13, 2014)
Bruce Henstell (email: June 5, 2014)
Gail Morgan Hickman (phone: May 21, 2004 and March 14, 2005)
Rod Holcomb (email: March 18, 2014)
Lance Hool (phone: May 2, 2014)
Alf Humphreys (phone: January 20, 2015)
Robert Joy (phone: July 13, 2007)
Pancho Kohner (phone: May 25, 2004)
Diane Ladd (phone: July 15, 2014)
Sheldon Larry (phone: March 14, 2014)
Laurence Luckinbill (email: May 26, 2014)
Robert F. Lyons (phone: May 24, 2014)
Denny Miller (email: July 2, 2014)
Harold Nebenzal (phone: March 30, 2014)
Sy Richardson (phone: May 27, 2014)
Robin Sherwood (phone: March, 2006)
Scott Spencer (email: May 10, 2014)
Catherine Mary Stewart (email: April 30, 2014)
Kirk Taylor (phone: July 12, 2014)
Angel Tompkins (phone: June 7, 2014)
Danny Trejo (in-person: March 29, 2015)
Kathleen Wilhoite (email: March 3, 2015
Barbara Williams (email: April 7, 2014)

Research Institutions:
New York Public Library for the Performing Arts (New York, NY)
Thomas Cooper Library, University of South Carolina (Columbia, SC)

Books:
Trevor Armbrister, *Act of Vengeance: The Yablonski Murders and Their Solution* (NY: Saturday Review Press, 1975)

Peter Biskind, *Easy Riders, Raging Bulls: How the Sex-Drugs-and-Rock 'n' Roll Generation Saved Hollywood* (NY: Simon and Schuster, 1998)

Harriett Bronson, *Charlie & Me* (Woodland Hills, CA: Timberlake Press, 2011)

Gilles Boulenger, *John Carpenter: The Prince of Darkness* (Los Angeles: Silman-James Press, 2003)

Rex Burns, *The Avenging Angel* (NY: Viking Press, 1983)

Larry Ceplair, *The Marxist and the Movies: A Biography of Paul Jarrico* (Lexington, KY: University Press of Kentucky, 2007).

Lewis Chester, *All My Shows Are Great: The Life of Lew Grade* (London: Aurum Press, Ltd., 2010)

Steve Chibnail, *J. Lee Thompson* (Manchester and NY: Manchester University Press, 2000)

David Downing, *Charles Bronson* (NY: St. Martin's Press, 1983)

Jack Early (pseudonym of Sandra Scoppetone), *Donato & Daughter* (NY: Dutton, 1988)

Roger Ebert, *Two Weeks in the Midday Sun* (Riverside, NJ: Andrews-McMeel, 1987).

Dwayne Epstein, *Lee Marvin: Point Blank* (Tucson, AZ: Schaffner Press, 2013)

Quentin Falk and Dominic Prince, *Last of a Kind: The Sinking of Lew Grade* (London: Quartet Books, 1987)

Frank D. Gilroy, *From Noon Till Three* (Garden City, NY: Doubleday & Company, Inc., 1973)

Frank D. Gilroy, *Writing for Love And/Or Money: Outtakes from a Life Spec, the Early Years* (Hanover, NH: Smith and Kraus, 2007)

Lew Grade, *Still Dancing: My Story* (London: Collins, 1987)

Lawrence Grobel, *The Hustons: The Life and Times of a Hollywood Dynasty* (NY: Scribner's, 1989)

James Heddon, *Love and Bullets* (novelization) (NY: Charter Books, 1979)

R. Lance Hill, *The Evil That Men Do* (NY: Times Books, 1978)

Jill Ireland, *Life Lines* (NY: Warner Books, 1989)

Jill Ireland, *Life Wish* (Boston: Little, Brown and Co., 1987)

Russ Kingman, introduction, *Jack London: Tales of the North* (Secaucus, NJ: Castle, 1979)

Denny Miller, *Didn't You Used to Be What's His Name?* (Las Vegas: To Health with You Publishers, LLC, 2004)

Charles Napier with Dante W. Renzulli, Jr., *Square Jaw and Big Heart* (Albany, GA: BearManor Media, 2011)

Gordon Newman, *Hard Times* (novelization) (NY: Dell Publishing Co., Inc., 1975)

Michael R. Pitts, *Charles Bronson: The 95 Films and the 156 Television Appearances* (Jefferson, NC: McFarland & Co., Inc., 1999)

Christopher Reeve, *Still Me* (NY: Random House, 1998)

Paul Talbot, *Bronson's Loose!: The Making of the 'Death Wish' Films* (Lincoln, NE: iUniverse, 2006)

Jerry Vermilye, *The Films of Charles Bronson* (Secaucus, NJ: Citadel Press, 1980)

John Walker, *The Once and Future Film: British Cinema in the Seventies and Eighties* (London: Methuen London Ltd., 1985)

Steven Whitney, *Charles Bronson Superstar* (NY: Dell Publishing, 1975)

Andrew Yule, *Hollywood a Go-Go: An Account of the Cannon Phenomenon* (London: Sphere Books Limited, 1987)

Articles:

"After Trouble With 'Swallowing,' Marketbound Cannon Is Calmer," *Variety* (February 25, 1987)

Elizabeth Aird, "Yes, Virginia, Stanley Park can pass for Central Park," *The Vancouver Sun* (June 14, 1991)

Nancy Anderson, "The hidden man in Charles Bronson is revealed," Copley News Service (April 22, 1979)

Stephen Aris, "Enter the mogul and his Muppets," *Sunday Times* [London] (April 20, 1980)

Associated Press, "Bronson hates wimpiness," Toronto Star (December 3, 1991)

James Bacon, *Hollywood Hotline* column (November 29, 1974)

James Bacon, "Lord Lew Economic Asset To Britain," *Lakeland Ledger* (June 27, 1977)

Ian Bailey, "It's smart to call him 'Sir': At 71, actor Charles Bronson's still tough as nails," *Kitchener-Waterloo Record* (April 19, 1993)

John Bartholomew, "Lord Grade: More than a fat cigar," *Financial Times* (August 21, 1978)

Marilyn Beck, "Bronson's 'Cabo Blanco' Script Ever-Changing," *Marilyn Beck's Hollywood* column (March 11, 1979)

Marilyn Beck, "Is Charles Bronson a pussycat at heart," *Hollywood Closeup* column (July 16, 1975)

Marilyn Beck, "Still No Separations for Bronsons," *Hollywood Closeup* column (January 2, 1976)

Tom Bierbaum, "Media Home Entertainment Lands Rights To 23 More Cannon Pix," *Variety* (May 7, 1986)

Jay Bobbin, "Bronson a father to 'Family of Cops,'" Tribune Media Services (November 24, 2014)

"Bob Tessier: The Villain Who Turns Hero," *Easyriders* (No. 162) (December 1986)

Steve Bornfeld, "Dana Delany considers Charles Bronson icon, tough cookie," *Albany Times Union* (September 21, 2014)

James Brady, "In Step with Catherine Mary Stewart," *Parade* (April 18, 1993)

Allan Bryce, "A Conversation with Jerry Goldsmith," *Soundtrack* (No. 25) (1981)

Tom Buckley, "James Bond visits United States," *New York Times* (July 8, 1979)

"Cannon Films, producer battle over title for Bronson picture," *Los Angeles Times* (July 23, 1986)

"Cannon Group Will Be Marketing A Score of Pics From '85 Sked," *Variety* (March 6, 1985)

Bill Carter, "CBS Struggling, Sinks in Ratings," *The New York Times* (February 13, 1995)

E. Graydon Carter, "Yeah, Bronson Would Love to Walk Away from a Fight or Two," *TV Guide* (Vol. 34, No. 16) (April 19, 1986)

Charles Champlin, "Charles Bronson: a long way from Il Brutto," *Los Angeles Times* (February 7, 1989)

Charles Champlin, "Bronson Finds Something To Say," *Los Angeles Times/Washington Post* News Service (February 23, 1986)

"Charles Bronson meets 'lost' Skid Row brother," *The Star* (January 6, 1976)

Lawrence Cohn, "Cannes To Know Cannon's There: 3 Pics Competing, Plus 16 Others, And Host of Execs Holding Court," *Variety* (May 7, 1986)

"Comeback may be real this time," *Spokane Chronicle* (March 12, 1986)

Harry Crews, "Charles Bronson Ain't No Pussycat," *Playboy* (October 1975)

Bill Davidson, "America Discovers a 'Sacred Monster,'" *The New York Times* (September 22, 1974)

Phil Davison, "Police keep out of girl kidnap drama," *The Glasgow Herald* (October 5, 1977)

Bernard Drew, "John Huston: At 74 No Formulas," *American Film* (September 1980)

Roger Ebert, "Life With Charles Bronson Right Role For Jill Ireland," *Chicago Sun-Times* (January 18, 1976)

Shirley Eder, "Secrecy surrounds film set to safeguard Bronson family," Knight-Ridder Newspapers (December 29, 1977)

Janis D. Froelich, "Dana Delany, Bronson team up for police thriller airing Tuesday," *Des Moines Register* (September 18, 1993)

Kay Gardella, "Bronson Uses Background In Portrayal of Yablonski," *New York Daily News* (April 19, 1986)

"Golan and Globus May Be Moguls, But Still Pitch From Mkt. Floor," *Variety* (October 22, 1986)

"Grapevine: What I Watch, Charles Bronson, macho movie star," *TV Guide* (Vol. 43, No. 47) (November 25, 1995)

Alan Guthrie, "Sandra Scoppettone Interview: A Creative Kind of Killer," criminal-e.blogspot.com (June 13, 2011)

David Hewson, "Over-priced, over-promoted, mid-Atlantic and sinking," *The Times* [London] (July 2, 1981)

William H. Honan, "Lester Persky, 76, Producer of 'Taxi Driver' and 'Shampoo,'" *The New York Times* (December 25, 2001)

Richard T. Jameson, "'I don't like those hard goodbyes'—Strother Martin," *Movietone News* (March 1981)

Gregg Kilday, "Play it again, Sam—but a little bit differently," *Los Angeles Times* (December 12, 1978)

Susan King, "Tossed at Sea: Jack London's 'Sea Wolf' Is A Natural Setting For Reeve," *Los Angeles Times* (April 18, 1993)

Milly Kocian, "Travels With Bronson; Snitch Fear Makes Pic A Secret," *Variety* (December 21, 1977)

Joel Kotkin, "Bronson at 54: last of the super-heroes," Times-Post News Service (June 10, 1977)

Bob Lardine, "The coal miner who struck it rich," *New York Sunday News: Coloroto Magazine* (February 11, 1973)

"Larry Joachim, Distributor of Kung Fu Films, Dies at 88," *Variety* (January 2, 2014)

Evan Levine, "Yes Virginia: There is a movie," TV Data Service (December 8, 1991)

"Lorimar Packing 5 First-Looks To Debut Mart With Telepictures," *Variety* (February 19, 1986)

Lynne McNamara, "Bronson coming here: Christmas story to be filmed on the North Shore," *The Province* (June 7, 1991)

Mike Malloy, Unpublished phone interview with Robert Axelrod (April 26, 2005)

Patrick McGilligan, "Walter Hill: Last Man Standing," *Film International* (No. 12) (June 2004)

Bart Mills, "Bronson has a soft spot, his family," *St. Petersburg Times* (December 19, 1977)

Bart Mills, "Tough Guys Don't Quit," *Los Angeles Daily News* (July 27, 1988)

Diane Joy Moca, "Yes Virginia, there is a positive message in new TV movie," *Los Angeles Daily News* (December 7, 1991)

Mary Murphy, "Yes, Virginia, there is a Charles Bronson," *TV Guide* (Vol. 39, No. 49) (December 7, 1991)

New York Times News Service, "Networks line up their best for sweeps month," *The New York Times* (May 14, 1995)

David Nolte, "Kathleen Wilhoite: The Murphy's Law Interview," http://crimsonceIluloid.blogspot.com (April 9, 2014)

John Patterson, "Walter Hill: a life in the fast lane," *The Guardian* (July 17, 2014)

Chris Poggiali, "Shock Cinema Talks with Perennial Psycho-Villain Paul Koslo," *Shock Cinema* (Spring/Summer, 1999)

Rex Reed, "The Most Popular Unpopular Actor," *New York Sunday News* (July 2, 1972)

Barry Rehfeld, "Cannon Fathers," *Film Comment* (November–December, 1983)

Bibliography

Vadim Rizov, "Tough Little Stories: Director Walter Hill at 92Y Tribeca," filmmakermagazine.com (Jan 29, 2013)

Vernon Scott, "Actor lives in fear of snips," United Press International (May 20, 1978)

Vernon Scott, "Bronson, Ireland Co-Star in 'Assassination,'" United Press International (January 23, 1977)

Vernon Scott, "Bronson: Tough image, a gentle man," United Press International (January 2, 1976)

Vernon Scott, "Charles Bronson takes aim at sequels," United Press International (November 10, 1987)

Vernon Scott, "Hollywood killer really a pussycat," United Press International (July 20, 1979)

Vernon Scott, "Jill's Career Ready To Role," United Press International (November 28, 1976)

Vernon Scott, "Jill's Career Ready To Role," United Press International (November 28, 1976)

Vernon Scott, "Macho Bronson trapped in tough guy roles," United Press International (April 15, 1986)

Tom Seligson, "How Jill Ireland and Charles Bronson share bad news and good: 'We don't lie to each other,'" *The Courier* (January 11, 1987)

Jay Sharbutt, "Playwright Frank Gilroy Returns To Broadway," Associated Press (November 11, 1979)

Liz Smith, "Poker-Face Bronson…He's Quite a Card," *New York Sunday News* (September 14, 1975)

Tom Smith, "Charles Bronson: I Cringe When I See Myself on Screen," *National Enquirer* (August 9, 1977)

Tom Stockman, "Interview: Harriett Bronson, first wife of Charles Bronson and author of 'Charlie and Me,'" WeAreMovieGeeks.com (January 19, 2011)

James M. Tate, "Kathleen Wilhoite," www.cultfilmfreaks.com (June 2, 2013)

Bob Thomas, "Bout with cancer enriched actress' life," Associated Press (January 27, 1987)

Bob Thomas, "Charles Bronson, Jill Ireland: A Dynamic Duo," Associated Press (May 16, 1975)

Bob Thomas, "Charles Bronson not just another pretty face," Associated Press (November 12, 1987)

Bob Thomas, "The Western: Riding Into the Sunset?" Associated Press (September 27, 1976)

"Tough guy Bronson just wants to be with the wife and kids," *The Star* (May 17, 1975)

Jan Ubelherr, "Action! Bronson film shot here," *Milwaukee Journal Sentinel* (September 8, 1995)

United Press International, "Loner Charles Bronson looks for marquee company," (March 16, 1989)

Mary Vespa, "Off the Screen: Charles Bronson Finally Becomes a Star at Home," *People* (August 19, 1974) (Vol. 2 No. 8)

Michele Wallace, "Charles Bronson Is Still Pleading Poverty," *The Village Voice* (January 12, 1976)

Robert Ward, "Hollywood's Last Angry Man," *American Film* (January–February 1982)

Wayne Warga, "Charles Bronson: Polite But Not Friendly," *Los Angeles Times/Washington Post* News Service (November 8, 1975)

Patience Wheatcroft, The humiliation of Lew Grade, *Sunday Times* [London] (April 25, 1982)

Rita Zekas, "Cops and daughters in Cabbagetown," Toronto Star (October 6, 1995)

Jon Zelazny, "Kicking Ass with Walter Hill," thehollywoodinterview.blogspot.com (December 8, 2013)

Elizabeth Zelvin, "Interview with Sandra Scoppettone," *Poe's Deadly Daughters: A Blog For Mystery Lovers* (April 26, 2007)

Pressbooks/Press Kits:

Assassination Press kit, Cannon Films, 1987

Borderline Pressbook, Associated Film Distribution, 1980

Cabo Blanco Pressbook and Advertising Manual, Avco Embassy Pictures, 1980

From Noon Till Three Pressbook, United Artists, 1976

Hard Times Pressbook, Columbia Pictures, 1975

Kinjite: Forbidden Subjects Press kit, Cannon Films, 1989

Love and Bullets Pressbook, Associated Film Distribution, 1980

Love and Bullets, Charlie Pressbook, ITC Entertainment, 1978

Screenplays:

From Noon Till Three, Screenplay by Frank D. Gilroy, draft dated May 9, 1975

Hard Times, uncredited, undated draft (The close resemblance to the final film and the dialogue references to Chaney's advanced age indicate that this is a very late draft written by Walter Hill.)

Messenger of Death, Screenplay by Richard Sale, draft dated August 6, 1987 (includes pages revised on August 17, 1987)

Murphy's Law by Gail Morgan Hickman, second draft dated February 18, 1985

The President's Wife by Richard Sale [released as *Assassination*], draft dated April 29, 1986 (includes pages revised on May 1 and May 5, 1986)

So Sorry (Gomen Nasai), Screenplay by Harold Nebenzal [later retitled *Kinjite: Forbidden Subjects*], draft dated March 1, 1987

Ten to Midnight Screenplay by William Roberts, revision dated September 28, 1982 (includes pages revised on October 1, 4 and 7, 1982)

Documentaries:

Lew Grade: The Persuader, producer: Louis Heaton. BBC. 60 minutes. 1994

The Making of Cabo Blanco, written and directed by Stephen Peck. A MVS Production. 25 minutes. 1979

Websites:

eBay (ebay.com)

Google News Archive

Internet Movie Database (imdb.com)

Index

A

Abbott, George, 20
Act of Vengeance (book), 253
Act of Vengeance (film), x, 145, 253–264, 292, 366
Affliction, 57
Against the Wind, 153
Alfred Hitchcock Presents, 4
Ali, Muhammad, 11
Alliance Communications, 402
Ambassador, The, 172
Amblin Entertainment, 111
America 3000, 162, 169, 171
American Film Market, 264

American International Pictures (A.I.P.), 13–15
American Ninja, 324
American Ninja 3, 350
Anderson, Ernie, 5, 87, 92
Anderson, Michael, 372, 376
Ansara, Michael, 305
Aphrodite, 102
Armbrister, Trevor, 253
Ash Wednesday, 28
Asner, Edward, 362, 363
Assassination, 104, 149, 262, 300–321, 347
Associated Film Distribution (AFD), 104–105, 149, 151, 232
Avenging Angel, 324–325, 326, 327,
Avco Embassy, 129–130, 131, 133
Axelrod, Robert, 347

B
Bacon, James, 88
Baldwin, Daniel, 402, 407
Ballard, Lucien, 66
Balsam, Martin, 250
Banner, Bob, 360, 372
Barra de Navidad, 117, 124, 131
Battle of the Bulge, 90
Beatty, Warren, 200
Beck, Kimberly, 331–332
Bergman, Alan, 72
Bergman, Ingmar, 4, 87
Bergman, Marilyn, 72
Bernstein, Elmer, 72
Big Bad Mama, 17
Big Score, The, 268
Bisharat, John, 290

Blasberg, Joel, 402, 407, 410
Blye, Maggie, 23–25, 27, 28–29, 30, 31, 34, 35, 36, 37, 39, 41, 42, 46, 49, 53–54, 57, 58
Bolero, 292
Bonanza, 4
Bonetti, Massimo, 366
Boorman, John, 89
Borderline, x, 23, 126, 127, 137–153, 223, 235, 256, 257
Boyd, Jan Gan, 300, 303–304, 305–307, 308–310, 311–312, 313–314, 317–319, 320–321
Boyle, Tony, 253, 254, 256, 257
Boys from Brazil, The, 90
Brando, Marlon, 248–249
Breach of Faith: Family of Cops II (a.k.a. *Family of Cops II*), 406–410, 416
Breakheart Pass, 23, 45, 64, 66, 73, 79, 80, 127
Breakin', 324
Breakout, 10–12, 42, 45, 56, 66, 90, 127
Breakwater, 402
Bridge in the Jungle, The, 90
Bright, Richard S., 42
Brimley, Wilford, 144–145, 198, 254, 256, 257
Bronson, Charles, ix–x, 1–12, 13, 17, 19, 20, 24, 26, 31, 33, 34, 47, 59, 60, 64, 67, 70, 73, 75, 79, 80, 81–82, 83, 84–86, 98, 109, 129, 131, 137–139, 158, 161, 162, 167, 173, 176–178, 186, 189, 190, 191, 192–194, 195, 196, 197, 198, 199, 202, 206, 209, 211, 212, 213, 215, 217, 218–219, 222, 223, 224, 229, 232, 235, 236, 240, 241, 242, 244, 251, 253, 254, 25, 255, 257, 258, 260, 262, 264, 265, 266, 272, 274, 281, 290, 292, 295, 299, 300, 301, 302, 312, 314, 318, 319, 322, 323, 324, 325, 326, 327, 328, 329, 334, 335, 336, 338, 339, 340–342, 344, 350, 354, 357, 358, 366, 367, 368, 369, 371, 381, 384, 387, 390, 392, 394, 399, 400, 402, 409
Death of, 417

Early career of, 2–3
Early stardom of, 4–7
Late career of, 357–416
Lifestyle of, 7, 22–23, 40, 44, 62–63, 141, 216, 311–312, 320, 327, 361
Military career of, 2
Mustache of, 23, 256–257, 260, 262, 363, 371
Personality of, 27, 32–35, 40–41, 57, 65–66, 68–69, 72, 85–86, 87–88, 92, 96, 99, 102, 120, 122, 124–126, 142–143, 146–147, 164–165, 187–188, 202–203, 208, 216, 225–227, 230–231, 234–235, 239, 245–246, 256, 258, 259–260, 273, 278–279, 280, 282, 283–285, 286, 287, 291, 297, 298, 303–304, 305–307, 308–309, 311–312, 313–314, 315–315, 320–321, 329–332, 345–346, 347, 348, 355–356, 357–358, 361, 362, 363, 364–365, 370, 373–374, 376, 377, 379–380, 385–386, 396–397, 401, 403, 404–406, 407–408, 410–411, 412–413, 416
Physical fitness of, 2, 22–23, 39, 43, 92, 415
Salary of, 5, 6, 10, 20, 64, 116, 142, 219, 255, 265, 305, 374
Self-image of, 1, 3, 7, 68, 260, 261–262, 315, 327, 333, 337, 418
Supporting roles of, 3–4
Unmade projects of, 50, 88, 219, 237–239, 402
Youth, 1, 36

Bronson, Harriett, 282–283
Bronson, Zuleika, 28, 77, 92, 222
Bronson's Loose!: The Making of the 'Death Wish' Films, ix, x, 155
Brosnan, Pierce, 371
Brynner, Yul, 303
Buchinsky, Dempsey, 357, 374
Buchinsky, Joe, 2
Buchinsky, Roy, 36–37, 330
Bullet to the Head, 31
Bundy, Ted, 200
Burns, Rex, 324–325, 326, 329–330, 332–333

Burstyn, Ellen, 254, 256, 259
Butch Cassidy and the Sundance Kid, 29
C
Cabo Blanco, 109–136, 138, 141, 192, 195, 219, 223, 403
Caine, Michael, 24
Canby, Vincent, 77
Candy Snatchers, The, 15
Cannes Film Festival, 84, 86, 88, 112, 147, 174, 193, 194, 272, 295, 312, 358
Cannon Films, ix, 158, 161–162, 167, 169, 170, 171, 172, 191, 192, 193, 194–195, 197, 212, 213, 214, 215, 216, 218–219, 237–239, 255, 260, 262, 265, 266, 269, 272–273, 280, 289, 291, 292, 295, 296, 297, 298–299, 301, 302, 305, 311, 301, 302, 305, 311, 312, 314, 315, 318, 319, 323–324, 326, 327, 329, 332, 333, 334, 335, 339, 340, 345, 347, 348, 349, 350, 353, 354, 356, 371, 381, 390
Cannon Video, 353
Can't Stop the Music, 151
Cape Fear, 114
Capone, 17
Captain America, 172
Carolco Pictures, 116
Carpenter, John, 131
Carson, Johnny, 209
Casablanca, 114, 115, 118, 120, 127, 131, 133
Cavett, Dick, 9
CBS/Fox Video, 152
CBS-TV, 117, 128, 152, 383, 389, 390, 404, 407, 409, 414, 415
Channel Z, 135
Charles Bronson, Superstar, 64
Charter Books, 106
Chartoff, Robert, 10, 186
Chase, Lorraine, 97

Chato's Land, 40, 348
Chattaway, Jay, 312
China Syndrome, The, 139, 142
Chinatown, 25
Chong, Rae Dawn, 275
Chorus Line, A, 303, 305, 318, 319
Church, Francis P., 359, 360, 361, 363
Cineplex Odeon Films, 262
Coburn, James, 19, 20, 22, 23, 25, 27, 29, 32, 37–38, 39, 40, 41, 43, 44, 45, 46, 49, 57–58, 102, 165, 172
Coffeyville Raid, The, 61
Cold Night's Death, A, 140, 148
Cold Sweat, 5, 98
Columbia Pictures, 10, 14, 15, 43, 45, 47, 56, 62, 128, 139, 156, 232, 328
Columbia Pictures Home Video, 235
Cobra, 170
Combat!, 4
Conners, Chuck, 305
Connery, Sean, 7, 371
Conway, Gary, 156, 157, 170
Cook, Fielder, 221–222, 224
Cook, T.S., 402
Cool Hand Luke, 29, 91, 100
Corman, Roger, 242, 243
Costa, Cosie, 198
Cowboy and the Cossack, The, 238–239
Cramer, Douglas S., 402, 408, 411
Creative Entertainment, 111, 117
Crews, Harry, 23
Crowther, John, 93–94, 95, 100, 101, 196–198, 199, 208, 219–222, 223–225, 226–227, 238, 229–230, 231, 236–237

Cruising, 200, 201

cummings, e.e.

D

Davis, Brad, 200

Davis, Gene, 199–202, 203–206, 208, 209–211, 212, 216, 332

Dead to Rights, 389, 390

Death Hunt, x, 127, 132, 147, 303

Death Sentence, 161

Death Wish, ix, 9, 10, 45, 85, 102, 137, 158, 161, 174, 176, 178, 234, 238, 303, 348, 392, 401

Death Wish II, 37, 155, 156, 157–169, 172, 173–183, 186–189, 192, 202, 214, 218, 235, 238, 240–253, 273, 276, 301, 316, 387

Death Wish 3, 169, 235, 238, 253, 255, 269, 272, 295, 301, 316, 374

Death Wish 4: The Crackdown, frontispiece, 296, 299, 301, 312, 318, 323, 326, 327, 344, 347, 348

Death Wish V: The Face of Death, 356, 390, 391–399, 401, 403, 416

Death Wish 6: The New Vigilante, 401

De Boer, Nicole, 412

De Crowl, Val, 359

Déjà vu, 171

Delany, Dana, 384–385, 386, 387

De Laurentiis, Dino, 86, 137–138, 211

Dell Publishing, 50, 64

Delon, Alain, 4

Del Ruth, Thomas, 163, 180, 387

DeNiro, Robert, 86

Delta Force, The, 265, 266, 295, 299, 324

De Palma, Brian, 254, 255

Diamonds Are Forever, 25

Diamonds for Breakfast, 24

Diary of a Mad Housewife, 287

Di Cicco, Bobby, 200

Dickens, Charles, 56, 58
Die Hard, 57
Dierkop, Charles, 330–331
Dietrich, Marlene, 4
Dillinger, 17
Dimitri, Nick, 31, 42–43
Dirty Dozen, The, 4, 114, 303
Dirty Dozen: Next Mission, The, 256
Dirty Harry (character), 268–269
Dirty Harry (film), 267
Doc Savage: Man of Bronze, 40
Dollar Ninety-Eight (a.k.a. *$1.98*), 50, 88, 219, 238
Donahue, Marc, 290
Donato and Daughter (film), 381–390
Donato and Daughter (novel), 382–383
Doubleday and Company, 61
Douglas, Michael, 139, 140, 142
Down, Lesley-Anne, 395–396, 398
Downhill Racer, 10
Driver, The, 32, 57
Drowning Pool, The, 14
Drum Beat, 3, 30, 344
Dudikoff, Michael, 297
Duffy, Thomas, 179
Dusty and Sweets McGee, 6
Duvall, Robert, 248

E

Early, Jack, 383
Easton, Robert, 94
Eastwood, Clint, 4, 79, 82, 102, 234, 238, 267–268, 271
Easy Rider, 31
Ebert, Roger, 45, 69

Eilbacher, Lisa, 198, 199, 207, 208, 209, 211, 212
EMI, 104
Enforcer, The, 267–268, 271
Engelbach, David, 155–172
Enriquez, Rene, 228
Epper, Tony, 125
Escape from New York, 131
Escape to Athena, 104
Evil That Men Do, The, (film), 101, 152, 192–193, 217–239, 272, 302, 316, 339
Evil That Men Do, The, (novel), 192, 217–218, 220, 228, 229, 232, 233

F

Fairmont Roosevelt Hotel, 26–27, 28
Family of Cops, 390, 400, 402–406, 416, 417
Family of Cops II (see: *Breach of Faith: Family of Cops II*)
Family of Cops III, 410–416
Farewell, Friend, 4, 95
Farmer, The, 156
Farmer, Frances, 72
Featherstone, Angela, 402, 403, 404, 411
Fenady, Andrew, J., 358–363, 364, 367, 369, 370–371, 372, 373, 374, 375, 376, 377, 379, 380
Fenady, Duke, 358, 370, 379
Fernandez, Juan, 345, 347, 353
Ferrer, Jose, 228
Filmways, 214
Fine, Morton, 115, 127
Firepower, 102, 104, 153
Firewalker, 289, 302
First Blood, 170, 257, 402
Fishburne, Laurence, 179, 180
Fleischer, Richard, x

Fonda, Henry, 28
Frankenstein, 204
Frankovich, M.J. (Mike), 62, 64, 65, 68, 79–80
Freedman, Jerrold, 139, 140–144, 145–147, 148, 150–151, 153
Friedkin, William, 254, 255
From Noon Till Three, (film) x, 59–80, 84, 260
From Noon Till Three (novella), 61–62
Fuentes, Miguel Angel, 229
Fugitive, The, 4
Fuhrman, Mark, 212
Fujimoto, Tak, 145
Full Metal Jacket, 249–250

G

Gable and Lombard, 17
Gallardo, Silvana, 163, 174, 175–177, 178, 179–180, 181, 182
Gang War, 3
Garcia, Inez, 176, 179
Gardenia, Vincent, 161, 164
Garfield, Brian, 161
Gazzo, Michael V., 104
Gelman, Milton, 113, 127
General Cinema, 89
Gere, Christina, 234–235
Getaway, The, 13, 14
Gilmore, Gary, 85
Gilroy, Frank D., 59–62, 64, 65–68, 70, 72, 73, 76–77, 79, 80
Gindoff, Bryan, 15, 17, 50
Gironda, Vince, 201
Globus, Yoram, 157, 174, 192, 213, 215, 218, 237, 239, 265, 266, 272, 273, 275, 292, 296, 299, 301, 302, 311, 312, 314, 323, 324, 325, 336, 340, 350, 354, 390
Glover, Bruce, 25, 32–33, 35, 37–38, 40, 41, 43–44, 45, 57–58

Godfather, The, 8

Golan, Menahem, 86, 157–159, 161, 162, 169, 170, 171, 172, 174, 192–195, 213, 215, 218, 237, 239, 265, 266, 272, 273, 275, 292, 296, 297, 299, 301, 302, 311, 312, 314, 323, 324, 325, 327, 336, 340, 350, 354, 356, 390, 401–402

Golden Globe Awards, 7, 77–79

Goldsmith, Jerry, 127

Goldstein, Allan, 393–394, 395, 398

Gone with the Wind, 6

Gordon, Larry, 13–15, 35, 41, 43, 45, 47, 56, 57

Gore Gazette, 234, 293, 335, 353

Gotti, Andrew, 157

Grade, Lew, 83–85, 86–90, 100–101, 102–103, 104–105, 108, 140, 142, 147–148, 149–152, 153, 219, 228

Great Escape, The, 3, 20, 72, 202, 258, 303, 309

Greek Tycoon, The, 114, 115, 118

Greene, David, 407

Gries, Tom, 10

Grimes, Stephen, 91

Grizzle, Sandy, 249

Guns of Navarone, 114, 202

H

Hackman, Gene, 140

Happy Birthday to Me, 132, 228, 233

Hard Times, x, 13–58, 68, 100, 141

Harris, Ed, 144

Harvey, Laurence, 23

Hayes, William "Billy", 305, 312

Hausu, 6

Hayakawa, Kumiko, 346–347, 353

Heather, Carol, 127

"Heaven Knows," 127

Heller, Lukas, 114, 127
"Hello and Goodbye," 72, 77
Hemdale Film Corporation, 272, 273
Hemingway, Ernest, 19
Henry, David Lee, 231
Henstell, Bruce, 15, 17, 50
Hickey and Boggs, 13
Hickman, Gail Morgan, 266–272, 273, 275, 280, 282, 289, 291, 296–297, 299, 326
Hill, R. Lance, 192, 217–218, 219, 220, 231
Hill, Walter, 13–20, 25, 29, 31, 32, 34, 38, 39, 42, 43, 44, 45, 46, 47, 49, 52, 57, 272
Holcomb, Rod, 384, 385, 386, 387
Holden, Hilary, 222–223, 230
Holden Bronson, Katrina, 231
Hombre, 23, 54
Home Box Office (HBO), 89, 117, 128, 135, 152, 215, 255, 260
Hool, Conrad, 118
Hool, Lance, 109–110, 111–118, 120–122, 124, 127, 129, 133, 135–136, 195, 198, 200, 212, 213, 219, 221, 223, 224, 228, 230–231, 235, 237–239, 357–358, 418
Hotel Des Bergues, 92
Hotel du Cap, 86
House of Wax, 348, 406
Howard, Kevyn Major, 164, 179, 180
Huffaker, Clair, 238
Humphreys, Alf, 257–260, 263
Hunt, Peter, 302–303, 304, 307, 310, 315
Hunter, 50
Hunter, James Granby, 109–110, 127
Hurricane Katrina, 31
Huston, John, 4, 90–91, 114, 227

Huston, Tony, 90, 91

I

I Love My Wife, 287

Indian Runner, The, 357

In Like Flint, 20

In the Heat of the Night, 99

Invasion USA, 313

Ireland, Jill, 4, 10, 16, 17, 22, 27, 28, 33, 34, 44, 45, 46, 47, 50, 52, 62–66, 67, 69, 70–71, 72, 75, 77–79, 80, 88, 91, 93–94, 98, 99, 102, 104, 124, 141, 158, 164, 178, 180, 188, 189, 192, 200, 211, 216, 218, 222–223, 230, 234, 235, 245, 272, 273, 276, 282, 290, 297, 298, 302, 305, 307, 308, 309, 310, 311–312, 314, 315, 320, 327, 330, 332, 355–356, 357, 361, 364, 374, 407

Isabelle, Katherine, 360, 364

Italian Job, The, 24, 54, 98

ITC (Incorporated Television), 83, 86, 101, 140, 147, 149, 151–152, 219, 220, 224, 228, 232, 235

I Thought We Were Making Movies, Not History, x

J

Jack the Stripper, 200, 216

Jacobs, Alex, 15

James, Clifton, 129

Jarrico, Paul, 328–329, 330, 331, 333

Jarrott, Charles, 362

Jaws, 12

Jesus of Nazareth, 84

Jett, Joan, 276

Joachim, Laurence, 81–82

Johnny Handsome, 31

Johnson, E. Lamont, 179

Joseph, Paul A., 111, 118, 135, 117

Joy, Robert, 391–399

Juarez, Benito, 85
Jubal, 99
Jubelirer, Noah, 410
Julienne, Remy, 98
Just Tell Me When to Cry, x

K

Kapalua Bay hotel, 234–235
Kassar, Mario, 116
Kennedy, Burt, 111, 114
Kennedy, George, 115
Kerby, Bill, 102
Key Video, 108
Kid Galahad, 42, 363
Kill and Kill Again, 219
King and I, The, 303
King of White Lady, 218
King Solomon's Mines, 295
Kinjite: Forbidden Subjects, 333, 338–356, 357, 358
Kirby, Bruno, 142, 143
Kleven, Max, 39
Kline, Steve, 139–140, 145
Kohner, Pancho, 85–86, 88, 90, 93, 98, 100, 101, 113, 114, 127, 191–195, 196, 197, 198, 217, 218–222, 223, 224, 225, 230, 272, 273, 275, 277, 282, 302, 304, 312, 318, 324, 327, 328, 340, 341, 350, 356
Kohner, Paul, 3, 5, 9–10, 50, 84–85, 88, 90, 113, 114, 191, 272, 302, 328, 336, 340
Komarov, Shelley, 278
Konigsberg, Frank, 255
Koslo, Paul, 95–96, 104
Kotcheff, Ted, 402, 403
Kotero, Apollonia, 276

L

Ladd, Alan, 3
Ladd, Diane, 407–408, 412
Larry, Sheldon, 410–411, 412–414, 415, 416
Last Detail, The, 42
Last Dragon, The, 242
Lathrop, Philip, 32
Legend of the Lone Ranger, The, 151
Leone, Sergio, 4
Lerner, Michael, 144
Levinthal, Malcolm, 111
Life Wish, 282, 302
Lightning Swords of Death, 56
Lloyd Williams and His Brother, 18
London, Jack, 369–370, 371
London Philharmonic, 148
Longest Yard, The, 40
Long Riders, The, 57
Lopez, Perry, 344, 351
Loren, Sophia, 86, 102
Lorimar Motion Pictures International, 255, 264
Losin' It, 50
Love and Bullets, 30, 83–108, 138, 140, 149, 151, 153, 192, 196, 219, 223, 235, 284, 314
Luckinbill, Lawrence, 330, 331
Ludlum, Robert, 86
Luisi, James, 282–283
Lund, Kevin, 397
Lyle, Ron, 11
Lyons, Robert F., 185–189, 202–203, 216, 274, 276, 280–281, 286, 297–298

M

Machine Gun Kelly, 3, 7
Mackie, Bob, 79
Mackintosh Man, The, 13
MacCorkindale, Simon, 115, 129, 402
Mackenzie, John, 256, 257, 258–259
Madeline, 356
Madonna, 275
Magnificent Seven, The, (film) 3, 20, 72, 165, 195, 242, 303
Magnificent Seven, The, (TV series), 416
Magnum Force, 267
Maher, Joseph, 220, 227–228
Maltese Falcon, The, 90
Mandingo, 32
Mandom, 6
Mann, Abby, 254
Man on Fire, 239
Man Who Shot Liberty Valance, The, 29
Man Who Would Be King, The, 42, 90
Man with a Camera, 3, 176
Marble Arch Productions, 140, 146
Marshall, Alan, 223
Martin, Strother, 22, 29–30, 32, 39, 40, 43, 44, 46, 49, 57, 100, 104
Marvin, Lee, 4, 256, 265, 303, 314
Mastroianni, Marcello, 24
Maximillian and Juarez, 84–85
Maximillian I, 85
Mayes, Wendell, 85, 90, 101
McCallum, David, 4, 297
McCallum, Jason, 256, 297, 357
McCallum, Paul, 146, 198, 256, 290
McCallum, Valentine, 290, 312

McGuire, Michael, 37
McQueen, Steve, 113, 305
McRae, Frank, 45
Mechanic, The, 8, 10, 20, 162, 186–187, 283, 297
Media Home Entertainment, 135, 296, 318, 335, 353
Mele, Gil, 148
Melson, John, 90, 101–102
Melvin Purvis: G-Man, 28
Messenger of Death, 216, 318, 322–337, 353
MGM, 80, 138
MGM/UA Home Video, 215
Midkiff, Dale, 243
Midnight Express, 305, 312
MIFED Film Market, 263, 312
Mifune, Toshiro, 147
Miller, Denny, 118, 119, 120, 124–126, 133
Miller, Frankie, 264
Minor, Bob, 24, 46
Mirisch, Walter, x
Misch, Laura, 32
Mishkin, Meyer, 40
Missing in Action, 135, 237, 324
Missing in Action 2: The Beginning, 198, 237
Mitchell, Frank, 363,
Mitchum, Robert, 171–172, 358, 380
Montand, Yves, 171
Moses the Lawgiver, 85
Movie Movie, 104
Mr. Majestyk, x, 8, 96
Mulligan, Robert, 91
Multimedia Motion Pictures, 383
Muppet Movie, The, 104, 149, 151

Murphy, Eddie, 50

Murphy's Law, x, 186, 197, 253, 255, 260, 265–299, 302, 312, 316, 318, 326, 347

Murray, Don, 23

My Affair with the President's Wife, 301, 312

My Bloody Valentine, 257

N

National Enquirer, 308

Nebenzal, Harold, 339–340, 341, 342–343, 347, 350

Nelson, James, 142

Newman, Paul, 14, 23, 111, 113

Nicholson, Jack, 64, 66, 79

Noble, Roy, 127

Norris, Chuck, 237, 239, 297, 313, 324

Number One with a Bullet, 269, 297

O

Oates, Warren, 20

Ohbayashi, Nobuhiko, 6

O'Hanlon, Virginia, 359, 360

O'Herlihy, Gavan, 244, 247

Once Upon a Time in the West, 4, 262, 348

One Man's Way, 23

Ortiz, Graziella, 92

Out for Justice, 43

Outlaw Josey Wales, The, 79

Over the Top, 156–157, 169–171, 324

P

Pacino, Al, 86

Page, Geraldine, 23

Page, Jimmy, 167

Paper Moon, 17

Paramount Pictures, 45, 195, 212, 254, 255

Pasadena Playhouse, 2, 34
Pat Garrett and Billy the Kid, 20
Patino, Antenor, 92
Pax, James, 343, 344
Peck, Gregory, 122, 187
Peck, Steve, 122
Peerce, Chris, 275
Pendulum, 185, 186
Penitentiary III, 348, 350
Penn, Sean, 357
Penny, Joe, 407, 413
People vs. Inez Garcia, The, 176
Perry, George, 348
Persky, Lester, 41–42, 47
Platoon Leader, 297
Playboy, 32
Poe, Edgar Allan, 49
Point Blank, 15, 32
Ponti, Carlo, 102
Pool, Robert Roy, 384
Power, Tyrone, 3
Predator, 57
President's Analyst, The, 20
Pressley, Elvis, 26
Preston, Kelly, 198
Prisoner, The, 84

Q
Anthony Quinn, 44

R
Rafelson, Bob, 91
Raffin, Deborah, 374
Ragland, Robert O., 312, 334

Raid on Entebbe, 85, 255, 366
Raiders of the Lost Ark, 111
Raise the Titanic (film), 151
Raise the Titanic (novel), 86
Rawhide, 4
Ray, Ola, 198
Red Devil Battery Sign, 44
Red Dragon, 211
Red Sun, 5, 6, 9, 91, 147, 195
Reeve, Christopher, 371–372, 375–376, 377
Reeves, Keanu, 256, 260, 263
Rehme, Bob, 129
Remsen, Bert, 144
Report to the Commissioner, 37
Rey, Fernando, 120
Rhodes, Phil, 36
Richardson, Sy, 344–347, 350–351
Richmond, Anthony, 96
Rider on the Rain, 4, 9, 23, 266
Ritchie, Michael, 10
Roadhouse, 231
Robards, Jason, 116, 119, 122
Roberts, William, 195
Robertson, Dale, 28
Robinson, Edward G., 370
Robinson, Stuart K., 179, 180
Rocky, 80, 170
Roman, Joe, 284–285
Roosevelt, Theodore, 26
Rosenberg, Stuart, 91, 94, 96, 99, 100, 101
Runaway Train, 295, 298, 348
Run of the Arrow, 99

S

Sahara, 292
Saint, The, 84
Saldana, Theresa, 223, 229
Sale, Richard, 301–302, 308, 310, 312, 326–327, 329, 332, 333
Sanda, Dominique, 112, 116, 119, 121, 136
Sandpiper, The, 4
Saturn 3, 151
Savalas, Telly, 371
Schaffner, Franklin J., 90
Schifrin, Lalo, 101
Schurr, Scott, 267
Scoppettone, Sandra, 383
Scott, George C., 314, 329
Scott, Vernon, 69
Screen Actors Guild, 329
Sea Wolf, The, (film), x, 368–380, 403
Sea Wolf, The, (novel), 369–370, 371
Seagal, Steven, 43
Shamata, Chuck, 397
Shampoo, 42
Shariff, Omar, 24
Sherman, Harry, 140
Sherwood, Robin, 174, 175, 176, 177, 178–179, 180, 181–183
Shootist, The, 79
Showtime, 295
Shout! Factory, x
Showdown at Boot Hill, 3
Siegel, Don, x
Siegel Film, A, x
Silva, Henry, 95, 97, 104
Simpson, O. J., 212

Sirtis, Marina, 247
Smith, Martin V., 117, 127, 128, 135
Smith, Liz, 70
Snodgress, Carrie, 287–288
Southern Comfort, 31, 57
Sparrow, Sharolyn, 397
Sparv, Camilla, 118
Specialist, The, 100
Speck, Richard, 195, 200
Spence, Sebastian, 402, 403
Spencer, Scott, 254, 259
Spiridakis, Tony, 244, 247, 251
Spottiswoode, Roger, 45
Stallone, Sylvester, 86, 169, 170, 324
Steadicam, 145–146, 231
Steiger, Rod, 99–100, 104, 111, 113, 114
Stevens, Andrew, 198, 199, 207, 209, 212, 216
Stewart, Catherine Mary, 372–373, 376–377, 380
Sting, The, 17
St. Ives, 37, 72, 73, 80, 88, 114, 192, 284
St. Jacques, Raymond, 225, 228, 235
Stone Killer, The, 8, 96
Streetcar Named Desire, A, 44
Streetfighter, The, 43, 56
Streetwalkin', 242, 243
Struzan, Drew, 149
St. Vincent de Paul Cemetery, 31
Subject Was Roses, The, 59
Summer and Smoke, 23
Sun, The, 359, 363
Superman, 371

Superman IV: The Quest for Peace, 371

Survival Run, 109, 135, 223

T

Target Zero, 30

Taylor, Albert "Ab," 139, 140, 145, 149

Taylor, Elizabeth, 4, 28

Taylor, Kirk, 240–252

Telefon, x, 23, 79, 106, 138, 257, 407

Telepictures Productions, 255

Teller, Ira, 111

10 to Midnight, x, 101, 145, 186, 189, 190–216, 219, 221, 228, 256, 276, 286, 291, 312, 316, 334, 339

Tessier, Robert, 40–41, 50

Thief Who Came to Dinner, The, 13

This Property Is Condemned, 4

Thomas, Richard, 360, 364

Thompson, J. Lee, 114–115, 119, 120, 127, 128, 135, 191, 195, 198, 200, 202–203, 205–206, 210, 211, 216, 218, 219, 221, 224–226, 227, 228, 233, 272, 273, 278–279, 281, 282, 283–284, 286, 289, 295, 296, 302, 329, 330, 332, 337, 341, 344, 345, 346, 348, 350, 356

Thompson, Peter-Lee, 211, 289

Thor, Jerome, 197

Three Stooges, The, 243, 244

Thunder Run, 296

Tightrope, 234

Times Books, 217

TNT, 377

Todd, Michael, 88

Tolan, Kathleen, 174

Tompkins, Angel, 268, 271, 276–278, 283–284, 285–286, 287–288, 296, 298

Travels of Jaimie McPheeters, 361

Travolta, John, 371
Trejo, Danny, 348
Trimark, 416
TriStar Pictures, 232, 233
Turner Home Entertainment, 379
Turner Pictures, 372, 379
Turner, Ted, 372, 377, 379
TV Guide, 260, 364
20th Century Fox, 3, 23, 128, 323
21st Century Pictures, 390
Twilight Zone, The, 4
Two-Lane Blacktop, 20

U

Ullman, Liv, 4
Union Bank, 117
United Artists, 64, 66, 73, 76, 79, 80, 137
United Mine Workers, 253, 261

V

Vajna, Andrew, 116
Valachi Papers, The, 8, 23
Van Devere, Trish, 329
Vanity, 276
Variety, 111, 112, 130, 151, 194, 196, 312, 333
Vaughn, Robert, 416
"Very Thought of You, The," 127
Vestron Video, 272, 273
Viacom Enterprises, 295
Video Software Dealers Association (VSDA), 318
Vidmark Entertainment, 390
View to a Kill, A, 303
Vincent, Jan-Michael, 20, 186, 297
Violent City, 5

W

Wallis, Hal, 23
Ward, Olivia, 246
Warner Bros., 69, 102, 104, 117, 128, 129, 253–254, 323, 370
Warriors, The, 57
Washington, Denzel, 239
Waterhole #3, 23, 25, 54
Wayne, John, 79, 82, 358, 380
Way We Were, The, 17
W.C. Fields and Me, 17
Weeks, Kim, 320, 374, 376, 379, 380, 386, 411, 412, 414, 416
Western Writers of America, 380
When Hell Broke Loose, 3
White Buffalo, The, 72, 79, 88, 114, 137, 192, 284, 302, 326
Wild Bunch, The, 29
Wild West, The, 81–82
Wilhoite, Kathleen, 276, 278–280, 281, 282, 285, 287, 290, 291
William Morris Agency, 358, 361, 371
Williams, Barbara, 402, 403, 406, 410, 412, 415, 416
Williams, Bert, 329
Williams, Paul, 79, 88
Williams, Tennessee, 44
Williamson, Fred, 268
Will Penny, 10
Will There Really Be a Morning?, 72
Wilson, Gerald, 102
Winkler, Irwin, 10, 186
Winner, Michael, 102, 159, 160, 161, 162, 163, 164, 166, 168, 172, 173, 174, 175, 176, 178, 179, 180, 181–183, 186–187, 188–189, 202, 242, 245, 247, 248–249, 251, 374
Winter, Alex, 244
Wolf Lake, 109, 111

Wood, Natalie, 4
World War II, 2, 4, 90, 110
Writers Guild of America, 101, 161, 166, 169, 231, 333, 341, 347
X
Y
Yablonski, Joseph "Jock", 253, 254, 255, 256, 257, 260, 261
Yes Virginia, There Is a Santa Claus (editorial), 359
Yes Virginia, There Is a Santa Claus (film), 357–367, 369, 370, 372, 373, 374, 403
Young, Robert, 156
You're in the Navy Now, 3
Yulin, Harris, 28
Z
Zuleika Farms, 222

Printed in Great Britain
by Amazon